Regional Partners in Global Markets: Limits and Possibilities of the Euro-Med Agreements

Regional Partners in Global Markets: Limits and Possibilities of the Euro-Med Agreements

Edited by
Ahmed Galal
and
Bernard Hoekman

المركز المصرى للدراسات الإقتصادية
E C E S
The Egyptian Center for Economic Studies

Centre for Economic Policy Research

The Centre for Economic Policy Research is a network of over 300 Research Fellows, based primarily in European universities. The Centre coordinates its Fellows' research activities and communicates their results to the public and private sectors. CEPR is an entrepreneur, developing research initiatives with the producers, consumers and sponsors of research. Established in 1983, CEPR is a European economics research organization with uniquely wide-ranging scope and activities.

CEPR is a registered educational charity. Institutional (core) finance for the Centre is provided by major grants from the Economic and Social Research Council, under which an ESRC Resource Centre operates within CEPR; the Esmée Fairbairn Charitable Trust; the Bank of England; the European Monetary Institute and the Bank for International Settlements; 18 national central banks and 39 companies. None of these organizations gives prior review to the Centre's publications, nor do they necessarily endorse the views expressed therein.

The Centre is pluralist and non-partisan, bringing economic research to bear on the analysis of medium- and long-run policy questions. CEPR research may include views on policy, but the Executive Committee of the Centre does not give prior review to its publications, and the Centre takes no institutional policy positions. The opinions expressed in this report are those of the authors and not those of the Centre for Economic Policy Research.

31 January 1997

25–28 Old Burlington Street, London W1X 1LB, UK
Tel: (44 171) 878 2900, Fax: (44 171) 878 2999
Email: cepr@cepr.org

© CEPR/ECES, 1997
ISBN: 1 898128 28 6
Typeset, printed and bound in the United Kingdom

The Egyptian Center for Economic Studies

The Egyptian Center for Economic Studies (ECES) is an independent, non-profit research institute. It was founded in 1992 by members of Egypt's private sector. Its objective is to promote economic development in Egypt by assisting policy-makers and the business community in the process of identifying and implementing reform.

ECES is keen to bring international experience to bear on Egypt's problems. By conducting and disseminating applied research and analysis of relevant issues, ECES is working to deepen understanding of the problems facing Egypt and to find appropriate solutions. Through its publications, lectures, conferences, and round-table discussions, ECES strives to increase awareness and generate discussion of economic policy. The views and findings expressed in ECES publications are those of the author(s) and should not be attributed to ECES or its board of directors.

Members of ECES

Directors

The Egyptian Center for Economic Studies, World Trade Center
1191 Corniche El Nil, Cairo 11221, Egypt
Tel: (20 2) 578 1202/3/4.
Fax: (20 2) 578 1205.
Email:eces@powermail.intouch.com

Contents

List of Tables

List of Figures

Preface

This volume contains a set of papers on preferential trade agreements commissioned by the Egyptian Center for Economic Studies. These papers were presented at a conference on 'How Can Egypt Benefit from a Partnership Agreement with the European Union', which was held in Cairo in June 1996, concurrent with Egypt's negotiations with the EU. The objective was to provide Egyptian policy-makers and other concerned parties with the outcome of recent preferential trade agreements elsewhere in the world, to analyse the likely impact of an Egyptian agreement with the EU on the economy in general and on selected sectors in particular, and to make policy recommendations accordingly.

Several individuals and organizations deserve our deep gratitude. We are especially obliged to the contributing authors, the discussants and participants at the conference for sharing their insights. We are also grateful to those who made it all possible, particularly Hisham Fahmy, Eman Mohsen and other staff at ECES for superb organization of the conference, Faten Hatab and Maha Philip for secretarial support and for coping with both of us, and Patti Lord for editorial work with a smile. In addition, we thank Hala Fares, Hala El Khamissi and Amal Rifaat (all of ECES) for excellent research assistance. Last but not least, we are especially indebted to the board of directors of ECES for having the wisdom to approve funding for this project, to John Page for providing World Bank support and personal encouragement, and to the UK Foreign and Commonwealth Office for its financial support to CEPR for the production of this volume.

Ahmed Galal and Bernard Hoekman
January 1997

Conference Participants
(Authors, discussants and session chairpersons)

Gouda Abdel-Khalek *Cairo University*
Moustafa Abd-El-Latif *ECES*
Mohamed Abdellah *Foreign Relations Committee, People's Assembly, Egypt*
Amr Amin *BC Hydro Canada and ECES*
Gamal El Din El Bayoumi *Egyptian Ministry of Foreign Affairs*
Adel Bishai *American University in Cairo*
Sayed El Bous *Egyptian Ministry of Economy*
Priscilla del Bosque *US Agency for International Development*
Alan Deardorff *University of Michigan*
Dean A DeRosa *ADR International*
Ishac Diwan *World Bank*
Mohamed El Erian *International Monetary Fund and ECES*
Ibrahim Fawzy *Egyptian General Authority For Investment*
Samiha Fawzy *Cairo University*
Joseph F Francois *Erasmus University, Rotterdam, and CEPR*
Ahmed Galal *ECES and World Bank*
Heba Handoussa *Economic Research Forum for the Arab Countries, Iran and Turkey*
Abdel Aziz Hegazi *Abdel Aziz Hegazi and Company*
Taher Helmy *Baker and McKenzie and ECES*
Bernard Hoekman *World Bank and CEPR*
Magdi Iskander *World Bank*

Hanaa Kheir-El-Din *Cairo University*
Karima Korayem *Al Azhar University*
Robert Z Lawrence *Harvard University*
Ahmed El Maghrabi *Accor Hotels and ECES*
Mahmoud Mohieldin *ECES and Cairo University*
Youssef El Mokkadem *Ambassador of Tunisia to Egypt*
Said El Naggar *New Civic Forum, Egypt*
John Page *World Bank*
Douglas Paterson *Embassy of Canada in Egypt*
Raouf Saad *Egyptian Ministry of Foreign Affairs*
André Sapir *Université Libre de Bruxelles and CEPR*
Mohamed El Sayed El Said *Center for Political and Strategic Studies, Al Ahram, Cairo*
Ali Soliman *Egyptian Ministry of Economy and International Cooperation*
Arvind Subramanian *International Monetary Fund*
Subidey Togan *Bilkent University*
Yakis Yasar *Ambassador of Turkey to Egypt*
Stephen Yeo *CEPR*
Galal El Zorba *Nile Clothing Company and ECES*
Mona Zulfikar *Shalakany Law Office, Cairo*

Foreword

Regional integration re-emerged on the agenda of policy-makers during the 1980s, and has now become a central feature of the international economy, as bilateral and regional liberalization initiatives proliferate, independently of the GATT and WTO process. This resurgence of regionalism stimulated a renewed interest among the research community, as evidenced by the burgeoning analytical literature on the economics and the political economy of regional integration.

While some people regard the recent proliferation of preferential trade agreements as a signal of global fragmentation into trading blocs, others hold the more positive view that it indicates a shift towards openness and market orientation. Regardless of the prevalent views, it seems clear that regionalism will remain an important element of global trade, at least for the near future. The forms it takes and the impact it has are thus worth investigating. This volume presents the findings of such an investigation, comparing new developments in the literature on regional integration, and examining some actual and potential effects of several recent preferential trade agreements, such as NAFTA, AFTA, and the agreements Morocco and Tunisia have concluded with the EU. It also covers policy options for Egypt as it negotiates an agreement with the EU, and examines possible consequences on distribution and welfare on three of Egypt's key economic sectors.

This book offers a number of valuable insights for countries contemplating preferential trade agreements. One such insight is that the modern breed of agreements can result in greater benefits than traditional ones, because the new agreements tend to promote market-oriented policies. Another is that an external agreement with a large trading partner can serve as an anchor to policy reform, providing credibility against policy reversal in economies in transition. An insight shared by several contributors to this volume is that Mediterranean countries would benefit most if they continue to open up to the global economy, as part of their overall growth strategies.

This project was initiated by the Egyptian Center for Economic Studies in response to the ongoing negotiations between Egypt and the European Union to form a trade agreement. ECES invited a team of accomplished economists to address many of the questions raised by the Euro-Med Initiative – and by experiences elsewhere. The outcome carries a broader scope than originally envisioned, and gives the findings much relevance to policy-makers, not only from the Mediterranean region, but also from the transitional economies of the former Soviet Union. In the pursuit of wide dissemination of the conference findings, ECES joined forces with the Centre for Economic Policy Research in publishing this book.

CEPR was a natural choice for this partnership, since it has for some years pursued a vigorous and wide ranging programme on research on regional economic integration, most recently through a large-scale initiative, funded by the Ford Foundation, on 'Market Integration, Regionalism and the Global Economy'. In 1992, the World Bank and CEPR jointly organized a key conference on regional integration. CEPR's interest in regional integration arises very naturally, since Europe has led the way in such integration efforts.

We believe that this volume demonstrates the potential for productive collaboration between international researchers and those based in the region. It also makes an important and timely contribution to the ongoing negotiations between the Egypt and the European Union and offers valuable insights for other countries contemplating similar agreements.

Ahmed Galal
Stephen Yeo
January 1997

1

Overview

Ahmed Galal
Egyptian Center for Economic Studies

Bernard Hoekman
The World Bank and CEPR

While the theoretical debate continues to rage over the costs and benefits of regionalism versus multilateralism[1], policy makers who have decided to integrate for political and other reasons confront a different set of questions. Which country or bloc of countries should they seek to integrate with? What form of integration is most desirable? Under what conditions will integration further the national interest? This book attempts to help answer such questions. Fundamentally empirical and policy oriented in nature, it is intended to assist policy makers looking to make the best of preferential trading agreements (PTAs) with other nations. Although the papers in this volume focus largely on Mediterranean countries, the issues analysed are quite general.

The importance of the questions addressed in this volume stems from the observed proliferation of preferential regional agreements, notwithstanding the insistence of multilateralists that national and global welfare would be maximized by opening up to all trading partners rather than to a few.[2] Over 100 PTAs have been notified to the World Trade Organization (WTO), and many policy makers appear tireless in their pursuit of more PTAs. It is therefore important to explore whether such agreements are actually beneficial, under what conditions they could be beneficial, and what can be done to maximize the benefits.

The move towards PTAs in recent years may, in fact, be a positive trend. There is a growing body of literature suggesting that the benefits of regional integration may be greater than traditional economic theory predicts. As Robert Lawrence elaborates in this volume, recent vintages of PTAs differ from those pursued in the past in most parts of the world. The 'new' regionalism is grounded more in a general process of increased openness to trade and investment, and less in import substitution, protection of national and regional markets and managed trade.[3] The recent PTAs that have emerged in the Americas and Europe involve countries that put greater reliance on market forces, support production for export to world markets, and actively welcome foreign investment. These agreements go beyond trade liberalization. To varying degrees they aim for 'deep' integration of member countries, and involve a mix of harmonization and mutual recognition of national regulatory systems and policies. As a result, the new agreements have the potential to generate greater dynamic benefits – that is, economic growth impacts – than traditional free trade agreements[4].

Whether these potential growth benefits are realized depends greatly on the contents of the PTA that is negotiated and on the policy stances of the countries that participate. There is therefore a great need for empirical analysis on a case-by-case basis. In itself this is nothing new, as the same conclusion applies with respect to more classic free trade areas: whether a free trade agreement is welfare improving depends on the extent to which it changes the volume and terms of trade of participating countries (through a mix of trade creation and trade diversion).[5] But the importance of empirical analysis is even greater if deeper integration is involved, as the static and dynamic effects are both more complex and more conditional on a wide range of variables.

The papers in this volume suggest that there are two key channels through which PTAs can affect growth; first, the extent to which implementation of a PTA improves the incentives regime confronting producers and consumers, thereby fostering economic growth; and second, the extent to which it enhances the credibility of the government's commitment to liberalize the economy and maintain an outward-oriented, investment-friendly policy stance. On the incentives front, political economy forces often make it difficult to liberalize unilaterally. It is partly for this reason that countries engage in reciprocal multilateral negotiations to reduce trade barriers, as export interests are then given an incentive to oppose protection granted to import-competing industries.[6] But a regional agreement may go much further than what is possible at the multilateral level. Not only is elimination of tariffs on the agenda, but on a wide range of regulatory, administrative and procedural fronts; cooperation and coordination between trading partners may help to remove bureaucratic red tape and associated transaction costs and uncertainty that inhibit private investment and production for export. The greater the focus on trade facilitation and nitty gritty regulatory issues, the greater the potential for gain associated with membership in a PTA, especially for countries with a history and reputation for extensive intervention in trade. The PTA may allow member countries to 'import' administrative reforms and efficient trade procedures at lower cost (both economic and political) than if unilateral reforms were pursued.

With respect to the credibility associated with a PTA, external agreements can act as an anchor for government policy; a PTA may help signal to the financial community – both domestic and foreign – that the government is unlikely to reverse its liberalization policies in the future. For countries with a history of intervention in trade and foreign investment, changing investor expectations and risk perception is difficult, but crucial, as the legacy of past policies is often reflected in high risk premiums, higher borrowing rates, and the higher propensity for capital to seek safe havens whenever shocks occur. This is detrimental to economic performance and can make the country more prone to macroeconomic instability. If credibility can be gained through a PTA, this may be one of the most valuable dimensions of the agreement.

Credibility is, of course, largely a function of what the PTA does to liberalize the economy and lock in policy reform. This will depend greatly on the countries that participate in the PTA and the disciplines that are imposed on 'backsliding.' A distinction can be made between two types of countries and PTAs in this connection. The first are nations wherein government has undertaken far-reaching liberalization on a unilateral basis. The main attraction of a PTA for such countries may then be related to the anchor role it can play, complemented by the greater security of access to partner country markets. For the PTA to be a credible anchor it probably must include a country's largest trading partners. This category includes Mexico and its participation in the North American Free Trade Agreement (*see* Chapter 3); and the so-called Europe Agreements between the European Union and the Central and Eastern European countries (Sapir, 1995). It is probably fair to say that most observers would regard these agreements as successes, and much of the discussion on deep regional integration is based on these PTAs.[7]

The second category includes countries wherein significant liberalization and policy reform remain to be achieved. Most Mediterranean countries belong to this category. Such countries could pursue PTAs (again with major trading partners) as part of a strategy to open the economy. Locking in reforms that are achieved is an important corollary of the PTA, but it is not the primary objective. Economic reforms have been pursued slowly and a great deal remains to be done to change policies and perceptions held by potential investors. Less experience has been obtained with PTAs that are 'process based' and it can be argued that the Mediterranean agreements being concluded by the EU are something of an experiment. Much therefore depends on both partners to make the agreements a success in terms of liberalization and locking in reform.

This volume of conference proceedings provides insights for both types of countries. It includes analyses of the NAFTA and the ASEAN Free Trade Agreement (AFTA), as well as the recent agreements concluded between the EU and Morocco and Tunisia. The authors use diverse methodologies, ranging from computable general equilibrium modelling to partial equilibrium approaches. A recurring theme in this volume is that Egypt and other Mediterranean countries must pursue 'deeper' integration and continue to open up to the world economy, not just the EU. For its part, the European Union should undertake all possible efforts to facilitate and support implementation and expansion of the partnership agreements. The papers herein should be of particular interest to policy makers from countries in the Mediterranean region, several of which are in the process of negotiating partnership agreements with the EU; others may start to do so soon. Along with Egypt, the list includes Jordan, Syria, and Lebanon. The analyses should also be relevant to the countries of the former Soviet Union and those Eastern European countries where EU accession is not on the medium-term agenda

Highlights of the book

The book is organized around a number of topical 'building blocks'. The first summarizes the new developments in thinking about regional integration, and provides evidence on the actual and potential effects of recent PTAs in North America and Asia: NAFTA and AFTA. The second part focuses on the possible impacts of the PTAs that were recently negotiated between the EU and Tunisia and Morocco, respectively. The remainder of the book focuses on the case of Egypt, in its process of negotiating a PTA with the EU. After analyses of Egypt's policy options, the likely impact on welfare of a Tunisia-type PTA, and the possible distributional consequences of an agreement, the implications for three key economic sectors are investigated: pharmaceuticals, textiles and services. The book concludes with a chapter by the editors dealing with the normative implications of the various analyses for Egypt. Throughout, the analyses and approaches that are taken are quite general, and can easily be transferred to other countries that are contemplating the pursuit of PTAs.

To begin, Robert Lawrence examines the economic case for and against PTAs. He notes that while some multilateralists fear that preferential arrangements may dull the appetite for more general non-discriminatory trade liberalization, others believe that PTAs are a stepping stone to global free trade. In comparing the traditional with the 'new' view of PTAs, Lawrence emphasizes that in contrast to the past, regional integration is often pursued by countries that have unilaterally liberalized trade and are seeking to increase their participation in the world economy. The new agreements go beyond liberalization of trade in goods; they imply opening the economy to investment, services and capital flows. However, he also notes – and was strongly seconded by his discussant André Sapir at the conference – that the types of agreements that are being concluded between the EU and Mediterranean countries, while having the potential to be (or to become) deep integration arrangements, are perhaps better characterized as more traditional trade agreements. As a result, until such time as the agreement liberalizes services and investment, the welfare implications of a PTA may be driven largely by classic trade diversion and trade creation tradeoffs.

In chapters 3 and 4, Joseph Francois and Dean DeRosa examine two recent regional agreements from different perspectives. Francois discusses the potential for PTAs to enhance the credibility of economic policy reform, exploring in particular the role of NAFTA in anchoring recent reforms in Mexico. He concludes that with the right ingredients – notably, a large partner to serve as a policy anchor – North–South regional agreements have the potential to benefit developing and transition economies by cementing policy reform and enhancing credibility. He also notes that the NAFTA experience suggests that the investment response sought by governments that conclude a PTA with a larger partner may well be conditional upon prior comprehensive economic reforms. In the case of Mexico, accession to NAFTA to a large extent involved locking in liberalization that was undertaken by the Mexican government unilaterally. In the Mediterranean context, and in Egypt in particular, the PTA is part of a strategy to attain liberalization. As a result, there is less certainty regarding the role of the EU and the PTA more generally as a 'policy anchor.'

Turning to East Asian regionalism and economic integration, Dean DeRosa compares the ASEAN Free Trade Area (AFTA) with the 'open regionalism' favoured by the Asia-Pacific Economic Cooperation forum. He estimates the potential welfare gains of these two policy options, concluding that open regionalism – liberalizing regional trade on a non-discriminatory basis – will result in greater gains by expanding agricultural production and trade. The gains from the AFTA plan are found to be modest.

In Part II the book turns to the economic implications of the PTAs that Morocco and Tunisia concluded with the EU in 1995. Druscilla Brown, Alan Deardorff and Robert Stern use a computational general equilibrium model to analyse the potential economic effects on Tunisia of the PTA with the EU. An innovative feature of their model is the explicit incorporation of Tunisia's policy regime towards foreign direct investment, and an evaluation of the possible responses of foreign investment to the preferential liberalization. Their results lead them to conclude that Tunisia will gain little or nothing from the PTA in the short run, and could experience significant adjustment problems stemming from labour and capital movement. Moreover, in the absence of complementary policy actions, no large inflow of foreign direct investment is expected. They suggest that Tunisia would do better to liberalize trade barriers and foreign investment policies multilaterally.

John Page and John Underwood next examine three dimensions of the potential dynamic effects of the EU's PTAs with Morocco and Tunisia. These may operate through the trade liberalization and the associated fall in the price of capital goods, through greater foreign investment and associated technology transfer and pro-competitive impacts, and through an increase in total factor productivity. Such growth stimulating effects of the PTA are not included in the analysis by Brown, Deardorff and Stern, as they are very difficult to model. Since both Morocco and Tunisia already had virtually free access to the EU market for manufactured goods, imposed relatively low tariffs on capital goods, and have done little to change their FDI regimes, Page and Underwood conclude that the PTAs in themselves will not have a great growth impact. For significant dynamic gains to materialize, the two countries must accelerate and deepen economic reforms, building upon and exploiting the principle of liberalization that is inherent in the agreements.

The following three chapters focus on the economy-wide implications of a PTA for Egypt. Bernard Hoekman and Simeon Djankov start with a summary of the main building blocks of the PTA, using the Tunisian agreement as a benchmark. They quantify the impact of existing trade policies by calculating effective rates of protection across industries, and explore the impact of alternative liberalization strategies on protection. Acknowledging the arguments against preferential liberalization, they assert that an agreement with the EU can do much more than liberalize trade – it could benefit Egypt in numerous ways, particularly by enhancing its structural reform and credibility. However, realization of this potential depends upon the contents of the agreement. Particularly important in this connection are liberalization and increasing competition in the services sector, and encouraging investment though guaranteeing the right of establishment and actively pursuing privatization.

In the next chapter Denise Konan and Keith Maskus analyse the implications of alternative trade liberalization strategies for economic welfare, trade, production and employment in Egypt. Using a specially developed numerical general equilibrium model of the Egyptian economy that takes into account not only the existing trade policy regime but also the tax system, Konan and Maskus conclude that while a PTA with the EU is inferior to non-discriminatory trade liberalization, the agreement will generate welfare gains as long as it actually leads to a reduction in administrative and transactions costs ('red tape'). Because trade reforms enhance efficiency, wages are expected to rise in real terms. The authors also note that expansion of the PTA to include neighbouring countries in the region as well as the United States (a major trading partner) will further increase the gains.

Ishac Diwan addresses the question of how the EU partnership agreement will affect income distribution in Egypt. He looks at how the agreement can contribute to redressing negative distributional effects related to globalization and facilitate the social transition towards a more open economy. In his view, Egypt's unemployment problem can be eased by the agreement if it instills good practices and commitment to 'the rules of the marketplace'. Given the socio-political risks involved in reform, the gradual nature of liberalization under the agreement – and the EU's offer of substantial financial and technical assistance – could make a significant contribution to advancing economic reform.

The next three chapters investigate the impact of the PTA on particular industries in Egypt. Arvind Subramanian and Moustafa Abd-el-Latif deal with the potential impact of stronger protection of intellectual property rights on Egypt's pharmaceutical sector. They argue that liberalization under the PTA will not have a great impact on the sector, because Egypt's tariff barriers on imports of pharmaceuticals are already low, the sector is already exposed to international competition, and Egyptian pharmaceutical exports to the EU already benefit from duty-free access. On the other hand, stronger intellectual property protection required under the agreement will have far-reaching effects on the sector, particularly concerning patent protection. The disciplines that are imposed in this connection are basically those of the WTO agreement on trade-related intellectual property rights (TRIPs). However, there are additional implications that result from the PTA, including the interaction between EU competition rules and the TRIPs disciplines. The probable short-term impact of stronger intellectual property protection on the Egyptian pharmaceutical industry is negative: prices are expected to rise, profits accruing to patent owners and foreign firms located in Egypt will increase while those of indigenous firms will deteriorate. Overall, welfare is likely to deteriorate. However, the predicted long-run impact is positive: greater foreign investment can be expected, and greater incentives for local research and development and transfer of technology will emerge.

The Egyptian textile industry is the nation's second largest manufacturing sector after food processing. This is also a major export industry for other countries in the Mediterranean region. Hanaa Kheir El Din and Hoda El Sayed discuss how this sector may fare after a trade agreement with the EU. Trade liberalization would benefit Egyptian consumers by affording more variety in products, prices and quality, but would threaten Egyptian producers with increased competition on the domestic market. The main conclusion drawn from the analysis is that Egyptian textile and clothing manufacturing and exports are competitive for the most part, but are constrained by a variety of domestic distortions. These can be addressed by more privatization and less government interference in the sector, which should result in greater efficiency and competitiveness.

A number of the book's contributors emphasize the importance of an efficient service sector and openness to foreign direct investment (FDI) in services in fostering economic growth. The services industry in Egypt, as in many other countries in the region, is relatively inefficient and subject to substantial government intervention that limits competition. Mahmoud Mohieldin surveys the Egyptian services sector – particularly financial services – in the light of the proposed partnership agreement. He notes that inefficiencies and protection in the services sector result in high transaction costs that reduce the competitiveness of other sectors, and argues that state domination of the services sector must be reduced. Assuming that the PTA will not differ significantly from those of Tunisia and Morocco, he predicts that the agreement will defer the liberalization of trade in services to the WTO, which may not be an effective catalyst for change. As a result, wider reforms must be undertaken at the domestic level to improve the sector's efficiency.

In the final chapter, Ahmed Galal and Bernard Hoekman discuss how the partnership agreement could become a catalyst for enhancing the performance of the Egyptian economy if it is seen as part of a coherent growth strategy. They compare Egypt's current growth strategy with those of the fast-growing economies in Southeast Asia and Latin America, and argue that Egypt is held back from achieving the high rate of sustained economic growth it needs by its limited trade openness, low savings and investment, and insufficient domestic competition. Since 50% of Egypt's exports go to the EU and 40% of its imports originate in the EU, liberalization under the PTA could have dramatic effects. Egypt's industries will have access to cheaper inputs sourced from Europe, which will reduce costs, but they will face greater competition, which should induce them to improve quality.

As argued in several chapters, Galal and Hoekman emphasize that a great deal depends on the unilateral, complementary policies that are pursued – these are crucial in signaling the government's commitment to reform, which, in turn, is vital to inducing greater investment, both domestic and foreign. The reforms necessary to enable Egypt to take full advantage of the agreement include increasing public sector savings, lowering tax burdens, pursuing comprehensive privatization, and continuing to open the economy to trade and investment from all parts of the world.

References

Baldwin, Richard (1994), *Towards an Integrated Europe, London*, CEPR.

Baldwin, Richard and Anthony Venables (1995), 'Regional economic integration,' in *Handbook of International Economics*, vol. 3. Amsterdam, North Holland, forthcoming.

Bhagwati, Jagdish (1993), 'Regionalism and multilateralism: an overview,' in De Melo and Panagariya, (eds).

Bhagwati, Jagdish and Anne Krueger (1995), *The Dangerous Drift To Preferential Trade Agreements*, Washington, DC, American Enterprise Institute.

Bhagwati, Jagdish and Arvind Panagariya (1996), *The Economics of Preferential Trade Agreements*, Washington, DC, American Enterprise Institute.

De Melo, Jaime and Arvind Panagariya, (eds.) (1993), *New Dimensions in Regional Integration*, Cambridge, Cambridge University Press.

Hoekman, Bernard and Michel Kostecki (1995), *The Political Economy of the World Trading System: From GATT to WTO*, Oxford, Oxford University Press.

Kowalczyk, Carsten (1990), 'Welfare and Customs Unions,' National Bureau of Economic Research Working Paper 3476, Boston, Mimeo.

Sapir, André (1995), 'The Europe agreements: implications for trade laws and institutions,' in Alan Winters (ed.), *Foundations of an Open Economy*, London, CEPR.

Viner, Jacob (1950), *The Customs Union Issue*, New York, Carnegie Endowment for International Peace.

World Trade Organization (1995), *Regionalism and the World Trading System*, Geneva, WTO.

Notes

1. See, for example, WTO (1995). The literature on preferential trade agreements is enormous, and dates back to Viner (1950), who introduced many of the concepts that are still used and debated today.
2. As argued strongly by Jagdish Bhagwati; see Bhagwati (1993); Bhagwati and Krueger (1995).
3. The contributions in De Melo and Panagariya (1993) provide a recent survey of the experiences with PTAs negotiated in the 1960s and 1970s in all parts of the world. See also WTO (1995).
4. See Baldwin (1994) for a discussion of the various types of impacts; Baldwin and Venables (1995) and Bhagwati and Panagariya (1996) are up-to-date discussions of the theoretical literature in this area.
5. See Kowalczyk (1990) for a critical analysis of the usefulness of trade diversion and creation as yardsticks for welfare analysis. See also Baldwin and Venables (1995).
6. See Hoekman and Kostecki (1995) for a survey of the literature on the political economy of multilateral trade negotiations.
7. This is not to deny that Eastern European countries still confront a significant reform agenda. However, as these countries have indicated that their objective is to join the EU, investors confront less uncertainty regarding the long-term policy regime.

PART I
Regionalism: Theory and Evidence

2

Preferential Trading Arrangements: The Traditional and The New

Robert Z Lawrence
Harvard University

2.1   Introduction

Over the past decade, a large number of regional economic arrangements have been negotiated. The most well known are the programmes of the European Union – to complete its internal market programme (EC92) – and the United States, Canada and Mexico to form the North America Free Trade Agreement (NAFTA), but these were only the most prominent of a rapidly growing number of preferential economic agreements which have emerged or been revitalized in recent years. A list of such agreements compiled by the International Monetary Fund (1994) numbered 67 in 1994. It covers all five continents, running virtually the full alphabet from the ASEAN Free Trade Area (AFTA) to the West African Economic and Monetary Union. It is estimated that about 90% of all members of the World Trade Organization (WTO) are signatories to such arrangements.[1]

Some pessimists see the current situation as an ominous precursor of what has come before. They believe that the world trading system is fragmenting in the same way it did in the 1930s and that the rule-based multilateral trading system that has developed under the General Agreement on Tariffs and Trade (GATT) will be destroyed as Europe, North America and Asia become 'fortresses' in which some trading partners obtain refuge, while others are excluded.[2] For example, in his bestselling book *Head to Head*, Lester Thurow (1992) proclaimed that 'the GATT is dead' and argued that the world would shift to a tripolar system, with three blocs centred on Europe, the United States and Japan which would have free trade internally but managed trade among them.

Multilateralists, such as Jagdish Bhagwati, are not willing to give the GATT its last rites, but remain concerned that the expansion of regionalism will undermine the multilateral system and weaken its thrust towards liberalization.[3] Bhagwati fears that if some countries are given a vested interest in preferential trade arrangements (PTAs), they will have less incentive to press for complete free trade. If leaders devote resources and political capital to their regional arrangements, they could be diverted from investing in the multilateral system. He concedes that PTAs may have played a role in spurring the completion of the Uruguay Round (1986–94) of multilateral trade negotiations, which led to the creation of the WTO. But he argues that the WTO should now be the sole locus of future trade liberalization. Bhagwati therefore calls for greater disciplines on PTAs and a more exclusive reliance on global initiatives.

There are, however, more sanguine views of the process. Regional arrangements have also been presented as a complement and supplement to liberalization under the multilateral trading system. Indeed, this is the traditional view enshrined in Article 24 of the GATT which permits the formation of PTAs such as free trade areas and customs unions provided that they meet certain conditions. It is also the view of many American and European trade officials. By following both regional and multilateral approaches, they argue, world trade liberalization can proceed more rapidly.[4] Such a multi-speed approach to freer trade can achieve greater gains for those willing to proceed faster and at the same time put pressure on the multilateral track to perform better.

2.2 Traditional theory

Both economic theory and experience provide reasons why this controversy is not easily resolved. A central result of international trade theory is that in a competitive global economy, complete free trade will maximize global welfare. However, theory provides a more ambiguous verdict of the welfare implications of a PTA which removes the barriers between only a few trading partners. Superficially, it appears plausible that if free trade is optimal for the world, any movement towards free trade will improve global welfare. Removing the trade barriers between a group of countries without raising barriers to other trading partners seems to be a step in the right direction. However, theory has demonstrated that such measures do not necessarily make the world better off, and do not even necessarily make those concluding such agreements better off.

The possibility that aggregate global welfare can be damaged even though the world as a whole is moved closer to free trade is a quite startling result with more general implications. It was thinking about the example of PTAs which led Lipsey and Lancaster (1956) to enunciate the 'general theory of the second best' which states that reducing some distortions while others remain in place does not necessarily increase welfare.[5] As Jacob Viner (1950) emphasized, eliminating the internal trade barriers in a customs union will lead to more trade between the partners, and this 'trade creation' should add to welfare. But a customs union could also reduce trade between the members and the rest of the world. This 'trade diversion' could misallocate global resources. If outside producers are actually more efficient than those inside the agreement, global efficiency declines when the producers within the agreement expand production and the producers in the rest of the world contract production.[6]

This argument can be illustrated by an example. Assume that prior to implementing a free trade agreement (FTA) with Europe, all television sets purchased in Egypt are subject to a tariff of 10%. Assume that Japan produces television sets under competitive conditions which it sells at a cost of $100 but Europe could only produce such sets at $105. Initially, all television sets sold in Egypt and elsewhere would be Japanese. These would be imported at a price of $100 from Japan and sold to Egyptian consumers for $110, with the additional $10 representing the tariff which would be paid by Egyptian consumers to the Egyptian government. Assume now that an FTA is signed between the EU and Egypt which removes tariffs between Egypt and the EU but retains Egypt's tariffs on other countries. Egyptian consumers will now have a choice between buying European televisions which will sell in Egypt at $105 or Japanese televisions which will sell at $110. They will buy European televisions and be better off. However, the Egyptian economy as a whole will be worse off. Prior to the agreement Egypt bought its televisions from Japan. While consumers laid out $110, $10 was just a transfer from Egyptian consumers to the Egyptian government. The economy as a whole, therefore spent only $100 per television. After the agreement, however, Egypt is spending $105 per television. Television prices in Egypt do not reflect their social opportunity costs. The impact of the FTA is to expand television production in the EU which is relatively less efficient and to reduce it in Japan which is relatively more efficient.

Of course, not all of the increased trade between partners will represent expansion from a less efficient source. Pure trade creation could also result. Assume in the example, that initially Egypt could produce television sets for $107. In this case, prior to the agreement Egypt would not have imported them from Japan but instead would have supplied these television sets domestically. In this case, Egypt would benefit from the FTA which would allow it to pay only $105 per television by buying from the EU – although of course it would have done even better by liberalizing fully and buying the sets from Japan.[7]

An implication of this theory is that the rapid growth in the internal trade between members of an FTA does not necessarily imply their welfare is being enhanced. The insights from this theory lead naturally to the prescription that only those PTAs which are net trade-creating should be concluded.[8] This has led economists to generalize about which countries are best suited to form preferential trading arrangements, or about rules which would offset some of the negative effects of these agreements. These have included (a) regional partners – since geographic proximity generally promotes trade, trade creation could be large; (b) partners at similar stages of development – since intra-industry trade flourishes between developed countries; and (c) large PTAs – since the more varied the members, the greater the opportunities for specialization.[9] However, an important insight that emerges from theory is that there are no rules that are foolproof. Indeed, it suggests that it is dangerous to try to rely on such generalizations as if they provide reliable guides of the likely extent of net trade creation. There are no hard and fast rules and thus no substitute for a case-by-case empirical analysis.

Theory does suggest that trading partners who do not participate in a PTA will be hurt, even when global welfare as a whole is enhanced (Mundell, 1964). Unless the outsiders are too large (or the preferential trading area too small) for the arrangement to affect world prices, outsiders as a whole will be harmed because their terms of trade are likely to deteriorate.[10] But again there could be exceptions. If the internal trade liberalization has dynamic effects which increase growth, or if there are scale economies which stimulate the demand for imports from outside the region, the income effects of liberalization could more than offset trade diversion, thereby raising outside welfare.[11]

2.2.1 Building blocks or stumbling blocks

Viewed statically, in the context of border barrier removal, PTAs are inferior to multilateral free trade. But they can also be viewed dynamically, as measures which move the world in the direction of global free trade. Indeed, over the post-war period the world has moved towards free trade partly through a series of GATT trade rounds which have successively lowered trade barriers and partly through preferential arrangements. One process of liberalization entails partial liberalization but full participation; the other, full liberalization but partial participation. An important question, for which the answer remains uncertain, is whether the rise of PTAs makes the achievement of full multilateral liberalization more or less likely. The literature provides some reasons which could tilt policies towards further liberalization and others which could tilt them towards further protection.[12] As might be expected, predictions depend on the manner in which the dynamics of trade liberalization are modelled, whether the arrangements considered are customs unions or FTAs (although there is no firm presumption that one particular type is more liberal), and on the rules of the international trading system.

There are many plausible considerations leading to opposite conclusions. Naive application of optimal tariffs, dangers of capture by protectionist interests, increased interest in protection, diversion of political capital and dilution of political support all make multilateral liberalization less likely. On the other hand, reactions by other major players demanding accession or liberalization, the greater ease of monitoring and negotiating, the ability to adjust in stages and thus reduce protectionist interests and the increased difficulties of capturing large arrangements – particularly   customs unions – all make it more likely. The rules of the game on compensation, protection and accession can all be important. In the end, there is no substitute to seeing which of these effects dominates in practice.

In sum, theory is useful in underscoring the considerations for empirical evaluation, but it does not settle the issue. Ultimately it is the task of empirical analysis to estimate the relative importance of trade creation and trade diversion and the effects on additional liberalization.

2.3   Traditional experience

The post-war experience with regionalism has been mixed. PTAs have had a checkered history. To be sure, the rapid growth and liberalization achieved by European countries between 1958 and 1973 coincided with the formation of the European Community (EC) and the European Free Trade Area (EFTA), but regional arrangements were also associated with the disastrous fragmentation of the world economy into trading blocs in the 1930s and with the ill-fated arrangements between developing countries in the 1950s and 1960s. In particular, the agreements between developing countries in the Middle East and elsewhere often failed miserably.[13] This might have been expected given their motivation. They were an extension of domestic import substitution and planning policies to the regional level and were usually proposed to achieve scale economies for protectionist policies. The theory was that participating countries would become more specialized. In practice, however, given the general philosophy of trying to produce everything at home, members tended to give each other access to their markets only in those products they imported from the rest of the world. In other words, the region as a whole became more self-sufficient, but in a most inefficient manner – by maximizing trade diversion. The bilateral protocol trade arrangements in the Middle East, in which countries selectively determine specific products and quantities to be traded, are examples of politically-driven trade that inevitably fails to yield much benefit.

Under these circumstances, it was no surprise that preferential trading agreements among developing countries often failed. It is difficult enough – many would say impossible – to manage resource allocation in a single economy. Planning for several simultaneously is impossible and inevitably becomes tangled in international politics. This was particularly the case when countries had similar patterns of specialization so that there were few opportunities for avoiding competition. However, even where there was scope for such specialization, once the extra-regional trade was diverted, the impact of the agreements were exhausted. If one partner ran surpluses, acrimony inevitably resulted.[14]

2.4   The new regionalism

Neither traditional trade theory nor this previous experience provide an adequate guide to current regional arrangements. The forces driving the current developments differ radically from those driving previous waves of regionalization in this century. Unlike the episode of the 1930s, most of the current initiatives represent efforts to facilitate their members participation in the world economy rather than their withdrawal from it. Unlike those in the 1950s and 1960s, the initiatives involving developing countries are part of a strategy to liberalize their economies in general and to open their economies to implement export- and foreign-invest-ment-led policies rather than to promote import-substitution. The current moves towards regionalization are, by and large, not responses to thwart the allocative process of the market but to strengthen its operation. They represent efforts to fill the functional needs of international trade and investment and the requirements of international governance and cooperation to which globalization gives rise. In particular, countries hope that by integrating with their regional partners, they will become more attractive export locations. Thus for example, firms in the United States who supported the NAFTA hoped to become more competitive internationally by sourcing some of their more labour-intensive activities in Mexico. They recognize, however, that such sourcing cannot take place if tariffs, regulatory differences and other legal barriers prevent the movement of components and finished products across the border. In addition, many important regional initiatives are not developing as arrangements with exclusive memberships in which insiders limit their contacts with outsiders. On the contrary, they are developing as inclusive arrangements in which members either allow outsiders to join or independently join them in developing similar arrangements. In sum, there are crucial differences between earlier and many of the current regional initiatives.

Some major aspects of the new regionalism are listed in Table 2.1. It is striking that recent regional agreements have been strongly supported by corporate leaders. In Europe, the initiative to establish a single market was promoted by large European firms who argued that a fragmented Europe deprived them of the scale economies they needed to be competitive. Similarly, the NAFTA was boosted by US business both large (as represented by the Business Round Table) and small (the US Chamber of Commerce).[15] Major FTA supporters in Canada were the Business Council on National Issues and the Canadian Manufacturers Association;[16] large Mexican industrial groups strongly backed NAFTA. Private foreign investors have led the informal regional integration in Asia. In addition, in the Asian Pacific Economic Cooperation (APEC) forum, political leaders explicitly institutionalized the role of business by creating an advisory Pacific Business Forum in June 1994. Both large and small firms from the 18 member countries are represented in this forum which is charged with providing proposals for facilitating trade and investment within the region.

Clearly, many multinational corporations view these regional arrangements as promoting their interests. This reflects the role of these arrangements as responses to the functional demands of multinational firms in the current economic environment. In particular, it is noteworthy that these initiatives are concerned with services and foreign direct investment (FDI) as well as goods trade and they focus on internal rules and regulations and institutional mechanisms to ensure implementation and enforcement as well as removing border barriers.

As global competition has intensified, market access has become increasingly important for success. Access for products is crucial because the international diffusion of innovations has become increasingly rapid. The diminished time before competitors respond to new innovations makes large global markets essential for spreading the fixed costs of innovation. But the ability to operate abroad has also become vital. Foreign

Table 2.1 Regionalism: old and new

Old	New
Import substitution; withdraw from world economy	Export orientation; integrate into world economy
Planned and political allocation of resources	Market allocation of resources
Led by governments	Led by private firms
Mainly industrial products	All goods, services and investment
Deal with border barriers	Deeper integration
Preferential treatment for less developed	Equal rules (different adjustment periods)

investment and exports have become increasingly complementary activities.[17] Firms selling sophisticated products find that a significant local presence can be a prerequisite for marketing, sales and service. The ability to follow market trends, respond to customer needs, and acquire innovative smaller firms in all major markets has also become important in determining competitive success.

There has also been a dramatic rise in FDI in services industries. Indeed FDI in services has grown more rapidly than in goods. As manufacturing firms move abroad, other firms providing complementary inputs and services (such as banking, advertising, management consulting) often accompany them.[18] Some of the rise in services FDI can therefore be understood as complementary to the manufacturing investment. However, there are also independent reasons. Developments in information technologies have increased global integration in many services sectors that were once isolated. Moreover, in the 1980s, there was a strong trend toward financial liberalization, privatization and deregulation in many economies which created investment opportunities in sectors such as banking, communications, utilities and transportation.[19]

2.4.1 Developing countries

As they seek to attract capital and at the same time pursue programmes based on export-led growth, foreign firms become increasingly attractive to developing countries. They bring knowledge about the latest technologies and ready-made access to major markets. Moreover, in many developing countries, accompanying the shift toward more open trade policies has been a reduction in the role of the state through privatization. In this context, foreign investors have become increasingly attractive as providers of capital, technology and operational skills. The demand for FDI emanating from the developing countries has corresponded with an increased supply from multinational corporations. As international competition intensifies, small cost advantages may have large consequences. Particular national locations are not necessarily well suited for the complete manufacture of complex products. With improvements in communications and transportation, firms are increasingly able to produce products by sourcing from multiple locations. Raw materials might best be sourced in one country, labour-intensive processes performed in a second, and technologically sophisticated processes in a third. Multinationals from many nations are therefore expanding their foreign investments.

Traditionally, FDI in developing countries occurred to gain access to raw materials. Later, in countries following protectionist import-substitution policies, it was attracted by the prospects of selling behind trade barriers in a large internal market. While the motive of an attractive domestic market persists, as developing countries have lowered their trade barriers, investment has increasingly been motivated towards servicing export markets (Wells, 1992). Those able to offer export platforms have become most successful in attracting FDI.[20]

2.4.2   Implications

The increased importance of international investment naturally shifts attention from trade to investment barriers and focuses attention on (a) national differences in the degree of ease with which foreign firms can enter new markets through both acquisition and new establishment, and (b) the effects of domestic regulations and taxes on the conditions under which such firms can operate. Similarly, firms that plan to source in one country and sell in others need security about the rules and mechanisms governing trade. Such firms also prefer secure intellectual property rights and technical standards and regulations that are compatible.

For developing countries, particularly those which were previously inhospitable towards foreign investment, establishing the credibility of new policies to attract investment and securing access to markets for exports becomes of major importance. In addition, for some developing countries, it may be easier to 'import' new institutions and regulatory systems than to develop them independently. While such institutions may not have the virtue of matching domestic conditions precisely they do offer the advantages of having been pre-tested and in addition of international compatibility. For nations in Eastern Europe for example, adopting policies which conform to EU norms is particularly attractive. Finally, entering international negotiations can affect an internal debate tilting it in favour of one side and against another. In many cases, domestic forces interested in liberalization will find their hand strengthened if they can present their policies as part of an international liberalization agreement.[21]

Given these developments, the reasons for the distinctive character of the emerging regional arrangements become clearer. They are motivated by the desire to facilitate international investment and the operations of multinational firms as much as the desire to promote trade. While liberalization to permit trade requires the removal of border barriers – a relatively 'shallow' form of integration – the development of regional production systems and the promotion of services investment require deeper forms of international integration of national regulatory systems and policies (for example, eliminating differences in national production and product standards which make regionally integrated production costly). Investment also requires credible and secure governance mechanisms, and secure access to large foreign markets that is unhindered either by customs officials or by domestic actions such as anti-dumping. Since much of the investment relates to the provision of services, the regulatory regimes governing establishment and operation become the focus of attention.

These developments have, without doubt, had an impact on the multilateral trade agenda. The Uruguay Round, for example, included agreements which (a) limited trade-related investment measures; (b) placed disciplines on the use of standards; (c) required enforcement of intellectual property rights; (d) liberalized trade in services; (e) clarified the rules on anti-dumping and subsidies; and (f) established a more binding mechanism for the resolution of disputes. But it is also not surprising that they have also been important in regional initiatives. Indeed, in several cases these agreements have gone much further than the GATT.

2.5   Deeper integration

As discussed in Section 2.1, theorizing about regionalism considers these arrangements in the context of a traditional paradigm in which trade policy is characterized by changes to barriers at the border. Regional arrangements are modelled either as customs unions (in which members have free trade internally and a common external tariff) or as FTAs, (internal barriers are eliminated while external tariffs differ). Many of the empirical studies of these arrangements similarly construct models which focus on the effects of lowering tariff and non-tariff barriers.[22] Traditional trade theory has largely ignored the existence of different national institutions. Trade policy is generally modelled as decisions to change border barriers while other governmental policies are usually ignored. One justification is that these differences can simply be subsumed as similar to differences in technology or climate. In fact, the paradigms of traditional theory and the GATT notion of sovereign national states fit quite neatly with each other provided that institutions (and regulations) can be taken as given. In traditional analysis, therefore, the dominant goal is the maximization of global welfare by multilateral free trade. Each nation exploits its distinctive features by freely trading with the rest of the world. Against this paradigm, PTAs are judged to be 'second best'.

While the removal of internal border barriers is certainly an important feature of PTAs, focusing only on these barriers overlooks much of what regional arrangements are about. The traditional perspective is at best incomplete, and at worst misleading. A more comprehensive view of these emerging arrangements acknowledges that they are also about achieving deeper integration of international competition and investment. Once tariffs are removed, there remain complex problems between nations relating to different regulatory policies. The traditional approach is that these should be determined and administered at the national level with foreign goods and firms accorded non-discriminatory national treatment – an approach I have termed 'shallow integration'. Increasingly, however, globalization has created pressures for deeper integration, to reconcile divergent national practices with common rules and policies and supra-national implementation mechanisms.

In a national context, there is an extensive theory dealing with the question of how to assign authority over different aspects of fiscal policy to different levels of government, in the literature on fiscal federalism. The optimal degree of integration to maximize public welfare will reflect two factors. The first is the technology of producing public services. The benefits and costs of different public goods and externalities will be realized on a variety of special scales. Purely private goods should be provided through decentralized markets. Other goods generate local externalities and should be provided by local governments. In still other cases, the externalities will span larger areas. Some goods are public, in the sense that consumption is non-rival. For example, an additional individual can obtain knowledge without detracting from the knowledge of others. Such goods may be provided locally, nationally or internationally, depending on the span of publicness. The mobility of factors and consumers dramatically complicates the ability of local authorities to internalize the costs and benefits of providing public goods. The second factor is diversity of consumer choice. If tastes vary widely, it is efficient to accommodate such variations in taste even when some advantages in production efficiency might be gained from a broad governmental authority.

No single answer seems to result from a general consideration of the factors that will affect this choice.[23] There will inevitably be tensions between realizing scale economies and internalization by increasing the scope of governance and realizing more precise matching of tastes and choices by reducing that scope. What does seem clear, however, is that the answer will not always be the nation state or the world. It is bound to differ, depending on the nature of the activity to be regulated.[24] In some cases, e.g. global warming or global financial networks, the appropriate level may be the world; in other cases, it could be the local community. The answers to this question are ambiguous and they will not be independent of technology, history, incomes and tastes. Indeed, there is no reason, a priori, to assume that the provision of regulatory regimes and other public goods should be the sole responsibility of the nation state. Some goods and rules are better provided locally, while for others bilateral and plurilateral international arrangements may be more appropriate.

What is critical for appraising the current regional initiatives, however, is the recognition that some emerging international regional arrangements reflect efforts to come up with solutions to this issue. This insight has both normative and positive implications. While multilateral free trade may result in an efficient allocation of international resources, a single global government is almost certainly not the ideal solution to providing all public goods. Accordingly, in principle, regional arrangements dealing with international governance need not be second best – they could be the first best.

Focusing only on border barriers could miss much of the effects of a deeper regional arrangement. The EU might do nothing to change its external tariffs, but the adoption of a single European product standard for example, could affect both intra- and extra- European trade flows. Given its reliance on the traditional theoretical approach, it is not surprising that economic modelling of regional arrangements has often been incomplete. Such modelling is useful in capturing the effect of incremental change on a given economic system. It is far less able to capture the effects of changes in a legal or institutional order. But these changes can be extremely significant in affecting resource allocation. Insecurity about access to foreign markets or the rights of foreign investors, for example, may act as a severe tax on the incentive to invest. Indeed, the concerns of regional arrangements have shifted away from incremental changes, toward changes in the rules of the game: defining property rights and permissible behaviour by governments and firms. But too little effort has been placed in analysing these dimensions. Also often neglected is the contribution that more effective enforcement mechanisms will make in ensuring adherence to the rules.

2.5.1   *First or second best?*

What is critical for appraising the current regional initiatives is recognition that some emerging international regional arrangements reflect efforts to come up with solutions to this issue. While multilateral free trade is an optimal solution given the institutionless setting of traditional analysis, a single global solution to deeper integration is surely not. Accordingly, in principle, regional (or plurilateral) deeper arrangements need not be second best, they could be the first best. Some activities may be best carried out on a global level, others on a plurilateral level, while some may best be left to sub-national level. Recognizing the deeper nature of these agreements provides important challenges for modelling their effects – a challenge which to date has not been adequately met.[25] A regional agreement which guaranteed domestic firms better access to large neighbouring markets and foreign investors more secure control could boost investment and give rise to important dynamic gains. Indeed a key Mexican motive for the NAFTA was to ensure that policies would be credible and permanent. But modelling such a process is not easy, and it is generally easier to estimate the impact of changes in tariffs and other prices than changes in rules.

Challenges for appraising welfare effects are also significant. The nature of policy changes under these arrangements suggests that the normal presumptions about trade creation and diversion may not hold. It is generally presumed, for example, that PTAs will reduce exports from outside the region. However, deeper internal agreements could actually stimulate such trade. For example, if members agree on tougher pollution controls or labour standards, their imports of products from nations with more lenient standards could rise. Similarly, the adoption of a common standard in the PTA may make it less costly not only for domestic producers but also for producers outside the region to sell their products. Likewise, the adoption of constraints on national state aids would provide benefits for both internal and external producers who compete with firms that might once have received such subsidies and tougher anti-trust enforcement could provide improved market access for both internal and external producers.

In empirical studies, a reduction in external trade is generally an indication of trade diversion – i.e. that a member of an agreement is buying products from a less efficient internal source. However, deeper agreements could actually make regional firms more efficient. This might lead to a reduction of external trade, but it would not represent trade diversion that reduced welfare. For example, changes in domestic regulations could give internal firms cost advantages over outsiders that resulted both in fewer imports from outside the region and in lower internal costs. This has important implications for proposals that outsiders should be compensated for their loss of trading opportunities when preferential trading arrangements are formed.

It is also possible, however, that even without raising border barriers, or increasing internal trade, deeper regional agreements could become more closed to outsiders. One example would be the adoption of a common standard which discriminated against external imports and raised internal costs. Another might be the adoption of common cartel-like industrial policies in the region as a whole which limited external producer access.

As these examples indicate, from an efficiency standpoint, deeper international agreements could be better or worse than the domestic policies they replace or discipline. *Deeper does not necessarily mean better or more efficient.* The choice of the level of government is a matter of judgement and balancing the costs and benefits of more centralized government.

Mistakes could be made and policies implemented by international agreement could violate the principle of subsidiarity. Much depends on the specific policies that are adopted. It may be much worse to harmonize on the wrong policy than to retain national policies which are not linked.

The European example is illustrative of the argument that deep integration, i.e. the achievement of harmonized regional policies, could lead either to more or less protection depending on the specific nature of the policies. In particular, the EC's choice of trying to thwart market pressures in sectors such as agriculture, steel and coal led to a Europe that was more protectionist to the outside world. In addition, the efforts by the Community to wrest control of external trade policies away from individual countries has probably also led to more protection for the Community as a whole. Similarly, the availability of anti-dumping rules has permitted producers one-stop shopping for protection that might have been more difficult to achieve in markets that were more fragmented. There is, thus, ample evidence of contamination. On the other hand, market conforming measures have had the opposite effect – leading to increased trade opportunities both internally and externally. European disciplines on state aids and other measures which favour domestic producers provide benefits for all who compete within Europe. Similarly, the achievement of common standards reduces costs for all who wish to sell in the market.

In sum, while traditional trade theory provides us with interesting insights into both the benefits and costs of regional arrangements and their dynamics, the deeper aspects of these agreements suggest that they need to be viewed through more than the narrow prism of conventional trade theory.

2.6   Implications

The traditional view of PTAs focuses on the impact of tariff and non-tariff liberalization. This view leads to an ambivalent verdict on such arrangements since they both divert and create trade. This perspective also provides an ambiguous verdict on whether the proliferation of these arrangements undermines or increases the chances of achieving multilateral liberalization. There are numerous arguments in both directions. An alternative view acknowledges that some PTAs are both broader and deeper than the coverage of the WTO. On the one hand, they may provide more extensive liberalization of investment and services; on the other, they may also involve efforts to adopt rules and governance in areas of domestic policy that affect trade and investment. Once tariffs are removed, there remain complex problems relating to different levels of subsidies and other industrial and regulatory policies. The traditional approach is to assume that these should be determined at the national level. Increasingly, however, globalization has created pressures to reconcile divergent national practices through international agreement and governance. Indeed, there is no reason, a priori, to assume that all public goods should be delivered at the level of the nation state. In some cases, the best outcome may be for such goods to be provided by groups of countries, either permanently, or until a broader multilateral arrangement can be concluded. In principle, some regional arrangements may well be first best.

The emerging regional arrangements are moving to deal with measures that have not been dealt with by the WTO. Some opponents of these regional arrangements actually see the 'deeper' integrative aspects of these arrangements as pernicious and undesirable. They view these as mechanisms for foisting inappropriate rules and restraints on weaker, smaller and in particular, developing countries. Jagdish Bhagwati, a free trade opponent of PTAs, views them as 'a process by which a hegemonic power seeks (and often manages) to satisfy its multiple trade-unrelated demands on other, weaker trading nations more easily than through multilateralism…'. Free trade arrangements seriously damage the multilateral trade liberalization process by facilitating the capture of it by extraneous demands that aim, not to reduce trade barriers, but to increase them (as when market access is sought to be denied on grounds such as 'eco-dumping' and 'social-dumping'.[26] It is indeed likely that, in negotiations between countries with differing market sizes, an asymmetrical power relationship will exist. However, this does not mean that poor small countries will lose in these associations. Indeed the power asymmetries reflect the fact that the gains, particularly those from realizing scale economies, are likely to be relatively larger for the smaller country. Similarly, economic integration generally leads to convergence, with poorer economies growing more rapidly than richer economies. Moreover, small countries join these agreements voluntarily.

Indeed, if the NAFTA or US–Canada FTA had been seen as US initiatives they would have been doomed politically from the start. In both cases, the governments and firms of these countries saw these agreements as in their own interests, and not simply because they feared American protectionism. The same is true of the Eastern European nations that are voluntarily seeking to join the EU and those in Latin America seeking a hemispheric arrangement with the United States. Finally, particularly in agreements with the EU, aid has been made part of the package.

Moreover, while countries seeking to join these arrangements may have to make 'concessions' by adopting some rules and institutions that may not suit their needs perfectly, they also enjoy benefits from adopting institutions without having to go through the costs of developing them. Just as several European countries have sought to import the credibility in fighting inflation enjoyed by the Bundesbank by pegging their exchange rate to the German Mark, so countries can make their regulatory policies more credible through international cooperation.

I have noted the strong role played by corporations in promoting regional integration. Recognizing this role provides insight into both the promise of and the problems with the current regional initiatives. The promise is represented by moves toward deeper economic integration than is currently feasible under the WTO. Regional agreements can make progress in harmonizing domestic policies and providing more credible and more effective supra-national governance mechanisms than the WTO. On the other hand, there is the concern of regulatory capture, that under the influence of companies new systems of rules will be set to help insiders and hurt outsiders. Sceptics such as Anne Kreuger, Bernard Hoekman and Raymond Vernon are particularly concerned that while masquerading as FTAs, the new arrangements have been severely compromised by intricate rules of origin and other loopholes that may actually represent a retreat from freer trade rather than a movement towards it.[27] In addition to the traditional problem of trade diversion, therefore, there are two other major risks with regional agreements. The first is that they could implement new forms of protection, not by erecting new tariffs but by implementing rules of origin and administering anti-dumping and countervailing duties which have protectionist effects. The second is that some countries may join regional arrangements even where the rules they provide are inappropriate.

2.6.1 The EU partnership agreements

It is instructive, in the light of this discussion, to briefly consider the agreement between Tunisia and the EU since the agreement with Egypt is likely to be similar. The traditional view looks at what the agreement does to border barriers.[28] Tunisia already has duty-free access for most of its exports of manufactured goods to the EU.[29] The agreement requires liberalization of Tunisian manufactured imports from the EU over a 12-year period. It also requires the adoption of basic competition policy rules in so far as these affect trade with the EU. In return, the EU will provide increased financial and technical assistance. However, the agreement provides little in improved access for agricultural products, requires no liberalization of government procurement, does not ensure free movement of capital, makes no commitments to liberalize services and retains the anti-dumping rules.

In terms of the traditional analysis of FTAs described above, therefore, the agreement will both create and divert trade. Tunisian consumers will benefit from duty-free access to European products. But there will also be trade diversion. On the one hand, the large market share of EU goods in Tunisian imports suggests trade diversion will be small. On the other hand, the high protection that will remain on other countries suggests it could be large. In addition, a particularly troubling feature is the positioning of the EU as a hub with the Mediterranean countries as spokes. This implies that diversion could come at the expense of regional trade – thereby undermining the goal of increased regional integration. This would particularly inhibit growth in exports of industrial products to the region, particularly from Israel and Turkey, but also from other Middle Eastern manufacturers. All told, therefore, a key issue is how the loss due to trade diversion compares with the gains from trade creation and additional financial and technical assistance. Simulations undertaken by Rutherford, Rutstrom and Tarr (1995) suggest the net effect would be positive – even without taking account of the financial aid, the agreement would raise welfare by 1.7%. Estimates by Brown et. al (*see* Chapter 5) suggest welfare could actually be damaged. Clearly this is an issue needing serious investigation.

There are, however, more dynamic implications of trade diversion which could actually be more positive. In particular, precisely because external barriers are high in Middle East–North Africa (MENA) countries, non-European nations such as the United States are bound to object to the preferential treatment to be conferred on their European competitors. In response, they may find it necessary to offer MENA countries improved access to their markets in order to be given similar access. This force could therefore impel additional liberalization.

What about measures for deeper integration? These are important because if the Euro-Med agreements are to succeed they must help change the general environment for entrepreneurship. They should help make the Mediterranean countries more attractive locations for both foreign and domestic producers to serve the European market and also make the economies more globally competitive by enhancing domestic competition and encouraging these economies to open up to the rest of the world. At the margin, however, the contribution made by the agreement signed by Tunisia in these respects does not appear to be large, particularly for manufactured goods exporters. Producers of manufactured goods already have duty-free access to the EU.[30] The technical assistance in bringing Tunisian standards up to the point where mutual recognition by Europe will be possible would bring benefits – but only in the long run. The adoption of competition policy rules will bring relief from countervailing duty actions but exporters will still have to be concerned about anti-dumping actions. Foreign investors, in particular, will be struck by the lack of commitments to liberalize services and to grant rights of establishment. Likewise, those investing in services will find it gives them no additional security. Producers of agricultural goods are also given very little. All told, therefore, the agreement is unlikely to provide a boon to new investment in export industries. On the other hand, the impacts on import-competing sectors will be larger, because the liberalization commitments will be more credible since they are backed by financial aid that is conditional. In addition, it could be hoped that once the trade regime changes for goods from the EU, once producers understand their government is restricted in providing them with protection, it could curtail their rent seeking activities.

Nonetheless, the political economy of the agreement remains troublesome. Liberalizing with respect to a few trading partners can be beneficial if it strengthens the sectors which are globally competitive and reduces the size of those which are not. But there is a distinct danger that while these agreements will succeed in reducing the size of the import-competing sector they will do too little to stimulate exports and foreign investment. While the agreement will make some contribution towards upgrading standards and policies, its impact is unlikely to have the dramatic impact on foreign investment that was achieved, for example, by the much deeper agreement on NAFTA.

In the long run, of course, the MENA countries will have to adjust to their increased imports by exporting more or by receiving more aid. Even if they do not benefit by the impact of the agreements, exporters could eventually benefit as the adjustment process operates. Ironically, however, the more generous the aid, the smaller and slower these benefits may be. Nonetheless, it would serve Egypt well if it tried to surpass what Tunisia achieved in its negotiations. In particular, it could seek additional concessions from Europe in two areas: first, additional entry in textiles and agriculture, and second, exemption from European antidumping rules, in return for adopting its competition policy rules. In addition it should also try to surpass the commitments made by Tunisia with respect to liberalizing services and foreign investment. These measures would help take advantage of the greater benefits which the new regional agreements can afford.

References

Baldwin, Richard (1989), 'On the growth effect of 1992', *Economic Policy*, 248–81.
Begg, David et. al (1993), *Making Sense of Subsidiarity: How Much Centralization for Europe?*, Centre for Economic Policy Research, Monitoring European Integration 4.

Bhagwati, Jagdish (1992), *Trading Choices: The Americas or the World?*, New York, Columbia University.

Bhagwati, Jagdish and Anne O. Krueger (1995), *The Dangerous Drift to Preferential Trade Agreements*, Washington, DC, American Enterprise Institute.

Bhagwati, Jagdish (1994), 'The demand to reduce diversity among trading nations', New York, Columbia University, Mimeo.

Cooper, Richard N. (1974), 'Worldwide versus regional integration: is there an optimal size of the integrated area?', Yale Economic Growth Center Discussion Paper 220.

Corden, W. Max (1972), 'Economies of scale and customs union theory', *Journal of Political Economy 80*, March/April 465–75.

Corden, W. Max (1984), 'The normative theory of international trade', in Ronald W. Jones and Peter B. Kenen, (eds.), *Handbook of International Economics*, 63–130, Amsterdam, North Holland.

Doern, G. Bruce and Brian W. Tomlin (1991), *Faith and Fear: The Free Trade Story*, Toronto, Stoddart.

Encarnation, Dennis J. (1992), *Rivals Beyond Trade*, Ithaca and London, Cornell University Press.

Fishlow, Albert and Stephan Haggard (1992), *The United States and the Regionalisation of the World Economy*, OECD Development Centre.

Frankel, Jeffery A (1995), 'Does regionalism undermine multilateral trade liberalization or support it? A survey of recent political economy arguments', Institute for International Economics, Mimeo.

Frankel, Jeffery, Ernesto Stein, and Wei Shang-jin (1993), 'Trading blocs: the natural, the unnatural and the supernatural', University of California, Mimeo.

Grossman, Gene and Elhanan Helpman (1993), 'The politics of free trade agreements', NBER, Working Paper 4597.

Haggard, Stephan (1995), *Developing Nations and the Politics of Global Integration; Integrating National Economies: Promise and Pitfalls*, Washington, DC, Brookings Institution.

Hazlewood, Arthur (1979), 'The end of the East African community: what are the lessons for regional integration schemes?', *Journal of Common Market Studies*, September, 40–58.

Hoekman, Bernard M. (1995), 'Regional versus multilateral liberalization of trade in services', *Journal of Economic Integration*.

Hoekman, Bernard and Simeon Djankov (1996), 'The EU's Mediterranean free trade initiative', *The World Economy*, 19, 1996, 387–407.

Hoekman, Bernard and Michael Leidy (1993), 'Holes and loopholes in regional integration agreements', in K. Anderson and R. Blackhurst (eds.), *Regional Integration and the Global Trading System*, London, Harvester–Wheatsheaf.

International Monetary Fund (1994), *International Trade Policies – The Uruguay Round and Beyond: Volume II. Background Papers*, Washington, DC, International Monetary Fund.

Japan, Industrial Structure Council (1995), *The WTO Consistency of Trade Policies*, Research Institute of International Trade and Industry.

Kreuger, Anne O. (1993), 'Free trade agreements as protectionist devices: rules of origin', National Bureau of Economic Research, Working Paper 4352.

Langhammer, Rolf J. (1992), 'The developing countries and regionalism', *Journal of Common Market Studies* 30 (2/1992).

Lawrence, Robert Z. (1996), *Regionalism, Multilateralism, and Deeper Integration*, Washington, DC, Brookings Institution.

Lipsey, Richard (1957), 'The theory of customs unions: trade diversion and welfare', *Economica* 24, 40–6, (93/1957).

Lipsey, R. G. and K. Lancaster (1956), 'The general theory of the second best', *Review of Economic Studies* 24, 11–32.

Lustig, Nora, Barry Bosworth and Robert Lawrence, (eds.) (1992), *North American Free Trade: Assessing the Impact*, Washington, DC, Brookings Institution.

Meade, James E. (1955), *The Theory of Customs Unions*, Amsterdam, North Holland.

Mundell, Robert A. (1964), 'Tariff preferences and the terms of trade', *The Manchester School of Economic and Social Studies* 32, 1–13.

O'Brien, Richard (1992), *The End of Geography: Global Financial Integration*, Chatham House Papers, London, Pinter Publishers.

Perroni, Carlo and John Whalley (1994), 'The new regionalism: trade liberalization or insurance?', NBER, Working Paper 4626.

Rutherford, Thomas, E.E. Rutstrom and David Tarr (1995), 'The free trade agreement between Tunisia and the European Union', World Bank, Mimeo.

Stoeckel, Andrew et. al. (1990), *Western Trade Blocs: Game, Set or Match for Asia–Pacific and the World Economy*, Canberra, Centre for International Economics.

Thurow, Lester C. (1992), *Head to Head: The Coming Battle Among Japan, Europe and America*, New York, William Morrow.

United Nations Centre on Transnational Corporations (1991), *World Investment Report*, 1991, New York, United Nations.

United Nations Centre on Transnational Corporations (1992), *World Investment Report*, 1992, New York, United Nations.

Vernon, Raymond (1994), 'Multinationals and governments: key actors in NAFTA', in Lorraine Eden (ed.), *Multinationals in North America*, Ottawa, Investment Canada.

Viner, Jacob (1950), *The Customs Union Issue*, Carnegie Endowment for International Peace, New York.

Wells, Louis T. (1992), 'Mobile exporters: the new foreign investors in East Asia', National Bureau of Economic Research, paper presented at NBER Conference on Foreign Direct Investment.

Whitman, Marina v. N. (1972), 'Place prosperity and people prosperity: the delineation of optimum policy areas', Mark Perlman et. al. (eds.), *in Spatial, Regional and Population Economics*, 359–93, New York, Gordon and Breach.

Notes

(This paper draws heavily on Lawrence (1996)).

1. Japan, Hong Kong and India among a mere ten or so exceptions (Japan 1995, P. 304).
2. For estimates of the impact of a fortress EC or USA see Stoeckel (1990).
3. See Bhagwati (1992), Bhagwati (1994), Bhagwati and Krueger (1995).
4. According to Mickey Kantor, the United States Special Trade Representative, 'regional trading arrangements ...can prepare developing nations for admittance to the global trading system ...[and] ...they can complement global trading and lubricate negotiations', 'Global Village Gathers Speed' in *Financial Times*, 13 October 1993, page 11.

5. If trade barriers were the only market imperfection in the world, their elimination would improve aggregate welfare. However, if not all barriers are removed, or if there are other market imperfections in addition to trade barriers, we cannot be sure that removing some barriers will be welfare improving. The reason is that in a world in which market imperfections remain after the trade barrier has been removed, prices will not reflect social opportunity costs. Resources could therefore shift away rather than towards their optimal allocation.

6. Viner's original presentation of this theory was couched purely in terms of the costs of production. As Meade (1955) and Lipsey (1957) later pointed out, the removal of tariffs also brings a benefit from less distorted consumption. Thus welfare in an FTA member *could* rise, even though it is buying from a higher cost source, if the benefits from more efficient consumption exceed the loss of tariff revenues.

7. The results obtained here are sensitive to the assumptions made. Corden (19~/2) shows that scale economies complicates the analysis. In addition to the traditional trade creation and trade diversion there can also be trade suppression and cost reduction effects. The former occurs when, as a result of access to a larger market, a producer expands and thus displaces goods which would have been imported. This is not necessarily efficient, since if it was, it would have occurred prior to the union. In addition, however, there could be cost reductions, which do raise efficiency.

8. Most theorizing about PTAs assumes that nations seek to maximi – their overall welfare. Increasingly, however, more attention has been paid to the distributional effects of trade policy. Under such circumstances, Grossman and Helpman (1993) have found in a median voter model, free trade areas are most likely to be supported under conditions when trade diversion outweighs trade creation. This is precisely the case when these agreements are harmful.

9. For discussion of the role of transport costs see Frankel, Stein and Wei (1993).

10. If the intra-union terms of trade are changed, the outsiders terms of trade can actually improve (Corden, 1984 p. 120).

11. See for example, Baldwin (1989).

12. See Frankel (1995) for a more complete survey.

13. See, for example, Hazlewood (1979).

14. The East African experience is a good example. See Langhammer (1992).

15. See Fishlow and Haggard (1992).

16. See Doern and Tomlin (1991).

17. See Encarnation (1992) for a study along these lines.

18. The second half of the 1980s, in particular, were marked by a massive increase in FDI that was initially concentrated in the developed economies. According to the United Nations (UNCTC 1991) between 1983 and 1989 the dollar value of FDI outflows grew at an annual rate of 28.9%, three times as rapidly as the 9.4% pace of world exports and 7.8 % rate of world GDP.

19. See O'Brien (1992).

20. In the 1970s, developing countries receiving the largest foreign investment flows were Brazil ($1.3 billion annual average inflow), Mexico ($0.6 billion), Malaysia ($0.3), Nigeria ($0.3), Singapore ($0.3) and Egypt ($0.3). Of these only Singapore was an open, export oriented economy. Between 1980 and 1990, the list of developing economies receiving the largest annual average inflows of FDI was headed by Singapore ($2.3 billion) followed by Mexico ($1.9), Brazil ($1.8), China ($1.7), Hong Kong ($1.1) and Malaysia ($1.1). Of these only Brazil did not emphasize export oriented investment. See UNCTC (1992, p. 317).

21. See for example, Haggard (1995).

22. For a discussion of these methodologies as applied to the NAFTA, see Lustig et al (1992).

23. For additional discussion see Begg (1993).

24. See Whitman (1972) and Cooper (1974) for discussions.

25. For additional discussion see Lustig et al (1992).

26. See for example, Bhagwati and Krueger (1995) and Perroni and Whalley (1994).
27. See Hoekman (1995), Hoekman and Leidy (1993), Kreuger (1993) and Vernon (1994).
28. See Hoekman and Djankov (1996) for a more extensive analysis reaching similar conclusions.
29. A notable exception being quotas on textiles which will be liberalized, but only as called for by the Uruguay Round agreement on the Multifibre arrangement.
30. Without doubt, there may be fears today about whether these benefits could be repealed which the agreement allays.

3

External Bindings and the Credibility of Reform

Joseph F Francois
Erasmus University and CEPR

3.1   Introduction

Over the last two decades, there has been a fundamental shift in the domestic policy and outward orientation of developing and transition economies. This shift has been away from inward-oriented development policies and toward a set of outward-oriented, market-based policies (good practices) believed to be conducive to sustained development and growth. This set includes good governance, macroeconomic stability, an open trade and investment regime, market orientation, protection of property rights, and enforcement of contract law (Rodrik, 1996). While the emphasis on particular aspects of this policy mix may vary, an emerging consensus is that the greater the overlap between actual policy and the optimal set of policies, the greater the chances for sustained growth and eventual convergence with OECD income levels. In this context, the recent round of policy reforms can be characterized as efforts to move the domestic policy mix closer to congruence with the good practice set.

This most recent movement to market-based policies has also served to highlight the importance of political economy constraints in the economic reform process. As North (1990) has emphasized, not all stable policy regimes are characterized by good practice. In fact, through most of history, and across most of the world, regimes conducive to stagnation and decline have been remarkably tenacious and even robust. At this point, the fundamental problem of development economics is perhaps not so much the identification of good practices, but rather the identification of the institutional arrangements necessary for the sustainability of such practices. Not surprisingly, given the demonstrated difficulties inherent in pursuing good long-run policies both through painful short- and medium-run adjustments, and through sustained pressures of rent seeking (and rent preservation), a common theme to emerge in some of the recent development literature is the potentially positive role, at least in the economic arena, that can be played by a strong, stable central government in anchoring such policies. Examples offered in this regard include Chile and Korea. This paper explores the alternative (or complementary) option of anchoring policy through regional or multilateral agreements that offer external bindings on trade, investment, competition, and related economic policies in contractual agreements.

Concurrent with the shift over the 1980s in development strategy, there has also been both a shift in the pattern of regionalism, and an increased participation by developing countries in the multilateral system. Both have ramifications for the institutional context of reform. In the 1980s, the most successful efforts at expanded regional integration involved OECD countries in North America and Western Europe. However, since then, these regional trading blocks have expanded their reach to developing and transition countries, resulting in North–South regional agreements. This differs from earlier preferential arrangements, in that the new set of agreements tends to be contractual, and involves requirements for economic restructuring and reform on the part of Southern members. In the case of both EU partner agreements and the North American Free Trade Agreement (NAFTA), motivation can be found in an expressed interest in economic and political stability at the borders.

The Europe Agreements aim to establish bilateral free trade agreements (FTAs) between the EU and several Central European countries. These agreements offer access to the EU market free of tariff and quantitative restrictions, and are linked to the Copenhagen European Council's decision in 1993 that associated countries could accede to the EU after political and economic criteria are met. Hence, the promise of preferential access to the EU has been linked closely to human rights conditions and mechanisms related to consultations on economic, monetary, and industrial policy cooperation. While the process of developing EU agreements with the Mediterranean countries is not as well advanced or as far reaching, the EU has explicitly linked its overall policy in the region to concerns about demographic, economic, and political trends (i.e. migration incentives and political stability). Cyprus and Malta are associated countries, while Turkey has entered in a customs union. Negotiating rounds have been held with Egypt since the approval of a mandate in December 1994, while various stages in the process, ranging from preparatory talks to initialed agreements, have been reached with Algeria, Lebanon, Morocco, and Tunisia (WTO, 1995a).

This chapter is concerned with the potential benefits to developing and transition economies of enhancing the credibility of economic policy reforms through external agreements that secure a role for large partners as regional policy anchors. At a concrete level, the role of NAFTA in anchoring recent policy reforms in Mexico is discussed. Emphasis is placed on the role of the United States as a policy reform anchor. This is in contrast to the earlier NAFTA literature, particularly the numerical modelling literature surveyed by Francois and Shiells (1994), which emphasized the impact of expected reductions in tariffs and non-tariff barriers (NTBs). The critical overview of NAFTA is followed by a more abstract treatment, with reference to the Mexican case, of how external policy bindings, through bilateral and/or multilateral agreements, may lend an air of credibility to economic reforms. In addition to helping secure the path of reform, such credibility signals may also have important effects related to assessments by international capital markets of reforms undertaken in the context of trade and investment agreements. The paper concludes with discussion of the insights for the potential role of the EU as a policy reform anchor in the context of the Europe Agreements and the EU agreements with the Mediterranean countries.[1]

3.2   The opening of the Mexican economy

Mexico started a dramatic process of restructuring and reorientation in the 1980s. In accordance with its 1986 GATT accession obligations, Mexico began dismantling its previously universal regime of import-licensing requirements in 1985. Manufactured products in particular benefited from this liberalization process. By the end of 1991, only 8% of its imports from the United States (though 30% of agricultural imports) were covered by these restrictions. Other reforms implemented prior to NAFTA related to intellectual property, foreign exchange restrictions, foreign investment, and privatization. By 1991, Mexican government holdings in three large steel interests had been divested, as had Telefonos de Mexico (TELMEX) and the Banco Nacional de Mexico (BANAMEX). (The banking system had been nationalized in 1982.) The government also repealed the peso's controlled exchange rate, abandoning official exchange controls that had been in effect since 1982. Improvements in intellectual property rules followed pressure by the United States. In 1989, the US placed Mexico on a priority watch list under Special 301, citing lack of intellectual property rights protection. Mexico was removed from the list following government promises to reform earlier law, a change implemented in 1991.

Formal consultation mechanisms with the US were also in place before the NAFTA negotiations. These reflected the pattern of bilateral disputes. In conjunction with its GATT accession, Mexico concluded the Framework of Principles and Procedures for Consultation Regarding Trade and Investment Relations in 1989. This framework established a mechanism for consultations on trade and investment issues. This was followed by the Understanding Regarding Trade and Investment Facilitation Talks (TIFTs). In some areas, work begun under the TIFTs served as the basis for NAFTA negotiations.

3.2.1 Mexico's tariffs

The overall pattern of Mexican tariffs for the period spanning 1982–91 is presented in Table 3.1. The level of tariffs in the table reflects the episode of liberalization following Mexico's 1982 financial crisis. As part of its accession to the GATT, Mexico agreed to bind its entire tariff schedule, including both industrial and agricultural products, at a 50% *ad valorem* rate.[2] In the year prior to accession (1985), the average tariff was 18.5%, with up to 100% for some products. The average tariff on consumer goods was 45%. Since accession, Mexico's average tariffs have ranged between 4% and 13.1%, and the range of tariffs has been capped by Mexico's ceiling bindings. A further cap on tariffs was imposed by Mexico's entry into the North American Free Trade Agreement (NAFTA). GATT accession and NAFTA membership significantly limits the scope for raising trade barriers through tariffs. There are now caps that, though often above current rates, are well below the historically observed peak rates. Through NAFTA and the GATT/WTO, Mexico has combined the process of import and foreign investment liberalization with the undertaking of external obligations that greatly limit its ability to dismantle these reforms.

3.2.2 The credibility of the reforms

What has been the effect of this binding of trade and foreign investment policy? Arguably, a partial (and somewhat harsh) credibility test was provided shortly after ratification of NAFTA, with the peso crisis. (The movement in foreign reserves associated with this crisis is presented in Figure 3.1.) This crisis followed financial and public relations mismanagement by the Mexican government. While not linked to the reforms *per se*, the ensuing financial market reactions nonetheless threatened the sustainability of the policy regime.

An important aspect of Mexico's policy of openness relates to liberalization of barriers to foreign investment (Kehoe, 1996). The surge of

Table 3.1 Trade-weighted structure of Mexican tariffs, 1982–91

Imports (US $ million)

Tariff rates	1982	1983	1984	1985	1986	1987	1988	1989	1990	1991
Duty-free	3075.1	3174.2	3586.7	368.2	3004.5	4836.9	7664.4	4893.4	5172.2	5771.9
2	0.0	0.0	0.0	0.0	0.0	0.0	0.0	0.0	0.0	0.0
5	1458.1	793.6	1135.3	1487.2	0.0	823.6	1537.8	247.1	290.3	388.8
10	5312.8	2853.7	4229.7	3269.7	3556.6	1452.2	1415.0	6979.0	7630.1	11531.5
15	216.6	0.0	0.0	0.0	0.0	0.0	2102.2	3085.4	4205.7	6954.1
17.5	0.0	0.0	0.0	0.0	18.5	742.8	0.0	0.0	0.0	0.0
20	1761.3	206	231.1	129.8	6.6	0.0	1861.2	2999.2	4266.0	6078.6
22.5	0.0	0.0	0.0	1522.7	1347.2	0.0	0.0	0.0	0.0	0.0
25	375.4	290	492.3	0.0	120.8	0.0	0.0	0.0	0.0	0.0
27.5	0.0	0.0	0.0	0.0	25.5	0.0	0.0	0.0	0.0	0.0
30	433.1	7.6	10.0	118	22.2	0.0	0.0	0.0	0.0	0.0
35	28.9	0.0	0.0	0.0	0.0	0.0	0.0	0.0	0.0	0.0
37	0.0	0.0	0.0	0.0	954.8	0.0	0.0	0.0	0.0	0.0
40	462.0	190.8	211.0	1133.1	4.6	0.0	0.0	0.0	0.0	0.0
45	0.0	0.0	0.0	0.0	394.9	0.0	0.0	0.0	0.0	0.0
50	534.2	22.9	70.3	365.9	0.0	0.0	0.0	0.0	0.0	0.0
60	115.5	0.0	0.0	0.0	0.0	0.0	0.0	0.0	0.0	0.0
70	0.0	0.0	0.0	0.0	0.0	0.0	0.0	0.0	0.0	0.0
75	173.2	30.5	10.1	0.0	0.0	0.0	0.0	0.0	0.0	0.0
80	14.4	0.0	0.0	0.0	0.0	0.0	0.0	0.0	0.0	0.0
100	476.4	61.0	70.3	94.4	0.0	0.0	0.0	0.0	0.0	0.0
Total imports dutied	14437.0	7630.3	10046.8	8489.0	9456.2	7855.5	14580.6	18204.1	21564.3	30724.9
Imports dutied over 50% over	1313.7	114.4	150.7	460.3	0.0	0.0	0.0	0.0	0.0	0.0
weighted tariff	16.4	8.0	8.5	18.5	13.1	4.0	6.2	9.7	10.5	11.2

Source: GATT (1993), Table IV.3.
Trade levels exclude imports subject to variable specific duties, which are only relevant for 1991, and cover less than 1% of imports.

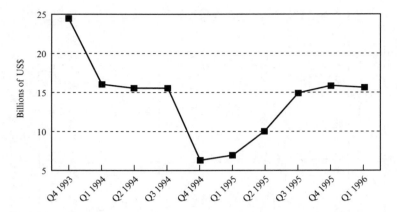

Figure 3.1 Net international reserves

investment in Mexico leading up to the crisis followed growing confidence in the Mexican reform process, and also a significant easing of restrictions on foreign investment grounded in the 1973 Law on Foreign Investment. However, much of the investment surge observed in this period (during NAFTA negotiation and ratification) was short-term investment, and much of this was borrowed by the government, in dollars, to finance public debt on a short-term basis. Kehoe provides a blow-by-blow account of the events leading to the rapid withdrawal of these portfolio funds following a series of political crises that were more or less unrelated to the basic structure of economic reform, but which still had the effect of conveying a profound sense of political instability. The crisis was linked to the politics of NAFTA in Mexico, though not directly to the policy mix itself. One result of this type of capital market crisis, under past regimes, would most certainly have involved exchange controls and a dramatic increase in levels of protection to address weakness in the capital account. This was the legacy of the crisis in the early 1980s, which in addition had been accompanied by nationalizations.

The actual outcome was quite different from past experience. With critical support (both financial and political) from its principal NAFTA partner, the United States, intervention was targeted at stabilization without sacrificing the move toward an open regime. President Clinton arranged for a $50 billion line of international credit in the spring of 1995, including $20 billion directly from the US (and additional funds 'coaxed' from the IMF). The Mexican government borrowed $12.5 billion of the American credit line. By January 1996, $2 billion had already been paid back, and currency reserve levels had largely recovered, though the

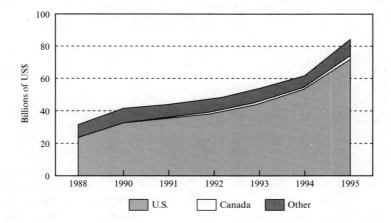

Figure 3.2 Mexican emports
Source: World Trade Organization (1995b)

government still owed $10.5 billion to the US Treasury and another $11 billion to the IMF. Also by January 1996, dollar denominated short-term government debt (Tesebonos) had been reduced from a peak of $29 billion in the beginning of 1995 to $115.7 million. The economy was recovering from a deep recession by early 1996, led by dramatic export growth, particularly to NAFTA partners (Figure 3.2). Kehoe states: 'It is important to note that, throughout the 1994–95 financial crisis in Mexico there was no serious discussion of imposing the sort of exchange rate restrictions as were used in 1982.'

3.3 The benefits of improved security

What benefits can a relatively small country expect to gain from pursuit of bilateral and multilateral bindings on its room to manoeuvre on trade and investment policy? In particular, do external bindings on domestic policy offer any advantages over unilateral liberalization? In Mexico's case, potential benefits relate to (i) security of current preferential access to the US market, (ii) improved access to the US market, and (iii) the role of the US as an external policy anchor for domestic reform. Among these, while improved access was clearly important, it was not the dominant element. Rather, the most important aspects of these effects relate to market security. In recent history, protection has been much higher on the Mexican side of the border than the US side. Prior to the NAFTA, most of Mexico's exports to the United States already benefited from duty-free or preferential access (Table 3.2). However, preferential access to the US

Table 3.2 US imports from Mexico, 1991 (value in millions of dollars, and percentage share)

	Value	Share
HTS 9802 (offshore assembly items)	6,751.4	47.1
GSP-imports	1,806.1	12.6
Petroleum (dutied at 0.7%)	2,178.8	15.2
Other	3,597.8	25.1
Total	14,334.1	100.0

Source: US International Trade Commission (1992).

market was not contractual (i.e. was not guaranteed). Rather, as can be seen in Table 3.2, these preferences resulted from offshore assembly provisions of the US tariff code, and from the US GSP programme. There was no obligation on the part of the United States to maintain Mexican eligibility for either of these programmes. Clearly, therefore, an important source of expected benefits related not to US tariff reduction *per se*, but rather to the reduction in commercial policy uncertainty associated with current preferential access. Combined with the locking of Mexico and its North American trading partners into commitments that anchored domestic reform, the result was a substantial increase in foreign direct investment, and a lowering of the risk premium for Mexico, in turn lowering interest rates.

This section briefly examines, analytically, some aspects of each of these mechanisms. The point is that policy reform, undertaken in the context of binding external agreements, may carry more credibility than otherwise. The net result is a reduction in policy uncertainty, which in turn has a number of important positive implications.

3.3.1 The expected cost of import protection

Since the establishment of the GATT in 1947, average industrial tariff protection in the OECD has fallen to less than 5%, while the variance of individual bound tariffs has been virtually eliminated. However, the stochastic nature of protection has remained strongly evident across individual sectors and instruments free from, or lightly constrained by, binding trade rules. Thus, protection rates have varied substantially in areas such as agriculture (in both developed and developing countries) and in industrial products in developing countries. When we look beyond bound tariffs on industrial goods, we find that a wide range of measures such as variable levies, import quotas, voluntary export restraints (VERs), import surcharges, and the various forms of contingent protection (such as balance of payments actions, anti-dumping and countervailing duties) continues to be used to generate time-varying rates of protection.

To deal with this inherent commercial policy uncertainty, a key feature of multilateral liberalizations has been the introduction of tariff and other instrument bindings which constrain the range and variability of protection rates. For example, while tariff bindings allow tariff rates to vary below the level of the binding, they reduce both the average applied tariff and the variability of the applied rate of protection. Drawing on the extensive literature on the political economy of protection for support, Francois and Martin (1995) have argued that the political economy pressures that cause protection rates to vary are likely to continue to generate varying rates of protection even after the introduction of new commercial policy bindings. In such a setting, the potential benefits of additional bilateral and multilateral liberalizations will be related to both the average level of protection *and its variance*.

Bindings are vital to the process of securing trade agreements. If an agreed tariff reduction could be unilaterally reversed, any liberalization offer would have to be weighed against the probability of backsliding. Exporting firms, which provide much of the political support for bilateral and multilateral trade and investment liberalization, are likely to be unenthusiastic about tariff cuts they expect to be short-lived. Bindings themselves are considered to be so important that, in the GATT/WTO context, countries agreeing to bind previously unbound tariffs are given 'negotiating credit' for the decision. This is true even if the tariff is bound above the currently applied level. Similar qualifications apply to investor enthusiasm under the threat of uncertain foreign exchange restrictions or similar measures.

Some of the welfare implications of bindings are illustrated in Figure 3.3 for the case of a small country, with symmetric variations in protection.[3] In the figure, the downward sloping line represents the compensated import demand curve. With a fixed tariff, the welfare cost of protection is defined by the Harberger triangle cab under the excess demand curve. Alternatively, consider symmetric variations around this tariff level, with a higher tariff yielding a higher domestic price P_h in one time period and a lower one P_L in another. The welfare cost of the higher tariff is cfg, and of the lower tariff is cde. The reader can verify that the average of these areas (the expected cost of protection) exceeds the cost of protection under a fixed tariff. Under more general conditions, Francois and Martin (1995) have shown that the expected cost of protection is a function of the first and second moments of protection. For this reason the expected cost of protection, for a given average tariff level, is higher when that tariff is uncertain. This benefit of binding relates to expected utility, and is distinct from investment-related benefits of reduced uncertainty (discussed below). It follows from the geometric aspect of the welfare costs of price distortions (Figure 3.3). The expected benefits of reduction in uncertainty will be further magnified, for small countries, when preferences reflect risk aversion.[4]

3.3.2 *The expected cost of protection in export markets*

By similar arguments, benefits can be identified related to secured market access conditions in export markets. However, the benefits depend critically on the nature of the security. Consider again a small exporter, with the excess import demand curve again represented in Figure 3.3. We now assume away home import policy variance, and focus instead on uncertainty in foreign market access conditions. Free trade is represented by price line P^*. We again assume symmetric variations in protection, though this time as reflected in market access conditions for exports. Exports are determined by the terms of trade and import demand, as reflected in the intersection of the world price line for importables. If protection in export markets is low, terms-of-trade are relatively favourable, and trade occurs along world price line P_l. Alternatively, with high protection in export markets, terms-of-trade are given by P_h. The welfare costs of these two states, compared to free trade, are $P_h P^* cf$ and $P_l P^* cd$ respectively.

What are the implications of price stability through bindings? Clearly, if market access can be secured at the lower level of protection, P_l, then the move is welfare improving. As the current example of China and unsecured MFN treatment in the US market has highlighted, secure

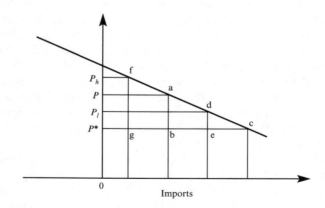

Figure 3.3 Welfare implications of protection

MFN access (i.e. secured access at the 'best available rate') is better than unsecured access. However, consider also a stabilized level of protection at the mean level P. In the present example, if we compare the welfare effects of the varied states (in terms of shifting terms-of-trade effects) with the fixed state P, in the absence of risk aversion, variable terms of trade are preferred. The reader can verify this by adding the relevant squares and triangles under the excess demand curve. Again, this is analogous to well known results in the price stabilization literature, this time for demand agents (or in our example the importer). The actual welfare implications of bindings on the part of trading partners will depend critically on the elasticity of demand, possibilities for consumption smoothing, and relative risk aversion.

Basically, in terms of expected utility analysis, commercial policy stability in both import and export markets is analogous to commodity price stabilization. For a small country, the benefits, analogous to the supplier benefits under commodity price stabilization, follow from the imposition of own-security. There may also be benefits from foreign market access security, but this hinges on the nature of commercial policy security on the export market side, as well as on relative risk aversion of home economic agents. A basic point here is that the national welfare benefits of secure commercial policy are much more evident for securing one's own policies than for securing partner policies.

3.3.3 Dynamic effects

Another set of effects is likely to follow from a generally improved commercial policy environment. In the case of Mexico, this has been emphasized by Kehoe (1994) and Young and Romero (1994). It is illustrated conceptually in Figure 3.4, where the curve MP_K represents the marginal product of capital, and where the line r^* represents current lending conditions on international capital markets. Conditions for international capital lending will reflect a number of factors, including risk of nationalization (e.g. Mexico in 1982), and the security provided by outside obligations (like the 1986 Mexican GATT accession and the 1993 NAFTA). As elements are added that reduce the underlying risk premium, this is reflected in a shift in r^* to $r^{*'}$. In Figure 3.4, the national income gain from this reduced risk premium is the area abcd. This is related to expanded production and rising labour productivity and wages. Arguably, this effect may be one of the most important medium-to long-run effects of investment-related external policy reform anchors.

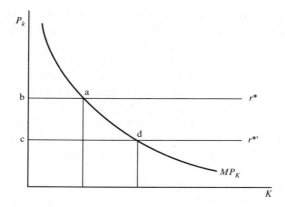

Figure 3.4 Implications of improved security

3.4   Can we generalize?

This chapter has drawn from the Mexican experience to develop a set of stylized effects that may follow from externally anchored policy reforms, particularly in the context of North–South trade agreements. The basic thesis is that reduced policy uncertainty, in terms of trade and investment policy, can have important effects, above those related to simple unilateral changes in the level of intervention. In the case of Mexico, GATT accession and the NAFTA both served to anchor domestic policy reform, lending credibility to the Mexican government's ongoing policy of openness or *apertura*.

The question left unanswered is whether these elements can be orchestrated in other trade and investment agreements entered by other developing regions. In particular, what lessons can we draw from this experience for the broader set of developing and transition countries? Can we reasonably expect that a mix of regional agreements with the EU and NAFTA blocks, combined with multilateral obligations, can serve as credible policy anchors? Based on the Mexican experience, *including the peso crisis*, the answer is a qualified yes. However, the market forced a testing of the credibility of the reform anchors, demanding strong intervention by the United States and IMF. It is unreasonable to expect the degree of financial commitment exhibited by the United States to hold in other situations. Hence, the Mexican experience highlights both the importance of external partners that value the internal policy reforms enough to force adherence to external obligations, and the importance of rational macroeconomic policies (like the exchange rate) as a backdrop to radical microeconomic reform. If the anchor is to provide macro credibility, then this in turn suggests that such external anchors must carry weight in financial markets and in international institutions.

Are these conditions met outside of Mexico? In some areas, particularly around the EU, the answer would seem to be yes. This includes Central and Eastern Europe, where there are parallels to the US concern about stability and prosperity at the border. The move toward EU integration can be viewed as a move toward cementing market reforms. What about the Mediterranean countries? Here again, there is a parallel with concerns about underlying demographic trends and migration. The model of anchored policy reform may potentially prove relevant in the long run for the Mediterranean countries as well. However, this will require both real commitment on the part of the EU, *and* (as Hoekman and Djankov 1996 have emphasized), real bindings on internal policies on the part of the Mediterranean countries. This includes binding, enforceable commitments on foreign direct investment regimes, and perhaps enough preferential liberalization in trade and investment to encourage commercial interest on the part of the anchor partner. Across the Mediterranean region, these steps have yet to be taken. Reform anchors only work if there are reforms to anchor. Otherwise, subsequent benefits related to improvements in the conditions imposed by international financial markets will not be realized.

References

Francois, J. and W. Martin (1995), 'Multilateral trade rules and the expected cost of protection', CEPR discussion paper 1214, July.

Francois, J. and C. Shiells (1994), *Modeling Trade Policy: Applied General Equilibrium Assessments of North American Free Trade*, Cambridge, Cambridge University Press.

GATT (1993), *Trade Policy Review – Mexico*, Geneva.

Hoekman, B. and S. Djankov (1996), 'The European Union's Mediterranean free trade initiative', The World Economy, 19, 387–407.

Kehoe, T. (1994), 'Toward a dynamic general equilibrium model of North American trade', in J. Francois and C. Shiells, (eds.), *Modeling Trade Policy: Applied General Equilibrium Assessments of North American Free Trade*, Cambridge, Cambridge University Press.

Kehoe, T. (1996), 'Capital flows and North American economic integration,' in J. Francois and R. Baldwin, (eds.), *Dynamic Issues in Applied Commercial Policy Analysis*, CEPR and Cambridge University Press, forthcoming.

North, D. (1990), *Institutions, Institutional Change, and Economic Performance*, Cambridge, Cambridge University Press.

Rodrik, D. (1996), 'Understanding economic policy reform,' *Journal of Economic Literature* XXXIV (March), 9–41.

US International Trade Commission (1992), *The Year in Trade – Operation of the Trade Agreements Program*, ASIATIC publication 2554, August.

World Trade Organization (1995a), *Trade Policy Review – European Union*, 1, Geneva.

World Trade Organization (1995b), *International Trade 1995: Trends and Statistics*, Geneva.

Young, L. and J. Romero (1994), 'A dynamic dual model of the North American Free Trade Agreement.' in J. Francois and C. Shiells, (eds.), *Modeling Trade Policy: Applied General Equilibrium Assessments of North American Free Trade*, Cambridge, Cambridge University Press.

This paper represents the views of the author, and is not meant to represent the position of any institution.

Notes

1. Hoekman and Djankov (1996), in their discussion of the Euro-Mediterranean Agreement between the EU and Tunisia, also place emphasis on credibility. In the case of the Tunisian EMA, they argue that there is an absence of binding commitments in a number of important areas, including services and investment.
2. The exception was any imports already covered by lower bindings. Mexico also negotiated quotas for certain products (primarily agricultural and wood-based products) under bound rates. See GATT (1993).
3. See Francois and Martin (1995) for a treatment with generalized temporal distribution of protection.
4. Note that this result will also hold in frameworks where consumption smoothing is possible, since reduction in policy uncertainty will reduce the expected costs of consumption smoothing (i.e. borrowing).

4

Economic Integration in East Asia: ASEAN

Dean A DeRosa
ADR International

4.1   Introduction

East Asia comprises the low- and middle-income countries of East and Southeast Asia and the Pacific, east of and including China and Thailand. During the last two decades the region has gained a great deal of prominence in the world economy and global trading system. Today, East Asia is arguably the most diverse and rapidly growing area in the world economy, led in particular by the newly industrializing countries (NICs) of the region – Hong Kong, South Korea, Singapore, and Taiwan – and their remarkable record of economic development and international trade[1] (Table 4.1).

Pursuit of 'open' or 'outward-oriented' economic policies is a major if not the principal element of the so-called East Asian Miracle (World Bank, 1993).[2] In presenting both consumers and producers with relatively undistorted prices for foreign and domestically produced goods, liberal trade policies and practices combined with stable (non-inflationary) macroeconomic policies have provided an environment conducive to robust expansion of internationally-competitive sectors in both industry and agriculture.[3] In particular, they have led many East Asian countries to follow their comparative advantage in labour-intensive production and, as investment in education accumulated, in production requiring greater intensity of human capital. Broadly speaking, they have also resulted in increased integration of the East Asian economies with one another and the economies of the major industrial countries.[4] Though greater specialization and division of labour, particularly between the East Asian countries and the major industrial countries, have resulted in occasional trade disputes and economic tensions, they have also resulted in greater economic welfare for both groups of countries.

Table 4.1 Indicators of fundamental economic factors for East Asian countries, 1993

	Population (millions)	Population density (sq.km)	Education (Index)[2]	Per capita GNP (US dollars)	Structure of production (Employment)[1]		GDP growth 1980–93(%)[3]	Export growth 1980–93(%)[3]
					Industry	Agriculture		
					(Percentage of GDP; labour force)			
China	1,178	123	54	490	48	19 (56)	10	12
Newly industrialising countries								
Hong Kong	6	6,000	148	18,060	21	0 (0)	7	16
South Korea	44	445	276	7,660	43	7 (15)	9	12
Singapore	3	3,000	169	19,850	37	0 (0)	7	13
Taiwan	21	583	n.a.	10,850	50	4 (11)	8	19
Southeast Asian countries								
Indonesia	187	98	63	740	3	19 (51)	6	7
Malaysia	19	58	92	3,140	39[4]	20 (21)[4]	6	13
Philippines	65	217	140	850	33	22 (46)	1	3
Thailand	58	113	108	2,110	39	10 (57)	8	16

Notes: 1. Values in parentheses are the share of agricultural employment in the domestic labour force.
2. Index of human resource development, calculated as the secondary school enrolment rate plus five times the university enrolment rate, both calculated in their respective age cohorts. Values reported are for 1989.
3. Average annual rate, in real terms.
4. 1989 value.

Sources: ADB (1995), DeRosa (1995) and World Bank (1995).

Within East Asia, the Association of Southeast Nations (ASEAN) countries – principally, Indonesia, Malaysia, Philippines, Singapore, and Thailand – are among the most prominent countries in the next tier of countries following the development path of the NICs.[5] Historically, ASEAN countries enforced higher levels of protection than the NICs, to promote faster industrialization. Since the 1970s, however, import-substitution strategies in ASEAN have been steadily eroded by gradual, unilateral adoption of more open trading regimes, with positive effects on growth of domestic output and exports.[6]

Although ASEAN was established during the late 1960s to strengthen political security in Southeast Asia, economic cooperation has come to play a primary role in the activities of the Association.[7] Most prominently, periodic economic policy dialogues are held among the ASEAN countries, and between ASEAN and its principal trading partners: the European Union, Japan, and United States. This cooperation has proven particularly successful in forging ASEAN positions in international economic fora, including the Bretton Woods institutions and the World Trade Organization (WTO).

Another centrepiece of ASEAN economic cooperation has been the pursuit of cooperative trade and investment arrangements, following the adoption of the ASEAN Preferential Trading Arrangement (PTA) system in 1977. Patterned after early regional trading arrangements in Latin America supported by the United Nations,[8] the PTA was unsuccessful in fostering significant expansion of intra-ASEAN trade and came to be eclipsed by a *de facto* policy of 'open regionalism,' whereby the ASEAN countries largely abandoned pursuit of their increasingly bureaucratic system of preferential trading arrangements in favour of gradual trade liberalization on a most-favoured-nation (MFN) basis.[9] Indeed, open regionalism is frequently offered as the explanation for the vitality of the economies of the ASEAN countries as well as East Asian NICs. As Drysdale and Garnaut (1993, p.187) have put it, open regionalism has given developing countries in Asia, and elsewhere, an alternative to being caught in the prisoner's dilemma of negotiated trade 'concessions'; specifically, it has given them the 'prisoner's delight' of observing the highly beneficial effects of each country's liberalization on its own trade expansion.

Notwithstanding this experience, in response to the overlong duration of the Uruguay Round negotiations, increasing regionalism in other parts of the world, and a perceived threat to ASEAN competitiveness in the formation of the North American Free Trade Agreement (NAFTA) by Canada, Mexico, and the United States, in January 1992 the ASEAN countries announced their intention to form the ASEAN Free Trade Area (AFTA).[10] The AFTA plan is technically consistent with the twin requirements of the General Agreement on Tariffs and Trade (Article XXIV) concerning customs unions and free trade areas, namely, that the regional trading areas cover substantially all intra-regional trade and not involve higher barriers to trade with countries outside the free trade area.[11] However, in specifying margins of tariff preferences for intra-bloc trade, the plan arguably marks a reversion to earlier protection policies in ASEAN, threatening continued progress of open regionalism and the full enjoyment of its benefits in Southeast Asia.

In greater East Asia, regionalism has come to be the domain of the Asia–Pacific Economic Cooperation (APEC) forum, which was established in 1989 by the East Asian countries (including ASEAN) and the major industrial countries bordering the Pacific Ocean. APEC is dedicated to promoting international trade and investment in the Asia–Pacific region, in particular through the reduction and, where possible, the elimination of impediments to all international transactions (APEC, 1991). APEC has little formal structure and only a small secretariat located in Singapore, but the bloc's annual meetings of economic ministers and heads of state are guided by a growing number of inter-government working parties on intra-regional trade and investment issues.

In recent years, APEC discussions have given prominent consideration to the formation of an Asia–Pacific free trade area to be founded explicitly on the concept of open regionalism, for principled but also pragmatic reasons.[12] The industrial-country members of APEC have set a general goal of dismantling their barriers to intra-regional trade by the year 2010, and the developing-country members of APEC by the year 2020. Given its adherence to preferential trading arrangements, the ASEAN Free Trade Area is at some odds with the 'higher' aspirations of APEC and East Asian countries to promote non-discriminatory trade liberalization not only in the Asia-Pacific region but also the world at large.

The remainder of this paper outlines the plan for the ASEAN Free Trade Area and presents the results of a quantitative analysis of the plan (DeRosa, 1995). Notably, the analysis investigates AFTA's implications for trade and national welfare, but also agriculture, which still contributes significantly to total output, and especially to total employment, in several ASEAN countries[13] (Table 4.1). By its methodology, the quantitative analysis also indicates the comparative implications of continued pursuit of open regionalism in Southeast Asia.

4.2   The AFTA plan and ASEAN trade simulation model

4.2.1   The AFTA plan

As outlined in the *Singapore Declaration of 1992* and related documents (ASEAN, 1992a,b,c), the elements of the AFTA plan are straightforward. Under what is termed the Common Effective Preferential Tariff scheme, beginning in 1995 each ASEAN country is to reduce the level of its tariffs on imports to a range of 0% to 5% by the year 2003. During the first five years of the plan, tariff levels are to be reduced substantially. Then, during the remaining three years of the plan, each member country will reduce tariff levels to the 0% to 5% range. Although the scheme makes provisions for safeguard measures in cases of 'serious injury' to domestic producers, it explicitly calls for the simultaneous elimination of quantitative restrictions and other non-tariff barriers to intra-bloc trade.

The plan singles out a mixture of industrial products of keen interest to exporters and policy makers in the ASEAN countries for accelerated tariff reductions (Table 4.2). The levels of protection associated with the products selected for accelerated trade liberalization are similar, on average, to protection in general for manufactures in the ASEAN countries.

The rates of protection for the selected manufactures also tend to be higher than those for primary commodities and agricultural raw materials.[14] This is symptomatic of what has been termed the 'bias against agriculture'. In particular, trade and macroeconomic policies often distort price incentives against agriculture with the objective of promoting more rapid industrialization. Studies by Cavallo and Mundlak (1982), Krueger, Schiff, and Valdés (1988, 1992), and Bautista and Valdés (1993), among others, reveal that this bias is manifest particularly in distortions in the real exchange rate, defined as the relative price of non-traded to traded goods. In giving rise to 'overvaluation' of the real exchange rate, import substitution policies and expansionary monetary and fiscal policies (under managed exchange rate regimes) cause agriculture and other exportable goods sectors, such as apparel and other labour-intensive industries, to be smaller and less internationally competitive than they would be under more neutral or open economic policy regimes. Also, the bias against agriculture causes the purchasing power of rural populations and unskilled urban workers to be lower than otherwise and thus imposes a significant demand-side constraint on economic growth in low-income countries.

4.2.2   ASEAN trade simulation model

The ASEAN trade simulation model was developed to gauge empirically the medium-term effects of the ASEAN Free Trade Area on economy-wide and sectoral variables in major Southeast Asian countries and is patterned after the 'Michigan model' of world production and trade (Deardorff and Stern, 1986).

For each ASEAN country, simultaneous linear equations depict the conditions for equilibrium in markets for 26 categories of traded goods, a non-traded good, and (assumed) homogeneous labour services (Table

Table 4.2 ASEAN import restrictions on manufactures selected for accelerated trade liberalization under the AFTA plan, 1987

	Average *ad valorem* tariff rates (NTB frequency rates) – percentage				
	Indonesia	Malaysia	Philippines	Singapore	Thailand
Selected manufactures	23 (92)	19 (2)	36 (55)	0 (12)	46 (14)
Vegetable oils	29 (100)	4 (0)	31 (36)	0 (4)	50 (96)
Cement, related products	26 (100)	18 (13)	41 (34)	0 (0)	48 (8)
Pharmaceuticals	5 (100)	3 (0)	18 (95)	0 (95)	31 (0)
Fertilizers	0 (100)	1 (0)	23 (100)	0 (0)	10 (0)
Rubber products	10 (66)	33 (0)	34 (46)	0 (0)	52 (0)
Leather products	28 (100)	28 (0)	39 (29)	0 (0)	64 (0)
Paper pulp	29 (85)	16 (0)	41 (58)	0 (0)	41 (22)
Textiles, apparel	33 (88)	29 (1)	48 (13)	2 (9)	62 (1)
Electronic components	25 (81)	21 (5)	37 (98)	0 (12)	43 (16)
Wooden furniture	42 (100)	40 (0)	52 (46)	2 (0)	64 (0)
Memorandum items					
Primary commodities	15 (99)	8 (5)	32 (41)	0 (15)	38 (24)
Foods	25 (99)	13 (6)	40 (60)	0 (22)	51 (37)
Cereals	4 (100)	2 (31)	42 (100)	0 (31)	15 (62)
Agricultural raw materials	10 (96)	7 (6)	28 (24)	0 (20)	34 (15)
Crude fertilizers, ores	4 (100)	4 (4)	18 (13)	0 (5)	19 (18)
Mineral fuels	5 (100)	6 (0)	21 (75)	2 (2)	21 (11)
Non-ferrous metals	9 (100)	7 (0)	26 (0)	0 (0)	25 (6)
Manufactures	20 (93)	16 (3)	34 (46)	0 (14)	43 (8)
Chemicals	11 (96)	9 (3)	23 (48)	0 (49)	36 (6)
Iron and steel	8 (99)	6 (8)	19 (20)	0 (0)	26 (8)
Machinery, equipment	17 (91)	12 (4)	29 (88)	0 (4)	33 (9)
Other manufactures	27 (92)	22 (2)	42 (28)	1 (5)	51 (8)
All goods	18 (95)	14 (4)	33 (45)	0 (15)	41 (12)

Notes: Tariff rates are inclusive of customs duties and other fiscal charges on imports. NTB frequency rates refer to the percentage of national tariff schedule lines affected by non-tariff barriers.

Sources: ASEAN (1992 a,b,c) and DeRosa (1995).

4.3). Goods satisfy demands for intermediate uses and final consumption. Primary factors of production are fixed in aggregate supply and fully employed at their respective value of marginal products. Labour is assumed mobile among sectors, but other factors of production, such as physical capital and natural resources, are assumed to be specific to individual sectors. Labour and other primary factors are substitutable for one another in value added, whereas purchased inputs and value added are combined in fixed proportions. On the demand side, expenditures on final demand are determined endogenously, with aggregate changes in revenues from import duties assumed to be redistributed to consumers. Finally, 'closure' of the model takes the form of an international payments constraint that, through adjustment of the nominal exchange rate and other variables, requires aggregate expenditures on domestic and foreign goods to equal the sum of revenues from production plus possible sources of external financing.[15]

Following Armington (1969), consumers differentiate traded goods according to their place of production. This results in a system of bilateral demands for traded goods that facilitates the analysis of preferential tariffs and non-tariff barriers applied to intra-ASEAN trade. A preferential reduction of tariffs on imports from ASEAN countries lowers the domestic price of the imported goods, thereby increasing demand for imports from ASEAN countries (trade creation) and reducing demand for imports from non-ASEAN countries (trade diversion). Non-tariff barriers are liberalized by increasing the quantity of administered imports from different trading partners.

4.2.3   Policy scenarios

Four policy scenarios are considered. The first two represent the basic variants of the AFTA plan announced in January 1992, namely, complete removal of tariffs and non-tariff barriers against intra-ASEAN trade in the categories of manufactures for accelerated trade liberalization (Scenario I) and in all manufactures (Scenario II). The third scenario represents the expanded AFTA plan endorsed in principle by the ASEAN economic ministers in late-1994, namely, complete removal of tariffs and non-tariff barriers against intra-ASEAN trade in all goods, including agricultural and other primary commodities. Finally, the fourth scenario represents non-discriminatory liberalization of ASEAN imports of all goods. This last policy scenario provides an MFN-based yardstick for judging the efficacy of the AFTA plan in reducing the bias against agriculture and, more generally, in improving national welfare. It can also be regarded as representing an alternative policy of complete open regionalism in ASEAN.

Under each scenario, *ad valorem* tariffs in the ASEAN countries for affected imports are reduced to zero. The elimination of non-tariff barriers, on the other hand, is represented simply by an increase in the volume of affected administered imports by 25%, on the assumption that NTBs restrict imports to levels in the neighbourhood of 80% of their free trade levels.[16]

4.3   Simulation results

In Vinerian terms (Viner, 1950), the AFTA plan represented by any of its variants (i.e., Scenarios I, II, or III) is trade-creating (Table 4.4).[17] Indeed,

Table 4.3 The ASEAN trade simulation model: goods categories and substitution elasticity values

Goods category	SITC[1]	Elasticity of substitution	
		Consumption[2]	Production[3]
Primary commodities	(0–4)+68	n.a.	n.a.
Foods	0+1+22+4	n.a.	n.a.
Cereals	041–045	4.0	0.6
Vegetable oils, oilseeds	22+42	4.0	0.6
Other foods	n.a.	4.0	0.6
Agricultural raw materials	2 less (22+27+28)	n.a.	n.a.
Textile fibres	26	4.0	0.6
Other raw materials	n.a.	4.0	0.6
Other primary commodities	27+28+3+68	n.a.	n.a.
Crude fertilizers, mineral ores	27+28	4.0	0.8
Mineral fuels	3	4.0	0.8
Non-ferrous metals	68	4.0	0.8
Manufactures	(5–8) less 68	n.a.	n.a.
Chemicals	5	n.a.	n.a.
Pharmaceuticals	54	3.0	0.8
Toiletries, perfumes	55	3.0	0.8
Manufactured fertilizers	56	3.0	0.8
Other chemicals	n.a.	3.0	0.8
Iron and steel	67	3.0	1.0
Machinery and equipment	7	n.a.	n.a.
Non-electrical machinery	71–75	2.0	0.6
Electrical machinery	76+77	2.0	0.8
Transport equipment	78+79	3.0	0.8
Other manufactured goods	(6+87) less (67+68)	n.a.	n.a.
Leather, travel goods	61+83	2.0	0.8
Rubber products	62	3.0	0.8
Wood products	63	2.0	0.8
Paper products	64	2.0	1.0
Textiles, clothing	65+84	3.0	1.0
Non-metal mineral products	66	3.0	1.0
Furniture	82	3.0	0.8
Footwear	85	3.0	1.0
Professional equipment	87+88	2.0	1.0
Other manufactures	n.a.	3.0	1.0
Non-traded goods	n.a.	n.a.	1.0

Notes: In addition to the ASEAN countries (Indonesia, Malaysia, the Philippines, Singapore, and Thailand), 21 countries and country groups are covered in the model. Other developing Asian countries include China, Hong Kong, Taiwan, and South Korea (East Asia); and Bangladesh, India, Pakistan, and Sri Lanka (South Asia). Industrial countries include Australia and New Zealand, Belgium, France, Germany, Italy, Netherlands, Switzerland, and United Kingdom (Europe); and Canada, Japan, and United States. Other developing and industrial countries are grouped into the rest of the world.

1. Standard international trade classification.
2. Elasticity of substitution in demand for similar traded goods differentiated by country of origin.
3. Elasticity of substitution among primary factors of production in value-added (ASEAN countries only).

if the AFTA plan is extended to cover all intra-ASEAN trade (Scenario III), the simulation results indicate that total intra-bloc trade expands by as much as 19% (US$2.9 billion in 1988), while total ASEAN (export and import) trade with industrial countries contracts by less than 1% (US$0.5 billion). In addition, the sectoral details of the simulation results presented in Table 4.5 indicate that the expansion of production and exports under the AFTA plan bears close similarity to that under MFN trade liberalization (Scenario IV). In other words, the expansion of production and exports tends to follow the widely acknowledged comparative advantage of the ASEAN countries in agricultural and other natural resource-based goods and in labour-intensive manufactures.

With regard to agriculture, the simulation results in Table 4.5 also indicate that the bias against agriculture in the ASEAN countries is reduced under the AFTA plan. Specifically, the domestic terms of trade for agriculture (relative to non-traded goods) are widely improved, giving rise to expanded agricultural production. Moreover, with the depreciation of the exchange rate in several countries and the preferential trade liberalization itself, incentive is also given to expansion of agricultural exports.

The circumstances of agriculture, however, are improved substantially less under AFTA than under MFN liberalization. Whereas the most liberal variant of the AFTA plan (Scenario III) results in expanded agricultural output in the four natural resource-based ASEAN countries of between 0.1% (Indonesia) and 0.6% (Thailand), MFN liberalization (Scenario IV) results in expanded agricultural output of between 2.3% (Indonesia) and 8.7% (Philippines). Similar results are seen for the expansion of agricultural exports, measured in terms of US dollars. Led particularly by expansion of agricultural exports in Indonesia ($1.3 billion) and Thailand ($1.2 billion), under MFN liberalization the total expansion of ASEAN exports of agricultural goods ($3.8 billion) is greater than the total expansion of ASEAN exports of manufactures ($3.2 billion). In contrast, the total expansion of ASEAN exports of agricultural goods under each variant of the AFTA plan is not only substantially less than under MFN liberalization but also substantially less than the total expansion of ASEAN exports of manufactures under any of the three variants of the AFTA plan.

These results reveal the limited potential of the AFTA plan for reducing the bias against agriculture in Southeast Asia. They also point to other questionable aspects of the simulated effects of the plan. In particular, the sectoral adjustment of *consumption and imports* under the AFTA plan diverges importantly from that under MFN liberalization, owing to the discriminatory nature of the trade liberalization. Overall, the AFTA plan is estimated to yield mainly small improvements in economic welfare

Table 4.4 Changes in economy-wide variables, international trade and economic welfare

Import liberalization scenario	Economy-wide variables (%)			International trade (millions US$)[1]					Economic welfare (percent)
	Expenditures	Wage rate	Exchange rate	Exports (imports) World	Exports ASEAN	Exports Industrial countries	Imports ASEAN	Imports Industrial countries	
I. AFTA – selected manufactures									
Indonesia	0.1	0.4	−0.3	130	102	27	134	−3	0.1
Malaysia	0.7	1.8	−0.4	213	239	−21	396	−145	0.8
Philippines	0.1	0.3	−0.5	70	56	14	103	−20	0.2
Singapore	1.0	2.1	1.3	427	595	−97	179	180	1.7
Thailand	0.1	1.1	−0.3	112	96	12	275	−119	0.2
ASEAN[2]	n.a.	n.a.	n.a.	952	1,088	−65	1,088	−107	n.a.
				(0.9)	(7.3)	(−0.1)	(7.3)	(−0.2)	n.a.
II. AFTA – all manufactures									
Indonesia	0.2	1.0	−0.8	213	127	77	223	−8	0.2
Malaysia	0.8	2.2	−0.4	273	315	−33	508	−181	1.0
Philippines	0.2	0.8	0.1	104	113	−6	141	−21	0.3
Singapore	1.6	2.8	2.4	680	1,002	−207	226	331	2.9
Thailand	0.3	0.9	−1.2	189	129	49	589	−306	0.4
ASEAN[2]	n.a.	n.a.	n.a.	1,459	1,687	−121	1,687	186	n.a.
				(1.4)	(11.3)	(−0.2)	(11.3)	(−0.3)	n.a.

Import liberalization scenario	Economy-wide variables (%)			Exports (imports)	Exports		Imports		Economic welfare (percent)
	Expenditures	Wage rate	Exchange rate	World	ASEAN	Industrial countries	ASEAN	Industrial countries	
III. AFTA – all goods									
Indonesia	0.2	1.3	-0.8	342	257	77	351	-8	0.2
Malaysia	0.8	3.1	0.5	536	716	-135	753	-167	1.3
Philippines	0.3	1.0	-1.2	171	128	37	262	-43	0.4
Singapore	2.1	6.3	3.2	993	1,520	-314	418	378	3.9
Thailand	0.6	4.2	-2.0	405	274	106	1,111	-393	0.6
ASEAN[2]	n.a.	n.a.	n.a.	2,446 (2.3)	2,895 (19.3)	-229 (-0.4)	2,895 (19.3)	-234 (-0.4)	n.a.
IV. MFN – all goods									
Indonesia	3.8	22.9	-23.2	3,102	213	2,484	288	2,004	2.3
Malaysia	5.8	22.4	-11.9	1,263	529	586	438	555	4.9
Philippines	4.8	4.6	-34.7	1,438	96	1,201	142	730	4.6
Singapore	0.2	7.1	-6.7	686	551	59	540	186	-2.1
Thailand	5.6	13.6	-26.8	2,572	344	1,836	325	1,374	4.4
ASEAN[2]	n.a.	n.a.	n.a.	9,061 (8.5)	1,732 (11.6)	6,167 (10.4)	1,732 (11.6)	4,849 (8.6)	n.a.

International trade (millions US$)[1]

1. Per annum, measured in 1988 US dollars.
2. Values in parentheses are percentage changes in ASEAN trade relative to baseline 1988 trade levels. The percentage changes in ASEAN trade with the world are average changes of ASEAN exports and imports with the world.
Source: DeRosa (1995). Simulations of the ASEAN trade simulation model using 1988 trade flows and circa-1987 import control measures as baseline data and assuming *ad valorem* customs duties are reduced to zero and non-tariff barriers are liberalized to increase the volume of administered imports by 25%, on a preferential basis (AFTA plan) and, alternatively, on a most-favoured-nation basis (MFN liberalization).

Table 4.5 Changes in production, consumption and trade in agriculture and industry

	Import liberalization scenario							
	AFTA			MFN	AFTA			MFN
	Scenario I	Scenario II	Scenario III	Scenario IV	Scenario I	Scenario II	Scenario III	Scenario IV
Indonesia	**Production**				**Consumption**			
Prices (%)								
Agriculture	0.0	0.3	0.4	9.0	−0.1	0.2	0.2	7.6
Industry	0.5	0.9	0.9	12.6	−0.2	−0.9	−0.9	−15.7
Quantities (%)								
Agriculture	0.0	0.1	0.1	2.3	0.0	−0.1	−0.2	−4.1
Industry	0.3	0.4	0.4	4.4	0.2	0.9	0.9	15.5
Similarity to MFN results cosine)	0.55	0.77	0.78	n.a.	0.47	0.75	0.73	n.a.
	Exports				**Imports**			
International trade (US$ millions)								
Agriculture	38	64	147	1,279	32	31	57	402
Industry	78	107	106	477	98	181	182	2,317
Similarity to MFN results (cosine)								
Trade with world	0.04	0.17	0.89	n.a.	−0.54	−0.69	0.79	n.a.
Trade with ASEAN	0.52	0.55	0.98	n.a.	0.61	0.73	1.00	n.a.
Trade with industrial countries	0.76	0.96	0.94	n.a.	−0.44	−0.64	−0.64	n.a.
Malaysia	**Production**				**Consumption**			
Prices (%)								
Agriculture	0.5	0.6	0.3	8.9	0.4	0.5	−0.5	6.0
Industry	0.6	0.7	0.0	7.7	−0.9	−1.2	−2.0	−1.3
Quantities (%)								
Agriculture	0.1	0.1	0.2	2.8	0.2	0.3	1.3	−0.3
Industry	0.6	0.7	0.5	3.7	1.5	1.9	2.7	6.7
Similarity to MFN results (cosine)	0.76	0.82	0.77	n.a.	0.79	0.87	0.83	n.a.
	Exports				**Imports**			
International trade (US$ millions)								
Agriculture	41	47	181	475	22	26	138	321
Industry	169	225	213	477	193	250	284	809
Similarity to MFN results (cosine)								
Trade with world	−0.14	−0.14	0.98	n.a.	−0.68	−0.67	0.91	n.a.
Trade with ASEAN	0.54	0.57	0.94	n.a.	0.54	0.56	0.86	n.a.
Trade with industrial countries	−0.58	−0.75	−0.91	n.a.	−0.82	−0.84	−0.86	n.a.
Philippines	**Production**				**Consumption**			
Prices (%)								
Agriculture	0.3	−0.1	0.6	19.6	0.2	−0.2	0.1	10.1
Industry	0.3	0.1	1.2	22.2	−0.7	−1.5	−0.9	−8.9
Quantities (%)								
Agriculture	0.1	−0.1	0.2	8.7	−0.1	0.3	−0.2	−11.5
Industry	0.4	0.6	0.9	11.6	0.5	1.2	0.7	5.3
Similarity to MFN results (cosine)	0.60	0.45	0.68	n.a.	0.22	0.02	0.34	n.a.
	Exports				**Imports**			
International trade (US$ millions)								
Agriculture	11	2	35	673	9	13	32	288
Industry	58	103	114	556	61	89	81	828
Similarity to MFN results (cosine)								
Trade with world	0.03	0.00	0.63	n.a.	−0.34	−0.21	0.87	n.a.
Trade with ASEAN	0.75	0.87	0.91	n.a.	0.47	0.51	0.98	n.a.
Trade with industrial countries	0.48	−0.06	0.85	n.a.	−0.36	−0.33	−0.57	n.a.

	Import liberalization scenario							
	AFTA			MFN	AFTA			MFN
	Scenario I	Scenario II	Scenario III	Scenario IV	Scenario I	Scenario II	Scenario III	Scenario IV
Singapore	**Production**				**Consumption**			
Prices (%)								
Agriculture	−1.0	−1.9	−1.9	5.6	−1.0	−1.9	−3.0	2.7
Industry	−0.5	−1.0	−1.6	6.4	−1.3	−2.2	−2.9	4.2
Quantities (%)								
Agriculture	−0.2	−0.4	−0.3	1.5	1.8	3.2	5.9	−0.0
Industry	0.4	0.6	0.5	1.2	2.3	3.8	4.9	−3.1
Similarity to MFN results (cosine)	0.40	0.37	0.39	n.a.	−0.38	−0.44	−0.40	n.a.
	Exports				**Imports**			
International trade (US$ millions)								
Agriculture	4	−5	45	113	48	79	232	106
Industry	440	715	693	384	368	584	623	530
Similarity to MFN results (cosine)								
Trade with world	−0.60	−0.70	0.93	n.a.	0.68	0.55	0.60	n.a.
Trade with ASEAN	0.54	0.63	0.98	n.a.	0.67	0.70	0.92	n.a.
Trade with industrial countries	−0.66	−0.75	−0.75	n.a.	0.48	0.26	0.25	n.a.
Thailand	**Production**				**Consumption**			
Prices (%)								
Agriculture	0.2	0.9	1.3	15.4	0.2	0.9	0.6	9.3
Industry	0.2	0.9	1.3	13.0	−0.4	-0.6	0.1	1.0
Quantities (%)								
Agriculture	0.2	0.4	0.6	5.8	−0.1	−0.5	−0.4	−7.6
Industry	0.3	0.5	0.8	7.2	0.4	0.8	0.4	3.1
Similarity to MFN results (cosine)	0.51	0.80	0.81	n.a.	0.35	0.48	0.21	n.a.
	Exports				**Imports**			
International trade (US$ millions)								
Agriculture	17	41	213	1,225	−2	−12	159	836
Industry	95	147	169	1,256	114	204	163	1,626
Similarity to MFN results (cosine)								
Trade with world	0.34	0.37	0.98	n.a.	−0.26	0.39	0.65	n.a.
Trade with ASEAN	0.44	0.52	0.99	n.a.	0.29	0.41	0.75	n.a.
Trade with industrial countries	0.79	0.97	0.89	n.a.	−0.49	−0.55	−0.65	n.a.
ASEAN	**Exports**				**Imports**			
International trade (US$ millions)								
Agriculture	110	148	621	3,765	109	137	619	1,954
Industry	840	1,297	1,294	3,151	834	1,308	1,332	6,110
Similarity to MFN results (cosine)								
Trade with world	−0.39	−0.47	0.87	n.a.	−0.32	−0.28	0.89	n.a.
Trade with ASEAN	0.52	0.58	0.95	n.a.	0.52	0.58	0.95	n.a.
Trade with industrial countries	0.07	0.20	−0.18	n.a.	−0.38	−0.68	−0.74	n.a.

Notes: Consumption refers to final demand. Changes in production and consumption in agriculture and industry are averages of changes in subsectors, using base period levels of production and consumption as weights. Similarity of AFTA to MFN results is measured by the same cosine of the angle formed between vectors of simulated changes in the variables indicated, across traded goods sectors.

Source: DeRosa (1995). Simulations of the ASEAN trade simulation model using 1988 trade flows and circa-1987 import control measures as baseline values and assuming that *ad valorem* customs duties are reduced to zero and that non-tariff bariers are liberalized to increase the volume of administered imports by 25%, on a preferential basis (AFTA) and, alternatively, on a most-favoured-nation basis (MFN liberalization).

measured in terms of real expenditures on final demand (less than 0.5%), except in Singapore and to a lesser extent Malaysia, which enjoy large improvements in their economic welfare (3.9% and 1.3%, respectively, in Scenario III).[18] Most important, in essentially targeting imports from the major industrial countries – the principal trading partners of the ASEAN countries by virtue of the sharp differences in resource endowments between the two sets of countries – for trade diversion, the AFTA plan limits an important source of *present* gains from trade to consumers in the ASEAN countries.[19] The plan also sacrifices an important source of *potential* gains from trade to ASEAN consumers – that is, the gains from trade they would enjoy under an alternative policy of nondiscriminatory trade liberalization, as indicated by the negative values of the similarity statistics in Table 4.5 for changes in ASEAN imports from industrial countries under AFTA versus MFN liberalization.

Liberalizing ASEAN trade relations on a non-discriminatory basis in fact results in significant gains in economic welfare for the four natural resource-abundant ASEAN countries,[20] ranging between about 2% (Indonesia) and about 5% (Malaysia and Philippines) in terms of real absorption (Table 4.4). For Singapore, however, economic welfare declines by nearly 2%. National welfare improves significantly in the former, so-called ASEAN-4 countries because the adjustment of *consumption and imports* as well as *production and exports* is consistent with the comparative advantage of the four countries. In other words, consumers as well as producers in the ASEAN-4 benefit to the fullest extent possible from the freedom that non-discriminatory trade liberalization provides individuals, within the constraints of their (more efficiently utilized) resource endowments and given international terms of trade, to purchase and sell goods abroad. In the case of Singapore, the welfare results reflect the reduced hegemony of Singapore in regional markets for manufactures under MFN liberalization. Reduced prominence in ASEAN markets of goods produced in Singapore would be a major but natural outcome of non-discriminatory trade liberalization in Southeast Asia, further reflecting the greater opportunity of ASEAN consumers to purchase goods from the world at large.[21]

Finally, although the liberalization of ASEAN trade relations on an MFN basis results in smaller gains in intra-ASEAN trade (US$1.7 billion), the simulation results indicate that ASEAN trade with the world expands by nearly four times more under non-discriminatory trade liberalization (US$9.1 billion) than under the AFTA plan (US$2.4 billion). Giving final testimony to AFTA's only modest potential for reducing policy-based disincentives to agriculture, the improvement of ASEAN trade in agriculture under the last policy scenario is even more dramatic; whereas total ASEAN exports of agricultural commodities expand by US$0.6 billion under the AFTA plan, total ASEAN exports of agricultural commodities expand by over six times more (US$3.7 billion) under MFN liberalization.

4.4   Concluding remarks

Regionalism is expected to remain an important factor in international trade relations during the next decade or more. Given the prominence of East Asia in the world economy, major issues are what form regionalism will ultimately take in East Asia, and how that form might influence the global trading system. East Asia's commitment to open regionalism, though practiced successfully during the past two decades by the East Asian NICs and, to a somewhat lesser extent, by the lower-income and still appreciably agrarian countries in Southeast Asia, is central to both these issues.

The new ASEAN Free Trade Area is a preferential trading arrangement at some odds with open regionalism and current discussions in the Asia–Pacific Economic Cooperation forum to expand international trade in East Asia and the greater Asia–Pacific area on a most-favoured-nation basis consistent with the founding principles of the General Agreement on Tariffs and Trade and World Trade Organization. This paper finds that the bias against agriculture – that is, economic policy-based disincentives to greater agricultural production and exports – will be reduced, and general economic welfare will be improved, in the ASEAN countries under AFTA. The extent of these improvements is very modest, however. Substantially larger gains in agricultural production and trade and national welfare are available to the labour- and natural resource-abundant ASEAN countries under open regionalism and non-discriminatory trade liberalization. Following the comparative advantage of ASEAN countries and through expansion of their trade relations particularly with major industrial countries, MFN liberalization of trade regimes in ASEAN improves the circumstances of agriculture and national economies in Southeast Asia by redirecting productive resources from protected industries (including some food-producing sectors) to internationally competitive sectors in agriculture and industry, and by providing consumers with greater freedom to purchase goods originating outside as well as in ASEAN.

These findings point to the superiority of open regionalism over the ASEAN Free Trade Area. They also point to the positive influence that the Asia–Pacific free trade area under discussion in APEC might have on the evolution of trade regimes in Southeast Asia and East Asia in general.

In requiring not only less-developed countries but also more-developed countries to pursue trade liberalization following the most-favoured-nation principle, steadfast commitment by APEC to open regionalism would ensure that all trading countries in East Asia will enjoy greater economic gains. With regard to the global trading system, it might also lead to greater progress in lowering barriers to international trade worldwide on a non-discriminatory basis. Specifically, an Asia–Pacific free trade area might stimulate greater institutional competition for achieving significant advances in liberalizing trade and other international transactions, by instigating greater competition between multilateralism (vested in WTO) and outward-looking regionalism (vested in APEC and possibly other large regional trading blocs such as the European Union and NAFTA).[22] In this eventuality, welfare in the world economy at large, and agriculture and other internationally competitive sectors in less developed countries, would gain even more substantially from APEC's continued commitment to open regionalism.

References

ADB (Asian Development Bank) (1995), *Key Economic Indicators of Developing Member Countries of ADB*, Manila.

APEC (Asia–Pacific Economic Cooperation) (1991), 'Seoul declaration', Asia–Pacific Economic Cooperation Forum, Singapore.

_____ (1993), 'A vision for APEC: towards an Asia–Pacific economic community', Report of the Eminent Persons Group to APEC Ministers, Asia–Pacific Economic Cooperation Forum, Singapore.

_____ (1994), 'Achieving the APEC vision: Free and open trade in the Asia-Pacific', Second report of the Eminent Persons Group, Asia–Pacific Economic Cooperation Forum, Singapore.

Armington, P. A. (1969), 'A theory of demand for products distinguished by place of production', *IMF Staff Papers* 16(1), 159–78.

Arndt, H.W. (1993), 'Anatomy of regionalism', *Journal of Asian Economics* 4(2), 271–82.

_____ (1995), 'AFTA and after', in J.L.H. Tan (ed.), *AFTA in the Changing International Economy*, Singapore, Institute of Southeast Asian Studies.

ASEAN (Association of Southeast Asian Nations) (1992a), 'Singapore declaration of 1992', *ASEAN Economic Bulletin* 8(3), 376–80.

_____ (1992b), 'Framework agreement on enhancing ASEAN economic cooperation', *ASEAN Economic Bulletin* 8(3), 381–5.

_____ (1992c), 'Agreement on the common effective preferential tariff (CEPT) scheme for the ASEAN Free Trade Area (AFTA)', *ASEAN Economic Bulletin* 8(3), 386–90.

Bautista, R.M., and A. Valdés. (1993), 'The relevance of trade and macroeconomic policies for agriculture', in R.M. Bautista and A. Valdés, (eds.), *The Bias Against Agriculture: Trade and Macroeconomic Policies in Developing Countries*, San Francisco, ICS Press.

Cavallo, D., and Y. Mundlak (1982), 'Agriculture and economic growth in an open economy: the case of Argentina', Research Report 36, Washington, DC, International Food Policy Research Institute.

Collier, P. (1979), 'The welfare effects of customs unions: an anatomy', *Economic Journal* 89, 84–95.

Deardorff, A.V. and R.M. Stern (1986), *The Michigan Model of World Production and Trade: Theory and Application*, Cambridge, Massachusetts, The MIT Press.

DeRosa, D.A. (1988), 'Asian preferences and the gains from MFN tariff reductions', *The World Economy* 11, 377–96.

_____ (1992), 'Protection and export performance in Sub-Saharan Africa', *Weltwirtschaftliches Archiv* 128 (1), 88–124.

_____ (1993). 'Sources of comparative advantage in the international trade of the ASEAN countries', *ASEAN Economic Bulletin* 10(1), 1–11.

_____ (1995), 'Regional trading arrangements among developing countries: The ASEAN example', Research Report 103, Washington, DC, International Food Policy Research Institute.

Drysdale, P. and R. Garnaut (1993), 'The Pacific: an application of a general theory of economic integration', in C. F. Bergsten and M. Noland, (eds.), *Pacific Dynamism and the International Economic System*, Washington, DC, Institute for International Economics.

Elek, A. (1995), 'APEC beyond Bogor', *Asian-Pacific Economic Literature* 9(1), 1–16.

Erzan, R., H. Kuwahara, S. Marchese, and R. Vossenaar (1989), 'The profile of protection in developing countries', *UNCTAD Review* 1, 29–50.

Krueger, A.O. (1995), 'NAFTA: strengthening or weakening the international trade system?', in J. Bhagwati and A.O. Krueger, *The Dangerous Drift to Preferential Trade Agreements*, Special Studies in Policy Reform, Washington, DC, American Enterprise Institute.

Krueger, A.O., M. Schiff and A. Valdés, (1988), 'Agricultural incentives in developing countries: measuring the effect of sectoral and economywide policies', *The World Bank Economic Review* 2(3), 255–72.

_____ (1992), *The Political Economy of Agricultural Pricing Policy*, Baltimore, The Johns Hopkins University Press for the World Bank.

Krugman, P. (1994), 'The Myth of Asia's miracle', *Foreign Affairs* 74(2), 62–78.

_____ (1995), 'Mything my point', *Foreign Affairs* 74 (2), 176–7.

Lee, T.Y. (1994), 'The ASEAN free trade area', *Asian-Pacific Economic Literature* 8(1), 1–7.

Mellor, J.W. (1995), *Agriculture on the Road to Industrialization*, Baltimore, The Johns Hopkins University Press for the International Food Policy Research Institute.

Riedel, J. (1991), 'Intra-Asian trade and foreign direct investment', *Asian Development Review* 9(1), 111–46.

Rieger, H.C. (1991), *ASEAN Economic Cooperation: A Handbook*, Singapore, Institute of Southeast Asian Studies, ASEAN Economic Research Unit.

Robinson, S. (1989), 'Multisector models', in H. Chenery and T.N. Srinivasan, (eds.), *Handbook of Development Economics*, Amsterdam, Elsevier Science Publishers.

Shoven, J.B. and J. Whalley (1992), *Applying General Equilibrium*, Cambridge, Cambridge University Press.

UNCTAD (United Nations Conference on Trade and Development) (1994), *Directory of Import Regimes*, United Nations, New York.
United Nations (1972), *Economic Cooperation for ASEAN*, Rome.
Viner, J. (1950), *The Customs Union Issue*, New York, Carnegie Endowment for International Peace.
World Bank (1993), *The East Asian Miracle*, New York, Oxford University Press.
____ (1995), *World Development Report* 1995, New York, Oxford University Press.
World Trade Organization (1995), *Regionalism and the World Trading System*, World Trade Organization, Geneva.
Young, A. (1995), 'The tyranny of numbers: confronting the statistical realities of East Asian growth experience', *Quarterly Journal of Economics* 110(3), 641–80.

The author acknowledges with thanks helpful comments on this paper by Mohamed El-Erian and other conference participants.

Notes

1. Though the remarkable record of the East Asian NICs (Hong Kong, South Korea, Taiwan, and Singapore) has been widely noted and frequently been held as an example for developing countries both within and outside Asia, the long-term sustainability of high economic growth in these countries is not without controversy. See Krugman (1994, 1995) and Young (1995).
2. As emphasized by the World Bank (1993), no single 'model' of economic reform underlies the East Asian Miracle. The record of the East Asian countries is dotted with different approaches and experiences with economy-wide and sectoral policy reforms. Yet, steadily increasing openness is a common and prominent feature of the record of the high-performing East Asian economies, achieved through both import liberalization and pro-export policies. While recognition of this fact leaves unanswered important questions about the political economy and sequencing of successful economic policy reforms, adoption of more open economic regimes appears to have been a major ingredient to the success of the East Asian economies. Above all, the resulting improvements to economic efficiency, welfare, and growth provided large economic gains that reduced previous, seemingly forbidding obstacles to initiating economic reforms and that increased appetites for undertaking further reforms, albeit gradually and subject to the constraints of the domestic political economy.
3. On role of agriculture in economic growth and development, see, for instance, Mellor (1995).
4. On increasing economic integration in East Asia, see Riedel (1991).
5. ASEAN also includes the Sultanate of Brunei and Vietnam.
6. An exception is the Philippines. During the 1980s, the Philippines experienced an appreciable slowdown in growth of output and exports that was related to the country's unsettled political circumstances and weak adherence to more appropriate macroeconomic policies.
7. See Reiger (1991) for an extensive discussion of economic cooperation in ASEAN.
8. See United Nations (1972) and DeRosa (1995).
9. More generally, as discussed by Arndt (1993), open regionalism emphasizes adoption of non-discriminatory trade relations to the point of undertaking unilateral trade liberalization without support from reciprocal bilateral or multilateral trade negotiations and arrangements.
10. See ASEAN (1992a,b,c) and also Lee (1994).
11. See, for instance, World Trade Organization (1995).
12. A central issue confronting APEC in establishing a free trade area based on open regionalism is whether reduced barriers to trade within APEC should be extended to

trade with countries outside APEC on an unconditional MFN basis, that is, without requiring reciprocal tariff or other trade 'concessions' from non-APEC trading partners. In addition to the economic benefits of pursuing open regionalism, a compelling reason for APEC's pursuing open regionalism is the likelihood of significant retaliation by the EU if an Asia–Pacific free trade area were to be established on a discriminatory basis. See, APEC (1993, 1994) and, for instance, Arndt (1995) and Elek (1995).

13. The share of agriculture in domestic production in low- and middle-income countries is often biased downward owing to the repression of prices for agricultural commodities by inappropriate trade and macroeconomic policies in these countries (*see* Section 4.2). Thus, the contribution of agriculture to total employment in such countries is often a more reliable indicator of the importance of agriculture to the national economy.

14. Consistent with the structure of protection in other developing countries, Table 4.2 also reveals that the ASEAN countries enforce rates of protection for food commodities and processed foods rivaling the rates of protection for many categories of manufactures. On levels of protection in less developed countries, see DeRosa (1988, 1992) and Erzan et al. (1989).

15. The non-traded goods in each ASEAN country is the numeraire (in local currency terms), and thus the nominal exchange rate is equivalent to the real exchange rate (Robinson, 1989). For non-ASEAN countries, the exchange rate, sectoral prices, and levels of primary commodity and industrial output are assumed constant.

16. In reality, non-tariff barriers in the ASEAN countries might be either more or less restrictive. The sensitivity of the simulation results under alternative values for the NTB and substitution elasticity parameters in the ASEAN trade simulation model is explored in DeRosa (1995).

17. As Collier (1979) demonstrates, net trade creation is not a reliable indicator of economic welfare in sophisticated economic models such as the ASEAN trade simulation model. Therefore, the effects of the AFTA plan on national welfare are considered further below in terms of changes in real absorption (expenditures on final demand) following the Hicksian approach to measuring changes in welfare used widely in CGE modeling (e.g. Shoven and Whalley, 1992).

18. By virtue of their relatively open economies (*see* Table 4.2), Singapore and Malaysia face little necessity to adjust the patterns of their import demands away from principal trading partners (a potential cost to consumers) under the AFTA plan. Moreover, given their initially greater industrial capacity, the two countries stand to gain substantially from the expansion of intra-ASEAN trade in manufactures under the plan, placing upward pressure on their respective exchange rates.

19. On ASEAN comparative advantage and its determinants in trade with the major industrial countries, see DeRosa (1993).

20. Indonesia, Malaysia, the Philippines and Thailand.

21. The simulation results suggest that Singapore's economic interest lies in wider multilateral trade liberalization, under the Asia–Pacific Economic Cooperation forum or World Trade Organization.

22. The eventual 'openness' of the European Union and NAFTA is subject to question, especially for political economy reasons. As Krueger (1995) argues, once preferential trading arrangements are adopted new vested interests are created, making political consensus in favour of adoption of non-discriminatory trading arrangements still more remote.

PART II
Agreements Under the Euro-Med Initiative

5

Some Economic Effects of the Free Trade Agreement between Tunisia and the European Union

Drusilla K Brown
Tufts University

Alan V Deardorff
University of Michigan

Robert M Stern
University of Michigan

5.1   Introduction

In this chapter, a specially constructed version of the Michigan Brown-Deardorff-Stern (BDS) Computational General Equilibrium (CGE) Model of World Production and Trade is used to estimate some potential economic effects on the Tunisian economy of the July 1995 free trade agreement (FTA) between Tunisia and the European Union (EU). The model provides measures of the effects of the FTA on trade, output, employment, welfare and returns to labour and capital in Tunisia and its major trading partners. As a key issue in evaluating the Tunisian–EU FTA concerns the impact on foreign direct investment (FDI) inflows, we investigate how the FTA may alter incentives for FDI and the resulting impact on the Tunisian economy.

Our analysis focuses exclusively on the static effects of reductions in tariffs and non-tariff barriers (NTBs) in the FTA and on several possible changes in FDI. We do not attempt to model possible effects arising from harmonization of standards, product quality improvements, and increased trading efficiency (*see* Chapter 6) because of the considerable uncertainties over how large the benefits may really turn out to be.

In Section 5.2, we outline some essential features of our model and the data used. Since our model-based approach is not altogether well suited to analysing issues relating to FDI, Section 5.3 briefly summarizes some recent literature on the determinants of FDI, especially in developing countries, and describes Tunisia's 1994 Investment Code. The results of various model scenarios are described in Section 5.4, and the aggregate and sectoral computational results of these scenarios are presented in Sections 5.5 and 5.6. Section 5.7 summarizes our conclusions regarding the possible implications of the FTA for Tunisia's trade and foreign investment policies.

5.2   The Michigan BDS CGE trade model[1]

The CGE model used in this paper is an extension of one constructed by Brown and Stern (1989) to analyse the economic effects of the Canada–US Trade Agreement (CUSTA), and later expanded by Brown, Deardorff, and Stern (1992a,b) to analyse the NAFTA.[2] For present purposes the following eight countries/regions are modelled: Tunisia; Greece/Portugal/Spain (MEU); France/Italy (FR–IT); the Other EU–7 countries (OEU); Other Europe (OEUR); Asia/Pacific (APAC); NAFTA; and South America (SAM).[3] All remaining countries of the world are consigned to a residual rest-of-world to close the model. The sectoral coverage in each country/region includes 1 agricultural sector, 21 product categories covering manufacturing, 1 mining sector, and 6 categories covering services, including government. All sectors are modelled as tradable. The individual sectors and corresponding International Standard Industrial Classification (ISIC) categories are listed in Tables 5.1 and 5.2.

The agricultural sector in the model is characterized as being perfectly competitive and the non-agricultural sectors are taken to be monopolistically competitive with free entry.[4] Agricultural products are differentiated by country of production. The products of the other sectors are assumed to be differentiated by firm to correspond to the imperfectly competitive market structure. Domestic demands by sector reflect the overall demands in the economies. The level of total demand is determined by income; there is no independent role for the government budget. The reference year for the data base of the model is 1990. The data base and documentation as well as a full statement and description of the equations and parameters of the model are available from the authors on request.[5]

There are several assumptions that are important to understand and interpret the results of our analysis.

- *Full Employment* The economy-wide level of employment is held constant in each country. This assumption is made because overall employment is determined by macroeconomic forces and policies that are not covered by the FTA. The focus instead is on changes in the *composition* of employment across sectors resulting from the liberalization of trade.

Table 5.1 Tunisia: basic data, 1990

Sector	ISIC	(1) Output (Mill. $)	(2) Labour (000)	(3) Capital (Mill. $)	(4) Imports (Mill. $)	(5) Exports (Mill. $)
Agriculture, forestry and fisheries	(1)	2,668.6	542.4	3,343.5	317.9	176.9
Manufactures						
Food, beverages and tobacco	(310)	2,487.6	35.3	579.4	286.2	234.3
Textiles	(321)	525.6	76.9	734.4	818.0	121.0
Wearing apparel	(322)	1,501.0	19.4	50.5	200.1	1,138.7
Leather products	(323)	88.2	2.6	22.2	55.7	30.4
Footwear	(324)	139.1	12.1	50.5	12.0	48.3
Wood products	(331)	141.9	6.6	13.5	104.0	5.1
Furniture and fixtures	(332)	33.6	1.7	12.7	28.0	9.3
Paper and paper products	(341)	176.6	4.6	177.2	101.1	23.7
Printing and publishing	(342)	82.9	5.0	29.5	24.5	2.2
Chemicals	(35A)	696.6	25.2	469.6	40.8	15.0
Petroleum and related products	(35B)	1,431.3	1.7	1,743.6	468.7	503.6
Rubber products	(355)	163.1	5.0	23.5	298.3	65.6
Non-metallic mineral products	(36A)	110.7	7.0	268.2	26.4	5.8
Glass and glass products	(362)	735.7	33.1	698.8	25.6	95.6
Iron and steel	(371)	136.2	3.4	48.6	236.3	35.3
Non-ferrous metals	(372)	23.5	0.5	11.1	69.1	16.8
Metal products	(381)	232.3	6.6	49.4	108.3	43.8
Non-electric machinery	(382)	459.0	19.3	152.7	751.2	30.7
Electric machinery	(383)	1,024.6	38.5	496.2	402.2	194.8
Transportation equipment	(384)	196.8	5.8	111.9	442.4	43.7
Miscellaneous manufactures	(38A)	148.2	5.3	39.4	273.7	90.0
Mining and quarrying	(2)	682.7	1.6	69.1	251.6	529.9
Services						
Electricity, gas and water	(4)	549.1	12.5	1,349.9	133.1	6.9
Construction	(5)	1,573.0	63.6	317.9	4.1	12.4
Wholesale and retail trade	(6)	1,057.5	267.6	3,918.7	140.3	803.3
Transportation, storage and communications	(7)	1,275.9	52.3	3,470.8	432.5	536.2
Finance, insurance and real estate	(8)	568.4	16.3	326.2	63.9	134.9
Community, social and personal services	(9)	5,247.1	721.0	2,863.8	70.8	106.4
Total		24,166.8	1,992.9	21,442.8	6,186.8	5,060.6

Notes: Column (1) refers to gross output; columns (1) and (2) are partly estimated for some sectors; column (3) is based on cumulative annual sectoral investment, measured in constant prices, less depreciation; columns (4) and (5) have been concorded from the Harmonized System to the ISIC sectoral categories.

- *Balanced Trade* The value of any initial trade imbalance is kept constant as trade barriers change. Thus implicitly the exchange rate can be thought of as flexible. Like the full employment assumption, it is appropriate as a way of abstracting from the macroeconomic forces and policies that are the main determinants of trade balances.[6]

- *Rents and Revenues* Revenues from tariffs are assumed to be redistributed to consumers in the tariff-levying country and spent like any other income. The same applies to the rents from NTBs. When trade barriers are reduced, income available to purchase imports falls along with their prices, and there is no overall bias towards expanding or contracting aggregate demand.
- *Fixed Relative Wages* While the economy-wide wage in each country is permitted to adjust to maintain full employment, wages across sectors are held fixed relative to one another. This permits the analysis to focus on the labour-market adjustments that might be required, independently of any relative wage changes that may facilitate those adjustments.
- *Fixed Labour Supply* The total labour supply in each country is assumed to be fixed, i.e. changes in labour supply are assumed to be independent of the FTA.
- *Role of Variety* A so-called Dixit–Stiglitz (1977) aggregation function is used, so that the elasticity of substitution determines both the degree of substitution among varieties of a good and the extent to which greater variety adds to consumer welfare and reduces costs of intermediate inputs. Such effects can be quite important, since liberalization provides greater access to foreign varieties and may increase welfare on that account alone.[7]

Because the model is static, the analysis compares the initial situation with the equilibrium after full elimination of the bilateral barriers on Tunisia/EU trade. When the policy changes are introduced into the model, the method of solution yields percentage changes in sectoral employment and other variables of interest for each country/region. Multiplying the percentage changes by the 1990 base year levels yields the absolute changes reported below.

We are aware that the FTA involves much more than negotiated reductions and/or removal of tariffs and NTBs.[8] While other facets of the FTA may be important, they are difficult to quantify.

- *Policy Input Data* An indication of the basic data for Tunisia is provided in Tables 5.1 and 5.2. Since data on collection rates were not available, we use the official rates based on Tunisian Government sources. To obtain the sectoral tariff rates, we first aggregated the import data to the 6-digit Harmonized System (HS) classification and then matched the import and tariff data at this level. We then concorded the 6-digit HS import and tariff data to the 3-digit ISIC categories that we use in our CGE modelling framework. Tunisia's bilateral tariff rates against the seven regions included in the model were calculated using bilateral imports as weights. Tunisia's weighted average official tariff rates show considerable dispersion, with some instances of rates below 10% and others in excess of 40% (Table 5.2).

Table 5.2 Tunisia: pre-Uruguay Round tariff rates (%)

Sector	ISIC	(1) Greece Portugal Spain	(2) France Italy	(3) Other EU-7	(4) Other Europe	(5) NAFTA	(6) Asia/ Pacific	(7) South America	(8) Rest of world
Agriculture, forestry and fisheries	(1)	21.9	19.7	22.1	28.1	20.2	13.8	19.9	18.0
Manufactures									
Food, beverages and tobacco	(310)	17.2	28.6	27.6	32.0	20.8	29.9	20.4	20.2
Textiles	(321)	38.2	37.3	37.9	31.1	32.2	30.2	29.5	34.2
Wearing apparel	(322)	40.0	40.7	40.4	38.4	40.9	41.1	43.0	38.8
Leather products	(323)	27.7	31.1	29.1	34.5	38.3	25.0	34.7	27.5
Footwear	(324)	39.0	39.6	42.4	42.7	43.0	42.1	0.0	41.9
Wood products	(331)	27.9	23.4	30.4	22.1	21.8	38.9	22.0	21.5
Furniture and fixtures	(332)	41.1	38.7	37.9	28.8	42.6	38.4	10.0	40.5
Paper and paper products	(341)	40.5	36.2	36.3	26.5	32.7	40.3	26.2	20.8
Printing and publishing	(342)	19.7	25.0	26.6	26.8	12.1	40.7	0.0	25.5
Chemicals	(35A)	17.4	18.9	19.9	18.5	19.4	20.4	16.2	17.8
Petroleum and related products	(35B)	10.3	10.3	20.3	28.5	18.0	31.0	0.0	10.2
Rubber products	(355)	33.3	30.9	33.4	33.8	36.4	32.2	28.7	24.9
Non-metallic mineral products	(36A)	34.9	33.3	35.9	37.5	31.2	24.6	42.0	39.0
Glass and glass products	(362)	23.3	15.1	25.3	20.9	5.9	22.4	20.0	27.4
Iron and steel	(371)	25.1	21.0	19.8	24.0	12.0	15.2	26.2	25.7
Non-ferrous metals	(372)	18.7	20.7	20.7	25.2	20.3	31.9	20.0	22.2
Metal products	(381)	32.9	32.4	32.5	32.6	28.5	31.8	36.3	31.7
Non-electric machinery	(382)	16.8	18.0	15.8	15.5	18.1	13.1	13.4	16.9
Electric machinery	(383)	26.7	28.6	22.7	36.8	18.8	19.4	27.8	27.3
Transportation equipment	(384)	24.1	25.9	24.8	34.3	22.3	27.0	27.7	32.9
Miscellaneous manufactures	(38A)	26.3	27.9	27.5	23.1	19.7	20.4	22.8	31.7
Mining and quarrying	(2)	16.2	20.1	38.9	20.1	17.2	17.0	20.0	10.2

Note: Tariff rates are based on official Tunisian data and do not reflect exemptions and other duty-free allowances. They are weighted by bilateral imports.

In 1992, 85% of Tunisia's imports were effectively unrestricted by NTBs (Nsouli et al., 1993, p.69). The remaining 15% were apparently subject to import licensing and annual import authorization;[9] we assume they apply only to imports of agricultural products. Estimates based on Stanton (1994) suggest that the *ad valorem* equivalents of these agricultural NTBs were 5.5% on imports from the EU and 12.3% from all other regions. These NTB *ad valorem* equivalents were added to the tariff rates for Sector 1 reported in Table 5.2, and are assumed to be eliminated as a result of the FTA.[10]

The EU maintains some quantitative restrictions on imports from Tunisia. These apply to such agricultural products as olive oil, oranges, potatoes, wine, apricot pulp, and sardines. In the absence of measures of the tariff equivalents of these restrictions, we decided to use a figure of 8% for the EU barriers on Sector 1 agricultural imports from Tunisia, based on the estimate in Harrison, Rutherford, and Wooton (1989). The EU also maintains certain seasonal restrictions on agricultural imports from Tunisia, which we assume to be included in the 8% tariff equivalent. With respect to manufactured goods, the EU has annual quotas limiting imports of cotton cloth and trousers from Tunisia. Since our textile and clothing sectoral aggregates cover a large variety of products and we do not have any information on the tariff equivalents involved, we assume that the EU quota restrictions are not binding.

5.3　The determinants of FDI and Tunisia's 1994 investment code

An important reason why many developing countries are anxious to enter into FTAs with advanced industrialized industries is the belief that this will stimulate inward FDI. The relevant literature – e.g. UNCTAD (1993), UNCTC (1992), Bajo-Rubio and Sosvilla-Rivero (1994), Lucas (1993) and Haddad and Harrison (1993) – provides some evidence that openness and trade barriers affect aggregate FDI inflows, but macroeconomic factors appear to play a dominant role. It is especially striking that FDI has not been shown to be responsive to the main microeconomic factor one expects to influence investment flows: the return to capital. This may be because returns to capital do not in fact influence FDI. Alternatively, FDI may respond so elastically to small variations in returns that the observed variations become too small to be picked up econometrically. Or, FDI may respond to variations in returns to capital separately by sector, so that measures of total FDI and average returns to capital hide the relationship. The literature also suggests that incentives designed to encourage FDI inflows do not appear to matter very much, although once it is decided to engage in FDI, the presence of incentives may affect the magnitude and geographic location of the FDI.[11]

Tunisia introduced a number of investment incentives in a new Investment Code 1994.[12] The Code is global in character and covers all sectors except domestic trade and investments in mining, energy, and finance. Foreign investors are permitted 100% ownership, with some exceptions in industries that are not wholly exporting, and in agriculture where long-term leasing is permitted. Incentives can be either fiscal (tax reductions or waivers) or financial (grants or subsidies). The tax incentives range from 35% for all activities covered by the Investment Code; 50% for activities related to environmental protection and investments in development support activities and services; and 100% for wholly exporting activities, companies located in regional development areas, and agricultural development projects. All activities covered by the Code are eligible for suspension of the value added tax (VAT) and the consumption tax on locally manufactured capital goods, and for reduction of tariffs to 10% and suspension of the VAT and consumption tax on imported equipment when no similar equipment is made locally. Accelerated depreciation on capital goods and income tax exemptions are available for revenues derived from export activities. Companies with off-shore status may import duty-free and can sell part of their production domestically subject to some restrictions. Partially exporting companies are allowed tax exemption and refunds of customs duties. There are special tax incentives for regional development projects, etc. Foreign nationals may account for up to 4% of the total employment in foreign investments, have certain personal tax advantages, are permitted free repatriation of profits, receive investment protection under treaty, are protected from double taxation, may invoke foreign arbitration processes, are covered for non-commercial risks, and are ensured protection of industrial property rights. While we have no way to determine how successful the Code may be in attracting FDI, the regime is clearly relatively open for FDI. In what follows we therefore allow for FDI to respond to the changes in relative prices caused by the FTA, and make an attempt to explicitly consider the impact of the various incentives of the Code in this regard.

5.4   Model scenarios

It is common in the international trade literature for some purposes to treat labour as perfectly mobile and capital as completely immobile, that is, sector specific. This may capture some of the short- and medium-run effects of trade liberalization as compared to the long run when all factors of production are mobile. In what follows, we will implement scenarios of both types since this helps determining how inward FDI may respond to the FTA. Given that the NTBs are confined to the agricultural sector, we modelled the elimination of both bilateral tariffs and NTBs in agriculture. Since it remains to be seen whether the FTA will involve the liberalization of both goods and services and since we do not have reliable estimates of bilateral services barriers, we confined our attention to goods liberalization. The following five model scenarios were evaluated:

*Scenario A. **Free Trade with Sectorally Specific Capital: Trade Only***
A Free Trade Agreement (FTA), involving bilateral removal of tariffs and NTBs on goods only, between Tunisia and the EU–12, assuming perfect labour mobility and sector-specific capital.

*Scenario B. **Free Trade with Sectorally Mobile Capital: Trade Only***
Same as A but with sectorally mobile capital.

*Scenario C. **Free Trade with Sectorally Mobile Capital: Trade and FDI***
Same as B but also including a flow of capital into Tunisia equal to 10% of the Tunisian capital stock, taken proportionally from the capital stocks of the EU–12.

*Scenario D. **Free Trade with Sectorally Specific Capital: Trade and FDI***
Same as A but also with an increase in the sectoral capital stocks of each sector in Tunisia that recorded a positive change in the nominal return to capital, r, in scenario A. The elasticity of FDI with respect to this return to capital is assumed to be 5.0. Thus, $FDI(j) = \max \{ 5Dr(j)/r(j) , 0 \}$, where $FDI(j)$ is foreign direct investment into sector j as a fraction of sector j's (specific) capital stock.

*Scenario E. **Free Trade with Sectorally Specific Capital and Capital Tax: Trade and FDI***
Same as D, but incorporating the Investment Code as follows: $FDI(j) = \max \{ 5a(j)Dr(j)/r(j) , 0 \}$
where $a(j)$ incorporates features of the Investment Code as follows:
1. To reflect excluded industries (page 1 of Code):
   $a(j) = 0$, (j = ISIC 2, 4, 6, 8 since the Code excludes the domestic trade, mining, energy, and finance sectors.)
2. To reflect tax exemptions for all other sectors:
   $a(j) = g(j)(1 + t) + (1 - g(j)) (1 + .35t)$, $(j^1 \neq ISIC\ 2, 4, 6, 8)$, where $g(j)$ is the export share of production and t is the tax rate for Tunisian capital income, which we have taken to be 35%.

To incorporate features of the Tunisian Investment Code we augment the incentive to invest in each sector $(Dr(j)/r(j))$ by a factor $\alpha (j)$ representing the tax incentive. The latter appears in the last equation as the 0.35 multiplying the tax rate τ. Coincidentally, this tax incentive of 0.35 happens to be equal to the value of the tax rate τ, which is also 35%. The above formulation also includes adjustments to reflect the exclusion of certain industries from the Investment Code and the fact that wholly exporting firms get a tax break of 100%.[13]

5.5   Computational results: aggregate effects

An overview of results on trade, terms of trade, welfare, and factor payments for each of the foregoing scenarios is reported in Table 5.3. Of considerable interest in evaluating the scenarios is the impact on economic welfare, defined as the 'equivalent variation' measure of the change in real gross domestic product (GDP).

5.5.1   Scenario A

Since the 1976 cooperation agreement between Tunisia and the EU eliminated trade restrictions against imports from Tunisia except for agriculture and textiles/clothing, the FTA practically amounts to a unilateral removal of tariffs by Tunisia. Because tariffs are eliminated only *vis-à-vis* the EU, these tariff reductions are discriminatory and need not necessarily lead to welfare improvement. Indeed, in Scenario A, which assumes that capital is unable to move among sectors, economic welfare in Tunisia declines by 0.2% of GDP (Table 5.3).[14] This result is best understood in terms of the traditional concept of trade diversion. When Tunisia eliminates its relatively high tariffs against all EU-members but keeps its tariffs in place against other ('third') countries, a first effect is to cause substitution away from the imports from third countries. The reason is that imports from the EU now appear cheaper to buyers within Tunisia, who no longer have to pay the tariff. But these imports are not cheaper to the country as a whole, since, if they had been cheaper, they would have been purchased before when all imports faced the same tariffs. Therefore, the country as a whole loses from this substitution.

The way that this loss manifests itself within Tunisia is through the loss of tariff revenue. Initially, buyers were paying high prices for imports from the third countries, but a part of these high prices was staying within the country in the form of tariff revenues collected by the government. This tariff revenue was available to be used by the government and therefore contributed to economic welfare. In our model, government revenues are formally assumed to be redistributed to consumers in some non-distorting way, so that consumer incomes include both earned factor incomes plus this transfer from the government, both of which are spent on goods and services. When tariffs against the EU fall, consumers pay less for the imports that they now buy from the EU instead of from third countries, but they lose even more as the transfer of tariff revenue is reduced as well.

Now trade diversion is only one of two effects of a discriminatory tariff reduction such as this. To the extent that trade is also created, welfare can

Table 5.3 Summary results of Tunisia–EU free trade – changes in country imports, exports, terms of trade, welfare and return to labour and capital

Country	Imports*	Exports*	Terms of trade (percentage change)	Equivalent variation		Percentage change	
				Percentage of GDP	Millions $	Real wage	Real return to capital
	(2)	(3)	(4)	(5)	(6)	(7)	(8)
A. Free Trade with Sector Specific Capital: Trade Only							
Tunisia	483.2	735.1	−5.0	−0.2	−26.8	2.5	6.6
Mediterranean EU	46.7	47.2	0.0	0.0	136.4	0.0	0.0
France–Italy	589.6	401.9	0.0	0.1	1542.0	0.0	0.0
Other EU	351.9	208.0	0.0	0.0	741.8	0.0	0.0
Other Europe	−31.4	−18.6	0.0	0.0	13.7	0.0	0.0
NAFTA	−28.2	2.1	0.0	0.0	54.3	0.0	0.0
Asia–Pacific	47.8	14.5	0.0	0.0	136.0	0.0	0.0
South America	0.0	−4.0	0.0	0.0	−0.6	0.0	0.0
B. Free Trade with Sectorally Mobile Capital: Trade Only							
Tunisia	911.6	1158.6	−4.9	3.3	430.3	−1.7	6.5
Mediterranean EU	52.8	58.7	0.0	0.0	172.3	0.0	−0.1
France–Italy	829.1	623.9	0.0	0.1	2186.3	0.0	−0.1
Other EU	481.3	317.8	0.0	0.0	1045.5	0.0	0.0
Other Europe	−8.5	−0.2	0.0	0.0	51.9	0.0	0.0
NAFTA	−15.5	13.9	0.0	0.0	−36.5	0.0	0.0
Asia–Pacific	71.4	26.1	0.0	0.0	147.6	0.0	0.0
South America	7.7	−1.7	0.0	0.0	17.0	0.0	0.0
C. Free Trade with Sectorally Mobile Capital: Trade and FDI							
Tunisia	533.3	1734.6	−7.0	−0.1	−15.0	4.6	7.1
Mediterranean EU	82.8	−9.4	0.0	0.0	284.3	0.0	−0.1
France–Italy	1037.0	493.8	0.1	0.2	3972.4	0.0	−0.1

Country	Imports*	Exports*	Terms of trade (percentage change)	Equivalent variation		Percentage change	
				Percentage of GDP	Millions $	Real wage	Real return to capital
	(2)	(3)	(4)	(5)	(6)	(7)	(8)
Other EU	657.9	-1.9	0.0	0.1	1662.4	0.0	-0.1
Other Europe	-17.2	-11.0	0.0	0.0	189.2	0.0	0.0
NAFTA	-34.5	-3.6	0.0	0.0	115.8	0.0	0.0
Asia–Pacific	68.3	24.8	0.0	0.0	336.5	0.0	0.0
South America	4.5	-2.9	0.0	0.0	43.5	0.0	0.0
D. Free Trade with Sector Specific Capital: Trade and FDI							
Tunisia	501.5	917.7	-5.1	0.9	122.4	3.5	6.6
Mediterranean EU	54.4	41.0	0.0	0.0	123.8	0.0	0.0
France–Italy	659.9	424.5	0.0	0.1	1597.8	0.0	0.0
Other EU	394.9	136.0	0.0	0.0	642.6	0.0	0.0
Other Europe	-34.2	-23.7	0.0	0.0	21.4	0.0	0.0
NAFTA	-34.5	-1.9	0.0	0.0	55.6	0.0	0.0
Asia–Pacific	45.2	11.0	0.0	0.0	144.3	0.0	0.0
South America	1.0	-3.8	0.0	0.0	4.1	0.0	0.0
E. Free Trade with Sector Specific Capital and Capital Tax: Trade and FDI							
Tunisia	498.0	931.4	-5.1	1.0	130.8	3.6	6.6
Mediterranean EU	55.1	39.4	0.0	0.0	124.1	0.0	0.0
France–Italy	664.8	423.5	0.0	0.1	1600.9	0.0	0.0
Other EU	398.0	130.9	0.0	0.0	646.6	0.0	0.0
Other Europe	-34.7	-24.3	0.0	0.0	22.5	0.0	0.0
NAFTA	-34.7	-2.3	0.0	0.0	60.1	0.0	0.0
Asia–Pacific	44.3	10.5	0.0	0.0	143.9	0.0	0.0
South America	0.9	-3.8	0.0	0.0	4.5	0.0	0.0

*Exports and imports in millions of US dollars, valued in US dollar base period prices.

rise. Trade creation occurs, in this case, when buyers substitute imports from the EU for purchases of domestically produced goods. Since these two sources both now face zero tariffs, imports from the EU must be cheaper than their domestic alternatives in order to be bought, and the country therefore gains from switching to the more efficient source. Formally, there is no loss of tariff revenue to offset the gain experienced by the purchasers. A limited amount of trade creation can occur to the extent that imports overall are made cheaper by the tariff reduction relative to domestic goods. But a greater scope for trade creation exists if the country is also able to increase exports, for then the revenues from increased exports can be spent on imports. Tariff reductions abroad (here only in agriculture), and a more general reallocation of factors toward export sectors, can therefore contribute to trade creation and cause the overall welfare effect of an FTA to become positive. In Scenario A, however, the sector-specificity of capital limits this reallocation, and it is perhaps not surprising that overall welfare falls in this short-to-medium run setting.

Tunisia's terms of trade – the relative price of its exports compared to its imports, or what it gets in return for its exports – fall by even more than welfare in Scenario A. This is the case in all of the subsequent scenarios as well, and is a normal effect of a discriminatory and largely unilateral tariff reduction, especially for a country with relatively high tariffs like Tunisia. Tunisia is of course quite a small country, and it is customary to argue that small countries are unable to influence their terms of trade.[15] But this is not the case for a discriminatory tariff reduction. To the extent that trade diversion occurs as discussed above, Tunisia substitutes toward higher cost imports, and this is a direct worsening of its terms of trade. In other words, while it is largely true that a small country cannot influence world prices, it can influence its terms of trade by changing the composition of its import bundle. Tunisia's terms of trade worsen, not because the prices of its exports fall or of its imports rise, but because it switches to higher priced imports from the EU and thus gets less in return for its exports. In quantitative terms, the terms of trade worsen by considerably more than overall welfare, however, because the country also benefits from the efficiency improvements that arise from trade creation.

The real wage and the real return to capital both rise, by 2.5% and 6.6% respectively. This may at first appear to be inconsistent with the overall decline in welfare. However, since economic welfare derives both from earned incomes and from redistributed tariff revenue, this is not that surprising. Furthermore, these changes in real factor returns, defined as the amount of goods that the wage and rent will buy, also include the effects of price changes and therefore contrast with the changes in nominal (money) factor returns which in this case are both negative (not reported). By substantially reducing tariffs, Tunisia lowers the nominal domestic prices of both imports and import-competing goods, and this feeds through the economy to reduce other goods prices and factor prices as well. However, the falling prices of goods also mean that the lower nominal factor prices can be used to buy an increased amount of goods, and real factor prices therefore can rise.

In Scenario A the return to capital rises relative to the wage, implying that the structure of tariffs in Tunisia protected labour more than capital, and the liberalization therefore causes a relative shift in favour of capital. However, both factors lose in nominal terms, which means that in terms of world prices (here essentially unchanged), capital simply loses less than labour. The reason is that domestic prices of goods and factors have been kept artificially high by the tariffs relative to world prices, and the liberalization therefore reduces them across the board.

Since Tunisia is small compared to its major trading partners, the effects of the FTA do not have a significant impact on the EU. Total imports and exports rise by less than $1 billion and changes in the terms of trade, welfare relative to GDP, and real returns to labour and capital are negligible. Nonetheless, in absolute terms the welfare gain for the EU-12 is $2.4 billion compared to the $26.8 million reduction in Tunisian welfare. France/Italy combined gain $1.5 billion.

5.5.2   Scenario B

In Scenario B capital is permitted to move among sectors, but is kept internationally immobile. Capital therefore exits from those sectors where its return has fallen the most and migrates to sectors where the relative return, inside Tunisia, has increased. The main effect of capital mobility is to cause greater changes in sectoral output, and therefore trade. This can be seen by comparing the export and import columns of Scenarios A and B in Table 5.3. Also, because trade creation is enhanced, the overall welfare effect of the FTA in Scenario B is now positive. Finally, the reallocation of capital in favour of the less protected capital-intensive sectors causes the ratio of the return to capital relative to labour to increase and actually leads to a fall in the real wage. That is, as capital migrates from previously protected labour-intensive sectors to capital-intensive sectors, labour is left with less capital to work with and its marginal product and real wage are reduced.[16] The asymmetry of the effects of the FTA is further evident here. While Tunisian welfare rises in absolute terms by $430.3 million, the absolute increase in welfare for the EU-12 amounts to $3.4 billion. These effects are larger than in Scenario A because of the more complete adjustments represented with full mobility of both labour and capital.

5.5.3   Scenario C

In Scenario C we allow for international capital movement, equal to 10% of the Tunisian capital stock.[17] The assumption is that it flows into Tunisia from the EU countries, in proportion to their own capital stocks. Our original intent was to select the capital flow as approximating that which would undo the effect of the FTA on the nominal return to capital in Tunisia. The rationale for this was two-fold. First, it is the relative nominal return in Tunisia compared to the rest of the world that should motivate capital to move. Second, we expected the FTA to raise the return to capital in Tunisia and to leave it essentially unchanged elsewhere. The latter expectation was borne out in the results of our model, as already noted in Scenarios A and B, but the former was not: there was a small reduction in the nominal return to capital in Tunisia in those scenarios. This suggests that capital would flow out of Tunisia, rather than in.

The model does not include certain considerations that might overcome these market signals and draw capital into Tunisia. Most frequently mentioned is the hope that an FTA between a small developing country and a larger, more advanced country or group of countries will lock into place certain market reforms in the developing country that accompany or precede liberalization. This in turn may reduce the risk that is associated with investment in the country and thus attract capital.[18] As our model does not include such effects, we impose an exogenous capital flow into Tunisia as a crude way of representing them. This is what is done in Scenario C. We have modelled the earnings on imported capital as being retained and re-invested in Tunisia, so that there is no effect on the balance of payments after the inflow itself is completed.

The results for Scenario C in Table 5.3 show a further worsening of the terms of trade, an increase in the expansion of exports and a decrease in the expansion of imports (needed to keep the trade balance unchanged when the prices of imports rise relative to exports), a rise (relative to Scenario B) in the wage-rental ratio, and a decline in overall welfare. All of these effects except the last are what one would expect from any capital inflow. The surprise may be the loss of welfare, which occurs because capital is flowing here in a direction opposite to market signals. That is, as noted above, the FTA drives the nominal return to capital in Tunisia down because it lowers prices in most sectors. Without evidence to the contrary, the model assumes that nominal returns on capital (adjusted for risk) were initially the same in Tunisia as elsewhere. Therefore the natural market response to the FTA would have been for capital to flow out of Tunisia to other countries where it would be more productive. By instead forcing capital to flow into Tunisia in Scenario C, we are moving capital to a location where its productivity has been reduced by the FTA, and it is now therefore below the return that is paid on it. The country is therefore paying more for this capital than it receives in increased output. This reduces welfare of the country as a whole.

This welfare result would change if the risk premium story noted above were to apply, as then a lower nominal return could be paid to foreign capital. The reduction in the risk premium could be much greater than any reduction in the marginal product of capital due to the FTA, and in that case the same capital flow would be welfare increasing. But we have no way of knowing how the risk premium might change, and therefore we are unable to quantify this possibility.

We again see the asymmetry *vis-à-vis* the EU in this Scenario. Tunisia has a welfare decline of $15.0 million, while the EU-12 gains $5.9 billion. Compared to Scenario B, the capital flow from the EU to Tunisia has increased welfare somewhat in the EU. This is because Tunisia is assumed to pay a market return on the capital even though its productivity within Tunisia is less than that. The real return to capital in all three EU groupings falls by 0.1%.

5.5.4 Scenario D

Scenario D assumes sector-specific capital. With capital unable to move among sectors, perhaps because it has already been installed and is not easily converted to other uses, returns to capital rise in some sectors and fall in others. Our assumption in Scenario D is that capital flows into the sectors where the return has risen, but does not flow out of the sectors where returns have fallen. As we cannot predict how much capital will respond to such signals, we assume for purely illustrative purposes that the elasticity of capital, with respect to its return, is equal to 5.0. That is, an increase in the nominal return to capital in a sector is assumed to cause a capital flow into Tunisia that is five times as large relative to the Tunisian sectoral capital stock.

What is shown in Table 5.3 is that the sector-specific capital flows cause largely very similar results to those of Scenario C, although the effects in this case are quite a bit smaller because the capital flow itself is smaller. Responding only to the sectors where the return to capital has increased, even with an elasticity of five, causes a capital flow of only 1.9% of the Tunisian capital stock, compared to the 10% in Scenario C. The one effect that is noticeably different, however, is on economic welfare. Here the small decline in welfare that we saw in Scenario A without the capital flow is turned into an also small but positive change in welfare by the sector-specific flow. The reason is simply that capital, in contrast to Scenario C, is now flowing only into sectors where it does earn a high enough return to pay for itself, and it thus creates a surplus for the economy.

5.5.5 Scenario E

Our final scenario takes account of the major features of the Tunisian Investment Code. The endogenous capital flows introduced in Scenario D are here expanded or contracted in response to various constraints and/or subsidies that are included in the Code. It is evident in Table 5.3 that the results differ hardly at all from those of Scenario D, although the fact that there is a slight increase in the welfare improvement from the FTA in the presence of the Code suggests that its features may have a small positive benefit. This suggests the Code is to some extent succeeding in directing capital to sectors where it can be most productive.

5.6 Computational results: sectoral effects

Sectoral results for Scenarios A, B, and D are given for Tunisia in Tables 5.4–5.6. The sectoral results for Scenarios C and E are available from the authors on request. The percentage changes in total exports and imports are shown in columns (2) and (3) of each table. The percentage changes in imports are decomposed bilaterally in columns (4)–(10). The percentage changes in sectoral output and number of firms are listed in columns (11) and (12). The change in output per firm, and thus the extent to which economies of scale have been realized, can be determined by subtracting column (12) from (11). Columns (13) and (14) record the percentage and absolute changes in employment of labour, and column (15) records changes in the return to capital or in the employment of capital, depending on the individual scenario.[19] The sectoral results for the three EU regions and the other regions are in general very small and are therefore not reported here.

5.6.1 Scenario A

There are sizable percentage increases in total Tunisian exports across all sectors (column 2, Table 5.4). Imports increase in all the goods sectors except wood products and mining; imports in all services sectors decline because the barriers in these sectors are assumed to remain intact. Since Tunisian goods imports will increase with the tariff removal, Tunisian exports rise in order for trade to balance. There are substantial percentage increases (reductions) in Tunisia's bilateral imports of goods (services) from the three EU groupings, reflecting the relative price changes following the removal of Tunisian tariffs on EU goods. There are sizable negative percentage changes in Tunisia's imports from all of the non-EU regions noted in columns (7)–(10), which is indicative of the trade diversion that occurs.

Output increases most in leather products, footwear, wood products, miscellaneous manufactures, and mining and quarrying (column 11). The largest declines in output occur in rubber products, furniture and fixtures, paper products, and transport equipment. If the percentage changes in number of firms in column (12) are subtracted from the percentage changes in output in column (11) to get changes in output per firm, there is evidence of positive scale effects in 20 sectors and negative scale effects in 8 sectors. The sectors with the largest absolute employment increases in number of workers are wholesale and retail trade and transportation services; those with the largest absolute employment declines are agriculture, textiles, and community, social, and personal services. There are positive changes in the nominal return to capital in 16 sectors, with the largest increases in mining and quarrying, wood products, miscellaneous manufactures, leather products and footwear, and clothing. The largest negative changes in returns to capital are in transportation equipment, rubber products, furniture and fixtures and paper products.

5.6.2   Scenario B

Scenario B can be interpreted as the longer-run effects of the FTA in that both labour and capital can move among sectors. Looking first at the percentage changes in total exports in column (2) of Table 5.5 in comparison to Scenario A in Table 5.4, there are evidently now relatively larger increases especially in exports of clothing and mining and quarrying, two of Tunisia's most important export industries. Four sectors now show reductions in exports: textiles; leather products; paper products; and rubber products. The percentage increases in sectoral imports (column 3) are larger than in Scenario A because both capital and labour can be reallocated among sectors. Services sector imports also fall by sizable percentages. Bilateral imports from the EU increase more in Scenario B than in Scenario A as indicated in columns (4)–(6), and there is less trade diversion (columns 7–10).

Allowing for full mobility of capital and labour has more pronounced effects on changes in sectoral output as compared to Scenario A. The sizable positive and negative changes in sectoral outputs suggest accordingly that there would be considerable intersectoral reallocation of capital and labour in response to the Tunisia–EU FTA, given Tunisia's relatively high manufacturing sector tariffs. This is evident from the results reported in columns (13)–(15). Comparing columns (11) and (12), there are indications of positive scale economies in 23 sectors and negative scale economies in 5 sectors.

Table 5.4 Scenario A: trade only with sectorally specific capital: sectoral effects on Tunisia of Tunisia–EU free trade (percentage change unless otherwise noted)

Sector	Exports	Imports	Bilateral imports							Output	No. firms	Employment		Return to capital
			MEU	FR-IT	OEU	OEUR	NAFTA	APAC	SAM			%	'000s	
	(2)	(3)	(4)	(5)	(6)	(7)	(8)	(9)	(10)	(11)	(12)	(13)	(14)	(15)
1 Agriculture	43.5	5.4	51.9	45.7	52.4	-20.3	-20.3	-20.3	-20.3	0.0	0.0	-0.9	-4.8	1.5
310 Food	18.2	17.4	22.0	53.0	50.1	-21.5	-21.5	-21.5	-21.5	-1.4	-1.3	-4.6	-1.6	0.0
321 Textiles	53.7	20.2	26.9	25.2	26.6	-44.6	-44.6	-44.6	-44.6	6.3	-4.7	-5.4	-4.2	-2.8
322 Clothing	14.8	66.5	66.0	67.9	67.1	-29.6	-29.5	-29.5	-29.5	3.7	3.6	6.5	1.3	7.7
323 Leather products	58.3	23.7	21.0	28.5	24.0	-36.9	-36.9	-36.9	-36.9	18.2	2.4	9.4	0.2	9.7
324 Footwear	45.2	54.6	56.8	58.2	65.2	-32.4	-32.4	-32.4	-32.4	13.7	0.6	11.0	1.3	9.7
331 Wood products	13.8	-6.7	62.5	49.2	70.0	-15.5	-15.5	-15.5	-15.5	12.5	1.9	7.9	0.5	11.4
332 Furniture, fixtures	4.9	34.8	65.5	59.6	57.5	-30.9	-30.9	-30.9	-30.9	-7.6	-5.7	-12.8	-0.2	-8.3
341 Paper products	17.6	19.9	61.4	51.0	51.1	-32.0	-32.0	-32.0	-32.0	-6.1	-2.0	-16.0	-0.7	-7.1
342 Printing, publishing	14.4	13.3	18.5	31.5	35.7	-27.7	-27.7	-27.7	-27.7	-2.2	-0.9	-6.0	-0.3	-4.5
35A Chemicals	8.0	18.2	27.3	31.4	34.3	-18.3	-18.3	-18.3	-18.3	-3.5	-1.8	-4.8	-1.2	-1.6
35B Petroleum products	8.8	8.4	10.4	10.2	38.4	-16.6	-16.6	-16.6	-16.7	1.7	-0.6	2.1	0.0	4.5
355 Rubber products	7.6	30.1	42.2	36.3	42.2	-32.9	-32.9	-32.9	-32.9	-15.2	-13.5	-20.2	-1.0	-9.6
36A Non-metal mineral products	1.2	56.4	76.9	72.0	79.6	-18.6	-18.6	-18.6	-18.6	-6.8	-5.9	-8.0	-0.6	-3.6
362 Glass products	6.0	5.2	42.6	20.0	48.4	-19.0	-19.0	-19.0	-19.0	-0.4	-0.8	-1.9	-0.6	1.1
371 Iron, steel	6.9	5.8	33.8	23.2	20.1	-26.8	-26.8	-26.8	-26.8	-5.1	-6.5	-8.5	-0.3	-3.4
372 Non-ferrous metals	13.9	4.0	10.5	15.3	15.2	-31.0	-31.0	-31.0	-31.0	4.7	0.6	5.0	0.0	6.0
381 Metal products	15.7	29.7	44.7	43.6	43.9	-31.1	-31.1	-31.1	-31.1	-5.2	-3.1	-9.3	-0.6	-6.8
382 Non-electrical machinery	14.6	5.5	12.8	15.8	10.3	-26.7	-26.7	-26.7	-26.7	-2.2	-2.9	-5.4	-1.0	-4.9
383 Electrical machinery	38.4	19.4	29.3	33.9	19.7	-31.2	-31.2	-31.2	-31.2	4.0	-1.3	-1.0	-0.4	0.7
384 Transport equipment	18.0	12.8	15.7	19.7	17.2	-35.4	-35.4	-35.4	-35.4	-6.1	-6.8	-8.5	-0.5	-18.9
38A Miscellaneous manufactures	33.5	11.9	18.4	22.1	21.0	-36.6	-36.5	-36.5	-36.5	13.5	2.0	11.6	0.6	11.0
2 Mining, quarrying	21.0	-5.1	21.4	32.2	85.0	-20.1	-20.1	-20.1	-20.0	13.5	12.7	20.0	0.3	14.4
4 Utilities	22.1	-16.6	-16.8	-16.8	-16.8	-16.7	-16.7	-16.7	-16.8	1.8	0.3	2.4	0.3	3.5
5 Construction	22.9	-22.7	-22.7	-22.7	-22.7	-22.7	-22.7	-22.7	-22.7	-0.5	-2.8	-4.1	-2.6	-1.0
6 Wholesale trade	3.6	-7.5	-7.5	-7.6	-7.5	-7.5	-7.5	-7.5	-7.5	1.3	0.4	14.1	37.8	8.2
7 Transportation	12.6	-10.5	-10.6	-10.6	-10.6	-10.5	-10.5	-10.5	-10.5	5.5	3.2	12.1	6.4	10.3
8 Financial services	11.8	-11.5	-11.5	-11.5	-11.5	-11.5	-11.5	-11.5	-11.4	2.8	1.9	7.5	1.2	6.7
9 Personal services	21.3	-19.6	-19.6	-19.6	-19.6	-19.5	-19.5	-19.5	-19.5	-2.0	-2.5	-3.5	-25.3	-0.5
Total	16.5	11.5	19.7	22.2	26.4	-24.9	-22.8	-29.6	-20.9	0.7	-1.8	0.0	0.0	3.5

5.6.3   Scenario C

The results of this scenario are not reported. They suggest that the assumed infusion of FDI from the EU results in larger percentage expansions of exports and smaller percentage reductions as compared to Scenario B. Total imports show smaller percentage increases as compared to Scenario B, since there is a worsening in the terms of trade that limits the imports that can be financed with an unchanged balance of trade. The percentage changes in Tunisia's bilateral imports from the EU are smaller than in Scenario B, which also reflects the change in terms of trade, and there is more evidence of trade diversion. The percentage changes in sectoral output tend to be larger with the assumed inflow of FDI, although this is not uniform. The reallocation of labour and capital remains substantial, even with the potential for proportional expansion in the sectoral capital stocks associated with an increased inflow of FDI.

5.6.4   Scenario D

This scenario considers an inflow of FDI within the context of the sector-specific capital framework. A comparison of percentage changes in total sectoral exports and imports in columns (2) and (3) of Table 5.6 with those in Table 5.4 suggests the results are not greatly different. This is because the calculated FDI inflows turn out to constitute only 1.9% of Tunisia's base-level total capital stock. (*See* above). Of course, some of the individual sectors are affected differentially because the FDI inflows are directed only at the sectors that show increases in the nominal return to capital. It is difficult to see many important changes in the bilateral import results between Scenarios A and D.

While the investment inflows that occur in this scenario have only relatively small effects on the various variables, it is of some interest to note that the largest increases in returns to capital (and therefore the largest FDI inflows under our assumptions) in manufacturing sectors occur in leather products, clothing, petroleum products, non-ferrous metals, miscellaneous manufactures, and footwear. There are also increases in returns to capital and hence capital inflows into all of the services sectors, including especially wholesale trade, transportation, and financial services, some of which includes components of tourism.

5.6.5   Scenario E

Scenario E incorporates some features of Tunisia's 1994 Investment Code. The results, which are not reported here, indicate that the inflow of

Table 5.5 Scenario B: trade only with sectorally mobile capital: sectoral effects on Tunisia of Tunisia–EU free trade (percentage change unless otherwise noted)

Sector	Exports (2)	Imports (3)	Bilateral imports MEU (4)	FR-IT (5)	OEU (6)	OEUR (7)	NAFTA (8)	APAC (9)	SAM (10)	Output (11)	No. firms (12)	Employment % (13)	Employment '000s (14)	Return to capital (15)
1 Agriculture	25.1	18.6	71.0	64.0	71.5	-10.3	-10.3	-10.3	-10.3	-4.1	0.0	1.8	9.7	-4.4
310 Food	5.3	34.1	39.6	75.0	71.8	-10.1	-10.1	-10.1	-10.1	-3.3	-3.8	6.6	2.3	-7.4
321 Textiles	-61.9	64.3	73.7	72.4	74.9	-24.4	-24.0	-24.1	-24.0	-85.9	-85.7	-85.1	-65.4	-86.2
322 Clothing	49.3	38.1	37.2	39.0	38.8	-41.7	-41.5	-41.5	-41.5	27.9	27.8	33.2	6.4	21.1
323 Leather products	-3.3	39.8	36.8	45.4	40.6	-28.7	-28.6	-28.6	-28.6	-22.5	-27.0	-25.4	-0.6	-29.2
324 Footwear	31.7	69.3	71.5	73.1	81.0	-26.0	-26.0	-26.0	-26.0	9.1	3.5	13.3	1.6	1.0
331 Wood products	10.0	-4.7	65.4	51.8	73.1	-14.0	-13.9	-13.9	-14.0	6.8	3.4	8.8	0.6	1.6
332 Furniture, fixtures	0.1	57.7	94.1	87.1	84.7	-19.0	-19.0	-18.9	-19.0	-13.8	-14.7	-10.2	-0.2	-18.0
341 Paper products	-6.8	50.2	104.4	91.2	91.3	-13.9	-13.9	-13.9	-13.9	-22.9	-25.0	-15.9	-0.7	-26.2
342 Printing, publishing	1.5	39.4	46.4	62.4	67.6	-10.7	-10.7	-10.7	-10.7	-7.2	-8.9	-3.5	-0.2	-9.6
35A Chemicals	2.8	25.4	35.2	39.5	42.5	-13.3	-13.3	-13.3	-13.3	-7.6	-7.5	-3.4	-0.9	-11.5
35B Petroleum products	6.2	15.6	17.9	17.7	47.5	-11.0	-11.0	-11.0	-11.1	2.1	-1.7	7.5	0.1	-0.8
355 Rubber products	-19.9	53.1	67.5	61.2	67.1	-21.2	-21.1	-21.1	-21.1	-30.4	-28.8	-27.4	-1.4	-36.4
36A Non-metal mineral products	1.0	59.2	80.1	75.1	82.8	-17.1	-17.1	-17.1	-17.2	-7.2	-6.5	-4.1	-0.3	-13.2
362 Glass products	5.2	28.6	50.0	26.2	56.1	-14.8	-14.8	-14.8	-14.8	1.9	-0.2	6.3	2.1	-4.0
371 Iron, steel	4.3	7.2	36.2	25.3	22.1	-25.6	-25.6	-25.6	-25.6	-9.6	-11.5	-7.1	-0.2	-16.9
372 Non-ferrous metals	11.8	0.1	6.6	11.1	11.0	-33.5	-33.5	-33.5	-33.5	1.4	-1.9	5.9	0.0	-5.0
381 Metal products	6.7	46.3	63.8	62.4	62.7	-22.0	-22.0	-22.0	-22.1	-8.4	-13.4	-8.6	-0.6	-15.3
382 Non-electrical machinery	10.2	12.3	20.2	23.3	17.4	-21.9	-21.9	-21.9	-21.9	-3.7	-8.0	-5.2	-1.0	-10.2
383 Electrical machinery	32.9	26.6	37.1	42.0	26.8	-27.1	-27.1	-27.1	-27.1	4.5	-2.8	0.9	0.4	-3.2
384 Transport equipment	4.4	28.4	31.9	36.5	33.5	-26.3	-26.3	-26.3	-26.3	-14.9	-16.9	-15.3	-0.9	-17.6
38A Miscellaneous manufactures	10.8	17.7	24.7	28.5	27.4	-33.2	-33.2	-33.2	-33.2	-4.7	-7.7	-0.9	0.0	-10.5
2 Mining, quarrying	94.4	-27.4	-17.1	-10.5	26.2	-45.3	-45.4	-45.4	-45.4	63.1	63.2	69.8	1.2	50.0
4 Utilities	17.6	-14.0	-13.8	-13.9	-13.9	-13.8	-13.8	-13.8	-13.8	1.5	-0.7	13.1	1.6	-5.7
5 Construction	24.1	-20.9	-20.9	-20.9	-20.9	-20.8	-20.8	-20.8	-20.9	3.1	0.4	3.5	2.2	-5.3
6 Wholesale trade	22.4	-17.2	-17.2	-17.2	-17.1	-17.1	-17.1	-17.1	-17.1	15.9	14.8	36.8	98.5	14.0
7 Transportation	34.4	-20.0	-20.2	-20.4	-20.3	-20.2	-20.2	-20.2	-20.2	17.9	16.5	26.1	13.7	12.2
8 Financial services	11.9	-13.3	-13.3	-13.3	-13.3	-13.2	-13.2	-13.2	-13.2	1.3	0.8	10.5	1.7	-3.3
9 Personal services	21.6	-17.1	-17.1	-17.2	-17.1	-17.1	-17.1	-17.1	-17.1	1.2	0.8	4.1	29.9	-4.6
Total	31.1	21.8	30.5	34.3	42.2	-20.6	-19.8	-23.7	-12.6	2.7	-20.1	0.0	0.0	1.4

FDI is only slightly larger than in Scenario D, amounting to an increase of 2.1% in the base level of Tunisia's total capital stock. The detailed sectoral results are very close to those in Scenario D.

5.6.6 Policies for adjustment

The foregoing disaggregated results all indicate the need for substantial intersectoral adjustment by the Tunisian economy in response to implementation of the FTA. The question then arises what policies, if any, should be used to facilitate that adjustment. Since this is inherently a dynamic issue, our model does not say anything about it directly. However, the world has considerable experience in adjusting to the dislocations that are occasioned by trade liberalization, and that experience warns of the pitfalls of programs to facilitate adjustment, even if it does not tell us clearly how to avoid those pitfalls. The greatest danger is that policies that are intended to reduce the burden of adjustment for industries whose output and employment must contract will instead permit them to avoid that adjustment entirely or delay it so that in fact the burden on the economy will be extended unnecessarily over time.[20] To avoid this, it is important that adjustment assistance policies be designed primarily to help workers accomplish the relocation and retraining that may be necessary to shift to expanding industries rather than merely to compensate them for the losses they incur in the contracting industries. Similar conditions apply to any assistance provided to owners of capital, although here the assistance might take the form of accelerated depreciation allowances and credits for investment in expanding sectors.[21]

5.7 Conclusions and implications for policy

Our chief findings are as follows:

1. The static welfare benefits for Tunisia of the FTA range from slightly negative to somewhat positive, depending on what is assumed about intersectoral capital mobility in Tunisia. Identifying capital mobility with the time horizon of the analysis, we therefore expect the FTA to reduce Tunisia's aggregate welfare somewhat in the short run but raise welfare in the longer run.
2. Depending on the length of time allowed for phasing in of the FTA, Tunisia could experience significant adjustment problems in connection with the intersectoral movements of labour and capital that the FTA would induce. We find that changes in output across sectors are substantial.

Table 5.6 Scenario C: trade and FDI with sectorally specified capital: sectoral effects on Tunisia of Tunisia–EU trade (percentage change unless otherwise noted)

Sector	Exports	Imports	Bilateral imports							Output	No. firms	Employment		Return to capital
			MEU	FR-IT	OEU	OEUR	NAFTA	APAC	SAM			%	'000s	
	(2)	(3)	(4)	(5)	(6)	(7)	(8)	(9)	(10)	(11)	(12)	(13)	(14)	(15)
1 Agriculture	40.0	8.5	56.3	50.0	56.8	-18.0	-18.0	-18.0	-18.0	-0.1	0.0	-1.1	-6.1	2.1
310 Food	16.3	20.4	25.2	56.9	54.0	-19.5	-19.4	-19.4	-19.4	-1.1	-1.5	-5.0	-1.8	0.7
321 Textiles	53.0	22.1	29.0	27.3	28.6	-43.7	-43.7	-43.7	-43.7	7.1	-5.1	-5.7	-4.4	-2.2
322 Clothing	11.9	71.8	71.3	73.3	72.5	-27.3	-27.2	-27.2	-27.2	2.1	1.9	3.6	0.7	6.4
323 Leather products	75.4	20.1	17.4	24.6	20.2	-38.8	-38.8	-38.8	-38.8	28.5	10.4	15.9	0.4	8.4
324 Footwear	60.0	44.5	46.5	47.8	54.3	-36.8	-36.8	-36.8	-36.8	20.1	7.2	12.4	1.5	5.6
331 Wood products	23.9	-13.0	46.1	34.1	52.9	-24.0	-23.9	-24.0	-24.0	19.5	17.2	13.8	0.9	-1.0
332 Furniture, fixtures	5.0	36.5	67.5	61.5	59.4	-30.0	-30.9	-30.0	-30.0	-6.2	-6.0	-12.6	-0.2	-7.3
341 Paper products	17.6	21.2	63.3	52.7	52.8	-31.2	-31.2	-31.2	-31.2	-5.1	-2.2	-16.2	-0.7	-6.4
342 Printing, publishing	13.6	15.7	21.0	34.3	38.6	-26.2	-26.2	-26.2	-26.2	-1.6	-1.2	-6.0	-0.3	-3.6
35A Chemicals	8.8	19.1	28.2	32.3	35.2	-17.8	-17.7	-17.7	-17.7	-1.3	-2.0	-3.5	-0.9	-0.4
35B Petroleum products	7.6	12.9	14.9	14.9	44.0	-13.2	-13.2	-13.2	-13.2	2.6	-0.9	2.5	0.0	5.9
355 Rubber products	8.8	32.1	44.5	38.5	44.5	-31.8	-31.8	-31.8	-31.8	-13.4	-13.5	-18.3	-0.9	-7.6
36A Non-metal mineral products	1.2	58.0	78.6	73.7	81.3	-17.8	-17.8	-17.8	-17.8	-5.7	-6.1	-8.2	-0.6	-2.9
362 Glass products	5.9	24.3	45.0	22.0	50.9	-17.6	-17.6	-17.6	-17.6	0.7	-0.8	-2.0	-0.6	2.0
371 Iron, steel	6.7	7.6	36.1	25.4	22.2	-25.6	-25.5	-25.5	-25.5	-7.0	-7.0	-8.3	-0.3	-2.3
372 Non-ferrous metals	13.1	5.9	12.7	17.5	17.4	-29.7	-29.7	-29.7	-29.7	-4.3	-0.2	3.5	0.0	5.9
381 Metal products	15.6	31.5	46.7	45.6	45.9	-30.1	-30.1	-30.1	-30.1	4.5	-3.2	-9.5	-0.6	-6.2
382 Non-electrical machinery	14.5	7.0	14.4	17.4	11.8	-25.7	-25.7	-25.7	-25.7	-4.3	-3.1	-5.5	-1.1	-4.2
383 Electrical machinery	37.9	21.2	31.2	35.9	21.5	-30.2	-30.2	-30.2	-30.2	-1.2	-1.5	-1.2	-0.5	1.3
384 Transport equipment	16.6	14.9	17.9	22.0	19.5	-34.1	-34.1	-34.1	-34.1	-6.5	-7.4	-9.1	-0.5	-19.8
38A Miscellaneous manufactures	50.9	6.1	12.2	15.7	14.7	-39.9	-39.9	-39.9	-39.9	25.9	15.6	19.7	1.0	5.7
2 Mining, quarrying	56.3	-15.2	1.6	10.8	54.9	-32.9	-32.9	-32.9	-32.9	39.4	38.8	40.1	0.7	4.9
4 Utilities	20.0	-14.3	-14.4	-14.5	-14.5	-14.4	-14.4	-14.4	-14.4	2.8	0.3	3.4	0.4	4.9
5 Construction	22.7	-21.6	-21.5	-21.6	-21.6	-21.5	-21.5	-21.5	-21.5	0.8	-2.8	-4.0	-2.5	0.0
6 Wholesale trade	4.8	-7.1	-7.1	-7.2	-7.1	-7.1	-7.1	-7.1	-7.1	2.6	1.6	12.5	33.5	7.9
7 Transportation	27.9	-17.3	-17.5	-17.6	-17.5	-17.5	-17.5	-17.5	-17.5	14.4	12.8	16.0	8.4	5.7
8 Financial services	8.8	-8.0	-8.0	-8.0	-8.0	-8.0	-8.0	-8.0	-8.0	2.9	1.6	7.3	1.2	7.6
9 Personal services	18.6	-17.2	-17.2	-17.2	-17.2	-17.2	-17.2	-17.2	-17.2	-1.5	-2.6	-3.2	-22.8	0.7
Total	21.4	12.1	20.6	23.0	27.6	-25.5	-23.6	-29.3	-20.7	2.6	-0.6	0.0	0.0	3.4

3. Our FDI-related scenarios are intended to be primarily illustrative since there is no straightforward way to integrate FDI inflows into the modelling framework. Our results suggest that even an approximate doubling of annual FDI inflows into Tunisia would be unlikely to make a significant difference for Tunisian welfare under the FTA. This also applies if allowance is made for FDI inflows to respond to changes in sectoral rates of return and the incentives in Tunisia's 1994 Investment Code are included into the analysis.
4. Our results imply that substantially greater FDI inflows are not necessary for the FTA to be beneficial to Tunisia in the medium term (once adjustment has occurred). Indeed, unless the induced FDI inflow is considerably larger than the flows that have been observed to date, and unless these flows are systematically targeted to sectors where yields exceed its cost, FDI should not make a noticeable difference to the economic success of the FTA. On the other hand, given the difficulty of observing the types of gain that the FTA is likely to yield, it may well be that a large visible flow of FDI is necessary for the FTA to be *viewed* as a success.

As noted earlier, we should reiterate that our CGE model does not make any allowance for dynamic efficiency changes and economic growth. Recent research suggests that static gains from trade, such as we have calculated here, may well be augmented by their effects over time on economic growth, so that the static changes, to the extent that they are positive, are really only lower bounds on what the economic benefits to an economy may turn out to be. On the other hand, the very few estimates of such effects that are available only suggest that the static gains will be increased by a small integer multiple, and this would not materially affect the conclusions we have reached here based on the estimates of the static model (see Baldwin, 1992). There are other theoretical models that explore the possibility that trade liberalization may have a permanent positive effect on a country's rate of growth, by stimulating technological progress or by taking advantage of various 'dynamic scale economies' (e.g. Grossman and Helpman, 1991). There is some empirical evidence for such an effect, but it is unclear whether the effects of trade on growth rates that have been found empirically are transitory or permanent.[22] We have also omitted from our analysis the possible reductions in trading costs with all countries that may be achieved through harmonization and other sources of increased trading efficiency (discussed by Page and Underwood (Chapter 6), Hoekman and Djankov (Chapter 8) and Konan and Maskus (Chapter 7) in this volume). This does not deny the potential importance of these other sources of benefit, but it remains to be seen whether and how this potential will be realized.

There are also forces that may act in the other direction. Since the mid-1970s Tunisia has benefited from preferentially low – if not zero – tariffs on most exports to the EU. The benefits to Tunisia from these preferences – which are not included in our analysis here since they are already present independently of the FTA – will be eroded as the EU continues to lower trade barriers multilaterally as a result of the Uruguay Round and future negotiations under the auspices of the World Trade Organization.

Overall, the analysis suggests that Tunisia may not have a great deal to gain in economic terms from entering into the FTA with the EU. The reason is that the FTA amounts essentially to Tunisia eliminating its bilateral tariffs *vis-à-vis* the EU, since Tunisia already has had duty free access to the EU except for some agricultural products and certain types of clothing exports. The trade diverting effects of such a discriminatory tariff reduction are likely to be harmful, especially in the short run. Further, the FTA does not in itself appear likely to generate an inflow of capital into Tunisia that would materially increase Tunisian welfare. The question thus arises as to whether Tunisia might pursue liberalization of its trade restrictions on a multilateral basis as well as preferentially with respect to the EU. This would avoid the trade diversion that might otherwise occur. Reducing its trade barriers multilaterally and reinforcing these actions with a liberalization of its foreign investment policies and maintenance of macroeconomic and political stability might in the end be the best path for Tunisia to follow.[23]

References

Bajo-Rubio, Oscar and Simón Sosvilla-Rivero (1994), 'An econometric analysis of foreign direct investment in Spain', *Southern Economic Journal*, 61, 104–20.

Baldwin, Richard E. (1992), 'Measurable dynamic gains from trade', *Journal of Political Economy*, 100, 162–74.

Brown, Drusilla K. and Robert M. Stern (1989), 'Computable general equilibrium estimates of the gains from US–Canadian trade liberalization', in David Greenaway, Thomas Hyclak, and Robert J. Thornton, (eds.), *Economic Aspects of Regional Trading Arrangements*, London, Harvester Wheatsheaf.

Brown, Drusilla K., Alan V. Deardorff, and Robert M. Stern (1992a), 'A North American free trade agreement: analytical issues and a computational assessment', *The World Economy*, 15, 15–29.

___ (1992b), 'North American economic integration,' *Economic Journal*, 102, 1507–18.

___ (1993), 'Protection and real wages: old and new trade theories and their empirical counterparts', Research Forum on International Economics, University of Michigan, Discussion Paper No. 331 (May).

___ (1995), 'Expanding NAFTA: economic effects of accession of Chile and other major South American nations', *North American Journal of Economics and Finance*, 6, 149–70.

___ (1996), 'Computational analysis of the economic effects of an East Asian preferential trading bloc', *Journal of the Japanese and International Economies*, 10, 37–70.

Brown, Drusilla K., Alan V. Deardorff, Simeon Djankov, and Robert M. Stern (1996), 'An economic assessment of the integration of Czechoslovakia, Hungary, and Poland into the European Union', in Stanley Black, (ed.), *Europe's Economy Looks East*, New York, Cambridge University Press.

Deardorff, Alan V. and Robert M. Stern (1990), *Computational Analysis of Global Trading Arrangements*, Ann Arbor, University of Michigan Press.

Dixit, Avinash K. and Joseph E. Stiglitz (1977), 'Monopolistic competition and optimum product diversity', *American Economic Review*, 67, 297–308.

GATT (General Agreement on Tariffs and Trade) (1994), *Trade Policy Reveiw: Tunisia 1994*, Vols. I and II, Geneva, GATT (September).

Grossman, Gene M. and Elhanan Helpman (1991), *Innovation and Growth in the Global Economy*, Cambridge, MA, MIT Press.

Haddad, Mona and Ann Harrison (1993), 'Are there positive spillovers from direct foreign investment? Evidence from panel data for Morocco', *Journal of Development Economics*, 42, 51–74.

Harrison, Glenn W., Thomas F. Rutherford, and Ian Wooton (1989), 'The economic impact of the European Community', *American Economic Review*, 79, 288–94.

Helpman, Elhanan and Paul R. Krugman (1985), *Market Structure and Foreign Trade: Increasing Returns, Imperfect Competition, and the International Economy*, Cambridge, MA, MIT Press.

Hoekman, Bernard, and Simeon Djankov (1995), 'The European Union's Mediterranean free trade initiative', *The World Economy*, 19, 387–407.

IMF (International Monetary Fund) (1996), *IMF Survey*, 4 March, Washington, DC, IMF.

Levine, Ross and David Renelt (1992), 'A sensitivity analysis of cross-country growth regressions', *American Economic Review*, 82, 942–63.

Lucas, Robert E.B. (1993), 'On the determinants of direct foreign investment: evidence from East and Southeast Asia', *World Development*, 21, 391–406.

Ministry of International Cooperation and Foreign Investment, Tunisian Government (1994), *Incentives for investment in Tunisia*, Tunis, MCIIE.

Nsouli, Saleh, Sena Eken, Paul Duran, Gerwin Bell, and Zühtü Yücelik (1993), *The Path to Convertibility and Growth: The Tunisian Experience*, Occasional Paper 109, International Monetary Fund, Washington, DC, IMF.

Page, John and John Underwood (1995), 'Growth, the Maghreb and the European Union: assessing the impact of the free trade agreements on Tunisia and Morocco', paper presented at the International Economic Association Eleventh World Congress, 18–22 December, 1995, Tunis.

Stanton, Julie (1994), 'Estimates of tariff equivalents of Tunisia's non-tariff barriers', unpublished manuscript, International Economics Division, World Bank.

United Nations Centre on Transnational Corporations (UNCTC) (1992), *The Determinants of Foreign Direct Investment: A Survey of the Evidence*, New York, United Nations.

United Nations Conference on Trade and Development, Programme on Transnational Corporations (1993), *Explaining and Forecasting Regional Flows of Foreign Direct Investment*, New York, United Nations.

Notes

1. Readers who are not concerned with the technical details of the model may wish to proceed to the results of the analysis reported in the sections below.
2. The extension of the NAFTA to some major trading countries in South America, the formation of an East Asian trading bloc, and the potential effects of integrating Czechoslovakia, Hungary, and Poland into the EU are also analysed in Brown et al. (1995, 1996) and Brown, Deardorff, Djankov and Stern (1996).
3. Other Europe includes: Austria, Finland, Norway, Sweden, Switzerland, Turkey and Israel. Asia/Pacific includes: Hong Kong, Japan, Singapore, South Korea, Taiwan, India, Australia and New Zealand. NAFTA includes Canada, Mexico and the United States. South America includes Argentina, Brazil, Chile and Colombia.
4. Issues of the modelling of market structure are discussed in Brown and Stern (1989). For the current model, we use a structure of monopolistic competition, following Helpman and Krugman (1985), for all of the non-agricultural sectors. There is free entry of firms, each producing a different variety of a good/service and producing it with a fixed cost and constant marginal cost in terms of primary and intermediate inputs.
5. The sectoral data for merchandise trade, production, and employment come primarily from United Nations sources and to a lesser extent from national sources. The model parameters are constructed from the trade and input-output data for the countries included in the model and from published studies of trade and capital/labour substitution elasticities. See also Deardorff and Stern (1990, pp. 37–45 and 61–79).
6. The results reported below for changes in total exports and imports do not contradict this assumption as these are measures of the changes in quantities traded, which are relevant for output and employment changes. It is the value of exports relative to imports (which are affected by changes in relative prices) that are held fixed by the balanced trade assumption.
7. The effect of variety in lowering costs can introduce an instability into the model, because an increase in demand for an industry can lead to entry, additional variety, lower costs to users, and hence additional demand. To avoid this happening we use an additional parameter to reduce the effect of variety on welfare to one half of what would occur in the Dixit–Stiglitz model.
8. For details on the Agreement, see IMF (1996, pp. 77–9) and Hoekman and Djankov (1995) and Chapter 8 in this volume.
9. For information on Tunisia's existing non-tariff restrictions, see GATT (1994, pp. 58–89). Tunisia also maintains export processing zones. We have no data on these zones, however, and have not included them in our analysis. For a brief description of the zones, see GATT (1994, Vol. II, pp. 40-41).
10. Tunisia's domestic tax system includes a value-added tax and a consumption tax. We chose not to represent these taxes in our modelling framework on the assumption that they would remain unchanged in the context of the Tunisia–EU FTA. For a brief overview of Tunisia's tax system, see Nsouli et al. (1993, especially pp. 5–9 and 70–2).
11. Effects may appear to be greater when FDI incentives are linked directly to exports, as in maquiladora-type export processing zones, but is not clear that Tunisia is moving very far in that direction. By the same token, there is reason to believe that such arrangements have little spillover to the domestic economy.
12. For details on the 1994 Investment Code, see Ministry of International Cooperation and Foreign Investment (1994).
13. There is much more to the Investment Code than this, of course, but it appears to us that most other features of the Code either are likely to be quantitatively insignificant (e.g. provisions that apply only to capital goods manufactured locally), or are related to activities that we are unable to isolate in our model (e.g. environmental protection, regional development areas).
14. This is in contrast to the positive welfare effect cited by Page and Underwood (1995) in a World Bank study of a Tunisian–EU FTA. That study reported an increase in wel-

fare (equivalent variation) of 1.7% due to trade liberalization alone, rising to 4.7% when effects of trade efficiency were included.

15. This is not entirely the case in our model, however, even for a non-discriminatory liberalization, because product differentiation by country of origin gives even small producers some leverage over their terms of trade. The effects on the terms of trade that appear in our scenarios are better understood as a by-product of trade diversion.

16. This is apparently a reflection of the Stolper–Samuelson effect, even though in our model we have found on other occasions that the Stolper–Samuelson Theorem does not necessarily hold, due to the effects of scale and variety. See Brown, Deardorff and Stern (1993).

17. This assumed capital inflow was $2,144 million in 1990 value. If, say, this was spread over a period of 10 years, it would amount to $214 million annually. This can be compared to the actual inflow of FDI in 1991, which according to GATT (1994, p. 52), was $133 million. Some 90% of this actual inflow went into energy-related sectors.

18. This argument was prominent in the discussions leading up to the NAFTA. Events starting in December 1994 unfortunately suggest that it may have been overly optimistic, at least for Mexico, and that perception may now stop it from working in other countries whether or not it would be justified. See also Francois (Chapter 3 in this volume).

19. Because our solution algorithm solves a log-linear approximation to the true model, when the changes in logs of variables (which average to zero) are converted to percentages they do not quite average to zero. This in turn means that the absolute changes in employment that are calculated from these percentages also fail to add exactly to zero.

20. According to Hoekman and Djankov (1995) and Chapter 8 in this volume, the tariff reductions for the least competitive Tunisian industries will be backloaded towards the end of the 12-year phase-in period. Since the effective protection for these industries will be increased due to cheaper imports as tariffs on inputs are reduced in the early phase-in period, they point out that this could lead to inefficient investment and resistance to market opening down the road.

21. According to the IMF (1996, p. 79), the Agreement provides for an industrial restructuring program that will cost an estimated $2.4 billion over five years and will be financed jointly by the Tunisian Government and contributions from the EU and the World Bank. It is interesting, though probably fortuitous, that the $2.4 billion corresponds to the estimated total welfare gain for the EU reported for our Scenario A in Table 5.3.

22. Levine and Renelt (1992), in a critical analysis of the empirical literature relating growth rates across countries to various determinants, find that the only robust conclusions are that growth responds to investment and that investment in turn responds to trade.

23. A similar conclusion is reached by Hoekman and Djankov (1995) and Chapter 8 in this volume.

6

Growth, the Maghreb and Free Trade with the European Union

John Page and John Underwood[1]
The World Bank

6.1   Introduction

Morocco and Tunisia have both recently signed comprehensive integration agreements with the European Union (EU). These agreements consist of two essential elements – increased aid flows and technical assistance in exchange for reductions in trade barriers and other impediments to the flow of goods and investment over a period of 12 years. The Euro-Med initiative, of which these agreements form a major part, is one element of a much broader European strategy to forge trade alliances with countries on Europe's periphery. Agreements with about 10 Eastern European countries in transition were signed in 1991, and the EU is at present actively negotiating with Egypt, Jordan and Lebanon to extend its web of integration agreements to the Mashreq. These initiatives are intended to promote more rapid convergence of incomes between Europe's transitional and developing economy neighbours and the EU.

Trade experts have traditionally viewed regional integration schemes as offering few benefits compared with universal trade liberalization (see the discussion by Lawrence in Chapter 2 of this volume). Nevertheless, efforts to create regional trading blocks proceed world-wide, suggesting that policy makers in both advanced and developing economies are persuaded of the potential dynamic benefits of integration agreements – their impact on long run economic growth. Broadly, these dynamic benefits fall into two groups – the possibility of increased investment flows and the positive impact of integration agreements on productivity and technological change. Both of these channels can raise growth rates.

Political economy arguments are now routinely brought forward to underpin the impact of integration agreements on investment behaviour.

The 'credibility' of the rules affecting domestic and foreign investment is viewed as greater in an integration agreement than from domestically-based rule changes alone, leading to a reduction in perceived political risks of investment (Hoekman, 1996). The opportunities for 'deeper integration' (including harmonization of standards, competition policies, taxation and regulations) are also cited as mechanisms by which investor behaviour can be changed (Lawrence, 1991). The means by which integration agreements can raise productivity growth rates have been less thoroughly explored. One strand of argument emphasizes that some of the deeper integration aspects of the agreements may reduce transactions costs and enhance measured productivity (Rutherford, Rustrom and Tarr, 1995). But the mechanisms by which these cost reductions take place are frequently only sketchily outlined and the resulting estimates of benefits are highly arbitrary. Another emphasizes improvements in learning and productivity change at the plant level arising from increased export rivalry or import competition. These impacts are of course dependent on the trade creation effects of the integration agreements themselves. Finally, where agreements include aid and technical assistance components, technology transfer and productivity enhancement can be explicit aid objectives.

This chapter examines three dimensions of the growth impact of the EU Partnership agreements on Morocco and Tunisia – gains from trade liberalization, increased foreign investment, and improvements in productivity. Section 6.2 looks briefly at historical trends in growth, investment, and productivity change in both countries between 1960 and 1994. Section 6.3 summarizes the results of recent estimates of the welfare effects of trade liberalization under the agreements. Section 6.4 examines the possible impact of the agreements on investment behaviour, especially on foreign direct investment (FDI). Section 6.5 concludes with a review of possible channels for the acceleration of productivity change.

6.2   Growth, investment and productivity change in the long run

Morocco and Tunisia are the star performers of the Middle East and North Africa (MENA) region in terms of growth.[2] Between 1960 and 1994, Tunisia grew by slightly more than 5% per year and Morocco by slightly more than 4.5%. As a result, Morocco has been able to more than double per capita income in the last 35 years, while Tunisia has tripled its per capita income. While these achievements are dramatic and visible, they fall short in comparison with the rapidly growing East Asian economies. If Morocco and Tunisia had grown, in per capita terms, as fast as the average for East Asia over the same period, per capita income would be $700 and $1,300 higher today in Tunisia and Morocco, respectively.

Countries grow by accumulating labour, capital, and human capital and by using these resources more efficiently. There is a substantial recent literature that advances evidence across countries on the relative contribution of these three basic inputs and of efficiency gains – total factor productivity (TFP) – to output growth.[3] In both Morocco and Tunisia, labour force growth has accounted for about 1% of GDP growth per year on average during the last 35 years (Table 6.1). In comparison, labour force growth contributed only about 1.5% to output growth in East Asia, where population growth dropped off earlier and more substantially. Human capital accumulation, proxied by average educational achievement, has been more important than labour accumulation, especially in Morocco, in contributing to economic growth. Although the level of education of the average Moroccan worker was and is substantially below that of the average Tunisian worker, the rate of accumulation of education was higher in Morocco between 1960 and 1994. In Morocco, human capital accumulation is estimated to have contributed about 2% annually to growth, more than the roughly 1.25% rate in both East Asia and Tunisia.

The most important contribution to growth in both Morocco and Tunisia has been the accumulation of physical capital. On average, net new investment added about 2.5% per year to growth. In this case, the two Maghreb countries lag behind the 3% average for East Asia, where savings rates have been consistently among the highest in the world.[4] Differences in physical capital accumulation cannot explain the difference between growth rates in Morocco and Tunisia and East Asia. Virtually all

Table 6.1 Determinants of long-term growth

	Morocco	Tunisia	East Asia	Portugal	Spain	France
Per capita income, 1994 (US$)[1]	1190	1821	n.a.	7890	13560	22360
GDP growth, 1960–94 (%)[2]	4.6	5.3	6.1	4.6		
Contribution to growth (%)[2]						
Capital accumulation	2.6	2.3	3	2.4		
Labour force growth	0.9	0.9	0.6	0.2		
Human capital growth	1.8	1.3	1.3	0.6		
Total factor productivity[3]	–0.7	0.8	1.2	1.4		

1. 1993 for Portugal.
2. 1960–87 for Portugal.
3. Authors' calculations, using the Nehru and Dhareshwar (1994) data set.

of the difference in growth rates between Morocco and Tunisia and East Asia can be explained by lower total factor productivity growth.[5] Morocco and Tunisia have, for the most part, achieved economic growth the hard way – through physical and human capital accumulation. Not only have efficiency gains been lower in Morocco and Tunisia than in East Asia, these gains have also been lower than in Western Europe, where total factor productivity contributed almost 1.75% to annual growth between 1960 and 1990.

Morocco and Tunisia have achieved better results in terms of total factor productivity in recent years. Between 1988 and 1994, total factor productivity growth is estimated at about 0.9% per year in Tunisia and 0.4% per year in Morocco. It is likely that these improvements can be linked to structural adjustment, which reduced trade protection substantially in both countries, and to a reduction in the share of public investment in total investment. However, the recent efficiency gains in Morocco and Tunisia remain insufficient to achieve the high rates of growth required to close the income gap between southern Europe and the Maghreb in a few decades.

6.3   How large are the benefits of trade liberalization?

Recent applied general equilibrium studies of the possible benefits of the Morocco and Tunisia free trade agreements (FTAs) with the EU suggest benefits are significant but not enough to imply rapid income convergence (Rutherford, Rustrom and Tarr, 1993, 1995). Using similar policy scenarios, the welfare gains are estimated to be about 1.5% of GDP in Morocco and 1.7% of GDP in Tunisia.[6] To put these numbers in perspective, the cumulative effect over ten years of these gains would be an increase of per capita income of about $25 per person in Morocco and $40 per person in Tunisia. The gains are, of course, larger if Morocco and Tunisia were to liberalize with respect to the entire world, rising to 2% and 2.5% of GDP. Currently, Moroccan and Tunisian non-agricultural exports (with a few small exceptions) enter the EU market duty free. Therefore, the major benefits of the FTAs come from lower prices to consumers of traded goods in Morocco and Tunisia. These gains to consumers more than offset the costs of adjusting labour and capital away from uncompetitive activities in traded-goods sectors and a small shift from non-traded to traded-goods production.

In essence, the models described above are exercises in comparative statistics. They do not take into account factors that might increase the overall efficiency of production or the level of investment, apart from the reallocation of resources away from some existing activities toward others. In the Tunisia exercise, the authors (who obviously believe that there would be some form of dynamic benefit) enhance the basic model to take into account benefits from harmonization of standards and a reduction in trading costs. They do this by an assumption that harmonization of standards with the EU will improve export prices by 2% and that improvements in trade-related services would increase export prices by a further 1% and would reduce import prices by 1%. The welfare benefits to Tunisia more than double, to 4.7% of GDP.

The actual FTAs are not identical to the assumed agreements modelled above. One important difference relates to the timing and sequencing of tariff reductions. Most of the model runs assumed instantaneous reductions in tariffs, although actual reductions will be phased in over 12 years, with faster reductions for imported inputs. The associated temporary increase in protection has an implied welfare loss. The only model run close to this scenario, an assumed reduction of tariffs on 40% of the products currently imported from Europe by Tunisia, did indicate a small net welfare loss.[7]

6.4   Will the agreements increase foreign investment?

Experience with other integration schemes suggests that a major potential benefit of the FTAs may come from substantially increased foreign investment. Mexico received some $30 billion of private capital inflow in the run-up to the NAFTA. Portugal and Spain saw private capital inflows increase by 2% of GDP following their integration with the EU and recently the more aggressive reformers in Eastern Europe have experienced large increases in investment (Dadush, 1995). Can Morocco and Tunisia realistically expect a major increase in foreign investment resulting from the FTAs?

6.4.1   Trends in foreign investment

Foreign savings played an important role in Morocco and Tunisia, notably in the 1970s and early 1980s, accounting for 33% and 27%, respectively, of total investment during 1960–87. In recent years, the overall role of foreign savings has declined in response to balance of payments difficulties in the mid-1980s. The bulk of foreign savings inflows in both countries has traditionally come in the form of loans from, or guaranteed by, official agencies of industrial country governments, supplemented by several purely private, syndicated loans from commercial banks. Foreign direct and portfolio investment was marginal in both countries, less than 1% of GDP annually, on average through the 1980s. Recently, the composition of foreign savings inflows has begun to change, notably in Morocco, towards FDI, in line with the growth in FDI to developing countries world-wide. This is in sharp contrast to largely stagnant FDI flows to MENA countries in general. In 1992 FDI flows were some $500 million or 2% of GDP. They reached 3% of GDP in 1994, probably because of transactions related to privatization. By and large Morocco's increase against the trend for the region reflects the fact that by the early 1990s Morocco had implemented all of the formal policies needed to attract FDI including current account convertibility, full repatriation rights for profits and dividends, no prior approvals, no controls on contracts covering licences, trademarks, management and technical co-operation, and no restrictions on foreign ownership except for agricultural land. Even in contrast with high performing East Asian economies, this was a remarkably liberal foreign investment regime (World Bank, 1995).

About two thirds of Morocco's FDI originates in Europe, nearly a quarter from France alone. Middle Eastern investors account for another 20% of total FDI. The share of foreign investment in manufacturing in Morocco has remained virtually unchanged since the 1980s, accounting for about a quarter of total FDI. Recent trends have resulted in expanding investments in financial services and corresponding declines in tourism and real estate.

Tunisia's FDI flows have also grown in the 1990s, primarily as a result of investments in the energy sector. Investment flows to other activities have been very low and stable since 1990, partly reflecting reservation of investment licensing to the state in such potentially attractive areas as chemicals, cement, mining, electricity, and telecommunications. Total FDI in 1992 was still less than $50 million. While the Unified Investment Code lifts restrictions on FDI for all export activities, many service and infrastructure sectors, such as telecommunications, tourism, computer services and information technology remain subject to prior approval. One feature of Tunisia's foreign investment regime which differs from that of Morocco is that the bulk of foreign and joint venture investments in manufacturing are concentrated in the so called 'offshore' sector. About 23% of wholly export-oriented offshore enterprises are foreign owned while another 24% are joint ventures. These firms have few direct links with the domestic Tunisian economy (World Bank, 1994a).

6.4.2 *Portfolio investment and macroeconomic management*

Integration with the EU may improve Morocco's and Tunisia's access to portfolio investments. If the agreements improve perceptions of macroeconomic management, capital may shift from other locations and/or the debt

service costs of existing portfolio flows may decline. Mexico benefited substantially from increased portfolio flows in the run-up to the NAFTA,
largely as a consequence of its ability to portray the agreement as enhancing the prospects of sustained good macroeconomic management, but the
impact of its failure to adhere to credible macroeconomic rules following
the NAFTA is well known (*see* Chapter 3 by Francois in this volume).
Thus, two key elements for Morocco and Tunisia to enhance access to portfolio investment are first, their historical performance in macroeconomic
management and, second, the likelihood that good performance will be
sustained or improved during the implementation of the FTAs.

How credible has macroeconomic management been in Morocco and
Tunisia? Three useful indicators of macroeconomic stability are the rate of
inflation, the budget deficit, and movements in the real exchange rate.
Morocco and Tunisia rank well in terms of both the rate and volatility of
inflation in comparison with other countries in the region, although the
EU has had marginally superior performance to both economies during
the past ten years (Figure 6.1). Both countries' fiscal performance validates
their performance on inflation (Figure 6.2). While it is difficult to judge the
adequacy of real exchange rate levels in a comparative context, Morocco
and Tunisia have shown a superior ability to manage the real exchange rate:
the extent of volatility is much lower than in most comparator countries
(Figure 6.3). External debt management in Morocco and Tunisia has been

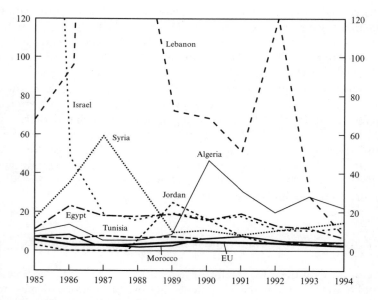

Figure 6.1 Change in consumer price indices

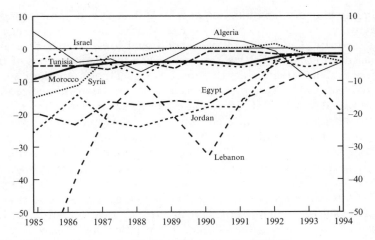

Figure 6.2 Central government balance (percentage of GDP)

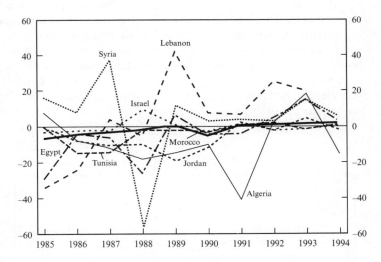

Figure 6.3 Real effective exchange rates (annual rates of change)

similar to other countries in MENA with debt to GDP ratios of about 60% of GDP. This contrasts with lower debt burdens in East Asia and Latin America in general, but is similar to the debt to GDP ratios of such rapidly growing East Asian economies as Indonesia and Malaysia.

In sum, relative to competitors in the region, Morocco and Tunisia appear to be well positioned to benefit from their reputation for prudent macroeconomic management. Both economies have established long run credibility in controlling inflation and fiscal deficits and in managing the exchange rate to accommodate external shocks. Debt management has been adequate. The FTAs will place additional stress on macroeconomic management because they are likely to require real depreciations of both currencies (compensating devaluations) as traded goods markets are liberalized and further fiscal prudence as capital markets are liberalized.

Compared to other MENA countries, the agreements may also enhance investors perceptions of the creditworthiness of Morocco and Tunisia in the future. The substantial aid packages embodied in the Euro-Med initiative can in part be used to facilitate macroeconomic adjustment. But additional effort will be required to shift perceptions of creditworthiness relative to emerging markets within the EU itself. Credit ratings compiled by *Institutional Investor* reveal that Tunisia and Morocco are seen as less creditworthy than Spain, Portugal or Greece. Investor attitudes have improved for both economies since 1986, reflecting improvements in macroeconomic management, but neither has recovered its creditworthiness levels of the early 1980s. There also has been no sharp upswing in investor evaluations in the past two years, despite the two countries active negotiations with the EU. Tunisia leads Morocco in the surveys throughout the entire 15 years, but the gap has narrowed substantially (Figure 6.4).

Financial markets in Morocco and Tunisia remain relatively undeveloped. Both are bank-based systems where direct instruments of financing – bonds or share issues – are rarely used by non-government entities. In both countries, the government and public enterprises absorb an inordinate share of the credit available. For example, in Morocco, the Treasury absorbs 35% of domestic credit. In both countries, the banking system

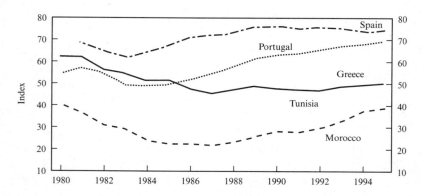

Figure 6.4 *Institutional Investor's* credit ratings, 1980–95 – selected Mediterranean and European countries
Source: Institutional Investor (1980–95), various issues.

has been modernized to a great extent, but banks are hampered in day-to-day liquidity management by the lack of functioning secondary markets for government securities. Local currency bond markets, which have been the conduit of portfolio inflows in many countries, including Spain and Portugal, are not deep in Morocco and Tunisia. The markets for government bonds are at an early stage of development, and there is no private bond market in the traditional sense.

Stock markets in both countries can best be described as nascent, although both have grown rapidly during the past three years. Market capitalization represented 14% of GDP in Morocco and 16% in Tunisia at the end of 1994. In comparison, many comparator countries have market capitalization to GDP ratios that are much higher, e.g. 30% for Turkey and about 100% for Jordan and Thailand. In Morocco, the recent rapid increase in market capitalization has been fuelled by the privatization program. Virtually all offers have been oversubscribed, implying a pent-up demand, including a foreign demand. As much as 25% of the shares offered in connection with privatization were reportedly purchased by Moroccans living abroad. Tunisia's stock market is dominated by bank shares. Again, there appears to be a strong demand for Tunisian portfolio equity from abroad. The problem is a lack of security offers. In many developing countries, before portfolio investors came to the local market, local firms went to the international bond market. (This was the pattern in major Latin American countries as they returned to international markets as the debt crisis ebbed.) Few Moroccan or Tunisian private borrowers are able to access these markets, as yet, partly because of their reluctance to bear the foreign exchange risk in the absence of helping mechanisms. To increase the ability of financial markets to attract and effectively channel new portfolio inflows to productive activities, a host of market development activities must be undertaken. These include the development and full implementation of a good regulatory framework for stock and bond markets, better management of Treasury issues, and the development of secondary bond markets. The single largest factor that will determine the evolution of stock market activity in both Morocco and Tunisia is the program of privatization. Large scale privatization through stock issues could rapidly develop these markets, making them a major conduit for foreign portfolio investment inflows.

6.4.3 Will the agreements improve credibility of investment rules?

One of the frequently cited motives for integration agreements is the ability to change perceptions of the investment climate by 'locking in' changes in rules and institutions affecting both foreign and domestic investors. We noted above that Morocco has undertaken a wide range of legislative and regulatory reforms designed to create a private investment friendly environment. Tunisia has similarly introduced domestic and regulatory changes, although they are not as wide ranging as those in Morocco.

Surveys of existing domestic and foreign firms and of prospective foreign investors in Morocco point to substantial differences in investor perceptions between foreign firms and domestic firms currently operating in Morocco (World Bank, 1992, 1994b). Domestic firms identify production-related constraints – financing costs, lack of skilled labour, access to industrial land, and high taxes – as the major impediments to expanded investment. In contrast they do not identify aspects of the administrative and regulatory environment bureaucratic red tape, licensing requirements, or an uncertain legal framework – as significant. Foreign firms identified fewer production related constraints, but also did not identify aspects of the administrative and regulatory environment as significant impediments.

The surveys of *potential* investors revealed that relative to other MENA economies Morocco ranks well with respect to perceptions of its legal system, lack of red tape, business attitude and government competence (Figure 6.5). It ranks below the regional average in such areas as infrastructure, political risk and foreign trade policy. There are some interesting differences between the perceptions of foreign investors currently operating in Morocco and potential investors, primarily reflecting implementation of policies intended to promote private sector development. Although the potential investors rate Morocco relatively highly in terms of government attitudes to private investment, foreign-owned firms in Morocco cite regulations and restricted entry in some sectors as evidence of less profound commitment to private investment. Existing foreign firms also express greater reservations about the efficacy of legal safeguards than prospective investors. Virtually all operating foreign firms cite the inadequacy of legal means for dispute resolution and lack of legal recourse on government contracts. Existing investors also identify lengthy, complex and uncoordinated administrative processes as significant constraints in contrast to prospective investors.

A survey of 124 potential European investors and firms currently operating in Tunisia point to similar concerns (Ministry of International Cooperation, 1995). Foreign investors rank political and social stability as the predominant factor determining investment decisions. Market size and macroeconomic stability are the primary economic considerations. Liberalization of the economy – including both trade liberalization and deregulation – was cited by nearly 20% of respondents as the single most important action the government could take to increase Tunisia's attractiveness to foreign investors. Another 8% identified reducing bureaucratic

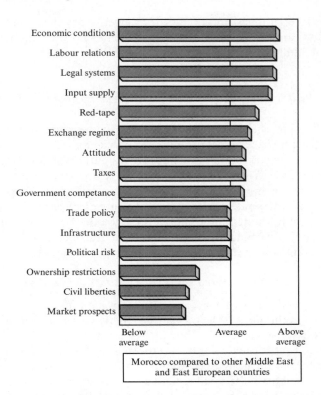

Figure 6.5 Perceptions of prospective foreign investors ('foreign survey')
Source: World Bank (1994b)

procedures as most important. Of the five leading actions identified by respondents more than 40% focused on reducing red tape and liberalization of the regulatory framework. As in Morocco domestic investors tended to focus on production related constraints – labour market regulations, absence of infrastructure, limited growth of the domestic market – rather than constraints arising from the legal and regulatory framework. The Tunisian survey also covered existing foreign investors. These respondents identified problems of the application of regulations and absence of systematic and transparent treatment by public officials as constraints on further investment.

These survey results suggest that improved credibility will not come automatically from the FTAs themselves. European investors' perceptions of government commitment to trade policy and regulatory liberalization may improve as a consequence of the agreements. And perceptions of political risk may decline, but many of the major constraints identified by existing foreign investors – red tape, discretionary decisions, and legal problems – are not covered by the agreements and will require sustained efforts at administrative and legal reform.

6.4.4 Will the agreements change strategic motivations for FDI?

Macroeconomic stability and improved legislative, regulatory and institutional structures are necessary but not sufficient conditions for increases in FDI. Surveys of foreign investors consistently report strong strategic motives for FDI (World Bank, 1992). Thus, if the agreements are to provide a basis for increased FDI in Morocco or Tunisia they must also result in changed strategic perceptions by foreign investors. In this section we therefore examine the possible impact of the FTAs on a number of strategic objectives identified by surveys of European investors as relevant to foreign direct investment decisions in the Mahgreb.

Natural resources (downstream processing)

Morocco's and Tunisia's trade specialization patterns, despite substantial change over the past 20 years remain highly concentrated in resource based activities (Table 6.2). Phosphate fertilizers and their derivatives have been a traditional source of exports for both economies and offer some potential for increased foreign investments. Similarly, for Tunisia investments in fossil fuels will remain attractive to foreigners. It is unlikely that the integration agreements will substantially change investors' perceptions of the desirability of investments in either sector, although investment volume may increase somewhat as a consequence of an

Table 6.2 Revealed comparative advantages and disadvantages

Morocco			Tunisia		
	1970	1991		1970	1991
Clothing	1.3	34.2	Clothing	0.3	95.5
Fish and prepared	8.7	27.0	Animal, vegetable oil	5.6	21.5
Fruits and vegetables	52.8	24.8	Fertilizers	13.7	20.9
Fertilizers	0.9	15.2	Mineral fuels	35.5	19.9
Crude fertilizers, minerals	33.4	9.9	Fruits and vegetables	12.1	6.6
Transport equipment	−13.8	−14.2	Transport equipment	−8.2	−15.4
Mineral fuels	−7.3	−22.8	Textile yarn, fabric	−8.4	−43.5
Non-electrical machinery	−21.2	−26.1	Non-electrical machinery	−21.7	−51.6
Cereals and preparation	−2.7	−6.0	Cereals and preparation	−17.9	−5.4
Iron and steel	−11.5	−10.4	Crude fertilizers, minerals	15.7	−7.4

improved overall investment climate. The agreements may provide some scope for increased downstream investments in agro-industrial processing. Both Morocco and Tunisia have strong revealed comparative advantage in agriculture and fisheries. Despite the restrictive nature of the agreements with respect to access to the European market in agricultural and processed agricultural products, both allow some scope for expanded agro-industrial exports.

Serving the domestic market

The guarantees of national treatment for foreign investors embodied in the agreements open up for European investors – especially in the case of Tunisia – possibilities for serving the Moroccan and Tunisian markets in previously restricted sectors. Major investments in activities to serve either market will be limited however by investors perceptions that their size is limited. Surveys of prospective investors in Morocco indicate that in comparison to other economies in MENA and Eastern Europe, investors perceive market prospects as well below average, reflecting small size and limited growth (Figure 6.5). Tunisia's market, which is only half of Morocco's, suffers from similar perceived deficiencies.

Serving the regional market

Because of the small size of both Tunisia's and Morocco's domestic market, one possible strategic option for investors is to establish capacity in one economy to serve both (and other potential entrants to the Euro-Med agreement). The nature of the agreements concluded thus far preclude such an investment strategy, however. Because there are no provisions for liberalized trade among Mediterranean partners with the EU, a 'hub and spoke' pattern of trade and investment is likely to arise in which investors choose to locate in Europe to serve several southern markets.

Niche export markets

The agreements may increase FDI in industries serving niche export markets in the EU. These are primarily in low end manufactures – textiles, clothing and footwear, and, in the case of Morocco, wood products. They are also the export industries in which existing foreign ownership is concentrated (Table 6.3). These niche exports previously enjoyed duty-free access to the European market, however. Thus, the primary motivation for new investment in these niches will not come from enhanced market access. Rather, it will have to come from increased cost competitiveness. Historical data suggest that Morocco especially, but also Tunisia, suffered from declining cost competitiveness in textiles, clothing, and footwear relative to such East Asian competitors as China, Indonesia, Malaysia and

Table 6.3 Percentage share of foreign ownership

	Export-oriented firms (export share > = 10%)		Domestic-market-oriented firms (export share < 10%)	
	Morocco	Tunisia	Morocco	Tunisia
Agro-industries	20.8	10.0	6.8	2.3
Less than 100 workers	23.3	0.0	5.1	1.7
100 workers and more	20.0	51.0	7.7	6.2
Textiles, clothing and footwear	16.8	52.9	15.3	n.a
Less than 100 workers	19.8	40.9	7.2	n.a
100 workers and more	16.0	62.0	21.6	n.a
Chemicals	70.0	10.6	18.3	5.7
Less than 100 workers	23.0	4.5	12.1	5.4
100 workers and more	72.3	25.0	21.6	6.8
Metals and machinery	38.9	37.7	19.5	6.8
Less than 100 workers	18.4	33.9	18.6	5.9
100 workers and more	42.4	42.8	19.9	9.1
Other manufacturing	n.a.	22.7	n.a.	4.5
Less than 100 workers	11.9	18.2	10.8	4.1
100 workers and more	n.a.	40.0	n.a	6.5

Source: World Bank (1994 c)

Thailand and to such European competitors as Portugal, Greece and Hungary (World Bank, 1994c).

Production sharing arrangements in which component production and assembly operations are distributed across a number of countries have become important magnets for FDI in East Asia. Prior to the integration agreements the outward processing facilities of the EU were designed to facilitate such production sharing. Components could be admitted temporarily in Mediterranean countries for assembly and then re-exported to Europe without payment of duties. Tunisia and Morocco led other countries in MENA in using these facilities, but neither have utilized outward processing arrangements as fully as Eastern European competitors (Table 6.4). Outward processing investments were heavily concentrated in clothing assembly in both countries. The integration agreements may facilitate some increase in production sharing based either on proximity (e.g. Morocco/Spain or Tunisia/Italy) or language (French), but the volume and diversity of production sharing investments directed at Eastern Europe, suggest that both economies will begin as relatively less attractive destinations for these investments.

An important niche export market for economies as diverse as India and Barbados has been information services exports based on low cost, English speaking skilled labour. Such services as back office operations,

Table 6.4 Exports to the EU under outward processing arrangements, 1994 (US$)

	Leather products	Clothing	Clay/glass	Machinery	Transport	Furniture	Total
Jordan	1	17	0	3	0	0	27
Lebanon	3	00	259	14	0	7	380
Syria	0	0	124	506	0	0	632
Tunisia	12,760	224,010	15	27,286	2,894	58	274,877
UAE	56	2,242	2,952	482	9,396	50	15,731
Morocco	13,001	169,732	2	13,328	519	554	200,922
Israel	95	42	493	1,898	104	0	4,162
Egypt	0	527	0	1,403	171	108	2,638
5 CEEC	305,478	2,409,770	13,190	396,891	70,121	166,832	3,577,955
MENA	29,516	396,747	3,845	46,665	14,950	781	503,347

Source: Hoekman, 1996.

medical transcription, and software development have been successfully exported. Both Morocco and Tunisia have the potential for French language services exports. The integration agreements provisions for harmonization of standards, approximation of laws and cross-border supply of services may help to promote such investments. Many information services exports, however, are heavily dependent on low cost, high quality telecommunications, the absence of which may limit the potential of both economies to attract such investments in the short run.

Summing up, the harmonization of laws and regulations combined with both economies' prior track record for good macroeconomic management may induce larger portfolio investments by European investors, but financial markets will require substantial strengthening if those increased flows are to be used efficiently. Expanded FDI will depend as much on changing strategic perceptions of investors and reductions in bureaucratic impediments to business as on macroeconomic stability and credible rules.

6.5 Will the agreements improve productivity?

A third channel by which the integration agreements may increase growth in Tunisia and Morocco is through improvements in technological acquisition and innovation. There is by now a large literature on the relationship between international trade and total factor productivity (TFP) change.[8] While there is little consensus, it may be fair to characterize the thrust of the literature as indicating that expanded international trade *may* improve TFP growth rates as a result of technological acquisition arising from increased exports and/or of improved cost discipline and innovation arising from increased competition (Pack and Page, 1994). In this section we present economy-wide estimates of long run TFP growth for Tunisia and Morocco compared with European and other developing economies. We then consider several mechanisms by which the integration agreements with Europe may improve TFP growth in both economies and assess their likely significance.

6.5.1 Comparisons of productivity growth rates

We estimate total factor productivity growth in a simple neo-classical framework by subtracting from output growth the portion of growth due to capital accumulation, to human capital accumulation, and to labour force growth. Because income share data is not available for most countries in our sample, output elasticities were estimated directly using a simple, cross economy production function. Annual log output growth was regressed on log capital growth, log human capital growth, and log labour growth between 1960 and 1990, specifying the production function to be Cobb–Douglas with constant returns to scale. Economy-specific dummy variables were used to estimate individual rates of TFP change for each of the sample's economies. Net investment is derived from constant price capital stock data (Nehru and Dhareshwar, 1993). Measures of human capital are incorporated in the specification using Barro and Lee's (1993) measure of educational attainment. TFP estimates are based on the parameters derived from an 85 country sample.

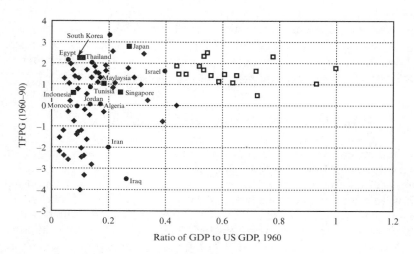

Figure 6.6 Total factor productivity growth and GDP per capita relative to US GDP, 1960

The contrast in productivity growth between Tunisia and Morocco and the major European economies is apparent in Figure 6.6. The diagram shows the TFP growth rate for the period 1960–90 for all 85 countries in the sample as a function of relative output per capita to the United States in 1960. High income, OECD economies are identified by the open boxes. Three broad patterns appear:

1. The range of TFP growth rates for high income countries is quite compact, especially in comparison with the low and middle income countries.
2. Nearly one third of the low and middle income countries in the sample had negative rates of TFP growth for the period 1960–89.
3. There is very little productivity-based 'catch-up' exhibited by the low and middle income countries.

These are not promising results for the developing world. Despite a substantial literature on the potential for developing countries to achieve rapid growth through the adoption of known, 'best practice' technologies, very few countries appear to have realized these potential gains.[9] Catch-up in per capita income, where it is taking place, is due primarily to higher rates of factor accumulation.

Tunisia and Morocco differ little from other MENA economies or developing countries in general. The estimated rate of TFP growth for Morocco is essentially zero and Tunisia's is less than 1% per year. Neither economy has rates of TFP change which equal the average for the high income countries of Europe and North America. Thus, despite the potential for both economies to adapt existing international best practice technologies to their economies, neither Morocco nor Tunisia have realized rates of TFP change which exceed those of European economies. In aggregate terms there is no productivity-based catch-up taking place.

Because TFP growth rates can be interpreted as rates of change in constant price average costs, it has become conventional to draw inferences concerning changing patterns of dynamic comparative advantage from international comparisons of TFP growth rates (Nishimizu and Page, 1986, 1991). For the economy in aggregate neither Morocco nor Tunisia reach the long run TFP growth rates of any European economy. Both Tunisia and Morocco have declining dynamic comparative advantage, relative to potential trading partners in Europe; constant price unit costs are declining in both more slowly than in Europe.

The economy-wide estimates presented in Figure 6.6 must be interpreted with caution, since much of the estimated productivity change may arise from sectoral reallocation of factors (particularly in Morocco and Tunisia) rather than from productivity enhancements within specific

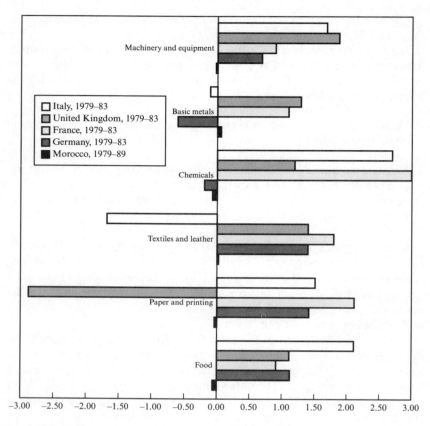

Figure 6.7 TFP growth rates, Morocco and EU countries

sectors (Pack, 1992). Figure 6.7 presents comparisons of industry specific rates of TFP change between Europe and Morocco for the late 1980s. The industry specific estimates tell much the same story as the aggregate data. TFP growth rates for Moroccan industry are all close to zero between 1985 and 1990, contrasted with sectoral TFP growth rates in major European economies in the range of 1–2%. In relative terms Morocco is lagging Europe least in textiles, clothing and footwear and in basic metals – sectors in which at least some European countries experienced TFP declines. But on the whole, the pattern at the industry level confirms that Moroccan industries are failing to move closer to European best practice technologies. Dynamic comparative advantage is also deteriorating at the industry level.

6.5.2 Will the agreements improve the acquisition of technology?

Countries face several alternatives for obtaining new technology which may be affected by the FTAs. These include: (i) the purchase of new equipment; (ii) FDI; (iii) obtaining licences for domestic production of new products or the use of new processes; (iv) the use of non-proprietary technology or reverse engineering; (v) obtaining information provided by purchasers of exports; and (vi) undertaking one's own R&D. All but the last represent an attempt to move towards international best practice by assimilating technologies available abroad and (vi) may have an element of aiding the identification, modification, and absorption of foreign technology rather than generating a genuinely domestic technology.

New equipment

The continuous importation of new, technologically superior equipment will increase measured TFP growth rates. In the East Asian countries showing superior TFP growth rates in Figure 6.6 investment rates were very high and much of their equipment was imported from the OECD countries, embodying the latest designs. In Taiwan, for example, embodiment accounted for roughly 1.25 points of the 5 point residual in the manufacturing sector (Pack, 1993). Cross-country evidence finds a significant impact of equipment investment in manufacturing on TFP growth rates (De Long and Summers, 1991). Clearly, the opening of both the Tunisian and Moroccan economies to capital goods imports from Europe at reduced duty rates will facilitate the import of new, improved equipment. But, because the liberalization of both economies is not universal with respect to capital goods imports, they run the risk of diverting imports away from suppliers of best practice technology in other regions. This risk is particularly acute in cases in which developing country machinery suppliers have adapted their equipment to skills and factor endowments more closely parallel to those of Morocco and Tunisia than in Europe.

Foreign direct investment

FDI permits local production to take place along the world best practice production function by substituting foreign physical and human capital for absent local factors, the best example of success being Singapore. FDI may also generate significant externalities as domestic firms become aware of new techniques and practices, workers move to other local firms, or establish their own, thus disseminating knowledge that originally was proprietary. In Tunisia, anecdotal evidence suggests that the techniques employed in the offshore sector (the principal locus for FDI in manufacturing), have resulted in few spillovers to the domestic economy and little technological upgrading (World Bank, 1994a). A recent cross-section, time series study of manufacturing industries in Morocco found that while foreign-owned firms had higher levels of total factor productivity – conforming to the technology transfer hypothesis – rates of productivity change for domestic firms in sectors with a high incidence of foreign investment were no higher than in sectors dominated by domestic investors suggesting an absence of spillovers (Haddad and Harrison, 1993). The evidence is less informative, however, as to whether the lack of technological spillovers form FDI is related to the pre-integration trade regime. The Tunisian study suggests that the *maquiladora* structure of the offshore enterprises – essentially transforming components supplied by European purchasers into finished products – provides few interactions with domestic suppliers, limiting potential purchaser supplier technological links. Similarly, there is little mobility of managers and workers between offshore firms and domestic firms limiting the transfer of skills embodied in workers (World Bank, 1994a). The Morocco study indicates that while spillovers are not related to the level of protection, the overall level of productivity of foreign firms is. Foreign owned firms in sectors protected by quotas have lower rates of productivity change (Haddad and Harrison, 1993). This is consistent with other studies of the relationship between trade policy and productivity change which have emphasized the negative impact of quantitative import restrictions on productivity growth rates (Nishimizu and Page, 1991).

Technology licensing

Licensing existing technological knowledge about production processes offers considerable opportunities to LDCs for improving the level of best practice, a possibility most thoroughly exploited by Japan in the 1950s and 1960s.[10] Stronger intellectual property protection under the FTAs may to some extent facilitate licensing of technology by firms in Morocco and Tunisia. But, there is some statistical evidence and a growing subjective sense that arms-length licensing is decreasing as an option for closing technology gaps. Potential licensers in the OECD countries have become wary of helping possible competitors, even if contracts preclude exports to third countries for the duration of the licence. Particularly in R&D-intensive sectors such as chemicals, machinery, and electronics, firms are increasingly unwilling to licence technology as they perceive royalties provide an inadequate return for an action which may impair their own long-term competitiveness. OECD firms increasingly prefer either cross-licensing agreements in which they obtain access to the licensee's technology or to its manufacturing skills.

Transfer of non-proprietary technology

The transfer of non-proprietary knowledge is more feasible if a country begins its industrialization effort in labour intensive sectors using relatively old techniques, precisely the conditions obtaining if exports are based on comparative advantage. Part of the success of Korea and Taiwan stems from employing older machinery and knowledge that was not hedged by proprietary restrictions.[11] The equipment was readily sold and the knowledge was available at low cost in engineering publications, trade literature, and from independent consultants. Some threshold level of competence is, of course, required to scan international markets but this is not very demanding in terms of skilled labour. Both Tunisia and Morocco have succeeded as exporters in labour intensive manufacturing, based on the transfer of non-proprietary technology. To the extent that the integration agreements reduce barriers to technology imports or encourage diversification of labour intensive manufactures, some additional technology transfers may occur. But given the high pre-existing access for labour intensive goods into the European market, the quantitative impact of these transfers on technological upgrading and productivity change may be limited.

6.5.3 Information provided by purchasers of exports

Information provided by purchasers can be quite important for firms.[12] The motivation of the purchasers is to obtain lower cost, better quality products from major suppliers. To achieve this they are willing to transmit tacit and occasionally proprietary knowledge from their other, OECD suppliers. Such transfers of knowledge are likely to characterize simpler production sectors such as clothing and footwear or more generally those older technologies that are not hedged by restrictions adopted to increase appropriability such as patents and trade secrets. Significantly, the knowledge transfer embodied in supplier purchaser relationships is generated only by exports. Firms in advanced economies have no incentives to transfer information to potential competitors in import substitution industries. Pack and Page (1994) conclude on the basis of both cross country evidence and a more detailed examination of Korea and Taiwan that manufactured exports work through several of the mechanisms listed above – primarily FDI, transfer of non-proprietary technology, and purchaser supplier relationships – to improve technical efficiency, and thereby contribute to rapid productivity change. They find a statistically robust relationship between manufactured export orientation and the rate of TFP growth. Export expansion resulting from the integration agreements may therefore provide a source learning for Tunisian and Moroccan firms independent of technology transfers embodied in equipment or FDI.

6.5.4 *Programmes for technological upgrading*

The mechanisms for technological upgrading outlined above, depend primarily on increased FDI and expansion of exports. The Euro-Med initiative also offers aid and technical assistance designed to improve local research and development capacity, broadly defined to include programmes for the technological upgrading of existing firms. Indeed, nearly half of the proposed assistance to the region from the EU's expanded aid programme is directed at preparation for free trade, including expertise for modernization, restructuring, venture capital and training. This assistance, if effectively used, could provide a basis for accelerated technological mastery by both economies.

Both Morocco and Tunisia are in the early stages of designing programmes of technical and financial assistance targeted at improving the competitiveness of existing firms. Experience with such 'industrial restructuring' programmes in East Asia, Latin America and Eastern Europe indicates that the central feature of successful technological upgrading programmes is the provision of diagnostic information to firms regarding product, process, marketing and technological changes required to meet quality and price standards of export markets or increased import penetration.[13]

In the case of large scale firms, governments have been most effective in solving the collective action problem among producers. Working with manufacturers' associations they have helped to identify international sources of consulting expertise, to define terms of reference for diagnostic studies at sub-sectoral or industry levels and to ensure the widespread dissemination of results. In some cases governments have also actively attempted to involve the financial sector in the design and dissemination of the diagnostics in a effort to improve the 'bankability' of projects arising from the studies.

Support programmes to small and medium enterprises have generally succeeded where government has restricted its activities to facilitating private provision of technical support to firms. Frequently these programmes have involved initial grant funding of a portion of the costs of technical assistance to the firm, but they have emphasized full payment of costs by the enterprise of any continued consultancy arrangements. Some governments in Asia have also sponsored the development of private productivity centres, usually on a cost sharing basis with manufacturers' associations (Levy, 1994).

6.6 Policies for accelerated growth

Our assessment of the EU integration agreements with Morocco and Tunisia leads us to conclude that while they offer both countries an important opportunity to accelerate growth and raise incomes toward Southern European levels, substantial benefits will not accrue to either country automatically. What can Morocco and Tunisia do to ensure that the EU agreements fulfil their promise? First, they can accelerate and generalize the liberalization of trade embodied in the agreements. Second, they can move aggressively to improve their investment climate; and third, they can adopt policies intended to accelerate the rate of productivity change.

6.6.1 Accelerating trade liberalization

The 12-year pace of liberalization of the trade regime permitted by both the Morocco and Tunisia agreements is slow relative to the pace adopted by Eastern European economies entering into similar arrangements with the EU – most of which are attempting to achieve full liberalization in five years – and relative to the pace of multilateral trade liberalization undertaken by the major Latin American economies in the last decade. In Tunisia, moreover, there is discussion of beginning the liberalization effort with capital goods and intermediates, which will have the effect of increasing effective protection to final goods producers. Delays in liberalization – and increases in effective protection to final goods producers – send perverse signals to potential investors and may delay or prevent domestic and foreign investment in export oriented industries. They also postpone the consumer benefits of the liberalization of imports. Both Morocco and Tunisia would benefit from substantially accelerated trade reform.

The agreements also provide the opportunity for both countries to move more forcefully in reducing barriers to trade with the rest of the world economy outside of Europe. The gains to universal liberalization of trade are approximately 50% higher than those from liberalization with respect to Europe alone. In addition more universal liberalization with respect to capital and intermediate goods imports will result in greater diversification of sources of technology, permitting accelerated productivity growth.

Finally, both Morocco and Tunisia should begin negotiations for a free trade agreement between themselves. As we noted, the existing 'hub and spoke' nature of the EU agreements provides no strategic motivation for investors to locate in either economy to serve both markets, nor does it facilitate production sharing arrangements. Both of these potential market structures would be enhanced by a parallel agreement which liberalizes trade between the two countries within the overall EU framework.

6.6.2 Improving the investment climate

There are a series of policy actions that could improve the investment climate in Morocco and Tunisia. These actions can be grouped under three broad headings: (i) deepening of financial markets; (ii) improvements in the judicial and administrative systems governing private activity; and (iii) further privatization. In fact, the distinctions are not clear-cut, as many of the suggested policy actions would have multiple benefits, as noted below.

Financial markets in the two countries do not, as yet, offer investors the variety of instruments or the kinds of services that are available in many other countries at roughly the same level of per capita income. More competition in banking markets would give banks more incentives to expand services. Further development of bond and equity markets would also spur banks to be more competitive. Privatization has already proven to be an effective means of developing equity markets; an acceleration of privatization would contribute to the rapid development of markets with a real critical mass.

Administrative and judicial reforms will be important in improving the investment climate in both countries. Most investor surveys indicate that the current judicial and administrative systems in Morocco and Tunisia deter investment. Respondents have few complaints concerning the laws themselves; they object to the way they are applied. Those that are actively involved in Morocco and Tunisia point to problems with the way commercial disputes are settled. Investors want quick and consistent decisions from a judicial system. They report that they receive neither. They report that administrative procedures are also heavy and sometimes murky. It can take months just to receive the necessary permits to open a relatively simple business (35 separate documents are needed in Morocco: World Bank, 1994b). Additionally, clearer interpretation and tighter enforcement of laws on collateral and on financial disclosure would greatly improve the function of financial markets.

Further privatization would contribute to a better investment climate in several ways. First, privatization provides immediate opportunities for foreign investors, either through direct investment or through non-controlling-interest portfolio investment. Second, a serious privatization programme sends a signal to potential investors concerning a government's perspective on private-sector-led development. Third, privatization of key input and service industries lessens potential investors' concerns with respect to the availability of these inputs. Fourth, in the Moroccan and Tunisian context, private provision of infrastructure (a form of privatization) could help remove existing infrastructure bottlenecks (ports and roads, for example). Simultaneously, privatization would reduce the burden of loss-making enterprises on the budget; and private provision of infrastructure would reduce the fiscal burden imposed when the state must provide these infrastructure services. Both would contribute to continued macroeconomic stability in a period in which tariff revues will be falling.

6.6.3 Accelerating productivity change

We have argued that the principal means by which the EU agreements may accelerate TFP change are increased foreign direct investment, expanded purchaser seller interactions and more absorption of non-proprietary technology. These channels all largely depend on an expansion of non-traditional exports. Thus, both Morocco and Tunisia should adopt an 'export push' strategy consisting of three essential elements: (i) accelerated trade liberalization to reduce anti-export bias; (ii) institutional reforms for trade facilitation including improvements in metrology and standards, streamlining of customs procedures, regulatory reforms to open up sea and air freight to increased competition and improved trade promotion; and (iii) targeted investments in trade related infrastructure including telecommunications, ports, export transport corridors, and power. In both Tunisia and Morocco the volume of investment required and the need for world class technology will also mean opening up these sectors to foreign investment.

Programmes for technological upgrading of existing industry can be a useful adjunct to the productivity enhancing outcome of an export push, but the implementation of the 'mise a niveau' in both economies will need to be well designed. There is a risk that highly targeted public programmes of venture capital or subsidized lending for technological acquisition will not succeed in raising productivity at the firm level. Rather, public support should focus on correcting information deficits with respect to new products, quality standards and techniques and on solving the collective action problem. Government can play a catalytic role in organizing producers to seek out high quality sources of information on industrial restructuring and in disseminating that information widely.

References

Barro, R. J. and J.-W. Lee (1993), 'International comparisons of educational attainment', Paper presented at the conference, 'How do national policies affect long-run growth?' World Bank, Washington, DC.

Dadush, Uri (1995), 'The Maghreb–EU agreement', Paper prepared for the World Bank–Middle East Forum, Washington, DC.

De Long, J. Bradford and Lawrence H. Summers (1991), 'Equipment investment and economic growth', *Quarterly Journal of Economics*, 106, 445–502.

Haddad, Mona and Ann Harrison (1993), 'Are there positive spillovers from direct foreign investment?' *Journal of Development Economics*, 42, 51–74.

Hoekman, Bernard (1996), *Economic Prospects for the Middle East and North Africa*, MacMillan, forthcoming.

Institutional Investor (1980–95), various issues.

Krugman, Paul (1994), 'The myth of Asia's miracle', *Foreign Affairs*.

Lawrence, Robert Z. (1991), 'Scenarios for the world trading system and their implications for developing countries', Technical Paper 47, OECD Development centre, Paris.

Levy (1994), 'Support systems for small and medium enterprise – comparative results', World Bank, Washington, DC.

Lieberman, Ira (1992), 'Industrial restructuring: policy and practice', Policy and Research Series, 9, World Bank, Washington, DC.

Ministry of International Cooperation (1995), 'Intensification des Relations D'Investissements Entre La Tunisie et L'Union Europeanne', Tunis.

Nagaoka, Sadao (1989), 'Overview of Japanese industrial technology development', The World Bank Industry and Energy Department, Industry Series Paper No. 6, Washington, DC.

Nehru, Vikram and Ashok Dhareshwar (1994), 'New estimates of total factor productivity growth for developing and industrial countries', Policy Research Working Paper 1313, World Bank, Washington, DC.

____ (1993), 'A new database on physical capital stock: sources, methodology, and results', World Bank, Washington, DC.

Nishimizu, Mieko and John Page (1986), 'Productivity change and dynamic comparative advantage', *The Review of Economics and Statistics*, Harvard University.

____ (1991), 'Trade policy, market orientation and productivity change in industry', in J. de Melo and A. Sapir (eds.), *Trade Theory and Economic Reform: North South and East: Essays in Honor of Bela Balassa*, Oxford, Blackwell.

Nsouli, S., S. Bassat and R. Kannan (1995), *Assessing the Impact of the Euro-Med Agreements on Morocco and Tunisia*, Washington, DC, International Monetary Fund (processed).

Pack, Howard (1992), 'Technology gaps between industrial and developing countries: are there dividends for latecomers?', *Proceedings of the World Bank Annual Bank Conference on Development Economics*, World Bank, Washington, DC.

____ (1993), 'Industrial and trade policies in the high performing Asian economies', Background paper for *The East Asian Miracle*, World Bank, Washington, DC.

Pack, Howard and John Page (1994), 'Accumulation, exports and growth in the high-performing Asian economies', Carnegie-Rochester Conference Series on Public Policy, 40, 199–236.

Ranis, Gustav (1979), 'Industrial development', in W. Galenson, (ed.), *Economic Growth and Structural Change in Taiwan*, Cornell University Press, Ithaca.

Rhee, Yung W. and Larry E. Westphal (1977), 'A microeconometric investigation of choice of technique', *Journal of Development Economics*, 4, 205–38.

Rodrik, Danny (1994). 'Miracle or design: Lessons from the East Asian experience', Policy Essay No. 11, 15–53, Overseas Development Council, Washington, DC.

Rutherford, Thomas F., E.E. Rustrom and David Tarr (1993), 'Morocco's free trade agreement with the European Community: a quantitative assessment', Policy Research Working Paper 1173, World Bank, Washington, DC

____ (1995), 'The free trade agreement between Tunisia and the European Union', Policy Research Department, World Bank, Washington, DC.

Westphal, Larry E., Yung Rhee and Gary Pursell (1981), 'Korean industrial competence: where it came from', World Bank Staff Working Paper 469, Washington, DC.

World Bank (1992), 'Attracting private investment: capitalists' perceptions of the investment climate in Europe, the Middle East and North Africa', Regional study by the EMENA Technical Department, Washington, DC.

____ (1994a), *Tunisia: Private Sector Assessment*, Middle East and North Africa Regional Office, Washington, DC.

____ (1994b), *Kingdom of Morocco: Preparing for the 21st Century – Strengthening the Private Sector in Morocco*, Middle East and North Africa Regional Office, Washington, DC,

____ (1994c), *Kingdom of Morocco–Republic of Tunisia: Export Growth: Determinants and Prospects*, Middle East and North Africa Regional Office, Washington, DC.

____ (1995), *Kingdom of Morocco: Country Economic Memorandum: Towards Higher Growth and Employment, Volumes I & II*, Middle East and North Africa Regional Office, Washington, DC.

Notes

1. The findings, interpretations and conclusions expressed in this paper are entirely those of the authors. They do not represent the views of the World Bank, its executive directors, or the countries they represent.
2. The Middle East and North Africa (MENA) region is used here to describe all Arab countries except Mauritania and Sudan plus Iran.
3. Nehru and Dhareshwar (1994) provide an extensive bibliography.
4. During the last 35 years, investment averaged 20% of GDP in Morocco and 26% in Tunisia.
5. Estimates of total factor productivity in Morocco and Tunisia show a low or negative average annual contribution to growth since 1960, ranging from 0.75% to a significantly negative number. There is a school of 'growth fundamentalists' who argue that more precise estimates in East Asia would yield substantially smaller residuals of TFP change. Krugman (1994) summarizes their argument. It is likely however that application of similar growth accounting methods to the data for Morocco and Tunisia would yield substantially lower or higher negative residuals, thus preserving the ordinal ranking.
6. Trade diversion is relatively small because more than 50% of Morocco's non-oil imports and more than 70% of Tunisia's already come from Europe.)

7. Obviously, the analogy is not complete, because tariffs will eventually be completely eliminated between Morocco and Tunisia and the EU, and welfare gains will predominate.
8. See Nishimizu and Page (1991) and Rodrik (1994) for reviews of the relevant literature.
9. For a concise review of the arguments for technologically based catch-up, see Pack (1993).
10. See, for example, Nagaoka (1989).
11. See Rhee and Westphal (1977) for evidence on the use of older technology to achieve exports and Ranis (1979) for Taiwan.
12. This was first noted by Westphal, Rhee, and Pursell (1981) in Korea and confirmed in Taiwan by a number of local researchers. For a discussion of Taiwan see Pack (1993).
13. See for example Lieberman (1992), Levy (1994).

PART III
Egypt and the European Union

7

Towards a Free Trade Agreement with the European Union: Issues and Policy Options for Egypt[1]

Bernard Hoekman
The World Bank and CEPR

Simeon Djankov
University of Michigan

7.1   Introduction

For some time now the Government of Egypt has been pursuing economic reform, as reflected most prominently in the Economic Restructuring and Structural Adjustment Program (ERSAP) and the liberalization commitments made during the Uruguay Round of multilateral trade negotiations. While economic adjustment efforts have led to great improvements in macroeconomic indicators,[2] the supply response by the private sector – in terms of investment in productive resources and employment creation – has been limited. There are a number of possible explanations for this, but two stand out: (i) uncertainty regarding the reversibility of reform; and (ii) reform efforts have not yet gone far enough to induce large-scale investment. The investment to GDP ratio is 18%, significantly below that of other lower-middle-income countries (World Bank, 1996). Foreign direct investment is negligible compared to the flows going to emerging market economies: Egypt obtained only 1% of the annual direct investment inflow into Indonesia in 1995.[3]

This chapter assesses the potential role of a Euro-Mediterranean Agreement (EMA) in helping to implement further structural economic reforms. An EMA can help address both of the factors noted above that impede investment since it can be much more than a trade liberalization agreement. It may also address liberalization of investment and services, and provide for extensive cooperation on regulatory and economic policies. Section 7.2 discusses the possible benefits and costs of preferential liberalization with the EU. Section 7.3 summarizes and evaluates the recently negotiated EMA between Tunisia and the EU and argues that significant additional actions will enhance the benefits for Egypt in terms of fostering sustainable economic growth. Key issues in this connection are liberalization of both inward foreign direct investment (FDI) and trade in services. Complementary policy actions that go beyond the EMA will increase the benefits of the free trade agreement (FTA). Two policy areas that are particularly important include reducing tariffs applied to the rest of the world and active pursuit of privatization. Section 7.4 analyses the possible implications of alternative approaches to reducing tariffs in the EMA context, and illustrates the importance of taking concurrent actions to improve the efficiency of the service sector. Section 7.5 concludes.

7.2 Benefits and costs of regional integration

There are three options to liberalize trade and investment regimes: unilateral action, reciprocal liberalization in the context of multilateral negotiations, and preferential (discriminatory) liberalization. For a small country that cannot influence its terms of trade, unilateral free trade is generally the best policy. If, in the context of multilateral negotiations, other countries reciprocate, this increases the gains from unilateral liberalization efforts. However, there are few if any gains to be expected from making liberalization conditional upon reciprocity by trading partners, as the relatively small size of the Egyptian market does not give the government much bargaining power. Preferential liberalization through the negotiation of an FTA will generally also be economically inferior to unilateral liberalization. The reason is simple: the world market is much larger than the regional one. By not discriminating across potential trading partners, domestic firms and consumers will be able to buy goods and services from the most efficient suppliers, wherever they are located. By granting preferential treatment to specific countries, trade *diversion* may occur (*see* Chapter 2). This may be offset by trade *creation*, as well as a number of other potential gains that are specific to the agreement with the EU. These include:

1. *Credibility and dynamic gains* An EMA may offer a strong mechanism for locking in (anchoring) economic reforms. The credibility associated with EMA-based reform may lead to greater investment and greater efforts to enhance productivity.
2. *Harmonization and mutual recognition* An EMA may involve harmonizing regulatory regimes and administrative requirements relating to product standards, testing and certification procedures, mutual recognition agreements, common documents for customs clearance (e.g. the

EU's Single Administrative Document), coordination and cooperation on linking computer systems of Customs, etc. While such cooperative efforts can be pursued unilaterally, formal agreements may be necessary to induce the administrative bodies involved to cooperate. The greater the share of trade with partner countries, the greater the benefits of elimination of such non-tariff barriers, which impose real resource costs.

3. *Security of market access* An EMA may allow agreement to eliminate the possibility of imposing contingent protection, such as anti-dumping actions against partner country exports. The greater the share of total trade that occurs between partner countries, the greater the value of enhancing the certainty of market access through bilateral agreement. In the multilateral context such an agreement is unlikely to be feasible any time soon (Hoekman and Kostecki, 1995). Harmonization or recognition of administrative requirements and procedures may also help to improve the security of market access. An important area in this connection are product standards and their enforcement.

4. *Transfers* The EMA involves transfers from the EU. Such transfers are both financial and in the form of technical assistance. To the extent they are *additional* to status quo ante flows they are a source of gain.

5. *Political economy* Non-economic considerations, especially foreign policy objectives may imply that there is a stronger political constituency for regional as opposed to unilateral or multilateral liberalization. Hence, the chances of attaining liberalization, albeit on a preferential basis, may be greater. In part this is because the set of issues on the table is large, including political, social and economic cooperation.

6. *Facilitation of general liberalization* If an EMA is part of a strategy to liberalize economic activity more generally, i.e. on a most-favoured-nation (MFN) basis this will generate greater gains. Adjustment costs associated with liberalization on an MFN basis are not likely to be much higher than those emerging from preferential liberalization with the EU (Konan and Maskus, Chapter 8). If financial and other assistance from the EU is used to facilitate the transition to general reductions in trade barriers, the EMA may enhance the political feasibility of MFN liberalization.

The extent to which these factors apply, and the magnitude of the associated welfare gains, are an empirical matter. Much depends on the contents of the negotiated agreement, the size of the additional financial and other types of transfers, and the longer-term economic policy stance of the government. Historically, preferential trade agreements generally have not gone much beyond the GATT. Allowance is frequently made for the re-imposition of protection; for various types of non-tariff measures; and for the use of contingent protection. Little progress is often made in harmonizing procedures or implementing mutual recognition arrangements (Hoekman and Kostecki, 1995). The probability that an EMA will be welfare enhancing increases the more the EMA goes significantly beyond the current WTO disciplines – especially in services; and the greater is progress in the area of trade facilitation – customs procedures, documentary requirements, product testing and certification. Cooperation and harmonization of standards and customs clearance procedures can do much to reduce the administrative costs of trade. Some administrative barriers may not differentiate between sources of imports. If these barriers are reduced or removed in the context of an EMA, they will also reduce the costs of trade with non-EU countries. This will further increase the gains from an EMA.

7.3   The EMA with Tunisia

Currently, economic relations between Egypt and the EU are governed by a Cooperation Agreement dating from the 1970s. This agreement, which is unlimited in duration, provides duty-free access to EU markets for industrial goods, and preferential access for agricultural commodities. The agreement is not reciprocal, and Egypt continues to apply MFN tariffs to goods of EU origin. The agreement is complemented by periodic Financial Protocols, which establish the amount of financial resources the EU provides over a five year period. These institutional arrangements will be changed with the implementation of an EMA.

The basic objectives of an EMA are to: achieve reciprocal free trade between the EU and Mediterranean countries in most manufactured goods; grant preferential and reciprocal access for agricultural products; establish conditions for gradual liberalization of trade in services and capital; and encourage the economic integration of Mediterranean countries. The goals and constraints imposed by Mediterranean countries are perhaps best stated in the EU Commission's request for negotiating authority: 'in order to be able to enter progressively into free trade with the Union and to take on board a wide range of trade-related Community regulations (customs, standards, competition, intellectual property protection, liberalization of services, free capital movements, etc.) ... Mediterranean countries ... insist on four fundamental aspects ...: the need for long transitional mechanisms and secure safeguards; the need to obtain improved access for their agricultural exports; the need for increased financial flows ... [and] the possibility to count on the Community's help to accelerate the modernization of their social and economic systems'.[4]

The first EMA, negotiated with Tunisia, was initialled in April and signed in July 1995. An agreement with Morocco followed in October 1995. In terms of what the EU is willing to offer, there is likely to be very little variance across EMAs. At the time of writing (summer 1996) the specifics of the EMA between Egypt and the EU are still under negotiation, but the initial drafts suggest that the agreement will closely resemble that of Tunisia and Morocco. What follows therefore briefly discusses the Tunisian agreement ('the EMA').

7.3.1 The terms of the agreement with Tunisia

The EMA is unlimited in duration and is to be implemented over a 12-year period. Its operation is overseen by an Association Council (meeting at ministerial level at least once a year) and an Association Committee (meeting at the level of officials, responsible for implementation of the agreement). The EMA has seven major elements:

1. Political dialogue.
2. Free movement of goods.
3. Right of establishment and supply of services.
4. Payments, capital, competition and other economic provisions (e.g. safeguards).
5. Economic, social and cultural cooperation.
6. Financial cooperation.
7. Institutional provisions.

Many of the provisions of the EMA are conditional upon the date it enters into force (e.g. timing of tariff reductions). This in turn depends on how long it will take the 15 EU member states and the Tunisian parliament to ratify the agreement.

Political dialogue

The EMA calls for the establishment of a regular political dialogue between the parties of the agreement is to focus in particular on regional security, stability and development, as well as the promotion of common initiatives.

Free movement of goods

There are four major dimensions regarding liberalization of trade in goods: trade in manufactures; trade in agricultural produce; safeguard mechanisms; and rules of origin. As noted above, Tunisia (like Egypt) already benefits from duty-free access to EU markets for manufactured goods under the 1976 Cooperation Agreement, and additional Protocols (1982, 1988) negotiated after the enlargement of the EU in 1981 and 1986. Thus, liberalization will mostly occur on the Tunisian side. Quotas are to be abolished upon the entry into force of the agreement – except as allowed by GATT rules. In contrast to the Europe Agreements with Eastern European countries, no special treatment was given to Tunisia as regards more rapid elimination of textile quotas than agreed under the GATT. However, Tunisia is reportedly only subject to two quotas, neither of which is fully utilized (World Bank, 1994).

Tunisian tariffs on industrial products of EU origin will be reduce to zero over a twelve year period. Four groups of products – at the 7-digit Community Common Nomenclature (CN) level – have been defined in Annexes. Tariffs on manufactured products that are not mentioned in one of these Annexes will be abolished upon the entry into force of the agreement. There are 470 six-digit tariff lines in this category, all of which are either intermediate inputs or machinery. They account for 10% of 1994 imports from the EU (Table 7.1).[5] Tariffs and surcharges on products listed in Annex 3 to the Agreement will be eliminated over a 5 year period in steps of 15%, starting from the entry into force of the Treaty. Products on this list, together with the group of goods to be liberalized immediately (i.e. those not mentioned in an Annex) account for some 35% of 1994 imports by Tunisia. Annex 4 of the EMA comprises a list of products that will be liberalized over the full 12 year transition period, in steps of 8% per year. Products listed in Annex 5 will commence tariff reductions four years after the entry into force of the agreement, with reductions spread out linearly over the remaining 8 years of the transition period (i.e. annual cuts of 11-12%). A final list of manufactured products contained in Annex 6 is exempted from tariff reductions. This list contains 37 six-digit tariff lines, comprising bread, pasta, and carpets.

Import weighted average tariffs applying to the groups of goods to be liberalized range from 21% to 34% (Table 7.1). Goods to be liberalized immediately have the lowest average tariffs, while those to be liberalized last have the highest average rates. Liberalization of intermediate inputs and capital goods is front-loaded, whereas liberalization of consumer goods has been back-loaded. Some 90% of the goods in Annexes 3 and 4 are intermediates or machinery; as compared to only 4% for Annex 5. About three quarters of Tunisian exports to the EU in 1994 involved Annex 5 goods, representing over 40% of domestic production. As Annex 4 covers another 20% of domestic output, much of domestic industry is subject to gradual and back-loaded liberalization. This might assist the domestic industries concerned to prepare for greater competition from imports in the future. However, increasing effective rates of protection (*see*

Table 7.1 Tariff liberalization commitments by Tunisia (industrial products)

	Share of trade		Share in domestic output	Share in total tariff revenue	Import weighted average tariff	Number of 6-digit lines		Share of machinery and intermediates	
	Exports	Imports				Total (=5019)	% of total	By line (%)	By import value (%)
Annex 3: 5 year transition	16	24	20	12.5	26.7	1810	41	93	87
Annex 4: 12 year transition	7	29	22	9.2	30.4	1127	26	94	89
Annex 5: 8 year transition starting in year 5	75	36	43	32.9	33.8	944	22	8	4
Annex 6: Exempted	1	1	1	n.a.	n.a.	37	1	0	0
Industrial goods not listed in an Annex: immediate liberalization	1	10	14	3.6	21.6	470	10	100	100

Source: Own calculations based on Comtext and World Bank data. All data is for 1994.

Section 7.4) may imply welfare losses as resource allocation incentives become more distorted. If the increase in effective protection of domestic industries during the first part of the implementation period leads to inefficient investment or non-adjustment, pressures may also emerge in the future to resist market opening or impose safeguard actions.

The approach taken by Tunisia with respect to tariff elimination is similar to that of the Central and Eastern European countries, albeit much more gradual. Poland committed itself to eliminate tariffs on about 30% of its imports from the EU in 1992, and to abolish the remainder over a seven year transition period, with duty reductions taking place during the last four years. Hungary agreed to liberalize 12-13% of its imports over a three year period in annual steps of one-third, another 20% between 1995 and 1997, again in steps of one-third and the rest (two-thirds) between 1995 and 2001, in steps of one-sixth per year. The Czech and Slovak

Republics dismantle tariffs over a seven year period (like Poland, but somewhat less front-loaded). The higher level of initial tariffs in Tunisia (and the Mediterranean more generally) may explain the longer transition path to free trade with the EU. Average protection levels in Eastern Europe are in the 6% range, as compared to 30% for Egypt.

An additional reason for the back-loaded nature of the tariff reduction process may concern the revenue implications of a more uniform move to free trade with the EU. Some 28% of government revenues are derived from trade taxes, with the EU accounting for 58% of total tariff revenue. Most of the tariff revenue generated from trade with the EU is currently collected on the imports of consumer goods (Annex 5), which account for 33% of total revenues, as compared to 12% and 9%, respectively, for Annexes 3 and 4 (Table 7.1). The goods to be liberalized immediately generate only 3.6% of total revenue. The dependence on trade taxes in Egypt is much lower than in Tunisia, but import duties still account for 10% of government revenues. As the EU share of total imports is also less than in Tunisia (42% compared to 68%), revenue implications are nonetheless not as far-reaching.

Safeguards In addition to anti-dumping and countervailing duties, which continue to apply, a general safeguard provision makes allowance for 'appropriate measures' to be taken if imports from a partner country injure import-competing industries. Necessary conditions for such actions are that products are 'being imported in such increased quantities and under such conditions as to cause or threaten to cause serious injury to domestic producers of like or directly competitive products in the territory of one of the Contracting Parties, or serious disturbances in any sector of the economy or difficulties which could bring about a serious deterioration in the economic situation of a region' (Article 25). The first of these criteria is drawn from the GATT; the second is specific to EU trade agreements. Article 25 allows substantial opportunity to (re-) impose protection.

Agriculture Little will change as far as agricultural trade is concerned. The objective of the EMA is to gradually liberalize trade in this sector. In concrete terms it mostly locks in the status quo (existing preferential arrangements), while offering limited improvements in access for specific products through expansion of tariff quotas and reduction/elimination of tariffs for specific quotas. Negotiations to improve on existing agricultural concessions are to be initiated after 1 January 2000. Continued restrictions on imports of agricultural products reduce the benefits of an EMA for Mediterranean countries. The unwillingness (inability) of the EU Commission to significantly expand export opportunities was an important stumbling block for Morocco in reaching agreement with the EU,[6] and has also emerged as a negotiating issue in the Egypt–EU negotiations. The relative importance of agriculture varies significantly across Mediterranean countries. It is least important to Jordan, where it accounts for 8% of GDP, and most important in Egypt, Morocco and Syria, where it contributes some 20% to GDP. The agricultural sector accounts for some 14% of total Egyptian exports, as compared to 30% for Morocco.

Rules of origin The EU supports greater integration of the economies of the Mediterranean countries. This is important, as the negotiation of bilateral agreements between the EU and each of the Mediterranean countries would otherwise lead to a so-called hub-and-spoke system. A problem with such an arrangement is that it creates incentives for firms to invest in the 'hub', i.e. the EU, as this gives them barrier-free access to all the 'spokes'. Partly for this reason a Central European Free Trade Agreement (CEFTA) was established by the Visegrad countries after conclusion of the bilateral Europe Agreements with the EU. To avoid a hub-and-spoke system from emerging, Mediterranean countries are well advised to pursue a similar strategy.

Intra-regional trade between countries of the Middle East and North Africa is limited. In part this reflects the similarity in endowments, in part the non-competitiveness of processed and manufactured goods that are produced. If the Persian Gulf states are included, intra-regional trade is not insignificant (it stood at some $8.3 billion in 1990, or 8% of total exports). Relative to the participation in world trade, these levels are actually quite high.[7] Thus, the trade of Egypt, Jordan, Syria and Turkey with other countries in the Middle East and North Africa is four times more intensive than trade with the world as a whole (Yeats, 1996). The only major economy in the region where intra-regional trade is clearly `too low' is Israel. However, if attention is restricted to Mediterranean nations (i.e. the Gulf countries are excluded), intra-regional trade represents less than 3% of total trade of Mediterranean countries. Given the differences in the factor endowments and per capita income between Israel and some of its neighbours, intra-regional trade should be able to grow substantially.

The rules of origin included in an EMA are important in this connection. Even though in principle Mediterranean countries already have duty-free access to EU markets for manufactured goods, in practice rules of origin may be such as to require the use of EU inputs in order to benefit from duty-free treatment.[8] Less restrictive rules of origin in an EMA may then imply an effective liberalization of trade in manufactures. The Tunisian agreement allows for cumulation for rules of origin purposes for products produced in Algeria and Morocco as well as the EU and

Tunisia. This may help create backward and forward linkages between the Maghreb countries and enhance the potential for intra-industry trade. The extension of cumulation to other Mediterranean countries as well as Eastern European nations would be more beneficial, helping to offset the hub-and-spoke nature of the EU's web of trade agreements. To be effective, more liberal rules of origin must be complemented with a reduction in barriers to intra-regional trade. This could be pursued by converting existing commodity-specific preferential trade agreements between Mediterranean countries into full-fledged FTAs.

Right of establishment and supply of services

The right of establishment (i.e. freedom to engage in FDI) is an objective in the EMA. Modalities to achieve this objective are to be determined by the Association Council. No specific language is devoted to this subject and no time path or target date is mentioned for its realisation. This contrasts with the Europe Agreements, where the EU has granted free entry and national treatment to all firms from partner countries from 1992 on, except in air and inland water transport and maritime cabotage. The Eastern European countries also grant free entry and national treatment to EU firms, with transitional periods for a limited number of sectors/activities. The absence of the right of establishment does not imply that FDI is restricted in Tunisia (*see* Chapters 5 and 6). However, the fact that the government chose not to lock in the status quo, let alone go beyond it is something that will not help attract potential foreign investors.

No specific commitments are made regarding liberalization of cross-border supply of services. As with the right of establishment, liberalization is an objective that is to be pursued by the Association Council. The EMA simply refers to the obligations of each Party under the General Agreement on Trade in Services (GATS). These do not imply much, if any, liberalization (Hoekman, 1996). Mediterranean countries made very limited commitments under the GATS, subjecting some 6% of their service sectors to the national treatment and market access principles, as compared to 26% for the EU.[9] The Europe Agreements are more concrete with respect to services than the EMA. They allow for temporary entry of natural persons and contain specific provisions dealing with air and maritime transport.

Payments, competition and other economic provisions

The EMA requires the adoption of the basic competition rules of the EU, in particular with respect to collusive behaviour, abuse of dominant position, and competition-distorting state aid (Articles 85, 86, and 92 of the Treaty of Rome), in so far as they affect trade between the EU and each partner country. Implementing rules are to be adopted by the Association Council within five years (as opposed to three under the Europe Agreements). Until then, GATT rules with respect to countervailing of subsidies will apply. For the first five years after entry into force of the EMA, Tunisia will be regarded as a disadvantaged region under Article 92.3(a) of the Treaty of Rome. This implies that state aids can be applied to the entire territory of Tunisia during this period. Rules to enforce competition policy and subsidy disciplines are to be adopted by the Association Council after the initial five year period. The EMA also provides for enhanced transparency of state aids, each party agreeing to provide annual reports on the total amount and distribution of the aid given. As mentioned, anti-dumping remains applicable to trade flows between partners, despite the agreement by Tunisia to apply EU competition disciplines. Liberalization of government procurement is not required; reciprocal and gradual liberalization of public purchasing is, however, an objective.

Economic and social cooperation

One third of the articles of the Tunisian EMA deal with cooperation in economic, social and cultural matters. The prime objective underlying economic cooperation is to target 'first and foremost' activities 'suffering the effects of internal constraints and difficulties or affected by the process of liberalizing Tunisia's economy as a whole, and more particularly by the liberalization of trade between Tunisia and the Community' (Article 43). Methods of economic cooperation mentioned in the EMA include information exchange, provision of expert services (consultants), joint ventures (e.g. the Euro-Partenariat program), and assistance with technical, administrative and regulatory matters. Specific areas mentioned in the EMA include regional cooperation, education and training, science and technology, the environment, modernization of industry (including agricultural processing), promotion and protection of investment (e.g. negotiating investment protection and double taxation treaties), standardization and conformity assessment (introduction of EU procedures/rules, upgrading Tunisian testing laboratories), approximation of economic legislation, financial services (supporting restructuring; improving auditing and supervision), agriculture and fisheries (modernization, diversification), transport (modernization and restructuring; management; quality upgrading), telecommunications and information technology (standardization, introduction of electronic data interchange), energy, tourism, and statistics. The various articles alluded to above are largely oriented towards upgrading Tunisian infrastructure broadly defined (both physical and regulatory) and providing support for restructuring of the economy. This support is not just reflected in technical assistance and advice, but is

supported by financial assistance as well (*see* below). The specific mentioning of an issue area under the economic cooperation chapter
presumably signals that this is a legitimate subject for using EU financial
resources.[10]

Financial cooperation

As mentioned earlier, Mediterranean countries have received financial
transfers from the EU under auspices of revolving five-year Financial
Protocols. The sums involved vary per country, but are significant.
During the period of the Fourth Protocol (1991–6), Tunisia was allocated
a total of ECU 284 million. Under the EMA approach, financial protocols will not be renewed. Instead, the EU envisages earmarking a total
amount of assistance – grants and loans – for all the Mediterranean
countries. Individual allocations out of this total would not be pre-deter-
mined, but would in part be endogenous – depending on country
performance, including the implementation of the EMA. Although not
spelled out explicitly in the EMA, the articles in the EMA on financial
cooperation put emphasis on the link between EMA implementation and
the provision of financial resources. The exact modalities of financial
cooperation are vague, the relevant procedures to 'be adopted by mutual
agreement between the Parties by means of the most suitable instruments
once the agreement enters into force' (Article 75). How future financial
transfers will compare to past flows remains to be seen. The European
Commission requested a total of ECU 5.5 billion for the region for a four
year period; ECU 4.7 billion was approved by the Council. An equivalent
amount is to be provided by the European Investment Bank.

Institutional provisions

As noted previously, the Association Council is the main body responsible for the implementation and operation of the EMA. It also deals
with disputes. If a dispute cannot be addressed through consultations,
one of the parties may appoint an arbitrator. The other party is then
required to appoint a second arbitrator within two months, and the
Association Council appoints a third one. Decisions by the three arbi-
trators will be taken by majority vote, with the parties required to
implement recommendations. However, it is not clear what the sanc-
tions may be in case of non-implementation of arbitration decisions.
Time will tell how this dispute settlement mechanism will work. In a
number of areas that are particularly relevant from a market access
viewpoint, binding obligations have yet to be established, e.g. as regards
product standards. Disputes on such issues, e.g. allegations that standards are used as non-tariff barriers, are perhaps better dealt with by

the WTO. Disputes on matters relating to state aid (in the first five years of the EMA), anti-dumping, and state trading are explicitly referred to the WTO by the Tunisian EMA (Article 36).

7.3.2   Evaluation of the Tunisian EMA

In principle, the liberalization of trade required under the EMA should induce firms to upgrade their production capacity and improve their efficiency. Although in the long run the EMA is likely to be beneficial to all of the countries involved, it may be economically welfare-reducing in the short- to medium-run due to its discriminatory nature (*see* Chapter 5).[11] The absence of binding commitments on FDI and trade in services, the exclusion of government procurement, and the maintenance of anti-dumping and broadly worded safeguard provisions implies that the EMA does not go significantly beyond existing multilateral (WTO) disciplines.

The transition path to free trade with the EU is a long one, with liberalization of goods competing with domestic production only starting five years after the entry into force of the agreements. By lowering tariffs on intermediates and capital goods first, domestic industries are granted some up front compensation for the adjustment costs that must be incurred later, and are given time in which to restructure. The tariff liberalization strategy ensures that tariff revenues will initially decline slowly, giving more time to mobilize alternative tax bases. But the backloaded nature of the tariff reductions may reduce the incentives to initiate rapid restructuring, and may create problems in implementing tariff reductions in the future (e.g. through pressure for safeguard protection). Much therefore depends on the credibility of the EMA. This in turn depends on the extent to which complementary actions are pursued to improve the functioning of the economy. Important in this connection is the fact that the EMA does little to ensure investors of national treatment or to grant the general right of establishment. This is a significant difference with the Europe Agreements, where such establishment is permitted immediately for most activities, and a transition path is spelled out for the remainder. By signalling their openness to FDI, the Central and Eastern European countries increased the incentives for foreign firms to establish and transfer much needed know-how. FDI is especially important in the services area, where establishment often remains the best way to contest a market. Efficient services are crucial in terms of being able to participate in the global economy: telecommunications, information technology, port services, financial intermediation, and business support services are all key elements underlying the ability to compete on world markets. By limiting commitments to those made in the GATS, the EMA risks sending a signal that liberalization is not on the immediate agenda. It also puts the burden on unilateral efforts to move forward.

7.4   Possible implications for Egypt of emulating the Tunisian agreement

Although the basic outline of the EMA between Egypt and the EU will be similar to the Tunisian agreement, the Government of Egypt has substantial discretion to determine the contents and time path of liberalization. This involves the modalities of the transition to free trade with Europe, actions to encourage FDI and open up the service sector to greater competition, and the policy stance that is taken regarding the rest of the world.

7.4.1   Liberalization

Table 7.2 'translates' the Tunisian commitments on tariff liberalization for the case of Egypt. It is assumed that Egypt would pursue an identical approach to free trade with the EU, based on the same grouping of commodities into Annexes, each of which is subjected to a different time path for tariff elimination. Compared to Tunisia, a greater share of domestic output is found in Annex 5 products (which comprises mostly consumer goods) – 50% as compared to 43% – while the relative importance in domestic production of the goods subject to immediate liberalization is less (8% compared to 14%). Thus, the liberalization process would be somewhat more gradual (backloaded) than in Tunisia. Egypt has a large merchandise trade deficit, but imports more from the rest of the world than from the EU. As noted earlier, it is therefore less dependent on the EU for tariff revenue than Tunisia.

Calculating the impact of alternative liberalization strategies on the levels and distribution of effective protection of Egyptian industry provides a useful measure of the change in incentive regime for industries. The effective rate of protection (ERP) is a measure of the extent to which trade barriers protect domestic value added in production.[12] The import-weighted average tariff is currently 30% (Table 7.3). At 70% (Table 7.3, last column), the average effective rate of protection is significantly higher than the average nominal rate. Effective rates are higher than nominal ones for 17 industries, all of which are final goods sectors. All agricultural sectors (not reported here) and the four intermediate sectors (crude petroleum, other extracting industries, iron and steel, and leather) have lower

Table 7.2 Tunisian tariff liberalization commitments applied to Egypt (industrial products)

	Trade with the EU value and share*		Trade with ROW value and share*		EU share of total trade		Share in domestic output	Share in total tariff revenue	Average tariff weighted	Number of 6-digit lines	% of total	Share of machinery and intermediates	
	Exports	Imports	Exports	Imports	Exports	Imports						By line (%)	By import value (%)
Annex 3: 5 year transition	642 (29)	1196 (25)	385 (19)	839 (14)	62	58	27	8.3	14.6	1140	29	83	79
Annex 4: 12 year transition	465 (21)	1291 (27)	527 (26)	2787 (46)	46	32	14	11.7	19.1	946	24	67	56
Annex 5: 8 year transition starting in year 5	907 (41)	1339 (28)	972 (48)	1738 (29)	48	43	50	20.2	31.7	913	23	8	7
Annex 6: Exempted	21 (1)	48 (1)	9 (0.2)	30 (0.5)	96	62	1	0.6	24.8	29	1	0	0
Industrial goods not listed in an Annex: immediate liberalization	177 (8)	909 (19)	142 (7)	659 (11)	55	58	8	3.5	8.1	802	23	89	85
TOTAL	2412	4783	2035	6053	54	43	100	44.3	19.4	3930	100	60	53

* Shares in brackets; values in US $ million
Source: Own calculations based on Egyptian Customs data (1994).

Table 7.3 Protection in Egypt, 1994

	EU share of imports	Nominal tariff	Share of services in total inputs	Current ERP, with tariff equivalents for service	Current ERP, without tariff equivalents for services
Chemicals and products, excluding petroleum	63	15	32	−12	21
Clothing	12	68	44	147	162
Cotton ginning and pressing	40	7	12	9	14
Cotton spinning and weaving	57	29	22	38	51
Crude petroleum and natural gas	63	9	89	−21	7
Food processing	26	36	23	59	72
Furniture	59	56	26	107	118
Glass and products	35	34	26	91	109
Iron, steel, other base metals	18	28	25	9	14
Leather products excluding shoes	62	35	28	13	28
Machinery and appliances	52	27	27	20	38
Mineral products, not included elsewhere	48	19	19	21	33
Other extractive industries	47	13	54	−25	−3
Other manufacturing	48	30	62	23	34
Paper and printing	45	31	52	52	90
Petroleum refining	43	13	32	45	83
Porcelain, china, pottery	16	37	34	98	115
Rubber, plastic and products	34	24	37	16	33
Footwear	37	56	24	267	301
Transportation equipment	33	40	43	65	90
Wood, wood products, excluding furniture	40	33	37	54	66
Average	42	31	36	51	70

Source: Trade shares from the Eurostat Comext database (1995); service shares from the 1994 input-output table; ERP from own calculations; nominal import-weighted tariffs from Subramanian (1995).

effective protection than what nominal tariffs would suggest. The structure of protection in Egypt is therefore skewed towards final goods.

Many inputs used by industries are not traded – services are often an important example. Analogous to tariffs on traded inputs, the higher the tariff-equivalent of regulatory policies for services, the lower the effective protection for industries that use the service inputs involved. Given the importance of services in the production process—for example, transportation of inputs and the goods produced, financial intermediation, insurance, business services, telecommunications – it is clearly necessary to take into account the extent to which regulatory regimes raise the costs of services, thereby imposing a tax on manufacturing and agriculture. These costs are not limited to direct price-increasing effects. In so far as their effect is to reduce quality of services, users are also confronted with an implicit tax.

The service intensity of Egyptian industries varies substantially, ranging from a high of almost 90% for crude petroleum/gas extraction to a low of 12% for cotton ginning and pressing (Table 7.3, column 3). Industries that are particularly dependent on services include 'other' manufacturing, extractive activities, paper and printing, clothing, transport equipment, wood products and rubber/plastics. If account is taken of the fact that service inputs used by Egyptian industry are less efficient and more costly than they might be (because of lack of competition), the magnitude of the ERP for most manufacturing industries falls significantly – from an average of 70% to 51% (Table 7.3, column 4). Indeed, for some industries it becomes negative, implying that the tariffs on intermediates combined with the implicit tariffs on service inputs outweigh the tariff protection applying to the goods produced. That is, the regulatory regime results in the effective taxation of Egyptian industry.[13]

The ERP is not a measure of the cost of protection, since all it does is provide information on differences in the level of protection across industries without taking into account the quantity of output that is protected (industry size) or divergences between private and social costs for each marginal unit of output (Corden, 1984). General equilibrium models are required to evaluate the welfare costs of protection, as these take into consideration quantities and interaction effects. Notwithstanding this, we focus on the ERP because it is useful in providing qualitative information on the change in the investment incentive regime over time that is caused by the gradual trade liberalization. An ERP framework also is useful to determine the relative sensitivity of industries to various types of domestic distortions, such as the implicit tax imposed by an inefficient services sector.

Three alternative tariff reduction strategies are compared in Tables 7.4–7.6: emulation of the Tunisian approach; a linear (proportional) reduction across-the-board over 12 years; and a 'concertina' approach under which the maximum tariff on EU imports is gradually compressed to zero over 12 years. In the proportional case it is assumed that all tariffs are reduced by one-twelfth each year; under the concertina the maximum tariff is reduced to zero in steps of one-twelfth. To facilitate comparisons the ERP is reported at three-year intervals. It is assumed for the time being that nothing is done to enhance the efficiency of services – i.e. the tariff equivalents for services are maintained unchanged throughout, MFN tariffs on the rest of the world remain constant, and no reduction in tariffs on agricultural products occurs. *Ex ante*, one expects the Tunisian approach to be most likely to result in increases in ERPs in the early stage of the transition to free trade with Europe, while this is least likely under the concertina.

Under the Tunisian approach, five industries with positive ERPs experience little change in protection until year 9: clothing, glass, ceramics, rubber/plastics and footwear (Table 7.4). Under the alternative approaches this occurs only for clothing. The Tunisian and proportional reductions lead to faster initial declines in ERPs, while the concertina leads to the most gradual decline in the average ERP. Noteworthy is that the Tunisian approach results in the lowest average ERP at the assumed mid-point (year 6), but has the highest dispersion of protection across industries. Under the concertina less change occurs up to year 9, and the change after year 9 is therefore more dramatic: the average ERP for manufacturing falls from 27% to –7% (Table 7.7). In contrast, the other two approaches imply an average ERP of close to 20% by year 9. The proportional approach results in a steady and uniform reduction in ERPs (Table 7.5). In all cases, after 12 years ERPs are mostly negative, reflecting the impact of the inefficient service sector. Trade (distribution), transport and storage, and hotels and restaurant services see their ERPs increase significantly (not reported), reflecting the gradual decline in the cost of tangible inputs. Manufacturing industries that continue to benefit from positive – sometimes substantial – ERPs at the end of 12 years are limited (clothing, ceramics, glass products, iron and steel, footwear).

The Tunisian approach gives rise to distorted incentives during the transition (ERPs for some industries rise), but the increases are relatively minor (with the exception of clothing). The results suggest that *if* nothing is done to improve the cost efficiency and quality of the service sector, the costs associated with the Tunisian approach may not be very high in comparison to alternative approaches given that it ensures that industries are compensated to some extent for the lack of improvement in services.

Table 7.4 Tunisia scenario (no reduction in service tariffs)

Sector	ERP0	ERP3	ERP6	ERP9	ERP12
Agriculture					
Vegetable foodstuffs	−5	−2	0	0	4
Other vegetable products	−5	−3	0	5	8
Animal products	18	24	26	52	64
Manufacturing					
Chemicals and products excluding petroleum	−12	−38	−85	−76	-60
Clothing: assembled and pieces	147	150	151	141	89
Cotton ginning and pressing	9	9	4	−5	−22
Cotton spinning and weaving	38	39	24	3	−23
Crude petroleum and natural gas	−21	−26	−34	−32	−28
Food processing	59	54	46	29	−10
Furniture	107	86	67	34	−12
Glass and products	91	88	90	61	3
Iron, steel, other base metals	9	8	3	3	4
Leather products excluding footwear	13	14	7	−6	−21
Machinery and appliances	20	−3	−41	−36	−29
Mineral products not included elsewhere	21	5	-31	−21	−5
Other extractive industries	−25	−20	-6	−15	−27
Other manufacturing	23	18	15	6	−8
Paper and printing	52	42	32	9	−29
Petroleum refining	45	24	−29	−24	−14
Porcelain, china, pottery	98	96	92	80	37
Rubber, plastic and products	16	15	16	7	−11
Footwear	267	275	251	186	47
Transportation equipment	65	58	55	33	−12
Wood, wood products excluding furniture	54	47	44	23	−13
Manufacturing average	51	45	32	19	−7
Services					
Construction	−64	−43	−2	16	58
Electricity, gas	−116	−97	−59	−56	−50
Transport, storage	−25	−9	24	29	42
Hotels, restaurants	−42	−39	−24	-6	19
Communications	−15	−7	8	14	25
Finance	−10	−7	−3	2	11
Distribution	−9	−7	−3	1	8
Insurance	−4	−3	−1	2	5
Services average	−36	−26	−8	1	16

Source: Own calculations.

However, this is of course very much a second best situation – it would be better to reduce the inefficiency of the service sector concurrently with the reduction in tariffs.

Table 7.7 reports calculations of the ERP at the *end* of the transition period under the proportional reduction approach, assuming that the cost inefficiency of the services industry is addressed to varying degrees (ranging

Table 7.5 Proportional scenario (no reduction in service tariffs)

Sector	ERP0	ERP3	ERP6	ERP9	ERP12
Agriculture					
Vegetable foodstuffs	−5	−2	0	0	4
Other vegetable products	−5	−3	−1	3	8
Animal products	18	24	33	51	64
Manufacturing					
Chemicals and products excluding petroleum	−12	−23	−36	−51	−64
Clothing: assembled and pieces	147	147	143	131	77
Cotton ginning and pressing	9	5	−1	−9	−23
Cotton spinning and weaving	38	26	12	−4	−24
Crude petroleum and natural gas	−21	−23	−25	−27	−29
Food processing	59	53	42	25	−11
Furniture	107	84	57	26	−10
Glass and products	91	82	69	46	4
Iron, steel, other base metals	9	9	8	7	2
Leather products excluding footwear	13	6	−1	−10	−22
Machinery and appliances	20	9	−3	−18	−28
Mineral products not included elsewhere	21	16	10	1	−10
Other extractive industries	−25	−25	−26	−26	−25
Other manufacturing	23	18	12	3	−8
Paper and printing	52	40	24	2	−29
Petroleum refining	45	36	24	5	−25
Porcelain, china, pottery	98	96	90	77	36
Rubber, plastic and products	16	14	9	3	−10
Footwear	267	247	212	151	33
Transportation equipment	65	57	44	24	−10
Wood, wood products excluding furniture	54	44	32	14	−10
Manufacturing average	51	44	33	18	−9
Services					
Construction	−64	−49	−27	4	58
Electricity, gas	−116	−105	−91	−72	−45
Transport, storage	−25	−15	−3	16	43
Hotels, restaurants	−42	−32	−19	−3	20
Communications	−15	−9	−1	9	25
Finance	−10	−7	−3	3	11
Distribution	−9	−6	−3	1	8
Insurance	−4	−3	−1	2	5
Services average	−36	−28	−18	−5	16

Source: Own calculations.

from a 25% to 100% reduction in the assumed tariff equivalents). It can be seen that the manufacturing average ERP becomes positive only if these price wedges are reduced by at least 40%. After elimination of the assumed 15% tariff equivalent for services (*see* Appendix on pages 153–4), two thirds of all industries would benefit from positive ERPs after free trade with the EU. Such reductions in the inefficiency of the service industries will require greater competition, in part through the encouragement of FDI, which will

Table 7.6 Concertina scenario (no reduction in service tariffs)

Sector	ERP0	ERP3	ERP6	ERP9	ERP12
Agriculture					
Vegetable foodstuffs	−5	−2	−1	0	4
Other vegetable products	−5	−3	2	5	8
Animal products	18	27	36	54	64
Manufacturing					
Chemicals and products excluding petroleum	−12	−12	−10	2	−58
Clothing assembled and pieces	147	135	122	112	69
Cotton ginning and pressing	9	9	9	5	−18
Cotton spinning and weaving	38	38	38	10	−22
Crude petroleum and natural gas	−21	−21	−20	−17	−28
Food processing	59	59	53	36	−3
Furniture	107	84	50	16	−15
Glass and products	91	91	83	51	10
Iron, steel, other base metals	9	9	9	8	4
Leather products excluding footwear	13	13	9	−5	−21
Machinery and appliances	20	21	23	0	−31
Mineral products not included elsewhere	21	21	22	15	−7
Other extractive industries	−25	−25	−23	−2	−17
Other manufacturing	23	23	25	14	−5
Paper and printing	52	52	53	23	−22
Petroleum refining	45	45	45	36	−12
Porcelain, china, pottery	98	98	94	77	46
Rubber, plastic and products	16	16	16	10	−6
Footwear	267	225	163	113	28
Transportation equipment	65	66	54	33	−7
Wood, wood products excluding furniture	54	54	50	28	−7
Manufacturing average	51	48	41	27	−6
Services					
Construction	−64	−64	−60	−34	56
Electricity, gas	−116	−115	−111	−102	−53
Transport, storage	−25	−24	−22	−6	43
Hotels, restaurants	−42	−32	−19	−7	20
Communications	−15	−14	−11	4	25
Finance	−10	−8	−5	2	11
Distribution	−9	−6	−4	1	8
Insurance	−4	−3	−1	2	5
Services average	−36	−33	−28	−17	16

Source: Own calculations.

only materialize if the regulatory and institutional environment is conducive to private sector investment. Indeed, in the absence of improvements in the legal and regulatory framework, opening up to trade with the EU may result in greater competition from imports without much in the way of new investment. If so, the potential negative impact of an EMA is significant and the political viability of its implementation may well decline.

Table 7.7 Impact on ERPs of reducing tariff equivalents for services, assuming full elimination of tariffs on imports from EU

Sector	Service share	0% cut	25% cut	50% cut	75% cut	100% cut
Chemicals and products excluding petroleum	32	−64	−56	−48	−40	−32
Clothing: assembled and pieces	44	77	81	84	88	92
Cotton ginning and pressing	12	−23	−22	−20	−19	−18
Cotton spinning and weaving	22	−24	−20	−17	−14	−11
Crude petroleum and natural gas	89	−29	−22	−15	−8	−1
Food processing	23	−11	−8	−4	−1	2
Furniture	26	−10	−7	−4	−1	2
Glass and products	26	4	9	13	18	22
Iron, steel, other base metals	25	2	3	4	5	7
Leather products excluding footwear	28	−22	−18	−14	−10	−6
Machinery and appliances	27	−28	−24	−19	−15	−10
Mineral products not included elsewhere	19	−10	−7	−4	−2	1
Other extractive industries	54	−25	−19	−14	−8	−2
Other manufacturing	62	−8	−5	−2	0	3
Paper and printing	52	−29	−20	−10	−1	9
Petroleum refining	32	−25	−15	−6	4	13
Porcelain, china, pottery	34	36	40	44	48	52
Rubber, plastic and products	37	−10	−6	−2	2	6
Footwear	24	33	42	50	59	67
Transportation equipment	43	−10	−4	2	8	15
Wood, wood products excluding furniture	37	−10	−7	−4	−1	2
Mean	33	−9	−4	1	5	10
Standard deviation	17	29	28	28	28	28

Source: Own calculations.

Much is likely to depend in this connection not only on actions to open service markets to greater competition but also on privatization efforts (*see* below) and on how EU financial assistance is used.

8.4.2 Complementary actions outside of the EMA framework

Liberalization and locking-in of regulatory regimes concerning services and investment can be done within the context of an EMA. Other reforms can be contemplated that go beyond the EMA – i.e. are neither required nor a longer-term objective of the EMA. These include reduction of MFN tariffs, liberalization *vis-a-vis* neighbouring countries, and privatization.

MFN tariffs

The foregoing results illustrate the need to reduce MFN tariffs significantly, especially those that support high rates of effective protection after the transition to free trade with the EU (e.g. clothing, ceramics). Of equal importance is a reduction in the dispersion of tariffs. Greater uniformity of tariffs combined with a substantial reduction in the average level will already do much to improve resource allocation and welfare. For example, Konan and Maskus (1996) estimate that a uniform, non-discriminatory tariff of 10% would increase welfare by 30% relative to the EMA alone.

Reducing hub-and-spoke investment diversion incentives

It was noted earlier that a free trade agreement may create incentives for firms not to invest in Egypt but to locate in the centre (hub) of the network of EU trade agreements (i.e. Europe). Trade barriers against regional trading partners should be eliminated as rapidly as possible to encourage investment by domestic and foreign firms that are interested in servicing regional markets and want to benefit from Egypt's geographical location and relatively diversified industrial base.

Privatization

The role of the state in Egypt is very large. The public sector accounts for 50% of GDP and 35% of total employment, with average wages in the public sector 20% to 40% above those in the private sector (*see* Chapter 12). The size of the public sector imposes a large burden on the economy. If maintained, it also reduces the credibility of the EMA-based liberalization program, as without significant restructuring and contraction, greater competition from imports will lead to greater public enterprise losses, fiscal pressures, and the possibility of macroeconomic problems. The Government is actively pursuing a privatization program. Privatization will not only provide a signal to international financial markets that there are substantial investment opportunities, but enhance the credibility of the liberalization program. Privatization of state-owned enterprises will generate revenue, create investment opportunities for foreign (and flight) capital, and limit possible claims on the budget as competitive pressures emerge. A strong case can be made that there may be a high payoff for using EU grants to fund worker compensation schemes to facilitate downsizing of the public sector and privatization (World Bank, 1995b). The wording of the Articles in the EMA on the scope and priorities for financial and economic cooperation implies that such funding should be possible.

7.5   Conclusions

A free trade agreement with the EU will give rise to greater competition in product markets and a more efficient allocation of resources. The extensive provisions in the EMA for technical cooperation aiming at harmonization and mutual recognition of regulatory procedures (e.g. in the areas of customs clearance, product standards) provide opportunities to reduce transactions costs associated with trade and to improve the investment climate. The magnitude of the benefits for Egypt clearly depend on the contents and implementation of the EMA. Two factors have been emphasized in this paper: the need to extend the EMA to include liberalization of foreign direct investment and services, and the possible implications of the design of the tariff liberalization program. Both dimensions have implications for investment incentives, adjustment costs, and national welfare over the transition.

If, as seems likely, the Tunisian approach to tariff reductions is followed, effective rates of protection may rise during the early years of the transition period. By lowering tariffs on intermediates and capital goods first, domestic industries will be granted some up front compensation for the adjustment costs that must be incurred later, and for the inefficiency of domestic service providers. Such a liberalization strategy also ensures that tariff revenues will initially decline slowly, giving more time to mobilize alternative tax bases. But the possible downside of the strategy is that the backloaded nature of the tariff reductions may reduce the incentives to initiate rapid restructuring, and may create problems in implementing tariff reductions in the future, especially if investment is induced in the sectors concerned. Moreover, although firms will obtain some 'compensation' on the domestic market, clearly this will not apply to export-oriented firms who will need to have access to low-cost, high quality services if they are to be able to compete on world markets.

The ERP analysis suggests that the opportunity cost of a Tunisian approach to reducing tariffs may be relatively minor. Of greater importance is the pursuit of supporting and complementary actions to improve the functioning of the economy. Upgrading the quality and reducing the costs of services is critical in this connection. This will require foreign direct investment, as establishment often remains the best way to contest service markets. Efficient services are crucial in terms of being able to participate in the global economy: telecommunications, information technology, port services, financial intermediation, and business support services are all key elements underlying the ability to compete on world markets. Further gains can be obtained by pursuit of complementary actions: reducing the average level and dispersion of tariffs imposed on non-EU products and negotiating fully-fledged free trade agreements with other countries in the region. This will reduce hub-and-spoke induced investment diversion incentives and allow Egypt to capitalize on its geographical advantages.

Appendix

Let Q_{EU} be the quantity of EU imports into Egypt, Q_{ROW} be the quantity of ROW imports, ε_{EU} is the own price elasticity of demand for EU imports, and ε_{ROW-EU} is the cross-price elasticity of ROW imports with respect to EU imports. Suppose that due to the FTA tariffs towards EU imports have been reduced by $\Delta T\%$. Then the change in the quantity of goods imported from the EU is:

$$\Delta Q_{EU} = Q_{EU}\,\Delta T\,\varepsilon_{EU} \qquad\qquad 1$$

Similarly, the change in ROW imports is

$$\Delta Q_{ROW} = Q_{ROW}\,\Delta T\,\varepsilon_{ROW-EU} \qquad\qquad 2$$

The new share of EU imports in total imports is then:

$$SHARE_{EU} = \frac{Q_{EU} + \Delta Q_{EU}}{Q_{EU} + \Delta Q_{EU} + Q_{ROW} + \Delta Q_{ROW}} \qquad\qquad 3$$

or

$$SHARE_{EU} = \frac{Q_{EU}\,(1 + \Delta T_{EU})}{Q_{EU}\,(1 + \Delta T\varepsilon_{EU}) + Q_{ROW}\,(1 + \Delta T\varepsilon_{ROW-EU})} \qquad\qquad 4$$

Equation 4 can be expressed as a function of the previous period's market share. Dividing the right-hand side by the numerator and manipulating the ratio of import quantities:

$$SHARE_{EU}{}^{t+1} = \frac{1}{1 + \left(\dfrac{1}{SHARE_{EU}{}^{t}} - 1\right)\dfrac{1 + \Delta T\varepsilon_{ROW-EU}}{1 + \Delta T\varepsilon_{EU}}} \qquad\qquad 5$$

The expression for the new weighted tariff becomes:

$$TARIFF_{NEW} = TARIFF_{EU}\,SHARE_{EU} + TARIFF_{ROW}\,(1 - SHARE_{EU}) \qquad 6$$

which is calculated for each sector.

The effective rate of protection is finally derived as follows:

$$ERP_i = \frac{TARIFF_{NEWi} - \sum_{j \neq i} TARIFF_{NEWj}\,a_j}{1 - \sum_{j \neq i} a_j} \qquad\qquad 7$$

where a_j is the input share of sector j in the production of good i taken from the 1994 input-output matrix for Egypt.

The data used to calculate ERPs have been adjusted to take into account the fact that extensive exemptions are granted to importers for imports of capital goods and certain intermediate inputs. The vector of nominal tariffs was adjusted downward for such goods by the proportion with which actual collected total tariff revenue falls short of 'predicted' tariff revenue, i.e. what would be collected in the absence of exemptions. Alcoholic beverages and tobacco products are excluded in the analysis given extremely high nominal rates of protection/taxation. The 1990 input-output table was used, adjusted to reflect 1994 aggregate output. Trade data for 1994 was obtained from the UN Comtrade database. Because no information is available on the magnitude of the implicit protection granted to services, the 'tariff equivalents' used to calculate the effective rates have been assumed, based on case studies and surveys. These have revealed that the costs for Egyptian businesses of services are substantially higher than in comparator countries (*see* also Chapter 11). For example, the Egyptian telephone company has 34 lines per employee as compared to 192 in high income countries. Restrictive entry and monopoly supply of certain port services results in handling costs per container in Alexandria that are almost triple those in Turkey (World Bank, 1995a, 1995b). Based on such information, a 15% tariff equivalent is assumed for service sectors (construction, communications, business services, transport and so forth). A 0% tariff equivalent is assumed for water, electricity and gas.

References

Corden, W. Max (1984), 'The normative theory of international trade', in R. Jones and P. Neary, (eds.), *Handbook of International Economics*, Vol. 1, Amsterdam, North Holland.

Hoekman, Bernard (1996), *Perspectives on Middle Eastern and North African Economics*, London, Macmillan, forthcoming.

Hoekman, Bernard and Michel Kostecki (1995), *The Political Economy of the World Trading System From GATT to WTO*, Oxford, Oxford University Press.

Konan, Denise and Keith Maskus (1996), 'A computable general equilibrium analysis of trade liberalization using the Egypt CGE-TL model', University of Hawaii, Mimeo.

Rutherford, Thomas, E.E. Rutstrom and David Tarr (1995), 'The free trade agreement between Tunisia and the European Union', The World Bank, Mimeo.

Subramanian, Arvind (1995), 'Effects of the Uruguay Round on Egypt', International Monetary Fund, Mimeo.

World Bank (1994), *Kingdom of Morocco-Republic of Tunisia. Export Growth: Determinants and Prospects*, Report No. 12947-MNA, World Bank, October.

___ (1995a), *Claiming the Future: Choosing Prosperity in the Middle East and North Africa*, Washington, DC, The World Bank.

___ (1995b), 'Egypt – country economic memorandum', World Bank, Mimeo. Washington DC.

___ (1996), World Development Report 1996, Washington, DC, World Bank.

Yeats, Alexander (1996), 'Export prospects of Middle Eastern countries', World Bank Policy Research Working Paper 1571.

Notes

1. The views expressed are personal and should not be attributed to the World Bank. We are grateful to Adel Bishai, Alan Deardorff, Simon Evenett, Ahmed Galal, Said El Naggar, Christian Petersen, Maurice Schiff, Bob Stern and Alan Winters for helpful comments and suggestions, and to Faten Hatab and Ying Lin for excellent research assistance.
2. For example, the fiscal deficit was 1.3% of GDP in 1995, down from 25% in 1987/88, inflation was around 6%, and foreign exchange reserves were $18 billion.
3. Financial Times Survey, 20 May 1996.
4. 'Strengthening the Mediterranean Policy of the European Union: Establishing a Euro–Mediterranean Partnership', Communication from the Commission to the Council and the Parliament, October 1994.
5. Trade data reported by EUROSTAT is either on a 6 or 8-digit level basis, making it impossible to relate exactly the tariff commitments (which use 7-digits) to publicly available trade statistics. However, in most cases, a concordance from the 7 to the 6-digit level was straightforward.
6. After lengthy negotiations, Morocco obtained improved access to EU markets for tomatoes, citrus, and cut flowers. For example, an additional 15,000 ton quota was given for tomatoes, of which 5,000 may be shipped in October and 10,000 during November–March. Preferential treatment ceases in April, when EU produce comes to market.
7. See Yeats (1996). Existing intra-regional trade is to some (unknown) extent driven by barter deals and a web of preferential, commodity-specific 'protocol trade' agreements. These involve preferential tariff rates on specific lists of goods of Arab origin. Some of the intra-regional trade may therefore consist of the 'wrong' goods, i.e. those in which countries do not have a comparative advantage.
8. Local content requirements are often 60%, i.e. to benefit from duty-free access to the EU, 60% of the value added must originate in either the EU or in the partner country. Alternatively, if a change in tariff heading criterion is used, the value-added equivalent may exceed 60%. See Hoekman and Kostecki (1995) for a summary discussion of origin rules.
9. The share of the service sector where commitments were made – even if not guaranteeing national treatment and market access also differed substantially. The EU scheduled 57% of its services; the Middle East and North African Members of the WTO only 16%.
10. One area of great importance for many countries in the region is cooperation on customs matters (Article 59). The aim of such cooperation is the simplification of procedures, the introduction of the EU's Single Administrative Document and linking EU and Tunisian transit systems. Active cooperation on these matters will be important for trade facilitation. Another issue that is important is standardization and conformity assessment. The longer run objective of the EMA is to conclude agreements for the mutual recognition of certification (Article 40).
11. However, Rutherford et al. (1995) conclude that the static impact is positive if account is taken of the reduction in administrative barriers through the improvement of the administration of regulatory regimes (e.g. customs; certification of product standards).
12. *See* the Appendix for more details on the calculation of ERPs used in this paper.
13. *See* the Appendix for a description of the methodology used.

8

A Computable General Equilibrium Analysis of Egyptian Trade Liberalization Scenarios

Denise Eby Konan
University of Hawaii

Keith E Maskus
University of Colorado

8.1   Introduction

The Egyptian government is considering the potential implications of various forms of further reforms in trade policies. Most immediately, Egypt and the European Union (EU) are engaged in bilateral discussions concerning some form of free-trade agreement (FTA) that would involve preferential trade liberalization. Because the discussions are ongoing, it is unclear at the time of writing what the terms of any agreement would be. At a minimum we would expect Egyptian tariff rates on merchandise imports from the EU to be reduced or eliminated over some period of time. For its part, the EU might be expected to provide free access to Egyptian manufactured exports (except perhaps in sensitive sectors, such as textiles and clothing) and greater access in agricultural commodities.

While impressive unilateral trade reforms have been undertaken since 1989, Egyptian trade performance continues to suffer from a variety of technical and administrative non-tariff impediments. Licensing requirements, inspection systems, customs procedures, and so on continue to act as a significant tax on Egyptian merchandise imports and, perhaps even more so, on merchandise exports. Export costs are further raised by inadequate financial and physical infrastructure. Bureaucratic constraints, such as the public monopoly in cargo shipping, through which exports of public-sector firms must be exported, are thought to be an important drag on exports.[1] Elimination or reduction of these administrative costs, which are just less transparent forms of non-tariff barriers, could promote efficiency and growth of Egyptian trade performance over the medium term, particularly in conjunction with further rationalization of the tariff structure. Accordingly, our analysis of trade liberalization simulates the impacts of tariff reform and reductions in administrative trade costs.

Subject to the usual caveats about data adequacy and parameter accuracy, we find that further non-discriminatory tariff reform and reduction of administrative costs would provide significant welfare gains for the economy. Bilateral liberalization with the EU would tend to reduce Egyptian welfare marginally from this point, though the impact depends on the form of market access the EU may eventually provide. Thus, trade-diversion effects would marginally outweigh trade-creation effects, though these losses could also be due to resource misallocation subject to distortionary taxes. However, our simulations indicate that if Egypt were to pursue an FTA alone, without prior reduction in administrative trade costs, it would enjoy small gains in overall welfare. Thus, the advisability of the FTA approach depends in part on what other policy options are adopted. Egypt could procure yet larger welfare benefits, according to our model, by expanding the scope of the FTA to include Middle East–North Africa (MENA) and the United States.

8.2   The simulation model

To study the intersectoral allocative effects of trade-policy reforms, along with the associated changes in economic welfare, a computable general-equilibrium (CGE) model of the Egyptian economy was constructed. The model was originally developed at the request of the World Bank. We assume Egypt is a small economy so that Egyptian policy changes do not significantly alter prices in other regions of the world. Four regions are modelled: the EU (including Turkey, reflecting its customs union agreement with the EU), the United States, MENA (including Israel) and the rest of the world (ROW).

Because Egypt's current tariff structure does not discriminate across sources of imports, tariffs are weighted across sub-sectors by their import shares. We assume that goods produced in Egypt and the other regions are differentiated. Thus, Egyptian export prices and import prices differ across regions. While the analysis is limited to trade policy scenarios, we do consider the impact on government finances. In Egypt, this concern is considerable because import duties constitute over 15% of tax revenues and over 10% of total current revenues (International Monetary Fund, 1994). We treat the government as operating under a fixed government deficit, wherein any change in tariff collections is compensated by a domestic tax change that makes the trade policy revenue neutral.

For each trade scenario analysed, we estimate the required increase in one of three taxes to make up tariff revenue losses. The first is the Goods and Services Tax (GST). The GST applies to final consumption and capital investment of domestic goods and imports, but does not apply to exports. The various GST rates are reported in Table 8.1 and range from 0% in food products, paper, petroleum refining and insurance to 25% for many luxury and investment goods. The standard tax rate is 10%. Exemptions and evasion of this tax are implicitly incorporated as tax rates are calibrated to total revenue collected in the benchmark year. A second tax is the corporate tax on operating surplus plus depreciation. This tax also varies across sectors and rates are again calibrated to benchmark year collected revenues. Finally, we construct an implicit lump-sum tax (which is non-distortionary) that transfers revenues from the representative agent to the government in order to maintain the initial government budget deficit.[2] Use of such a tax would provide the greatest welfare gains, or least welfare losses, in revenue-compensated trade liberalization and is included here in order to provide a framework for reference.

The impacts of liberalization on the nominal exchange rate, balance of payments, or monetary policy and conditions are not evaluated. Such analyses are infeasible within the context of CGE models, which focus strictly on the real economy and do not entertain monetary variables. However, in our model real exchange rates do adjust to maintain the benchmark-year current-account position. It is possible in this context to interpret the change in the exchange rate as the endogenous change in the real current account if the real exchange rate is fixed.

There are 38 sectors in the model producing outputs, each using production and non-production labour, capital, and intermediate inputs. The sectors include 3 in agriculture, 2 in mining and quarrying, 21 in manufacturing and 12 in services. They are listed in Table 8.1, along with acronyms for use in the simulation exercises. It is assumed that production exhibits constant returns to scale and firms operate in a perfectly competitive environment. We allow for free entry in each sector in long-run equilibrium. Intermediate inputs, as well as final goods, are differentiated by country of origin according to the Armington assumption. We assume a single household is representative of domestic consumers. The representative consumer receives income from primary factors (production labour, non-production labour, and capital), net transfers from the government and the current-account deficit. The consumer is also assumed to receive any net economic rents from the operation of non-tariff barriers to trade. Changes in aggregate consumption are used as a direct measure of the 'equivalent variation' of a policy change and measure welfare changes here.[3]

Sector-specific proportionate import and export costs are incorporated, which reflect administrative non-tariff barriers (NTBs) or 'red tape'. These costs, such as licensing fees, inspection delays, monopoly port charges, and difficulties due to inadequate transport facilities, are estimated to be a significant component of trade costs in Egypt (World Bank, 1995). These costs drive wedges between home and foreign prices. We assume that there are no resource-using rent-seeking costs in the economy, so that NTB revenues represent a pure transfer among domestic agents. We allocate these revenues to the representative agent.[4] When red-tape costs are removed, distortionary costs or deadweight losses are recovered to the benefit of the consumer.

An important feature of the model concerns the determination of balance of payments. We hold the current-account imbalance fixed at its benchmark level throughout the simulations. Foreign currencies are scaled so that the appropriate GDP deflator ('world' price index) is unity. Because the current account is in deficit, it represents an addition to the representative agent's income through exogenous capital inflows. To hold the deficit fixed requires a balancing item, which is accomplished by means of a change in the home 'real exchange rate.' This refers implicitly to a change in the home price index (generated by changes in price of home-produced goods) sufficient to sustain a constant current-account deficit measured at world prices.[5]

8.2.1   Data

The data for the model consists of a Social Accounting Matrix (SAM) and other parameters, such as elasticities of substitution and transformation, import and export trade flow shares by region, and tax and tariff rates.[6] We use the 1989/1990 Input–Output (IO) table for Egypt (CAPMAS, 1994b). As may be seen in Table 8.1, the most important Egyptian sectors in terms of shares of total output are vegetable food products, animal products, food processing, trade, transport, social services, construction and cotton textiles. There are some differences between these output shares and sectoral shares of total employment and capital. Services, for example, employ a disproportionately large amount of the work force. Columns (4) and (5) indicate the breakdown, for each sector, of employment into production and non-production labour types. We use this distinction as a preliminary effort to understand the impacts of trade liberalization on different skill classes of labour.

Table 8.2 presents data on trade shares by sector and region. We begin with import and export shares (of total trade) for each sector, using the trade data reported in the IO table itself, in columns (1) and (2). Despite

Table 8.1 Sectoral output and factor and tax rates (%)

Sector	Output (1)	Labour (2)	Capital (3)	Share of labour type		GS tax (6)	Capital tax (7)
				Production (4)	Non-production (5)		
Agriculture							
1. Vegetable products, food (VG1)	12.4	11.3	21.4	57.8	42.2	0.0	0.0
2. Vegetable products, non-food (VG2)	1.7	1.7	2.9	57.8	42.2	10.0	0.0
3. Animal products (ANI)	8.0	5.6	10.5	57.8	42.2	0.0	0.0
Mining and quarrying							
4. Crude petroleum and natural gas (OIL)	2.7	0.7	2.3	59.2	40.8	0.0	18.0
5. Other extractive industries (MIN)	0.9	0.5	2.0	42.0	58.0	10.0	18.0
Manufacturing							
6. Food processing (FOO)	7.7	2.8	4.3	68.5	31.5	0.0	18.0
7. Beverages (BEV)	0.6	0.3	0.3	58.5	41.5	10.0	18.0
8. Tobacco products (TOB)	1.9	0.4	0.7	76.2	23.8	10.0	18.0
9. Cotton ginning and pressing (TX1)	1.2	0.1	0.1	77.0	23.0	10.0	18.0
10. Cotton spinning and weaving (TX2)	5.2	4.9	3.0	71.8	28.2	10.0	18.0
11. Clothing: assembled and pieces (CLO)	1.4	1.5	1.1	84.6	15.4	10.0	18.0
12. Leather products, excluding shoes (LEA)	0.2	0.1	0.1	66.6	33.4	10.0	18.0
13. Shoes (SHO)	0.4	0.4	0.2	86.3	13.7	10.0	18.0
14. Wood and products, excluding furniture (WOO)	1.1	0.3	0.9	85.5	14.5	5.0	18.0
15. Furniture (FUR)	1.4	0.8	1.5	68.0	32.0	10.0	18.0
16. Paper and printing (PAP)	1.5	0.8	0.9	56.5	43.4	0.0	18.0
17. Chemicals and products (CHE)	3.1	1.7	1.6	34.3	65.7	5.0	18.0
18. Petroleum refining (PET)	2.7	0.8	3.2	49.0	51.0	0.0	18.0

Sector	Output (1)	Labour (2)	Capital (3)	Share of labour type		GS tax (6)	Capital tax (7)
				Production (4)	Non-production (5)		
19. Rubber, plastics and products (RPL)	0.8	0.4	0.4	68.6	31.4	10.0	18.0
20. Porcelain, china, pottery (POR)	0.3	0.2	0.2	71.0	29.0	10.0	18.0
21. Glass and products (GLA)	0.3	0.2	0.4	58.2	41.8	10.0	18.0
22. Mineral products, not included elsewhere (MPD)	1.7	1.0	1.8	66.0	34.0	5.0	18.0
23. Iron, steel, base metals (MET)	2.8	1.4	2.5	58.8	41.2	10.0	18.0
24. Machinery and appliances (MAC)	3.5	2.7	1.7	57.5	42.5	25.0	18.0
25. Transportation equipment (TRA)	1.0	0.9	0.5	62.5	37.5	25.0	18.0
26. Other manufacturing (OMF)	0.1	0.1	0.0	61.9	38.1	10.0	18.0
Services and other							
27. Electricity, gas and water (ELE)	1.7	2.4	0.8	33.0	67.0	25.0	23.0
28. Construction (CON)	5.5	5.0	4.3	55.5	44.5	10.0	23.0
29. Trade (TRD)	7.1	5.0	14.2	61.6	38.4	8.0	23.0
30. Restaurants, hotels (RES)	2.3	1.8	1.8	54.0	46.0	8.0	23.0
31. Transport and storage (TRN)	6.0	5.3	5.4	50.9	49.1	0.0	23.0
32. Communications (COM)	0.8	0.9	1.5	0.0	100.0	5.0	23.0
33. Financial establishments (FIN)	1.5	3.7	1.4	17.1	82.9	8.0	23.0
34. Insurance (INS)	0.3	0.6	0.2	13.0	87.0	0.0	23.0
35. Real estate, business services and housing services (HSG)	2.8	2.1	4.7	17.5	82.5	8.0	23.0
36. Social and community services (SER)	6.0	29.3	0.3	23.0	77.0	10.0	23.0
37. Recreational and cultural services (REC)	0.5	1.2	0.2	46.0	54.0	8.0	23.0
38. Personal services (PER)	0.9	1.4	0.7	30.3	69.7	10.0	23.0

Sources: CAPMAS (1990, 1994a), World Bank (1995).

Table 8.2 Trade shares by sector and region (%)

Sector	1990 Import (1)	1990 Export (2)	1994 Import shares				1994 Export shares			
			EU (3)	US (4)	MENA (5)	ROW (6)	EU (7)	US (8)	MENA (9)	ROW (10)
Agriculture										
1. VG1	13.3	2.6	11.7	47.9	2.3	38.2	27.0	1.5	64.4	7.1
2. VG2	0.0	0.1	37.0	16.5	1.8	44.7	49.3	13.4	16.1	21.3
3. ANI	0.8	0.3	82.7	0.0	10.4	6.8	35.2	2.3	53.3	9.3
Mining and quarrying										
4. OIL	1.2	18.5	52.0	7.0	25.4	15.5	30.6	4.6	21.3	43.4
5. MIN	2.0	0.2	17.7	14.8	3.5	64.0	56.8	9.2	22.7	11.3
Manufacturing										
6. FOO	15.1	1.3	40.3	10.6	2.7	46.3	20.1	4.5	51.4	23.9
7. BEV	0.0	0.0	41.7	16.3	39.3	2.6	1.2	0.0	91.3	7.5
8. TOB	1.0	0.0	27.0	27.4	2.7	42.9	0.4	0.7	95.9	3.0
9. TX1	0.5	4.2	36.9	0.3	0.9	61.9	33.7	0.2	1.6	64.5
10. TX2	2.4	10.3	33.4	7.1	3.8	55.7	72.4	10.9	7.6	9.1
11. CLO	0.0	1.2	12.4	0.9	19.1	67.6	34.7	49.1	8.6	7.6
12. LEA	0.0	0.1	25.7	0.9	13.8	59.6	48.8	1.5	31.0	18.7
13. SHO	0.0	0.0	16.0	2.9	12.0	69.0	20.5	1.9	60.7	16.9
14. WOO	5.0	0.1	39.8	1.4	0.5	58.4	1.5	0.1	92.0	6.4
15. FUR	0.0	0.5	57.0	34.7	2.3	6.1	14.9	10.6	60.9	13.7
16. PAP	3.3	0.9	46.8	17.1	3.0	33.1	1.6	0.8	94.5	3.0
17. CHE	10.8	1.8	62.6	12.2	8.4	16.8	31.3	3.5	39.5	25.7
18. PET	1.2	3.3	48.4	6.2	33.7	11.7	58.5	0.6	8.9	32.1
19. RPL	2.3	0.3	42.8	20.4	10.3	26.5	41.3	0.7	46.2	11.8
20. POR	0.4	0.1	47.4	7.8	11.5	33.3	42.2	1.5	32.5	23.8

their relatively large presence in production, vegetable foodstuffs and food processing are major import goods. So also are machinery and chemicals. On the export side, Egypt's trade flows are dominated by transport (because of the Suez Canal), oil, and textiles. Columns (3) to (6) provide import shares in 1994 for our four regions: the EU, the United States,

Sector	1990 Import (1)	1990 Export (2)	1994 Import shares				1994 Export shares			
			EU (3)	US (4)	MENA (5)	ROW (6)	EU (7)	US (8)	MENA (9)	ROW (10)
Manufacturing cont.										
21. GLA	0.5	0.1	63.3	5.3	3.8	27.6	9.3	5.5	62.9	22.2
22. MPD	0.4	0.0	61.6	3.8	4.1	30.5	4.8	2.0	82.1	11.1
23. MET	2.6	0.8	35.5	11.8	9.1	43.6	68.3	1.9	24.4	5.4
24. MAC	23.1	4.6	59.4	17.4	2.5	20.7	9.5	3.9	58.6	28.0
25. TRA	5.9	0.4	33.8	12.1	0.8	53.3	3.6	0.3	90.0	6.1
26. OMF	0.5	0.1	47.6	11.2	3.6	37.6	25.4	3.2	63.6	7.9
Services and other										
27. ELE	0.2	0.7	44.6	16.8	4.6	34.0	44.7	6.7	24.0	24.6
28. CON	0.2	0.8	44.6	16.8	4.6	34.0	44.7	6.7	24.0	24.6
29. TRD	0.3	5.6	44.6	16.8	4.6	34.0	44.7	6.7	24.0	24.6
30. RES	0.0	5.0	44.6	16.8	4.6	34.0	44.7	6.7	24.0	24.6
31. TRN	1.3	31.9	44.6	16.8	4.6	34.0	44.7	6.7	24.0	24.6
32. COM	0.1	0.4	44.6	16.8	4.6	34.0	44.7	6.7	24.0	24.6
33. FIN	1.1	0.0	44.6	16.8	4.6	34.0	44.7	6.7	24.0	24.6
34. INS	0.0	0.5	44.6	16.8	4.6	34.0	44.7	6.7	24.0	24.6
35. HSG	3.9	0.0	44.6	16.8	4.6	34.0	44.7	6.7	24.0	24.6
36. SER	0.1	0.2	44.6	16.8	4.6	34.0	44.7	6.7	24.0	24.6
37. REC	0.2	3.2	44.6	16.8	4.6	34.0	44.7	6.7	24.0	24.6
38. PER	0.0	0.0	44.6	16.8	4.6	34.0	44.7	6.7	24.0	24.6

Note: Regional trade shares in services are assumed to equal their respective shares in merchandise imports and exports.
Source: World Bank data and authors' concordance.

MENA, and ROW. The 1994 imports data is aggregated from the 8-digit Harmonized System (HS) classification into a consistent IO basis using a concordance developed by the authors. However, there is no data available on services trade or on its breakdown by region. Accordingly, we make the assumption that services trade is closely complementary to merchandise trade in terms of its sources. Therefore, regional shares of services trade are taken to be equal to each region's share in total imports or exports of merchandise. Egypt evidently exports far more services to MENA than it imports from that region, which is consistent with available evidence on net tourism and transport flows.

Egypt's merchandise trade structure is strongly diversified on a regional basis. For example, the EU's share of both Egyptian merchandise imports and exports is around 45%, while ROW provides 34% of imports and takes 25% of exports. The US is a significant supplier to Egyptian markets, while MENA serves as a major buyer of Egyptian exports. The importance of this observation is that Egypt's trade patterns are not as heavily focussed on the EU as are some other key North African countries, such as Morocco. As a result, the potential for trade diversion from a preferential trade agreement is more evident for Egypt.

The 1994 imports data also included information on 1994 tariff rates by 8-digit HS line. We aggregate these tariff rates to the IO basis by developing import weights consistent with the concordance. It should be noted that Egypt does not realize full revenue on its legal tariff rates because of various exemptions for duty-drawback provisions, investment incentives and performance requirements. We therefore scale the weighted legal tariff rates downward by approximately 20% in order to be consistent with total import duty collections in 1994.[7] The resulting tariff rates are reported in Table 8.3 and are the primary object of the Egyptian liberalization scenarios we analyse. We take the tariff rates on services to be zero.

As discussed earlier, it is claimed that Egypt places significant costs, in various forms of administrative 'red tape,' on importers and exporters. The World Bank (1995) has indicated that a conservative estimate of the cost impact on exports is 10%, which we incorporate as an NTB export-tax equivalent in merchandise. With little information on this score, we take 5% as the import-tax equivalent of red tape. It is difficult to develop quantitative measures of the price impacts on restrictions on services trade. There is little published information on this issue in Egypt, though conversations with Egyptian experts indicated that the service markets remain largely closed to foreign competition. We allow a conservative representation of this situation in the benchmark by imposing a 15% tax equivalent on prices of both exported and imported services.

To simulate potential trade reforms, the benchmark year (1990) was updated to 1994, in order to base the exercises on recent trade restrictions and taxes. In doing so, we impose tax neutrality by proportionately scaling a revenue-replacement instrument. For example, if the GST is the replacement tax then GST rates are scaled up or down to be consistent with revenue changes from all taxes and tariffs. For example, if the set of reforms implemented by 1994 implied a movement of resources into agri-

Table 8.3   Import-weighted tariff rates (scales for collections in 1994) and assumed NTB rates

Sector	Scaled tariff rate	NTB tariff equivalent	NTB export tax equivalent
Agriculture			
1. VG1	2.5	5.0	10.0
2. VG2	6.7	5.0	10.0
3. ANI	4.4	5.0	10.0
Mining and quarrying			
4. OIL	8.2	5.0	10.0
5. MIN	7.0	5.0	10.0
Manufacturing			
6. FOO	6.8	5.0	10.0
7. BEV	953.2	5.0	10.0
8. TOB	65.5	5.0	10.0
9. TX1	17.3	5.0	10.0
10. TX2	23.3	5.0	10.0
11. CLO	53.7	5.0	10.0
12. LEA	34.8	5.0	10.0
13. SHO	51.8	5.0	10.0
14. WOO	8.1	5.0	10.0
15. FUR	46.9	5.0	10.0
16. PAP	13.3	5.0	10.0
17. CHE	8.9	5.0	10.0
18. PET	7.1	5.0	10.0
19. RPL	15.6	5.0	10.0
20. POR	43.5	5.0	10.0
21. GLA	29.6	5.0	10.0
22. MPD	18.1	5.0	10.0
23. MET	17.2	5.0	10.0
24. MAC	17.9	5.0	10.0
25. TRA	41.2	5.0	10.0
26. OMF	19.3	5.0	10.0
Services and other			
27–38. (all)	0.0	15.0	15.0

Sources: Egyptian Customs Office, World Bank Data and authors' assumptions.

culture, Egypt would have experienced a loss in tax revenue from the capital tax, which does not place a levy on agriculture. The GST rates would be raised to make up for this shortfall.

We assume that the 1990 SAM adequately represents production technologies and preferences for 1994. Moreover, because our model is static we do not consider any changes in the economy outside fiscal policy changes between 1990 and 1994 in performing the updating. Accordingly, the updated SAM should not be expected to match actual 1994 figures because numerous other events happened over that period, including labour force growth and reform in public enterprises. In brief, we do not attempt to replicate the 1994 economy, rather we compare our liberalization scenarios to the updated equilibrium structure, given the 1994 tax system, holding constant other variables outside the model.

8.3   Simulation exercises and results

The set of simulation exercises we undertake is as follows.[8]

1. TRDREF involves removing the various NTB costs associated with 'red tape,' as discussed earlier. In the model, this is equivalent to a 5% cut in tariffs on merchandise imports, a 10% cut in export taxes, and a 15% cut in restrictions on international services transactions. Because this 'grease the wheels' scenario removes all restrictions on services trade, it may be optimistic as to Egypt's ability or willingness to reduce administrative trade costs. In most ensuing scenarios Egypt is assumed to undertake this NTB reform first and then to add trade liberalization. Note that this means the trade liberalization cases involve cutting average tariffs from a fairly low basis, given the zero tariff on services. However, we also consider trade liberalization experiments without this prior cut in red tape.
2. TARREF is a unilateral tariff reform by Egypt, setting a uniform tariff rate of 10% on all merchandise imports, though retaining the existing tariffs on beverage imports. The exception for beverages reflects Egypt's social-policy preference for maintaining rigorous barriers against imported alcoholic beverages. This treatment is maintained throughout all scenarios.
3. EUPA is a situation in which Egypt eliminates all tariffs on EU products. The EU responds by providing more liberal access to domestic markets that provides an 8% price increase for Egyptian agricultural, clothing, and textile exports to the EU and a 1% increase in all other Egyptian export prices in the EU. The former price assumption could well be conservative, given the large price wedges between EU domestic and international prices in agricultural goods and apparel. The latter price increase is meant to capture the possibility of the EU providing benefits in terms of accepting Egyptian inspection practices, recognizing Egyptian standards of production, and the like. It is likely that such a policy would procure significantly larger benefits for Egyptian exporters in the long run.[9]
4. FTAREF involves a major expansion of the EU partnership agreement. It includes reciprocal liberalization by Egypt, on the one hand, and the EU, the United States and MENA on the other hand. Here we raise all Egyptian export prices to the United States and MENA by 1%, along with those to the EU (there is no special treatment of agri-

cultural and apparel). At the same time, we simulate a tariff reform in which Egypt imposes a common 10% tariff on all merchandise imports from ROW.
5. LIBALL involves unilateral tariff elimination by Egypt against all trading partners. Here, however, there is no increase in export prices simulated. Thus, this case is meant to capture a unilateral movement by Egypt to free trade, with no reciprocal trade concessions from abroad.

It is possible to consider varying degrees of intersectoral capital mobility and different types of tax reform in conjunction with these scenarios (see Konan and Maskus, 1996). To conserve space here, however, we report the results of only two central cases. First, we undertake the TRDREF-inclusive simulations allowing for perfectly mobile capital, allowing for calculations of long-run effects of liberalization, and without prior tax reform.[10] Second, we repeat this analysis without reforming red-tape costs. In each case, we allow for the three tax-replacement rules discussed earlier.

We present calculations for changes in the following variables (again, all changes are relative to the 1994 updated benchmark):[11]

1. WELFARE = percentage change in welfare (equivalent variation as a percentage of 1994 benchmark GDP).
2. ERATE = percentage change in the real exchange rate (the shadow price of foreign currency) required to maintain a constant real current account imbalance; alternatively it is the percentage change in the real current-account deficit required to maintain a fixed real exchange rate.
3. TAU_C; TAU_K; TAU_X = percentage change in the replacement tax rates (consumption, capital), or level (lump-sum).
4. AVGTAR = the level of the average tariff rate, defined as total tariff revenue collections divided by manufactured imports.
5. TRCHG = absolute change in tariff revenues in billions of real Egyptian pounds.
6. PLWAGE = percentage change in the real wage of production workers.
7. NLWAGE = percentage change in the real wage of non-production workers.
8. KPRICE = percentage change in the real rental rate on mobile capital.
9. PLADJ = percentage of the production labour workforce that must change jobs (production labour force turnover).
10. NLADJ = percentage of the non-production labour workforce that must change jobs (non-production labour force turnover).
11. KADJ = percentage of the capital stock that moves among sectors (capital stock turnover).
12. XQUAN = percentage change in the aggregate quantity of exports.
13. MQUAN = percentage change in the aggregate quantity of imports.

Table 8.4 reports the results of the simulation involving perfectly mobile capital and no prior tax reform. Elimination of red-tape costs on exports and imports, which we call TRDREF, results in a rise in welfare of from 1.785% of GDP to 1.932% of GDP. It also causes a real appreciation of the exchange rate of from 6.339% to 6.865% and generates an average tariff rate of perhaps 12.3% and raises real tariff revenue from LE 411 million to LE 426 million. This increase in tariff revenue comes about from the higher quantities of trade that result. In turn, the model estimates that the consumption tax could be lowered by 17.7%, the capital tax by 5.2%, and the level of the lump-sum transfer by LE 2.367 billion. TRDREF also results in greater efficiency in the economy, raising all three factor prices by from 4.5% to 6.1%, while around 2.7% of the production labour force changes jobs, 2.3% of the non-production labour force changes jobs, and 3.9% of the capital stock moves in the long run. The quantity of exports is simulated to increase in the long run by nearly 30%, with real imports rising by over 22%. These trade impacts reflect the substantial improvement in economic efficiency that would result from removal of these NTB costs imposed on international business.

At this point, we must remind the reader that TRDREF is maintained throughout the other trade liberalization experiments in Table 8.4. Thus, the impacts of other scenarios listed here include those of TRDREF. The marginal impacts of the other cases are the difference between the results listed for them and those for TRDREF.

In this light, consider the column labelled, 'TARREF,' which refers to the impacts of setting a uniform 10% tariff level on merchandise imports (except for beverages) in addition to removing the red-tape NTBs. With the consumption-tax replacement, Egyptian welfare gains rise to 2.155%, or an additional 0.223%, due to the tariff reform. There is a further appreciation of the real exchange rate (or reduction of the real current-account deficit), while there is an aggregate tariff revenue loss of LE 153 million (compared to the 1994 benchmark), implying that, relative to TRDREF, the tariff reform reduces tariff revenue by LE 574 million (421–(–153)). The decline in revenue requires a rise in the GST rates by 8.619% relative to the 1994 benchmark. Obviously, the average tariff rate in this case is 10%. There is a slight reduction in all of the factor-price increases, while intersectoral factor adjustments are somewhat higher. However, labour wages rise in comparison with TRDREF when a capital tax rule is used, while the capital price falls due to the implied reduction in demand for capital. When a lump-sum tax rule is employed all three factors enjoy a further rise in price because of the greater economic efficiency in this solution. In all simulations, the combination of scenarios TRDREF and TARREF provide more welfare benefits than does an association agreement with the EU, and nearly as

Table 8.4 Impacts of trade liberalization with prior trade reform

Consumption Tax replacement

	TRDREF	TARREF	EUPA	FTAREF	LIBALL
WELFARE	1.932	2.155	1.767	2.196	2.445
ERATE	−6.339	−7.248	−6.971	−7.169	−7.006
TAU_C	−17.682	8.619	64.422	85.223	115.045
AVGTAR	12.448	10.001	4.350	2.590	0.001
TRCHG	0.421	−0.153	−1.518	−1.972	−2.669
PLWAGE	5.177	4.669	4.845	4.937	5.201
NLWAGE	6.056	5.934	6.496	6.899	7.506
KPRICE	5.917	5.835	5.883	6.124	6.434
PLADJ	2.688	3.195	3.931	4.448	5.001
NLADJ	2.335	2.664	3.309	3.643	4.054
KADJ	3.851	4.071	4.973	5.325	5.944
XQUAN	29.801	31.663	48.262	46.742	46.739
MQUAN	22.229	23.618	29.501	31.411	34.863

Capital Tax replacement

	TRDREF	TARREF	EUPA	FTAREF	LIBALL
WELFARE	1.785	2.011	1.485	1.874	2.070
ERATE	−6.865	−6.857	−4.536	−3.993	−2.757
TAU_K	−5.211	12.914	52.178	66.939	87.992
AVGTAR	12.240	10.001	4.342	2.591	0.001
TRCHG	0.426	−0.130	−1.539	−1.998	−2.697
PLWAGE	4.541	4.942	6.917	7.696	8.929
NLWAGE	5.519	6.228	8.545	9.604	11.152
KPRICE	6.066	5.132	3.447	3.045	2.458
PLADJ	2.740	3.212	3.853	4.308	4.782
NLADJ	2.382	2.653	3.211	3.500	3.843
KADJ	4.065	3.955	4.227	4.329	4.594
XQUAN	29.957	30.613	44.622	42.512	41.366
MQUAN	22.523	23.016	27.307	28.580	31.100

Lump-sum replacement

	TRDREF	TARREF	EUPA	FTAREF	LIBALL
WELFARE	1.907	2.221	1.949	2.428	2.746
ERATE	−6.701	−7.070	−5.653	−5.437	−4.678
LUMP	−2.367	−1.772	−0.599	−0.168	0.440
AVGTAR	12.330	10.001	4.345	2.590	0.001
TRCHG	0.411	−0.133	−1.494	−1.946	−2.644
PLWAGE	4.743	4.917	6.506	7.117	8.122
NLWAGE	5.659	6.173	8.108	9.016	10.351
KPRICE	5.504	6.016	7.299	7.999	8.965
PLADJ	2.686	3.199	3.948	4.451	4.996
NLADJ	2.344	2.661	3.310	3.642	4.050
KADJ	3.817	4.052	5.029	5.392	6.046
XQUAN	29.801	31.632	48.576	47.165	47.301
MQUAN	22.211	23.576	29.709	31.690	35.254

many benefits as a major FTA (involving the EU, the United States and MENA) or full trade liberalization. The Egyptian government might be well advised, therefore, to devote efforts to improving the efficiency of the trading system itself.

Consider now EUPA, the Egyptian association agreement with the European Union. The scenario involves elimination of Egyptian tariffs on EU commodities in return for greater access in the EU, captured by higher prices for Egyptian goods in the European market. In conjunction with TRDREF (the elimination of NTB red-tape costs on trade), this scenario is simulated to raise Egyptian welfare by 1.767% in the case of replacement of tariff revenues by the consumption tax. In fact, this result should be interpreted to mean that the agreement with the EU would reduce Egyptian welfare by 0.165% (1.932–1.767) in relation to solely undertaking TRDREF. Of course, this does not necessarily mean that the agreement would lower welfare in the absence of TRDREF, because of the second-best nature of this calculation, as we show in Table 8.5. Note that the average tariff rate becomes 4.35% and there is a tariff revenue loss of LE 1.518 billion, necessitating a rise in GST rates by 64.4%. With capital-tax replacement, the loss in welfare compared to TRDREF is 0.3%, with a rise in the distortionary corporate tax rates by 52.2%. However, when a lump-sum replacement rule is incorporated, scenario EUPA actually raises Egyptian welfare in relation to TRDREF by 0.042%. The implied tariff revenue loss is slightly smaller in this case than in the other two tax rules, while the transfer from the representative agent, relative to TRDREF, is LE 1.768 billion (–0.599–(–2.367)).

An interesting difference emerges between the various tax-replacement cases with respect to the real exchange rate. In scenario EUPA, and in all subsequent cases of trade liberalization, the real exchange rate is simulated to appreciate even more than it does under TRDREF when revenues are replaced with higher consumption taxes. In EUPA, for example, the exchange rate appreciates by 0.632% (6.999 – 6.339) beyond the change in TRDREF, while full liberalization (LIBALL) causes a marginal appreciation of 0.667% (though the total appreciation is 7.006%). Again, it is possible to interpret these results equivalently as percentage reductions in the current-account deficit at a fixed real exchange rate. However, in the case of capital-tax replacement, EUPA induces a real depreciation of the exchange rate by 2.329% relative to TRDREF, and LIBALL induces a marginal depreciation of 4.108%. With lump-sum replacement the implied depreciation amounts are 1.048% and 2.023%, respectively. The alternative view would be of an increase in the real current-account deficit. The difference in these cases is that the consumption tax operates on imports and not exports, implying that as GST rates rise there is a further reduction in import demand relative to export supply, placing pressure on the real exchange rate to appreciate. This situation does not emerge in the other two tax regimes.

With consumption tax replacement, the partnership agreement is simulated to reduce production labour real wages and real capital prices, while raising non-production labour real wages, in comparison with TRDREF. Factor-price effects are qualitatively different in the other cases. With the capital tax replacing tariff revenues, an agreement with the EU would raise wages of both labour types considerably, while reducing returns to capital. On the other hand, the lump-sum transfer is least distortionary and operating under this rule would actually raise real returns to all three factors in the event of an association agreement.

The possibility of lower Egyptian welfare, relative to that from trade reform, coming about from an association agreement with the EU bears explanation. There are two potential sources of these welfare losses. First, is that the tax system is distorted across sectors; both the GST and the corporate tax vary across industries due to various exemptions and different legislated rates. Trade liberalization in the face of such intersectoral distortions clearly runs the risk of moving economic resources into sectors that would not expand under greater competition except for the fact that they are lightly taxed. This possibility, which is confirmed by smaller welfare losses in simulation analysis when there is limited prior tax reform (Konan and Maskus, 1996), is a clear example of the so-called, 'Economics of the Second-Best.'

A second, and probably more important, source of potential welfare loss is familiar trade diversion effects in the case of an association agreement with the EU. Recall that Egypt has a highly diversified trade structure, with the EU accounting for less than 50% of Egyptian merchandise exports and imports. Accordingly, the potential for costly trade diversion is more in evidence here than, say, for Morocco in its agreement with the EU or for Mexico in its agreement with the United States. Moreover, our treatment of services trade, which is important in the Egyptian trade structure, may be contributing to this result. For one thing, we have assigned service trade shares equal to merchandise trade shares by region, which may not be accurate. If, instead, Egypt's services trade were 100% with the EU, welfare gains from an association agreement would be considerably more likely. For another, we treat the full 15% import restriction in services in the benchmark as an administrative NTB that is removed under TRDREF. As a result, an agreement with the EU has no impact in the model on services 'tariffs', which means that the aggregate tariff level that Egypt cuts in the liberalization scenarios begins at a fairly low level. If, instead, we were to consider 10% of the 15% trade restrictions to be 'tariffs' on services, then prior trade reform would not eliminate the price wedges on services trade. In this case, liberalization with the EU would involve removing 10% tariffs on services against the EU as well as merchandise tariffs. This case would lead to greater potential for trade creation and welfare gains.

The final two columns of Table 8.4 refer to broader Egyptian trade liberalization, first an FTA with the EU, the United States and MENA, and reforming tariffs against ROW, and second a full elimination of tariffs. Scenario FTAREF is sufficient to procure net welfare gains for Egypt under any tax replacement rule, and these gains rise further with additional liberalization in LIBALL. Again, the welfare gains are largest in the case of the lump-sum transfer. For example, scenario FTAREF provides a welfare gain of 2.428% in conjunction with TRDREF (a marginal gain of 0.521%). With lump-sum taxes the increases in real factor prices are largest as well. While the lump-sum tax is not a viable policy option in Egypt, this indication of greater benefits from trade liberalization in the presence of an efficient tax system should be viewed as an argument in favour of minimizing inefficiencies in the economy.

The model also calculates sectoral impacts of our scenarios, including output, imports and exports (in total and by region), and employment changes. Sectoral results are provided in the broader analysis (Konan and Maskus, 1996).[12] While it is difficult to characterize these impacts in a few statements, because they vary considerably with different structural variables, it seems that Egyptian trade liberalization would favour output expansion in the service sectors, especially transport and community and personal services. These services include the Suez Canal and tourism, which would be favoured by closer integration with the world economy. The latter two service sectors also include much of the public employment in the economy. Output would tend to fall in agriculture and many manufacturing sectors, while it would rise considerably in crude petroleum and natural gas. Manufacturing sectors that would see output increase include clothing, petroleum refining and other manufacturing. We should note that reforming the NTB costs on trade (TRDREF) tends to raise output quantities in numerous manufacturing sectors with service sectors declining. Again, such a reform bears considerable promise for raising the efficiency of the Egyptian economy.

Our discussion of the results so far indicated that Egypt would procure a sizeable gain in efficiency and welfare from simply reducing its administrative NTBs on imports and exports. Having made such a trade reform, the calculations suggested that an association agreement with the EU might reduce Egyptian welfare slightly from that point. An alternative view, of course, is that Egypt would choose not to reform its trade practices in this way prior to undertaking an association agreement. In this context, it is not necessarily the case that an FTA alone would reduce

Egyptian welfare because resource flows and price effects, starting from a basis of no trade reform, could clearly be different from the marginal resource flows and price effects starting from a basis of prior trade reform.

To investigate this case, we calculate the various impacts of our trade liberalization scenarios without first undertaking TRDREF. The results are presented in Table 8.5. It appears that the simple tariff reform scenario would raise welfare by about 0.3% of GDP and appreciate the real exchange rate (or reduce the real current-account deficit) by around 1.0% when the GST is used to replace lost tariff revenues. Note that the consumption tax rate would have to rise by 26.4%. The impacts on trade quantities are fairly small. Of more interest here are the EUPA simulations, which suggest that an agreement with the EU would actually raise Egyptian welfare slightly, by 0.2%, in contrast to the earlier finding of a welfare decline.[13] The real exchange rate would appreciate by 0.59%, while the GST rate would need to be raised by 76% as real tariff revenues would decline by LE 1.7 billion. This form of agreement would reduce production labour wages by 0.3%, raise non-production labour wages by 0.29%, and have virtually no impact on capital rents. Export quantity would rise by 15.9% and import quantity by 6.0%. Some of these results depend on the form of tax replacement, as may be seen. For example, if the capital tax were used, the real exchange rate would depreciate (or the real current-account deficit would rise), each labour group would receive a higher real wage and trade quantities would expand by less. In fact, overall welfare would decline in scenario EUPA. Again, this finding points out the importance of judiciously selecting the appropriate offsetting fiscal instrument. Were a lump-sum replacement instrument available, EUPA would provide a doubling of the welfare gain from the consumption tax and all factor prices would rise.

The remaining liberalization scenarios provide a consistent ranking. Establishing FTAREF could raise Egyptian welfare by nearly 1%. The largest welfare gains are to be had from full unilateral liberalization, denoted as LIBALL.

To summarize the results of this analysis, it is evident that a partnership agreement with the EU would provide some scope for welfare gains on its own, without the necessity for undertaking a prior trade reform. This is a significant finding from the standpoint of policymaking, as it may be politically difficult to engineer a decline in the administrative red tape limiting trade growth that was the subject of TRDREF. Nonetheless, the larger overall welfare gains from prior trade reform still point in that direction as a sensible policy objective. It is conceivable that some mixture of more-limited trade reforms and an EU association agreement could generate yet higher gains than those simulated here.

Table 8.5 Impacts of trade liberalization without prior trade reform

Consumption Tax replacement

	TARREF	EUPA	FTAREF	LIBALL
WELFARE	0.287	0.206	0.696	1.804
ERATE	−0.970	−0.570	−0.805	−0.628
TAU_C	26.380	75.989	96.049	123.183
AVGTAR	10.001	4.460	2.602	0.001
TRCHG	−0.531	−1.668	−2.075	−2.670
PLWAGE	−0.521	−0.299	−0.282	−0.045
NLWAGE	−0.088	0.286	0.635	1.145
KPRICE	−0.029	0.004	0.234	0.494
PLADJ	0.994	1.142	1.709	2.109
NLADJ	0.639	0.856	1.218	1.561
KADJ	0.872	0.997	1.424	1.902
XQUAN	1.854	15.949	14.051	14.195
MQUAN	1.383	6.030	7.740	10.588

Capital Tax replacement

	TARREF	EUPA	FTAREF	LIBALL
WELFARE	0.226	−0.058	0.353	0.637
ERATE	0.037	2.450	3.008	4.276
TAU_K	20.180	58.922	74.815	96.341
AVGTAR	10.001	4.454	2.602	0.001
TRCHG	−0.522	−1.692	−2.103	−2.697
PLWAGE	0.310	2.041	2.671	3.736
NLWAGE	0.697	2.550	3.491	4.799
KPRICE	−0.394	−2.556	−2.992	−3.617
PLADJ	0.896	1.140	1.524	1.951
NLADJ	0.564	0.755	1.048	1.324
KADJ	1.046	1.333	1.843	2.192
XQUAN	0.846	12.851	10.423	9.609
MQUAN	0.636	4.006	5.162	7.224

Lump-sum replacement

	TARREF	EUPA	FTAREF	LIBALL
WELFARE	0.371	0.408	0.949	1.407
ERATE	−0.398	1.086	1.277	2.035
LUMP	−1.413	−0.364	0.055	0.614
AVGTAR	10.001	4.457	2.602	0.001
TRCHG	−0.510	−1.644	−2.049	−2.644
PLWAGE	0.127	1.550	2.045	2.928
NLWAGE	0.522	2.053	2.866	4.007
KPRICE	0.526	1.584	2.228	3.046
PLADJ	0.897	1.079	1.547	2.014
NLADJ	0.579	0.826	1.172	1.512
KADJ	0.757	0.994	1.363	1.931
XQUAN	1.868	16.230	14.422	14.679
MQUAN	1.393	6.228	8.002	10.940

8.4 Concluding remarks

Our main findings are as follows.

1. Significant welfare gains appear to be available from reducing or eliminating the NTB administrative costs on trade, or what we have called 'red-tape costs'. Further, Egypt would benefit from reform of its tariff structure on a non-discriminatory basis, selecting a low and uniform tariff rate across sectors. Such trade and tariff reform could combine to raise Egyptian welfare by as much as 2.2% of GDP. The extent of such gains depends on the tax instrument used to replace lost tariff revenues.
2. Beyond that point, the results present a useful lesson in the economics of the second-best. Feasible forms of an association agreement with the EU could worsen Egyptian welfare slightly (perhaps by 0.2%) in relation to significant trade reform. This possibility comes about in our calculations due to trade diversion and the potential for further misallocation of resources associated with intersectoral distortions in tariffs and consumption and capital taxes.
3. However, taken on its own, an association agreement bears potential to raise Egyptian welfare to a fairly small degree, perhaps up to 0.2% to 0.3% of GDP in real terms. Over time, this bonus would accumulate to a worthwhile contribution to economic growth.
4. The broader is the trade liberalization, the more likely are significant welfare gains. At the extreme, full unilateral trade liberalization could raise Egyptian well-being by nearly 3% of GDP.
5. Because trade reform enhances Egyptian efficiency, we often find that all factor prices increase in real terms. With respect to labour, it appears that non-production labourers enjoy a relatively greater rise in real income than do production labourers. This may seem surprising, but given the dominance of the service sectors (especially public employment) in Egyptian employment, non-production labour is the most abundant factor.
6. Sectoral impacts of trade liberalization tend to favour output and employment expansion in service sectors relative to manufacturing sectors. However, reduction of NTB trade costs expand trade, output, and employment in the merchandise industries.

References

CAPMAS (1990), 'Employment, wages, and working hours report, 1990', October.
___ (1994a), 'Egypt: consolidated accounts, 1989–90', May.
___ (1994b), 'Egypt: input-output tables 1989–90', June.

International Monetary Fund (1994), *Government Finance Statistics Yearbook.*

Konan, D. and K. Maskus (1996), 'A computable general equilibrium analysis of scenarios for trade liberalization using the Egypt CGE-TL model', The World Bank, Mimeo.

Harrison, G.W., R. Jones, L. Kimbell, Jr. and R. Nigle (1993), 'How robust is applied general equilibrium modelling?', *Journal of Policy Modelling*, 15(1) February, 99–115.

Lofgren, H. (1994), 'Elasticity survey', Institute for Food Policy Research, Mimeo.

Rutherford, T., E.E. Rutstrom, and D. Tarr (1993), 'Morocco's free trade agreement with the European Community', The World Bank, Policy Research Working Paper WPS 1173, September.

World Bank (1995), 'Egypt: Into the Next Century: Volume I, Macroeconomic Framework.'

Notes

We are grateful to Nader Majd, Christian Petersen, Thomas Rutherford, David Tarr and Alan Winters for helpful comments.

1. Interview with Dr Heba Handoussa, Managing Director, Economic Research Forum, Cairo, 26 March 1995. *See also* Chapter 8 by Hoekman and Djankov and Chapter 11 by Mohieldin.
2. There are other taxes in Egypt, of course. Most significant in terms of revenue is the payroll tax for social-security contributions. We do not model this tax as a replacement instrument because the government does not propose to use it for such purposes; rather we implicitly hold its structure constant, as we do for other taxes.
3. The formal equations of the model may be found in Konan and Maskus (1996).
4. It could well be argued that rent-seeking is significant in Egypt, in which case there would be additional efficiency losses in the economy. In the absence of information to this effect, we ignore this possibility in order to be conservative about welfare gains from reducing NTBs. Further, it may well be that the recipients of these NTB rents are different (and in a higher income class) than those who pay them. Thus, their elimination could improve income distribution. Again, we ignore this complication.
5. A more accurate interpretation is that the real exchange rate is the shadow price of foreign exchange (a 'commodity') required to maintain a constant current-account imbalance. A rise in the real exchange rate is consistent with a depreciation of home currency, in that the per-unit price of foreign exchange rises. An alternative interpretation of the international balancing item comes if we hold the real exchange rate fixed and allow the current-account imbalance to vary at constant international prices. Thus, we can imagine an implicit shift in the real current account brought about by fixing the real exchange rate relative to the numeraire price index. In this context, a simulated percentage depreciation of the real exchange rate would correspond one-for-one with a percentage increase in the current-account deficit.
6. The benchmark values of trade elasticities are the central cases in Rutherford et al. (1993) and are consistent with the ranges reported in Lofgren (1994). The substitution elasticity between domestic and imported consumption is 2.0, while the Armington substitution elasticity between regional imports is 5.0. The transformation elasticity between domestic and exported output is 5.0, while the transformation elasticity between regional exports is 8.0. The labour-capital substitution varies across sectors, as taken from Harrison et al. (1993). Labour-labour substitution is set at 0.50 to be conservative in this parameter. Given the substantial uncertainty about these parameters, we perform systematic sensitivity analysis with the various trade elasticities, as reported briefly below.

7. The scaling factors differ somewhat by industry because we kept them proportional to a similar scaling in the benchmark year. It is interesting to note that the tariff reform in the early 1990s appears to have markedly increased the revenue yield from Egypt's tariff system, because the prior scaling factors had averaged around 40%. Thus, Egypt appears to have tightened its exemptions system successfully. In fact, this situation resulted in higher applied (scaled) tariff rates in 1994 than in 1990 for some sectors.
8. Further liberalization scenarios are analysed in Konan and Maskus (1996).
9. This scenario is the most generous we entertain as regards potential market access in the EU. Less generous EU offers result in smaller welfare gains (or larger welfare losses) in our model.
10. While there are interesting exceptions, as a general rule allowing for immobile capital in resource-intensive sectors (an intermediate-run scenario) generates welfare gains of perhaps 65% of long-run gains and allowing no capital mobility (a short-run scenario) generates welfare gains of around 40% of long-run gains. Prior reform of the capital tax results in slightly larger welfare gains, while prior reform of the GST results in marked additional gains. Thus, it is important to note that the prospective efficiency gains from trade liberalization depend strongly on the tax system.
11. In the broader analysis we also calculate impacts on relative adjustment costs and real trade values, along with sectoral effects.
12. We also perform extensive sensitivity analysis on the trade elasticities, which indicates little qualitative change in any interpretations listed here.
13. In these cases the association agreements do not build on the tariff reform exercise, so all results may be read as changes from the benchmark scenario.

9

The Egypt–European Union Partnership Agreement and the Egyptian Pharmaceutical Sector [1]

Arvind Subramanian
International Monetary Fund

Mostafa Abd-El-Latif
Egyptian Center for Economic Studies

9.1 Introduction

As part of its efforts to integrate with the world economy, Egypt has undertaken to negotiate a free trade agreement (FTA) with the European Union (EU). This initiative follows close on the heels of the completion of the Uruguay Round and the creation of the World Trade Organization (WTO). At the same time, the Egyptian economy is poised to embark upon serious structural reforms, including privatization, deregulation, and reduction of general trade barriers. This chapter seeks to examine the potential impact of these developments on the pharmaceutical sector in Egypt, focusing on, but not restricted to, the Trade-Related Aspects of Intellectual Property Rights (TRIPs) and EU agreements. In view of the EU agreement's pre-nascent state, and in so far as it is not a *fait accompli*, it seeks to draw certain normative conclusions about what can be done in the agreement to maximize the benefits for the sector. More importantly, broader policy conclusions for Egypt are also drawn.

It is essential to clarify at the outset that the EU agreement *per se* will have limited incremental impact. The pharmaceutical sector is affected by international agreements of this ilk in two possible ways. First, there is the competitive impact that will result from the progressive elimination by Egypt of its trade, especially tariff, barriers. In the case of Egypt, tariff barriers in the pharmaceutical sector are very low, and the industry is already exposed to international competition from European and non-European sources of supply.[2] Further, Egyptian exports of pharmaceutical products to the EU already benefit from duty-free access under existing arrangements, and hence the proposed agreement will add nothing by way of additional access.

The second and more important impact will emanate from the changes to Egypt's legal regime governing patent protection. However, here too the causation for change should be assigned not to the EU agreement, but to its multilateral forebear – the WTO Agreement on TRIPs. The FTA with the EU will entail relatively few (additional) changes to Egypt's intellectual property regime. To understand the impact on Egypt's pharmaceutical sector, it is to the TRIPs agreement that we should turn.

This paper is organized as follows. Section 9.2 describes the main provisions of the TRIPs agreement that will affect the Egyptian pharmaceutical sector. Section 9.3 outlines the main theoretical arguments related to patent protection, particularly how it affects small developing countries such as Egypt. Section 9. 4 describes the structure of the Egyptian pharmaceutical industry. Against this background, Section 9.5 assesses the short run, static impact on Egyptian industry, while Section 9.6 assesses the long run or dynamic impact. Section 9.7 briefly looks at what the EU agreement will add to TRIPs by way of additional obligations for Egypt. Section 9.8 examines various options facing policy makers with regard to the pharmaceutical sector and the options facing the industry. Section 9.9 concludes.

9.2 Changes in the legal regime as a result of TRIPs[3]

The TRIPs agreement will have the following far-reaching implications for the legal regime governing the Egyptian pharmaceutical sector.

General obligations

The most important general obligation under the TRIPs agreement is national treatment, which requires all members to treat nationals of other countries no less favourably than their own nationals on all intellectual property (IP) matter standards, enforcement, and acquisition, subject to certain exceptions. However, this obligation is not likely to require legislative changes, as most countries, including Egypt, already grant national treatment in their domestic laws.[4]

Patents

Under TRIPs, no field of technology can be excluded from patent protection, effectively disallowing any exemption for pharmaceuticals from protection. The key advance here is that Egypt will have to grant protection for pharmaceutical products, and it will no longer be enough to provide process protection for pharmaceuticals.[5] Egypt will have to provide a minimum term of protection of 20 years from the date of filing of the patent application. Egypt cannot favour the pharmaceutical sector through more permissive rules on 'compulsory licensing,'[6] or by stipulating that firms should produce the pharmaceutical invention locally rather than importing it.

While TRIPs does not specify the reasons for which a compulsory licence may be granted, Egypt will have to comply with a series of stringent conditions when a compulsory licence is granted (Article 31). Notable among these are the requirements to establish that normal channels of obtaining a voluntary licence have proved unsuccessful and that the patentee be provided adequate compensation for a compulsory licence.

To comply with TRIPs, Egypt has had or will have to undertake extensive reform of its patent laws in each of the areas described above to protect pharmaceutical products, to increase the term of patent protection to 20 years, and to eliminate the discrimination in the system of compulsory licensing against pharmaceutical inventions and against imported patented products. This includes ensuring that all these obligations are enforced effectively, in the sense that patent owners can prevent unauthorized use of their patent rights and be adequately compensated in the event of infringements of their rights

Transitional arrangements

Like all developing countries, Egypt has had to implement the national treatment and most-favoured nation (MFN) provisions beginning 1 January 1996. Other provisions of the agreement, including those on enforcement, will have to be implemented by 1 January 2000. Patent protection for biotechnological products will have to be implemented by 2005. In the critical area of pharmaceutical product protection, the transitional provisions are complex and explained in the box on page 192.

9.3 The economic impact of TRIPs: theoretical arguments

The rationale for a system of intellectual property rights (IPRs), particularly patents, has to do with the 'public good' nature of knowledge; once created, its benefits can be relatively easily 'appropriated'[7] by agents other than its creator. This in turn can blunt the incentive to undertake the effort to create knowledge in the first place, leading to an under-production of knowledge from society's point of view. IPRs therefore represent an arrangement whereby society mitigates the appropriability problem and reduces the divergence between the private and social returns to knowledge creation. Although IPRs create a distortion by reducing the degree of competition, it is assumed that the dynamic benefits from the incentives to R&D creation will offset the static efficiency losses. This rationale for IPR protection at the national level gets more complicated at the international level for a variety of empirical and theoretical reasons (see Siebeck 1990).

Small country/countries care

Suppose, as is likely to be true of Egypt, that a country or a group of countries is predominantly a net importer of technology and maintains a low level of IP protection to facilitate cheap or costless imitation by indigenous producers in a highly competitive environment. In addition, if one postulates that the country in question is 'small,' in the sense that the level of IP protection has no appreciable effect on global R&D creation, then an increase in IP protection will displace local producers and render the market less competitive, leading to a rise in prices and a consequent rent transfer from local consumers and producers to foreign title holders. The absence of an appreciable R&D effect will mean that the country will not derive any dynamic benefits in the form of reduced costs and prices, so that in welfare terms the individual country will be worse off (Chin and Grossman 1988; Deardorff 1990, 1992; Helpman 1993; Maskus 1990).

Imitation and large country effect

On the other hand, in a country or a group of countries that is sufficiently large, the level of IP protection could have a significant effect on R&D. An example of this could relate to the development of drugs for the treatment of diseases specific to developing countries, or technologies, such as seeds and chemicals, designed for agriculture in developing countries. The possibilities of *ex post facto* copying, in the absence of IP protection, could dent incentives to undertake R&D. This case is examined in Diwan and Rodrik (1991), who show that if R&D inducement effect is sufficiently strong, higher IP protection could lead to gains for individual countries and for the world.

Technology transfer effect

Where an invention can be copied easily, for example, through reverse engineering, it cannot be plausibly argued that patent protection is necessary for the transfer of technology (Subramanian 1990). Where, however, the assistance of the inventor is required, there may well be cases where patent protection creates the conditions for a voluntary transfer of technology which might not exist in the absence of a patent regime. The patent enables its owner to control the diffusion of the related secret know-how required to utilize the invention protected by the patent. In the absence of the patent, there would be little legal means of preventing persons, once trained in the use of the know-how, from setting up competing units, leading possibly to an uncontrolled diffusion of the technology. While *ex post facto* such diffusion might be in the national interest, the risk of such diffusion would deter the technology owner, forestalling the technology transfer in the first place. Thus the country could lose out on the benefits to employment, skills and growth, by not providing a climate conducive for the transfer of technology or foreign direct investment (Maskus and Konan 1994).

R&D effects

In principle, there are three distinct R&D effects, know-what, know-who and know-where, that could be instigated by higher patent protection. Know-what effects relate to whether higher IP protection would lead to greater R&D on products consumed (actually or potentially) by developing countries (or on processes used in the production of products consumed in developing countries). For example, will higher pharmaceutical protection accorded by developing countries lead to greater R&D on the range of diseases typically found in Egypt and other developing countries?

Know-who effects relate to whether higher IP protection will lead to greater R&D by indigenous firms; and know-where effects relate to whether protection will lead to a shift in the location of R&D investment in favour of developing countries such as Egypt. These three effects determine the welfare calculus of higher IP protection in different ways. Know-what effects determine costs, prices, and product variety, thereby affecting consumer welfare. Know-who effects determine who – foreigners or domestic nationals – would receive the rents from successful R&D activity; and know-where effects have implications for the rent effects (if R&D takes place locally, rents can be taxed by the country), but arguably also for the extent of diffusion of technology – that is, the more R&D generated in Egypt, the more likely its economy-wide diffusion.

9.4 Structure of the Egyptian pharmaceutical industry[8]

Aggregates

The market for Egyptian pharmaceuticals is among the largest in the Middle East, estimated to be about £E 3 billion in 1995, or some 20% of the Middle East market. The Egyptian market grew at an average rate of about 20% per annum between 1985 and 1995, with particularly rapid growth in the 1990s averaging close to 30% (Figure 9.1). These nominal growth rates signify a sharp increase in real consumption, especially since the pharmaceutical sector has been subject to price controls. Accordingly, per capita expenditures on drugs reached £E 35 in 1994, compared to £E 7 in 1980.

The direct contribution of the pharmaceutical sector to the economy is relatively modest. The sector's value added represented less than 1% of Egypt's total GDP in 1995;[9] its exports constituted less than 1.5% of Egypt's non-oil exports in 1994; its imports in 1994 of final products accounted for about 1% of total imports, which increases to about 3% if imports of inputs are taken into account. Total employment in the sector is estimated at about 50,000–60,000, or less than 1% of Egypt's total labour force of 16 million.

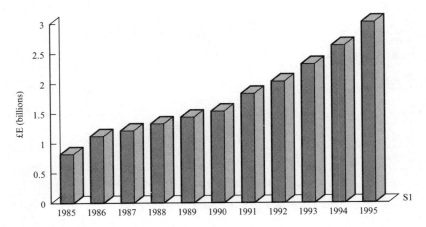

Figure 9.1 Egyptian pharmaceutical market evolution (*Source*: IMS Q4 95)

Ownership

The industry is comprised of three distinct categories of manufacturers based on the ownership of production – 9 multinationals (of which 3 are fully foreign owned, and 6 are majority-owned); 8 private companies and 11 public sector companies. Over time, the shares of the foreign companies and especially of the indigenous private sector have grown at the expense of the public sector. The public sector share in total production fell from 70% in 1984/5 to about 53% in 1990/1 (Table 9.1) and stands at about 40% today. The rest of the market is shared by the foreign companies and the local private sector. The industry exhibits a fair degree of concentration. In 1995, the top five firms accounted for 26% of market share, while the top 10 firms accounted for 43%.

Trade performance

At £E 94 million in 1994, exports accounted for less than 5% of output, comprising mainly generic products and vitamins. However, exports have grown rapidly since the early 1980s, from £E 3.5 million in 1980/81 to £E 103.4 million in 1991/92, an annual average rate of 27.7% (Table 9.2). Exports as a share of total output grew from 1.7% in 1980 to 5.3% in 1993 (Table 9.3).

Imports of final pharmaceutical products amounted to £E 405 million in 1994 and comprised 10% of final consumption. Imports have grown less rapidly than exports, from £E 49.4 million to £E 195.6 million in 1992/93,

Table 9.1 Ownership structure of the industry: values (£E million)

	1984/1985	1985/1986	1986/1987	1987/1988	1988/1989	1989/1990	1990/1991
Public sector	304.0	331.7	370.1	442.0	520.6	553.8	628.3
Joint venture	102.5	117.5	128.55	158.2	194.2	215.6	224.7
Private sector	28.4	61.9	82.0	146.2	197.4	284.4	334.9
Total	434.9	511.1	580.6	746.4	912.2	1053.8	1187.9
Percentage of change		17.5	13.6	28.6	22.2	15.5	12.7

Ownership structure of the industry: share percentage

	1984/1985	1985/1986	1986/1987	1987/1988	1988/1989	1989/1990	1990/1991
Public sector	69.9	64.9	63.7	59.3	57.1	52.6	52.9
Joint venture	23.6	23.0	22.1	21.2	21.3	20.5	18.9
Private sector	6.5	12.1	14.1	19.6	21.6	27.0	28.2

Source: Pharmaceutical Industry in Egypt (1980–1991) – A Case Study

at an average annual rate of about 7% (Table 9.2). Imports, which accounted for almost 19% of consumption in 1980/81, now constitutes about 10% of consumption, reflecting progressive import substitution over time (Table 9.4).[10] Imports of raw materials used in local production are estimated to be about 25% of total sales, approximately £E 750 million in 1995. The industry imports some 80–90% of its total raw material requirements in the form of active ingredients. Local production of active ingredients is very small, a feature that distinguishes the Egyptian pharmaceutical industry from the more mature industries in other developing countries such as India. Thus, Egypt has consistently been running a trade deficit in pharmaceutical products (Table 9.2), a deficit that is actually substantially larger if imports of raw materials are also taken into account.

Table 9.2 Pharmaceutical sector trade ('000 £E)

Year	Exports	Rate of growth(%)	Imports	Rate of growth (%)	Balance (deficit)
80/81	3,500		49,400		45,900
81/82	4,200	20	107,700	118	103,500
82/83	9,500	126	109,100	1	99,600
83/84	7,900	−17	131,600	21	123,700
84/85	8,600	9	150,800	15	142,200
85/86	10,400	21	161,300	7	150,900
86/87	12,600	21	191,800	19	179,200
87/88	25,800	105	163,400	−15	137,600
88/89	37,800	47	132,100	−18	94,300
89/90	29,100	−23	146,600	11	117,500
90/91	53,600	84	178,600	22	125,000
91/92	103,400	93	182,400	2	79,000
92/93	103,400	0	195,600	7	92,200

Source: Scientific Research Institute '94

Table 9.3 Share of exports in production

	1980	1985	1989	1993
Production				
Total	173.8	597.9	1059.9	1700
State	122.1	378	580.7	765
% Total	70.2	63.2	54.8	45
Private	51.7	291.9	479.2	935
% Total	29.8	36.8	45.2	55
Exports	2.9	10.2	51.4	90.4
% Export/ production	1.7	1.7	4.8	5.3

Source: Egyptian Export Promotion Centre

Table 9.4 Share in consumption

Year	Domestic (%)	Imported (%)	Total
1980	81.4	18.6	100
1982/1983	77.6	22.4	100
1985/1986	79.2	20.8	100
1987/1988	85.1	14.9	100
1989/1990	89.5	10.5	100
1990/1992	90.0	10.0	100

Source: *Pharmaceutical Industry in Egypt (1980–1991) – ACDIMA'93*

Protection

The simple average tariff for pharmaceutical products in 1994 was 8%, compared to 32% for the economy as a whole and 27% for industry sector. This pattern is found in most countries due to governments' desire to maintain easy, cheap access to products that safeguard health and safety. Effective protection is not high, owing to low output tariffs and comparable tariffs on intermediate inputs.[11] Although there are no explicit quantitative restrictions or non-tariff barriers, there could be *de facto* protection through import licensing system implemented by the Ministry of Health.

Structural attributes: A schizophrenic industry?

It is difficult to speak of the Egyptian pharmaceutical industry or generalize about the impact of international developments because, from an analytical perspective there are at least two, perhaps even three, pharmaceutical industries in Egypt, with antithetical interests in relation to IP protection.

The foreign-owned segment of the industry produces most or virtually all of its drugs under licence from the parent company. A large portion of these drugs (about 70%) are currently under patent in the industrial countries. On the other hand, the domestic private sector and the public sector produce only between 40 and 50% of their products under licence, the remainder being accounted for by generics (Tables 9.5 and 9.6). The latter offer a cheaper avenue of production because no payment of royalties are required (these typically vary between 7–10% of sales). Production under licence happens only because indigenous firms cannot buy the active ingredients from cheaper sources or because the technology and know-how are not easily available from other sources. One feature of significance from the perspective of assessing the impact of higher patent protection is that a growing share of generic production of indigenous firms is based on the use of inputs that would be deemed to be infringements had Egypt observed high levels of patent protection.

An interesting feature of the market is that, historically, and even today, the share of 'infringing activity' – or production based on imitation – has been low and is currently estimated at about 4% of total sales. In part, this has reflected the embryonic state of the local industry, which has needed the cooperation of the original drug producer in the form of inputs, technology and know-how transfer, to assist in production. Although the local industry is not geared to manufacturing the

Table 9.5 Financial indicators for representative firms, 1995

	Private	MNCs	Public
Total production	261,600	111,794	174,277
Sales	249,911	154,119	167,508
Rate of growth (%)	18	27	2
Wages and benefits	19,621	14,287	27,866
Rate of growth (%)	17	23	0
Percentage of operating costs	14	16	20
Percentage of value of production	8	13	16
Operating costs	141,017	88,182	137,866
Gross margin	108,894	65,937	29,642
Gross margin upon sales (%)	44	43	18

Source: Financial Accounts of Selected Firms and Authors' Calculations

Table 9.6 Economic indicators for representative firms, 1995

	Private	MNCs	Public
Exports ('000 £E)	31,200	0	16,865
Exports (% of sales)	12.50	0.00	10.10
No. of products	157	87	210
Generic products	107	0	141
Under licence	50	87	69
Imports of raw materials ('000 £E)	63,541	64,516	55,204
Imports (% of operating costs)	45	73	40
Wage rate/hr (£E)	6.01	7.87	4.75
US$	1.77	2.31	1.40
Rate of growth (%)	14	13	9
R&D (% of revenues)	1.50	n.a	0.70
No. of employees	1547	860	2777
Rate of growth (%)	2	9	–8
Value added	140,204	52,186	64,277
Rate of growth (%)	17.40	29	11
Labour productivity[1]	90.63	60.68	23.15

[1] Defined as value added per worker.
Source: Financial Accounts of Selected Firms and Authors' Calculations

active ingredients, it has now matured enough to be able to produce generics without the help of foreign producers by importing the active ingredients. Correspondingly, the extent of infringing activity is expected to increase over the next few years and could account for between 10% and 30% of the total market. It is this segment of the market that will become vulnerable once the obligations of the TRIPs agreement have to be observed.

The contribution of the foreign-owned pharmaceutical manufacturers to total exports is minuscule on account of restrictions imposed by the parent company on its Egyptian affiliates. Global marketing strategies, involving international market segmentation and consequential price variation according to market demand, could explain this behaviour.[12] About two-thirds of Egypt's pharmaceutical exports are accounted for by the private sector, and the remaining one-third by the public sector (Table 9.3). Exports consist of generics and vitamins and are mainly destined for the countries of the former Soviet Union, Eastern Europe, and some Arab countries.

Efficiency

The efficiency of the Egyptian pharmaceutical industry varies enormously across the different categories of producers. Predictably, the public sector lags significantly behind the private and foreign-owned companies, as reflected in a variety of economic and financial indicators depicted in Tables 9.5, 9.6 and 9.7.[13] The most profitable private company had a gross margin of about 44% in 1995, compared with margins of about 18% for the two best performing public sector companies, and 43% for the foreign company.[14] Wage costs as a share of total operating costs were also lower for private and foreign companies (14%) than for public sector companies (20%). It is important to note that the pharmaceutical sector as a whole is *not* a labour-intensive industry, as exemplified in the low share of wages and salaries in operating costs and in value of production (about 11% for the three types of firms combined). This has implications for the extent to which Egypt can base its competitive advantage on its endowment of cheaper labour.[15]

Economic indicators paint a similarly stark picture. At 17%, value-added growth in the private sector was more robust than in the public sector, where growth was negative. Labour productivity, as measured by value-added per worker, was about four times higher in the private and foreign sectors than in the public sector, which more than compensated

Table 9.7 Financial and economic indicators (total public sector)

Financial Indicators (value in '000 £E)

	1992/1993	1993/1994	1994/1995
Capital	202,200	229,300	331,280
Sales[1]	1,779,182	1,859,199	1,986,799
Rate of growth (%)		4	7
Wages and benefits	208,854	228,525	243,836
Rate of growth (%)		9	7
Net profit	−23,713	54,179	98,534
Rate of growth (%)[2]		144	82
Net profit (% of sales)	−1	3	5

Economic Indicators

	1992/1993	1993/1994	1994/1995
No of workers	29,608	29,247	28,485
Rate of growth (%)		−1	−3
Wage rate/hr			
£E	3.34	3.7	4.05
US$	0.98	1.09	1.19
Rate of growth (%)		11	9
Exports ('000 £E)	n.a	n.a	63,606
Exports (% of sales)	n.a	n.a	3
Value added ('000 £E)[3]	640,506	669,312	715,247
Rate of growth (%)		4	7
Labour productivity	21.63	22.88	25.11
Rate of growth		6%	10%

[1] Official figures of sales are reduced by 10% to take account of revenues accruing from sales of non-operational assets.
[2] Rate of growth using 1993/1994 as a base year.
[3] Value added is calculated applying the value added to sales ratio for two public sector firms to sales of the entire public sector.

Source: Financial Accounts and Authors' Calculations

for the fact that wages in the former sectors (US$ 1.77 per hour) are 26% above those in the public sector (US$ 1.40). Employment growth was positive in the private sector but negative in the public sector. The private sector exports more, both in absolute terms and as a share of total production. The share of imported raw materials in total operating costs tends to be substantially higher for the foreign companies, inviting the question of whether this is due to higher prices for patented products or to transfer pricing and an indirect mechanism for the transfer abroad of profits.

Research and development

The extent of R&D activity carried out by Egyptian firms – foreign and local – is negligible; less than 2% of revenue, compared with about 12–20% in industrial countries. R&D expenditures were higher in the private sector although the absolute levels remain low. While R&D can encompass a range of activities, in the case of Egypt, there is a larger dose of 'D' than 'R', and a fairly elastic definition of 'D' is used to encapsulate activities such as training of physicians, and participation of medical personnel in international conferences.[16] Overall, and at least for the moment, the Egyptian industry would not remotely qualify as an R&D-based industry.

Regulation

Concerns about health and safety contribute to extensive regulation of the pharmaceutical sector the world over, including Egypt. Two important aspects of Egyptian regulation are worth mentioning. First, prices of *all* pharmaceutical products are controlled and set by the government. In principle, pricing decisions are taken by a committee comprising the ministries of Health, Economy and Finance, and industry representatives. Prices are apparently set according to a cost-plus formula (where costs are based on submission by the concerned manufacturer) with a mark-up of about 10–12% earmarked for profits. There is no automatic adjustment to reflect cost inflation (or indeed deflation if prices of the imported active ingredients fall).[17] As a consequence, manufacturers frequently resort to product variation as a means of forcing a review of prices. In practice, the mechanism for price-setting is perceived as non-transparent and vulnerable to discretion.

The second aspect of regulation concerns product registration, which is a pre-requisite for commercial marketing. Egypt, like many developing countries, does not have an independent and fully-fledged system for regulatory approval of pharmaceuticals. Consequently, it relies on approval procedures in five other industrial countries; a product can be introduced in Egypt if it has obtained a 'free sales certificate' in one of these five markets. Registration procedures in Egypt can be initiated only after this certificate is obtained, which results in a typical lag of between two and three years between introduction of a product in an industrial country and its marketing in Egypt.

9.5 The short-run economic impact

As explained earlier, the main impact of introducing patent protection for pharmaceutical products is that all activity based on imitation of patented products will have to cease or cede to licence-based production. In the short-run, the effect of this is to lessen the degree of competition in the market. How much depends on the structure of the market, the demand and supply elasticities, number of competitors, etc. Table 9.8 quantifies this impact for a number of alternative scenarios. The numbers in the table represent the annual price, welfare and profit effects conse-quent upon the TRIPs agreement.[18] Unsurprisingly, the short-run impact is negative: prices are likely to rise,[19] economic welfare to fall, and profits accruing to patent owner – which in the case of Egypt are likely to be the foreign companies – to increase. As imitation-based production cedes to patent-based production, the share of indigenous firms in total sales will fall, while that of imports and foreign firms located in Egypt will increase.[20] These numbers are subject to two important qualifications. First, as explained in the box on page 192, these effects will not be felt until 2015. Second, in view of the arbitrariness of the assumptions and the sensitivity of results to these assumptions, the numbers should be viewed as illustrative, suggesting broad indications rather than precise outcomes (Subramanian 1995a, 1995b).

Two parameters in particular may drastically alter the nature of the conclusions. The first is the proportion of drugs that will be patented in the future. This is something that is impossible to predict since it will depend on the nature and rapidity of R&D over the coming years. According to data that we have collected, including interviews with indus-try experts, about 15–30% of the market would be affected, because that is roughly the magnitude that would have been based on imitation had there been no patent protection. If 15% of the market is likely to be affected (Scenarios I and III in Table 9.8), price rises of patented drugs could vary between 5% and 67%, resulting in an overall drug price impact of between 0.8 and 10.1%. In these cases, welfare losses to the country in the form of reduced consumer and producer surplus could vary between US$ 28 million and US$ 114 million; these losses are partially reflected in gains to patent owners (presumed to be foreign-owned companies) of the order of US$ 18 million and US$ 76 million.

The results are also sensitive to how competitive the market is assumed to be and what policies are followed after implementation of the TRIPs agreement. For example, in the limiting case where the pre-patent situa-tion is perfectly competitive and the post-TRIPs regime is a perfect

Box Timing of impact of the TRIPs provisions on pharmaceuticals

It is important to understand when the economic effects – be they positive or negative – are likely to be felt under the TRIPs agreement, especially since the general impression seems to be that legislative changes and economic impacts will occur immediately.

Although developing countries appear to have a ten-year transition period for the introduction of pharmaceutical patent protection (Article 65.4), the effective period of transition will be determined by the combination of Articles 65 and 70.8. The latter effectively requires all patent applications filed after 1 January 1994, to be granted protection. Figure 9.2 explains how these complicated transition provisions apply.*

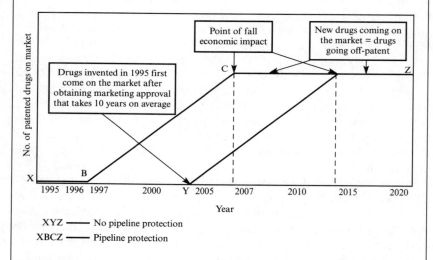

Figure 9.2 Timing of impact of TRIPs

*Although the agrrement requires patent applications made after 1 January 1995 to be accorded patent protection, patents filed in industrial countries after 1 January 1995 could in effect be eligable for protection because of the operation of the provision relating to the 'priority date' of an application.

monopoly, the adverse impact is large (compare Scenario II with Scenario III in Table 9.8). This represents an upper bound to the economic impacts. If, on the other hand, the pre-patent situation is a duopoly with one foreign and one domestic producer, and the post-TRIPs regime is a monopoly with one foreign producer, the impacts become less adverse (this is the model analysed in Chin and Grossman (1988) which is illustrated by a comparison of Scenarios II and IV).

If, more realistically, competition between patented therapeutic classes is assumed and allows governments to use compulsory licensing to regulate the post-TRIPs pharmaceutical market, adverse effects shrink further in magnitude. In Subramanian (1995a) this is modelled as a Bertrand duopoly in the pre- and post-patent situations, with one domestic and one foreign producer. The TRIPs agreement forces an increase in the cost of the domestic producer, as royalty payments to the foreign patent holder are incurred for use – under compulsory licensing – of the patent. This model yields annual welfare losses (price increases) considerably less than the results shown in Table 9.8.[21]

9.6   The long-run dynamic impact

The calculations in Table 9.8 ignore potentially important dynamic benefits stemming from TRIPs-induced R&D effects. The evidence on these R&D effects is unfortunately neither extensive nor systematic. A number of studies for industrial countries do, however, show that IP protection is important in R&D decisions in the pharmaceutical and chemical sectors, but less so in other sectors (Levin et al. 1987; Mansfield 1986, 1994).

In the case of Egypt, what are the prospects for the know-what, know-who, and know-where effects? Tables 9.5–9.7 shed some light on the know-who and know-where effects. Currently, there is very limited R&D in Egypt and very little by Egyptian firms; and, as discussed above, the little that there is tends to be of a very special, limited nature. It could be argued, however, that this outcome reflects in part the current legal regime that has not provided the incentives for R&D. On this view, future R&D activity cannot be extrapolated from current performance because of the regime shift that will occur. Even if this were true, the prospects for developing a genuine R&D-based industry in Egypt in the medium-term are not very bright. The development of one new patentable drug today costs about US$ 250–400 million or about £E 850–1360 million, which represents almost half the revenues generated by the entire Egyptian pharmaceutical industry. The Egyptian industry is not even at a stage of development at which it manufactures important active ingredients. Attaining R&D capability is therefore some time away.

This is not to say that certain kinds of R&D, such as clinical training and testing, cannot be carried out in Egypt, but attempts at assessing their magnitude are extremely speculative. Proponents of the view that R&D will be stimulated invoke the example of Italy, where it is claimed that

Table 9.8 Impact of TRIPS on the pharmaceutical market in Egypt in 2015[1] (in US$ million at 1996 prices, unless otherwise stated)

	Elasticity		
	e= −0.75	e= −1	e= −2
Scenario 1[2]			
Average price rise			
patented drugs (%)	67.0	50.0	25.0
all drugs (%)	10.1	7.5	3.8
Welfare loss	114	85	43
Profit transfer to foreign firms	76	57	28
Scenario II[2]			
Average price rise			
patented drugs (%)	67.0	50.0	25.0
all drugs (%)	20.1	15.0	7.5
Welfare loss	455	341	171
Profit transfer to foreign firms	303	227	114

	Elasticity		
	e= −2.5	e= −3	e= −5
Scenario III[3]			
Average price rise			
patented drugs (%)	10.0	8.0	5.0
all drugs (%)	1.5	1.2	0.8
Welfare loss	59	48	28
Profit transfer to foreign firms	36	30	18
Scenario IV[3]			
Average price rise			
patented drugs (%)	10.0	8.0	5.0
all drugs (%)	3.1	2.4	1.5
Welfare loss	117	96	113
Profit transfer to foreign firms	73	60	35

Memorandum item	
Annual sales of pharmaceutical products	1516

1 'e' refers to the price elasticity of market demand; in the case of a duopoly this translates into different perceived elasticites for individual duopolisits. In all scenarios, marginal costs remain the same in pre-and post -patent. The theoretical models used for deriving these numbers are described in Subramanian (1995b).

2 Share of patented drugs = 15% in Scenario I and 30% in Scenario II. In both scenarios pre-TRIPs market is perfectly competetive, and post- TRIPs is a foreign monopoly.

3 Share of patented drugs = 15% in Scenario lll and 30% in Scenario IV. In both scenarios pre-TRIPs market comprises two duopolists, one foreign and one domestic, and post-TRIPs market comprises a foreign monopolist.

Source: Subramanian (1995b)

patent protection improved the situation of local companies and encouraged R&D while at the same time restraining price increases. On the other hand, the Canadian Drug Manufacturers Association argues that the promise of higher R&D after the strengthening of the patent law in 1991 was belied by subsequent experience. International evidence is too mixed to allow any easy generalization that would apply in the Egyptian case.

While the know-who and know-where R&D effects may not be promising at this stage, the same need not be true of the know-what effects. Improved patent protection in Egypt and other similar developing countries could stimulate R&D by foreign and local firms in finding cures for diseases found predominantly in these countries.

9.7   What will the EU agreement add to TRIPs?

The draft agreement requires Egypt to provide protection for IPRs in line with 'the highest international standards' and to adhere to a non-exhaustive list of multilateral conventions (Loutfi, 1996). Although the deliberate ambiguity of the former requirement has raised some concerns, it appears that neither of these two obligations will have any significant consequences for the pharmaceutical sector.[22] However, another set of provisions may have some impact on the pharmaceutical sector, in particular on the ability of the government to regulate it. The draft agreement adopts the principles of competition policy that govern the free movement of goods within the EU. Once the agreement enters into effect, these principles would also govern the conditions of competition between the EU and Egypt. The implications, although uncertain at the moment, could be potentially significant, in terms of circumscribing the options that Egypt would otherwise have to regulate the pharmaceutical sector.

An example might help illustrate this point. Suppose that an European pharmaceutical company was charging a price that could be considered high or abusive under Egyptian competition law; however, under EU competition policy rules, such a price could be deemed normal. The question would then arise of whether Egypt would be forced by the EU agreement to implement the latter standards. Another example relates to the freedom provided under the TRIPs agreement to use compulsory licensing to mitigate any abusive use of the patent right. Would the EU agreement's provisions on competition policy preserve or eliminate this freedom? These are uncharted legal waters and need to be carefully explored before Egypt undertakes commitments in the area of competition policy.

9.8   Policy options for the government and industry

Pipeline protection and implementation of legislation

The box on page 192 indicates that the impact of the TRIPs agreement will be felt fully only in 2015–20 years after the implementation of the agreement. This should provide sufficient time for industries that are likely to be affected to adjust to the harsher environment. Two policy choices – neither of which is required by the TRIPs or EU agreements – confront the authorities: first, whether to grant patent protection for pharmaceutical products that were invented prior to 1995 (the 'pipeline protection' issue); and second, whether to accelerate the domestic implementation of the patent laws from 2005 (the 'black box' issue).

These are two distinct issues – the former will have a strong economic impact because it will shift forward by about 7–8 years the effects described in the box on page 192; in other words, pipeline protection would disallow imitation-based production by local manufacturers from now onwards.[23] But economic logic suggests that pipeline protection may not have merit. Pipeline protection would induce the short-run economic impact of higher consumer prices and lower consumer welfare, but would *not* have any attendant dynamic benefits. Dynamic benefits arise when the improved IP regime induces greater R&D activity; but by definition the products that will be introduced have already been invented, so there can be no incremental impact on R&D activity. The second advantage of not implementing pipeline protection is that it would afford a longer time period for local producers to adjust to the new patent regime, and to re-orient their production strategy from imitation-based production to licence-based production.

On the other hand, the acceleration of the domestic implementation of laws (the black box issues) would have no economic impact; it would merely introduce transparency and certainty into the patent system and provide guarantees that from 2005 onwards Egypt's patent protection for pharmaceutical products will be in line with international standards.[24]

Compulsory licensing

While the TRIPs agreement has significantly limited the use of compulsory licensing (which was, for example, the preferred tool in Canada for regulating drug prices), countries retain some margin of manoeuvre in using this form of regulatory control. In particular, two of the more stringent conditions attached to compulsory licensing (the need to demonstrate that the patent owner has refused to make available a voluntary licence on reasonable commercial terms and conditions, and the criterion of adequate compensation) can be waived if it can be shown that an IPR holder's actions have resulted in an anti-competitive practice. Hence, Egypt's national competition law can specify standards of abuse, encompassing such outcomes as high prices. Egypt retains enough latitude – subject of course to the caveat that this might be circumscribed or eliminated by the EU agreement – in determining where these standards could be set, for example, the point at which a price would constitute an abuse of the patent right. In the event that these standards are flouted, compulsory licensing could be used to redress the abuse and bring prices down to reasonable levels.[25]

However, in order to be able to implement compulsory licensing, Egypt needs to have a competition law in place that would allow explicitly for the regulation of the pharmaceutical industry. The current draft law, according to our understanding, does not provide for this possibility, and needs to be remedied. In the long run, it is probably preferable to regulate drug pricing through competition policy rather than through administrative fiat.

Price controls

Neither the TRIPs agreement nor the EU agreement would preclude the use of price controls which are already so pervasive in Egypt. Price control regimes co-exist with strong patent regimes in many developed countries, including those in Europe. If higher drug prices are a source of concern, the European model could serve as an exemplar; this policy, however, is a double-edged sword (*see* below).

Upgrading Egyptian industry

This would require other policy efforts that are currently seen as hampering investment in and development of the industry. The first of these relates to price controls. Successful regulation requires the institution of an independent body that takes into account and balances the interests of producers against the needs of the consumers and that follows a transparent process which engenders confidence and credibility. While the current system of pricing has contributed to remarkable price stability, it has not necessarily been transparent or adequately reflected the needs of producers. This will need to change.

The second aspect of regulation relates to registration procedures. The current system, whereby registration in Egypt can only be initiated after a product has been marketed abroad, leads to a time lag of between two and three years before the drug is introduced in Egypt, depriving consumers of access to potentially life-preserving medication. This is just a deadweight loss to society. Registration procedures need to be speeded up through a transparent mechanism, possibly by the independent drug regulatory body.

Finally, upgrading of the pharmaceutical industry also requires a careful review of whether the government has any comparative advantage in engaging in the production of pharmaceuticals. The analysis in Section 9.4 demonstrates that the public sector has been underperforming relative to its private sector competitors. It is estimated that public sector companies receive about £E 150 million annually in subsidies from the government, and that, in addition, these companies carry 'excess' (i.e. unserviceable) debt to the extent of £E 230–350 million. The question that needs to be debated is whether the legitimate regulatory and health concerns require government ownership and management of the pharmaceutical industry, or whether these objectives can be better accomplished through the combination of private-sector ownership and management coupled with effective government regulation.[26] In other words, the government should reconsider its current strategy of restricting privatization in this sector to minority divestitures.

Some of the above options are damage limitation options, stemming from the assessment that international developments are on balance likely to have a negative impact on the pharmaceutical industry. But there is a strong strand of opinion that views these developments as opportunities to be seized rather than threats to be contained. From the point of view of the pharmaceutical companies, particularly those that currently thrive on the lack of patent protection, the need for adaptation is a reality that is imminent and that will have to be contended with. There is also sufficient time – between 10 and 20 years – over which these adjustments can be made.

Industry's options

The Egyptian industry engages in what might be characterized as the equivalent of the completely knock-down (CKD) mode in the automobile sector. Essentially, all raw materials are imported, and Egypt serves as a base for mixing, packaging, and marketing, with very little R&D undertaken. From this base, a graduated approach to adaptation and upgrading could be considered. In the first phase the industry would have to gear itself to acquiring capability in manufacturing bulk generic drugs. This may have to be done in collaboration with foreign companies through licensing of technology and know-how. Egypt's competitiveness in this phase would derive from its cheap and skilled pool of manpower;[27] lower marketing and packaging costs which are in turn also related to Egypt's cheap labour, that allow for the replacement of automated processes by manual ones (Economic Research Forum, 1996), and the relatively large size of its market compared with other markets in the region.

Once this capability has been acquired, there could be greater scope for Egypt's industry to invest in R&D of which there are many facets. One immediate possibility would be to increase training and skill of personnel with a view to attaining manufacturing capability that complies with ISO-9000 standards. Another promising, if more distant, possibility would be the development of treatments for tropical diseases that are found in countries such as Egypt. The incentive to invest in finding cures for such diseases could be provided by the improved system of patent protection.

In building up technological, marketing, and R&D capability, Egyptian companies could also explore partnerships with foreign companies. Another possibility for deepening R&D effort is for Egypt's science and technology institutes to collaborate more closely with local companies to identify areas of mutual interest and advantage. For example, these institutes could identify locally available natural products with medicinal properties, and help in supporting research related to diseases specific to Egypt.

9.9 Conclusions

The pharmaceutical sector in Egypt is entering a critical phase and confronting choices as a result of the confluence of a number of developments – external and internal. The most important external factor is the WTO TRIPs agreement which will fundamentally alter the legal regime – and hence the nature of competition and market structure – and force producers to move away from imitation-based production. In Egypt, the balance of competitive advantage will shift away from indigenous private and public companies toward the foreign-owned companies that specialize in R&D-based production. However, the magnitude of the impact needs to be kept in perspective, as only a small share of the current market will be affected.

The domestic private sector and the public sector produce a much smaller fraction of drugs under licensing than the foreign private sector. These two sectors are most vulnerable to the TRIPs agreement, because a small but growing share of their production is based on imitation. All companies invest relatively little in R&D, and even the limited investment is of a fairly basic nature. All companies import virtually all their inputs of active ingredients. The industry as a whole is not very labour-intensive. Finally, financial and economic indicators suggest that the public sector is highly inefficient compared with the other two sectors.

Against this background, the static impact of the TRIPs agreement will be negative for the economy – owing to higher prices and associated loss in consumer welfare; negative for the private sector and public sector whose imitation-based production will have to cease; and positive for the foreign-owned companies who will make larger profits. Imitation-based production by indigenous firms will be replaced by a combination of increased production by foreign companies and increased imports. However, this static impact will be small in magnitude (because of the limited amount of imitation-based production) and backloaded in timing, with the full impact only felt by 2015. The dynamic impact is more uncertain, but the presumption is in favour of a limited rather than large impact. The prospects for greater and high-quality R&D *by* Egyptian firms and *in* Egypt appear limited at the present juncture. A possible exception could be research on diseases prevalent in Egypt which could be encouraged by the new legal regime

Against this background the following tentative policy recommendations can be made:

1. The government should not introduce pipeline protection, both on economic grounds and to provide enough time for affected industries to adjust to the new environment. The government should implement domestic laws and regulations consistent with or even more accelerated than, the TRIPs schedule, to remove uncertainty about the future legal regime.

2. The government should consider seriously the possibility of using competition law – and compulsory licensing – to regulate a future pharmaceutical sector, particularly to redress abusive uses of patent rights. This would imply that the current draft competition law should be amended to encompass the pharmaceutical sector within its scope. If so, care should be taken to ensure that the EU agreement's provisions on competition policies do not circumscribe Egypt's ability to use its competition policy appropriately.

3. While equipping itself to more effectively regulate this sector in the future, the government should also take measures to foster the development of the industry. To this end, it should introduce greater transparency in regulating the sector, particularly as regards pricing. One possibility would be to institute an independent drug regulatory authority that could balance competing interests, namely legitimate health and security concerns and the industry's profitability.

4. The government also needs to reconsider its engagement in the ownership and management of the industry in view of the financial unviability and economic unprofitability of the public sector companies. A superior alternative could be full privatization of these companies coupled with effective government regulation.

Turning to the options facing the industry, the key issue is how to adapt to the changing environment over a sufficiently long period of time. A possible sequential strategy would be to focus initially on building a strong generic industry based on Egypt's labour cost advantage and comparative advantages in marketing; subsequently, a more R&D-based industry could be developed, including through cooperative links with foreign companies and local science and technology institutes.

It is important to understand *when* the economic effects, be they positive or negative, are likely to be felt under the TRIPs agreement, since the general impression seems to be that legislative changes and economic impacts will occur immediately. Although developing countries appear to have a 10-year transition period for introduction of pharmaceutical patent protection, the effective period of transition will be determined by the TRIPs Articles 65 and 70.8. The latter effectively requires all patent applications filed after 1 January 1994 to be granted protection.[28] Figure 9.2 shows how these complicated transition provisions apply.

All patent applications for pharmaceutical products filed after 1 January 1995, will have to be put into a 'black box' by countries that did not earlier grant pharmaceutical product protection. By 2005, countries will have had to pass legislation that would allow patents to be granted for such black box applications. However, no commercial benefits would have been lost during the 10-year interval because the products for which patents had been granted in industrial countries, but which were in the black box in developing countries, would have been going through the process of obtaining regulatory approval prior to commercial marketing. This process is estimated to take an average of 10–12 years for new chemical entities, giving each patent a commercial life of 8–10 years.

This means that the patent applications that went into the black box in 1995 in Egypt would emerge in 2005; in 2005 the Egyptian patent authorities would have to examine these applications under the new TRIPs-consistent laws; concurrently, the drug would also be ready for commercial marketing in Egypt. As the line XYZ in Figure 9.2 shows, no patented drugs would be on the Egyptian market until 2005 and hence no *economic impact* of the TRIPs agreement would be felt until 10 years after the agreement.[29] Drugs that enter the market over the next 10 years, and certainly drugs already on the market, will be unaffected by the TRIPs agreement. If 100 of the applications in 1995 were to be granted patents in 2005, these 100 patented drugs would be on the market in 2005. Assuming a uniform rate of successful drug patents, the number of drugs on the market by the year 2006 would be 200 (the 100 granted patents in 2005 plus the 100 in 2006), 300 in 2007, and so on. After 2015, the number of patented drugs on the market would be constant because the number of new drugs coming onto the market would be balanced by those going off-patent after the expiration of their 20-year patent term. Thus only in 2015 – 20 years after the WTO enters into force – will Egypt have a full roster of patented drugs comparable with that in countries that currently provide patent protection.

Finally, if pipeline protection were to be granted, say for all inventions made after 1987, the effect would be to shift the graph from XYZ to XBCZ. The first impact would be felt next year and the full impact in 2007 instead of 2015. The consequences would be enormous because essentially the economic impact would be shifted forward by seven years, leaving that much less time for domestic industry to adjust.

References

Chin, J.C. and G.M. Grossman (1988), 'Intellectual property rights and north–south trade', Research Working Paper Series No. 2769, Cambridge, MA, National Bureau of Economic Research.

Deardorff, A.V. (1990), 'Should patent protection be extended to all developing countries?' *The World Economy*, 13 (4), pp. 497–508.

___ (1992), 'Welfare effects of global patent protection', *Economica*, 59, pp. 35–51.

Diwan, I. and D. Rodrik (1991), 'Patents, appropriate technology and north-south trade', *Journal of International Economics*, 30, pp. 27–47.

Economic Research Forum (1996), 'Study on the Pharmaceutical Sector'.

Helpman, E. (1993), 'Innovation, imitation, and intellectual property rights', *Econometrica*, 61, pp. 1247–80.

Levin, R.C., A.K. Klevorick, R.R. Nelson, and S.G. Winter (1987), 'Appropriating the returns from industrial R&D', Brookings Papers on Economic Activity No. 3, pp. 783–820.

Loutfi, M.H. (1996), 'Intellectual property protection, direct investment and technology transfer: the case of Egypt and the EU', Paper presented at the seminar on 'The Partnership Agreement and the EU', Alexandria, May 1996.

Mansfield, E. (1986), 'Patents and innovation: an empirical study', *Management Science*, 32, pp.173–81.

___ (1994), 'Intellectual property protection, foreign direct investment, and technology transfer', IFC Discussion Paper No.19, Washington, DC, World Bank.

Maskus, K.E. (1990), 'Normative concerns in the international protection of intellectual property rights', *The World Economy*, 13, pp. 387–409.

Maskus, K.E. and D. Konan (1994), 'Trade-related intellectual property rights: issues and exploratory results', in Deardorff and Stern (eds.), *Analytical and Negotiating Issues in the Global Trading System*, Ann Arbor, University of Michigan.

Siebeck, W.E., (ed.) (1990), *Strengthening Protection of Intellectual Property in Developing Countries: A Survey of the Literature*, Washington, DC, World Bank.

Subramanian, A. (1990), 'TRIPs and the paradigm of the GATT: a tropical, temperate view', *The World Economy*, 13 (4), pp. 509–21.

___ (1995a), 'Putting some numbers on the TRIPs pharmaceutical debate', *International Journal of Technology Management*, 10, No. 2/3, 1995, pp. 252–68.

___ (1995b), 'The impact of the TRIPs agreement on Asia: an analytical view', paper presented at the conference on the Impact of the Uruguay Round on Asia, Asian Development Bank, Manila, April 1995.

Notes

1. The views are those of the authors and should not be attributed to their institutions. The authors would like to thank Ahmed Galal for helpful comments. The usual disclaimer applies.
2. The time frame for the phase-out of tariffs on the imports of pharmaceutical products into Egypt has not yet been decided. Some indication of this can, however, be gleaned from the EU's agreements with Morocco and Tunisia which have committed to eliminate tariffs on most pharmaceutical products over three years and five years, respectively.
3. This section draws heavily on Subramanian (1995a, 1995b).
4. The second general obligation, an innovation in the field of IP is that of MFN treatment. This requires countries to treat nationals of any one country no less favourably than nationals of another country.
5. Process protection provides limited exclusivity to the creator because a given therapeutic product can be produced by different processes.
6. Compulsory licences need to be distinguished from voluntary licences that are negotiated between the patent owner and the agent who wishes to use that patent. A compulsory licence is granted by the Government to an agent other than the patent owner, permitting the use of the patent for a price that is usually less than what would have been voluntary negotiated between the patent owner and user. The compulsory licence results in the dilution of the exclusivity conferred on the patent owner.
7. In more emotive language, 'appropriability' goes by the names of 'theft', 'robbery' and 'piracy'.
8. This section is based on data compiled by the authors from the financial accounts of firms and those obtained from interviews and responses to questionnaires. All this data is available from the authors upon request.
9. Based on disaggregated data obtained from three enterprises, value added for the sector is estimated at about £E 1 billion, and nominal GDP at market prices at £E 212.8 billion.
10. In part, this import substitution could reflect the choice of foreign suppliers to service the Egyptian market by locating within (i.e. through foreign direct investment) rather than exporting to Egypt.
11. Tariffs on the active ingredients that constitutes the large bulk of inputs into production are 5%, while tariffs on imported packing materials range between 10% and 40%.
12. Foreign companies justify these export restrictions on the ground that price restrictions in Egypt create artificial and unfair export opportunities.
13. Tables 9.5 and 9.6 contain data for three pharmaceutical firms, one each from the public, private and foreign sectors. The choice of firms was dictated by data availability, but they were all amongst the best performing firms in their respective categories, which provides a plausible basis for generalizing about the sectors. Table 9.7 depicts data for the 11 public sector pharmaceutical companies as a whole.
14. The lower gross margin for the foreign company might give a misleading impression about profitability because of the possibility that imported raw material costs incorporate a margin of profit.
15. The comparable figure for the textile industry is about 21%.
16. A small share of 'development' includes conventional activities such as clinical trials.
17. Price controls were a particularly serious problem in the 1980s because of the frequent adjustments in the exchange rate which increased the costs of imported raw materials.

18. The methodology used for these calculations is described in detail in Subramanian (1995a). In one set of calculations (Scenarios I and II in Table 9.8), the pre-TRIPs situation is modelled as being perfectly competitive and the post-TRIPs situation as a perfect monopoly. In the other set of calculations (Scenarios III and IV), the pre-patent situation is modelled as a duopoly with one foreign and one domestic duopolist; in the post-TRIPs situation, it is posited that the domestic duopolists costs go up because he has 'work around' his competitor's patent. Market demand is assumed to be linear and production is characterized by constant marginal costs.

19. Of course, in a situation of binding price controls, the adverse impact will be fe~t through lower profitability of firms whose imitation-based production has been displaced.

20. Imports of final pharmaceutical products are predominantly undertaken by the foreign firms.

21. Maskus and Konan'(1994) calculate the economic impacts under other scenarios.

22. One of the conventions to which adherence is required – the International Convention for the Protection of Plant Varieties (UPOV, 1991) will, however, have important ramifications for the agricultural sector.

23. Egypt does not have the choice of not introducing patent protection. In fact, even if Egypt wished to renege on its international commitments, it will not be able to because the it would not have access to the imported raw materials – which could not be legally produced in the country of origin – on which Egyptian imitation depends. The only real question is not whether but when to introduce such protection.

24. According to legal experts, the TRIPs agreement is self-executing in Egypt in the sense that it has the force of domestic law overriding all previous relevant laws. However, there is still a need for domestic law if only to elaborate on and specify in greater detail the provisions of the TRIPs agreement.

25. That the use of such compulsory licensing by governments can reduce the adverse impacts was noted above. In such a case, the adverse price and welfare effects are considerably less than those obtained under scenarios III and IV in Table 9.8.

26. One of the arguments advanced against privatization is that it would lead to cessation of local production of certain essential product lines (e.g. insulin) that are unprofitable. However, even in this case, it is not clear why these products cannot be imported or sufficient incentives provided to private sector firms to produce them without increasing Government subsidies.

27. However, the competitive advantage derived from cheap labour should not be over-emphasized because labour costs account for a relatively small share (less than 10%) of the total costs of production.

28. Although the agreement requires patent applications made after 1 January 1995, to be accorded patent protection, patents filed in industrial countries after 1 January 1994, could in effect be eligible for protection because of the operation of the provision relating to the 'priority date' of an application.

29. The one significant caveat to this is that if regulatory approval for a drug takes less than ten years, countries will still have to protect that drug by granting an exclusive marketing right – a patent by another name – until such time as they can receive formal patents (Article 70.9). Such drugs will enjoy a commercial patented life greater than ten years, depending on how quickly they obtain regulatory approval.

10

Potential Impact of a Free Trade Agreement with the EU on Egypt's Textile Industry

Hanaa Kheir-El-Din
Cairo University

Hoda El-Sayed
Al Azhar University

10.1   Introduction

Egypt and the European Union (EU) are engaged in bilateral negotiations concerning a free trade agreement (FTA) that would involve preferential trade liberalization. Although the specific terms of this agreement are still unknown, it is expected to be very similar to the recently completed bilateral agreements between the EU and Tunisia and Morocco, respectively. All restrictions on industrial products exported from Egypt to the EU will be eliminated, while Egypt will gradually abolish trade barriers against European exports over a 12-year period.

As Egypt's industrial exports are already allowed free access to the EU – with the exception of exports beyond a quota imposed on yarns and fabrics – the economic argument against this arrangement is clear. By discriminating in favour of EU countries, the possibility of trade diversion arises. The elimination of tariffs on imports from the EU may induce Egyptian consumers and producers to import from EU less efficient suppliers than from other sources of supply in the rest of the world. Offsetting trade creation, although beneficial to Egyptian consumers who would enjoy lower priced, better quality and more diversified imports, would hurt Egyptian producers confronted with increased competition on the domestic market.

This paper examines the implications of preferential liberalization on the Egyptian textile and clothing industry. It is organized as follows: Section 10.2 assesses the export performance of the cotton textile industry, with particular emphasis on its relative position in EU markets. Production efficiency and extent of protection given to various stages of this industry are also considered. Section 10.3 presents an assessment of potential impacts of a FTA with the EU on the competitiveness of this industry in EU markets and domestically. Section 10.4 turns to the changes required to face the post-FTA environment, and asks how the EU can help in the transition period to full liberalization. A final section sums up the findings and policy recommendations.

10.2   The present performance of Egypt's textile industry

The textile industry is one of the oldest industrial activities in Egypt. Although its relative importance has been declining in recent years, it is the second largest manufacturing sector after food processing. It accounted for 22% of total industrial (non-oil) output and one third of total export earnings in 1993/4, down from 30% of output and 40% of exports in the 1980s. Imports of textiles are very limited, averaging only 3.7% of total imports during 1989–94. With some 500,000 workers, the industry accounts for a quarter of total employment in manufacturing. Of this total, 210,000 were engaged in the public sector (of which 186,000 in public sector cotton textile companies).[1]

With the exception of ready-made garments, production of all Egyptian textile products has been on a declining trend since 1991/2. This reflects the world textile recession coupled with a domestic recession resulting from the macro-stabilization program launched in 1990/1. Textile exports – not including clothing – stagnated in the early 1990s, with raw cotton exports declining dramatically. In addition to the demand factors noted, low procurement prices, an increase in consumption by local spinning mills, and high export prices (as these were based on a 5-year average of Egyptian cotton prices) were factors underlying poor export performance. Finally, the loss of Eastern European markets for fine count yarns induced spinning mills to shift their production to coarser yarns. Egypt is not competitive in this area, as reflected in a persistent decline in cotton yarn exports after 1990 (Table 10.1). Exports of cotton fabrics were also affected negatively as a result of these factors, although less than yarn exports. In contrast to the gloomy export performance of cotton lint, yarns and fabrics, manufactured clothing exports performed better, increasing at an average yearly rate of 24% during the first half of the nineties.

10.2.1   The share of the private sector in textile exports

Trade in textiles is highly regulated all over the world. In Egypt, cotton lint exports were under direct government control until 1994/5. Trade channels for textiles have been less rigorously regulated. Yarn production and trade was a public sector monopoly until the mid-1980s, when two large investment companies were allowed to establish operations. However, minimum export prices of yarn and fabrics are set by the Cotton Textile Consolidation Fund for both public and private sales. This price setting seriously interfered with export sales – particularly in times of textile recession – and were subject to *ad hoc* adjustments. Prices for exports of knitted fabrics and ready-made woven products by the private sector are not regulated. Quantitative export restrictions are not imposed on textile exports.

The private sector has increasingly contributed to exporting high value-added textile products. It currently accounts for around 70% of total knitted exports, 35% of terry cloth and 30% of garments.[2] Furthermore, its export performance was not as severely hit by the world textile recession as that of the public sector. Data on the composition and trends of exports (as shown in Table 10.1) indicates that textile products for which the public sector is the only or main supplier (cotton lint, yarns) lost ground while segments of the industry with higher value-added products and in which private sector participation is high, tended to expand (clothing and other textile manufactures). The share of cotton lint fell from 28% in 1989 to 7% in 1993[3] and that of yarn fell from 46% to 34%, while that of manufactured clothing jumped from 8% to 20% and that of fabrics and other textiles rose from 8% and 10%, to 11% and 14%, respectively. This reveals the private sector's ability to adapt to changing conditions and to penetrate external markets.

Table 10.1 Textile exports by component, 1989–94 (million £E)

	1989		1990		1991	
Cotton, raw	594.2	28%	562.2	23%	193.4	8%
Cotton yarn	990.2	46%	1045.8	43%	986.5	42%
Cotton fabrics	176.5	8%	219.7	9%	309.1	13%
Manufactured clothing	169.8	8%	465.2	19%	554.0	24%
Others	225.5	10%	152.8	6%	303.9	13%
Total textile exports	2156.3	100%	2445.7	100%	2346.9	100%

	1992		1993		1994	
Cotton, raw	175.2	8%	146.6	7%	791.1	21%
Cotton yarn	819.8	39%	720.5	33%	1279.5	34%
Cotton fabrics	236.9	11%	272.3	13%	409.0	11%
Manufactured clothing	542.8	26%	665.3	31%	780.3	20%
Others	327.5	16%	354.9	16%	552.1	14%
Total textile exports	2102.3	100%	2159.8	100%	3812.1	100%

Source: *Statistical Yearbook*, CAPMAS.

10.2.2 The share of the EU in textile exports

The EU constitutes the major export market for Egyptian textiles and clothing (Table 10.2), accounting for almost 53% of total exports of these items. During 1988–95, exports of yarn, fabrics and knitted garments to the EU increased by 40%, 187%, and 332%. Export prices in European markets also rose more rapidly than on world markets, reflecting a boom in European demand in 1994–5, a sharp decline in Asian cotton and textile exports in 1994, and an increase in duty-free quotas of 50% for yarn and 90% for fabrics.[4] Exports of yarns and fabrics are admitted to the EU duty free within negotiated quotas. These have not been a serious constraint to Egyptian exports of yarn and fabrics, as the utilization ratio averaged about 87% and 96% of their respective quotas. The same is true in the US market.[5] This suggests that the export performance of Egyptian textiles is mostly constrained by domestic factors rather than by limiting conditions in export markets.

10.2.3 Export potential

It is generally claimed that Egypt's comparative advantage relies on its natural resources, its location and its labour. Its natural resources yield a variety of extra long (ELS) and long (LS) staples (over $1\frac{1}{4}$ inches long) and medium-long staples (MLS) ($1\frac{1}{8}$ to $1\frac{1}{4}$ inches). Long staple production

Table 10.2 EU share of Egyptian textile exports according to 2-digit HS classification 1994 ('000 US$)

HS No.	Textile products	Exports to the world	Exports to EU	% Share of EU
50	Silk yarn and fabrics	40	0	0.00
51	Wool yarn and fabrics	556	231	41.55
52	Cotton yarn and fabrics	736 504	419 335	56.94
53	Other natural fibre yarns and fabrics	13 630	7 016	25.74
54	Man-made filament	4 698	375	7.98
55	Man-made staple fibres	3 032	786	25.92
56	Wadding, yarn, twine	5 902	4 245	71.92
57	Carpets and other floor coverings	34 069	18 796	55.17
58	Woven fabrics, laces,...	1 807	787	43.55
59	Impregnated, coated,... fabrics	1 122	347	30.93
60	Knitted or crocheted fabrics	1 013	269	26.55
61	Knitted or crocheted clothing	84 055	35 962	42.78
62	Clothing, not knitted or crocheted	145 650	44 708	30.70
63	Made-up textile articles	67 060	48 139	71.78
Total		1 099 138	580 996	52.86

Source: Compiled from COMTRADE

has been falling since the mid-1970s. By 1992, medium-long varieties accounted for over 70% of total cotton output. Egypt's share of world premium extra long staples has fallen dramatically. In 1980/1 Egyptian output of this variety amounted to 59.2% of global output, by 1989/90 Egypt's share had fallen to 27%. In contrast, India's share rose from 12.2% to 24%.

Egypt's comparative advantage does not lie in the simplest, most labour intensive goods where it is unable to compete with East and South Asia. However a comparison of labour costs in garment production puts Egypt among the lowest labour cost producers (Table 10.3). While it cannot compete with China, Indonesia, Pakistan, Sri Lanka and Vietnam in terms of labour cost, it can easily compete with India, the Philippines, or Thailand, particularly if location and transport costs are accounted for. Egypt is close to the Europe, giving it an advantage in these markets.[6] This suggests what is required is to find a suitable niche where Egypt could differentiate its products and capitalize on its locational advantages and the quality of its cotton endowment.

Simple indicators of significant export potential are positive trends in exports and increasing market shares in major export markets. Inspection

Table 10.3 Comparison of labour costs in the garment sector in selected countries, summer 1993

Country	Average cost per operator/hour as % of US cost	Indirect charges as % of gross wages
Brazil	13.0	70.0
China	3.0	33.0
Egypt	5.0	43.0
Hong Kong	33.0	16.0
India	5.0	38.0
Indonesia	4.0	26.0
Italy	140.0	99.0
Japan	204.0	68.0
Rep.of Korea	32.0	44.0
Malaysia	10.0	46.0
Pakistan	4.0	49.0
Philippines	7.0	29.0
Singapore	31.0	22.0
Sri Lanka	3.0	20.0
Taiwan	50.0	34.0
Thailand	9.0	11.0
Turkey	30.0	71.0
United States	100.0	33.0
Vietnam	3.0	27.0

Source: Werner International Inc., *Spinning and Weaving Cost Comparisons*, Summer 1993 (New York)

of the average annual percentage rate of change over the period 1990–4 of the export value, quantity, unit value and EU market shares of different product items at the 2-digit level of the Harmonized System classification shows this. Although the trends for particular textile products diverged considerably, they all point to the existence of export potential for items in all product groups with the exception of group 53 where Egypt seems to be losing ground with respect to other sources of supply.

Another measure of international competitiveness is a positive trade balance for disaggregated product categories. The 'revealed comparative advantage' (RCA) index is often used in this connection. This is a measure of a country's relative specialization in particular products.[7] By construction, the country has comparative advantage in products with RCA > 0. The higher the RCA index, the more successful is the trade performance of the industry in question. Egypt appears to have a comparative advantage in all 14 groups of textile products considered in Table 10.4.[8] Its comparative advantage in the EU is higher than in the rest of the world for all textile and clothing products except for woven fabrics (item 58) and knitted fabrics (item 60).

10.2.4 Efficiency of the industry

The issue of economic efficiency of the Egyptian cotton textile and clothing industry is now of particular importance. Aggressive competition is expected to prevail in both domestic and international markets, both as a result of trade liberalization under the WTO and the implementation of a

Table 10.4 Revealed comparative advantage of Egypt, 1994

HS No.	Textile products	RCA(%)	
		World	EU
50	Silk yarn and fabrics	25	
51	Wool yarn and fabrics	−196	−184
52	Cotton yarn and fabrics	425	609
53	Other natural fibre yarns and fabrics	226	297
54	Man-made filament	−149	−230
55	Man-made staple fibres	−190	−285
56	Wadding, yarn, twine	23	76
57	Carpets and other floor coverings	365	547
58	Woven fabrics, laces,...	89	73
59	Impregnated, coated,... fabrics	−109	−156
60	Knitted or crocheted fabrics	165	118
61	Knitted or crocheted clothing	438	603
62	Clothing, not knitted or crocheted	531	571
63	Made-up textile articles	397	592

partnership agreement with the EU. Indicators to assess economic efficiency include financial returns, labour productivity, input waste rates, and capacity utilization. A comprehensive indicator is the domestic resource cost per unit of foreign exchange (DRC). A recent audit reports that the rate of defective output of a sample of major items produced by 13 cotton textile companies (accounting for 64.65% of total production and 61.92% of exports of the 25 public sector cotton textile companies) increased in 9 firms between 1992/3 and 1993/4, ranging from 6.2% and 57.7% for individual products. Input waste rates were found to exceed the standard rates in 10 of the 13 companies. Efficiency in using cotton lint as measured by the amount of lint per ton of yarn was reported to have increased in 12 companies. The average count number of yarn never exceeded 35, a relatively thick medium-count yarn.

A great deal has been written on the issue of the efficiency of using domestic long staple cotton as an input to the domestic textile industry. Egyptian ELS and LS cotton varieties are best suited for producing yarn counts of 51 and higher.[9] The consensus has long been that unless the very high quality – and hence opportunity cost – ELS and LS cotton is used to produce a high quality output which yields a high international price, spinning activity in Egypt will not be competitive. Egypt is mainly spinning and exporting coarse and medium count yarns, thus underspinning the fine quality lint it is using and raising raw material costs of yarn produced (Table 10.5).

Labour productivity measured in terms of real output per worker and in terms of production at constant 1992/3 prices per £E of wages shows diverging results. The first measure shows an increase in labour productivity in 1993/4 in 15 companies while it declined in 10 others (with three

Table 10.5 Cotton cost of yarn in various countries, 1995

Country	Cotton costs (US$ per kg of cotton)	Cotton cost as % of total yarn cost
Brazil	2.01	42
India	2.04	47
Italy	2.27	43
Egypt	2.21	62.5
Japan	2.32	41
Korea	2.30	51
Thailand	2.31	51
USA	2.15	43

Source: Various countries, 1995 *International Production Cost Comparison*, International Textile Manufactures Federation. Figures for Egypt have been derived from accounts of public sector companies for 1994/5, fob price of the qualities used by the companies, according to CAPMAS, 1995.

of the latter achieving negative value added in constant 1992/93 prices). The second measure of labour productivity points to a decline in wage productivity in 1993/4 – compared to the previous year – in 20 companies while it increased in only 5. These observations suggest that wage cost per worker increased faster than both real production and real value-added per worker, pointing to an increase in wage costs of cotton textiles due to declining labour productivity.

The rate of capacity utilization varies considerably among companies and production processes. For yarn, it has ranged from as little as 40% to about 85%, with a number of spinning mills being concentrated within the range of 65% to 70% rate of capacity utilization. In weaving, the reported range was 50% to 90% with a large number of cases exceeding 70%. The main reasons for the low rate of capacity utilization are either related to internal problems such as the unavailability of major inputs, poor maintenance of machinery and equipment, inadequate supervision, lack of incentives, negligence or insufficient demand.

All of these factors result in high costs of production relative to domestic and export sales prices. Domestic sales prices and export prices barely cover total costs of the majority of products considered, sometimes do not cover production costs and in a few instances even fail to cover direct raw materials and labour costs. No information is available on the relative importance of the selected manufactured products in total production of the companies concerned. However, the audit report refers to them as being the 'major products'.

10.2.5 Domestic resource cost (DRC) estimates

The DRC measures the amount of domestic resources required to earn (or save) one unit of foreign exchange through export (or import substitution).[10] Domestic resources that enter this measure are essentially the costs of labour, capital and land required – directly or indirectly – in the production process. As domestic prices and incentives may be distorted due to government intervention and to market imperfections, costs have to be measured in appropriate prices reflecting their opportunity costs. Foreign exchange earned (or saved) is measured by the value added at world prices, i.e. the difference between the foreign exchange earned (or saved) from exporting (import substituting) a commodity and the foreign exchange spent on all the intermediate inputs used to produce this commodity.

DRCs for yarn, fabrics and ready-made garment production in eight public sector companies have been calculated.[11] These companies include one that exclusively produces cotton yarn, one that produces only knitted garments, and six others that are integrated units producing yarn, fabrics, ready-made garments and miscellaneous products such as bed linen and terry products. The share of yarn production varies between 96% and 23% of total output of these six companies. The eight companies together accounted for 47% of total public sector production in 1993/4, and 59% of total exports.

Efficiency of cotton yarn production

Yarn production is mainly coarse and medium-count. For the first (specialized) company medium yarn accounts for 77% of its total production while coarse and fine count yarn account for 14% and 9%, respectively. Although detailed data on the product mix in the other companies were not available, the average prices of their products suggest that most of their production consists of coarse and medium yarns.

Despite reform measures undertaken since the late 1980s to liberalize this sector, yarn input prices remain highly regulated. The production of yarn has traditionally benefited from high cotton subsidies: cotton selling prices to the spinners have always been set at levels far below their respective export prices, and often below their farm-gate prices.[12] Subsidy rates have fluctuated from year to year and differ from one variety to another. Thus, in 1993/4, medium-long staple varieties were the most subsidized, while in 1994/5 extra long staples (ELS) were the most highly subsidized. The traditional high subsidy for ELS has resulted in the wasteful use of this fine variety of cotton to produce coarse and medium yarns. Although domestic prices of yarn have been raised to approach their export prices, in several cases, domestic and even export prices of yarn were set at levels below their costs of production.

Table 10.6 shows the DRC ratios calculated for yarn production. Of the seven companies, only two are considered efficient in producing cotton yarn, i.e. have DRCs that are less than one. This implies that if these two companies produce for the domestic market the same yarn vari-

Table 10.6 DRC in cotton spinning industry

Company No.	DRC ratios
1	0.710
2	0.863
3	1.028
4	1.061
5	1.082
6	1.315
7	NIVA
Coarse yarn	1.331
Medium yarn	0.824
Fine yarn	0.950

NIVA = negative international value added
Source: Authors' calculations

eties they are exporting and sell them at the same export price, and if they use inputs without any subsidy, they would be efficient, Thus, it would be beneficial to the whole economy to proceed in this activity as it is a net foreign exchange earner. It is worth noting that the first company is the largest producer in this sector while the other is specialized in yarn production. Of the others, four companies appear inefficient at the existing level and structure of production and input mix, while the last company is extremely inefficient; its spinning activity involves an absolute loss of foreign exchange as its value added at world prices is negative and should be stopped.[13]

These differences among companies might be attributed to several factors, including the technical efficiency of using a given input mix – which depends on the degree of capacity utilization and the degree of control over waste;[14] the input mix employed (the extensive use of highly subsidized cotton, such as ELS, results in less value added at world prices than the use of cheaper less subsidized cotton); differences in labour, wages and capital productivity; and differences in the product mix.

The latter plays an important role in determining efficiency of production. This can be shown by estimating DRCs for different qualities of yarn: as shown in Table 10.6, coarse yarn production is highly inefficient while the production of medium and fine count yarn is clearly efficient. Furthermore, it appears that the use of ELS in producing coarse yarn involves a relative loss of foreign exchange. If we assume that ELS cotton is replaced by cheaper Egyptian cotton (MLS) for the production of coarse yarn, the DRC will fall from 1.3 to 1.106, which indicates that Egyptian cotton should not be used to produce coarse yarn, and should be replaced by cheaper imported qualities. Accordingly, we may conclude that improving yarn production efficiency requires to change the product mix to produce qualities with higher world prices and to use appropriate cotton input mix. In addition, improving technical efficiency is a pre-condition for the industry to be economically profitable. The necessity of ensuring regular availability of other intermediate inputs and spare parts, of improving maintenance and imposing strict discipline on labour standards may not be overemphasized. Increasing the private sector participation in this activity may stimulate efficiency increases in the spinning process.

Economic efficiency of cotton weaving

Table 10.7 reports estimated DRCs for cotton weaving in four public sector companies, in which cotton fabrics production accounts for 12% to 32% of total production. The estimates indicate that cotton fabrics production is an efficient activity in all the companies, as DRCs vary between 0.36 and 0.78. Differences in estimates mainly reflect the wide variation in the product mix in each company as well as their prices.

Greater efficiency is related to improved production quality and hence higher prices and value added. It should be noted that inputs have a smaller impact on the DRCs of fabric production than in yarn production. All the companies in the sample use mainly coarse yarn, which is the cheapest quality produced domestically and represents a relatively small portion of total costs of production.

Efficiency of other textile and clothing production

Other textile and clothing industries include garments, knitted garments, bed linen and terry products. Results are shown in Table 10.8. The calculations for ready-made garments were made for only two companies. They reveal that both are inefficient in producing cotton ready-made garments. This may be explained by the use of expensive Egyptian cotton fabrics to produce cheap cotton clothes. Knitwear and other products in contrast all seem highly efficient; their export unit values are high, and so is value added at world prices relative to the resources used in production.

Protection of textile and clothing industries

Restrictions in Egypt are much greater on textile imports than exports. With few exceptions, imports of cotton fabrics and ready-made textile products are prohibited. Even when exceptions to import bans are granted, tariffs are generally around 70%.[15] For cotton yarns, however, there are no quantitative restrictions on imports and the tariff is a flat 30% to which is

Table 10.7 DRC in cotton weaving industry

Company No.	DRC ratios
1	0.36
2	0.61
3	0.75
4	0.78

Table 10.8 DRC in other cotton textile and clothing manufacturing

	Company No.	DRC ratios
Ready-made garments	1	1.420
	2	1.142
Knitwear		0.350
Bed linen		0.753
Terry fabrics	1	0.180
	2	0.284

Source: Authors' calculations

added an additional 10% of sales tax and a surcharge of 3%. Yarn imports have provided private sector weaving companies with cheaper and more appropriate types of yarns and enabled private sector weavers to adjust to global price competition for fabrics – particularly during the textile recession. When yarns are imported to be woven for export, they are exempt from tariffs under the temporary admissions or duty drawback systems.

This selective partial liberalization with the continued ban on cotton lint imports – except for spinning mills outside the Delta region – is denying public sector companies an important alternative for meeting international and even domestic competition. Freedom to use appropriate raw cotton in the Egyptian spinning sector is necessary to enable it to compete effectively.

Tariff rates on textiles are typical of tariff structures found in other countries. Raw materials – cotton lint – receives nominal protection of 5%, yarn is taxed at the rate of 30%, fabrics are subject to a 60% tariff, and ready-made garments and other made-up textiles are taxed at the rate of 70%. The weighted average nominal tariff on textile imports from the EU is 27.21% compared with 39.11% for the whole world.[16] Imports from the EU account for 24.5% of all textile imports, the share of imports from the EU of various HS items varying from 2.4% (item 53) to a maximum of 68.8% (item 60). The difference observed between nominal protection against imports from Europe and those from the world are due to the differences in import mix, not to differences in the actual tariff rates applied.

As mentioned, the textile and clothing industry suffered from intensive government interference in the prices of inputs and outputs. This interference resulted in a distorted incentive structure which led to a misallocation of resources. The concept of effective rate of protection (ERP) can be used as a measure of the structure of incentives given to a certain activity. Although not a measure of efficiency, high ERPs are usually associated with inefficiency while low ERPs indicate that activities are quite efficient.

ERPs were calculated for the same activities as the DRCs. Two sets of estimates have been made: the first one (ERP_1) takes into account all elements of protection including the effect of interference in prices and of quantitative restrictions on imports. In this case, calculation of value added at world prices was made according to the same methodology applied in measuring DRCs. The second set (ERP_2) is based on the assumption that tariffs are the only means of protection and intervention in the domestic price system. This is a hypothetical case where domestic price for any product is equal to its world price augmented by the respective tariff rate. Results are shown in Table 10.9, which also reports implicit and nominal protection coefficients for outputs and inputs in each activity.

Estimated ERP_1 for spinning reveals that two companies are slightly taxed, one is enjoying huge protection (value added at world prices is negative), while the others enjoy relatively limited protection ranging between 4% and 19%. Companies with negative ERP_1 are generating domestic value added that is less than what could be realized in the absence of protection. This implies that, in spite of the escalating tariff structure, other elements of protection have had an adverse effect on the incentives to this industry. However, the absolute value of the negative ERP_1 is low, suggesting that the company is producing close to free market conditions. Calculations for different yarn qualities indicate that coarse yarn is enjoying significant protection, fine yarn is slightly protected and medium yarns are slightly taxed. These differences in ERPs can be attributed to the fact that the world price of coarse yarn is very close to its domestic price, while the world prices for fine and medium yarns are higher than their domestic prices.

The ERP_1 in other activities, including weaving, ready-made garments and miscellaneous products, are all negative. This is due to wide quality differentials between lower-priced yarns produced for the domestic market and those exported at higher prices and thus yielding higher value added. If these companies were to produce the same qualities designated for exports and sell them at the same price, they would substantially increase domestic value added and ERP_1 would not be negative.

Finally, a wide gap – and sometimes inconsistency – exists between ERP_1 measured on the basis of actual domestic and world prices and ERP_2 calculated on the basis of tariff data alone. Estimated ERP_2 suggest that tariffs provide huge protection to all production activities in the public cotton textile and clothing sector. They imply further that some of these activities would not continue producing in the absence of tariffs, as value added would be negative.

In theory, tariffs increase domestic prices of tradable products over their international equivalent by an amount equal to these tariffs. However, this is not the case in practice. For example, with a tariff rate of 30% the domestic price of yarn should equal the world price plus 30%. The actual domestic price of yarn was always less than the fob price, and the average implicit nominal protection was about (7.1%). This can be explained by differences in quality and costs and non-tariff measures of protection. The latter isolate the domestic market from external influences and may make tariffs redundant.

10.3 Potential impact of the partnership agreement

According to the 1977 Cooperation Agreement between Egypt and the EU, Egyptian textile and clothing products have duty-free access to EU markets. Although in practice duty-free access for cotton yarn and

Table 10.9 Effective protection in textile and clothing industry (%)

Company No.	ERP$_1$	INP$_j$	INP$_j$	ERP$_2$	NP$_j$	NP$_i$
Spinning industry						
1	(2.9)	(9.5)	(15.2)	76.9	30	6.7
2	(16.6)	(11.2)	(11.5)	81.4	30	6.2
3	4.0	(8.8)	(12.9)	104.8	30	6.1
4	11.0	(2.8)	(4.5)	86.8	30	7.1
5	17.9	(3.2)	(10.8)	97.1	30	5.8
6	19.1	(7.3)	(15.0)	110.9	30	5.7
7	NIVA	2.4	(12.5)	NIVA	30	6.2
Coarse yarn	55.0	2.4	(15.2)	----	30	
Mediumyarn	(4.8)	(11.0)	(15.2)	----	30	
Fine yarn	11.0	(6.5)*	(15.2)	----		
Weaving industry						
1	(39.0)	(11.6)	2.5	123.1	60	28.9
2	(61.0)	(25.9)	3.4	97.5	60	28.6
3	(62.0)	(15.9)	2.9	105.9	60	28.5
4	(71.0)	(23.3)	3.2	82.8	60	24.9
Ready-made garments						
1	(3.1)	(1.5)	2.4	115.2	70	55.8
2	(22.0)	(12.9)	(10.6)	132.0	70	56.7
Knitwear						
1	(31.0)	(13.7)	(5.9)	124.7	70	28.3
Bed linen						
1	(32.0)	(8.3)	2.1	146.4	70	55.1
Terry fabrics						
1	(10.0)	(4.7)	3.4	82.5	70	58.2
2	(57.0)	(34.0)	(1.0)	85.9	70	56.7

Notes: ERP$_1$ = Due to all elements of protection. ERP$_2$ = Due to tariff only.

- INP$_j$ = Implicit nominal protection of product j $\dfrac{P_d - P_w}{P_w} \times 100$.

  NP$_j$ = Nominal protection of product j.
- INP$_i$ = Implicit nominal protection of the input i.

  NP$_i$ = Nominal protection of protection of input i.

Positive INP$_j$ means that domestic price of output is higher than the respective world price, which increases the ERP.

Positive INP$_i$ decreases effective protection through taxation input, whereas negative INP$_i$ increases protection through input subsidization.

* It should be noted that according to the companies' reports, the differences between the export price for fine yarn and its domestic price was much less than the corresponding one for the medium yarn. This was not the case in previous years as in 1991/2, where the INP$_j$ for medium yarn was (14.5%), where the INP$_j$ for fine yarn was (28.6%).
NIVA = negative international value added.

cotton fabrics is subject to quota limits. As mentioned earlier, between 1989 and 1995 tariff quotas in EU markets were not fully utilized (Table 10.10). In Egypt, in addition to the escalating system of tariffs, clothing imports are subject to tight quantitative restrictions. These restrictions were not fully effective; tariffs were not applied in free zones like Port Said and continuous smuggling from the free zones made these products domestically available.

As Egypt and the EU are members of the Agreement on Textile and Clothing (ATC), they are committed to the liberalization of trade in textile and clothing products negotiated in the Uruguay Round (UR). The main provisions of the relevant UR agreement is the gradual phasing out of quotas or any equivalent quantitative restrictions over a period of ten years starting in January 1995. Egypt has maintained the right to keep bans on imported fabrics until January 1998, and those on clothing until January 2002.[17] In addition, tariffs are to be gradually reduced. Pre-Uruguay average weighted most favoured nation (MFN) tariffs in the EU averaged 7% on yarn, 10.5% on fabrics and 13.5 on clothing.[18] While the average reduction of tariffs is expected to be about 22% in the industrialized countries, Egypt is committed to reduce bound tariffs in 1995 by almost 45%. By January 2005, tariffs will be reduced to 15, 30, and 40% for yarns, fabrics and clothing, respectively.[19]

10.3.1 The EU partnership agreement

The main elements of the proposed partnership agreement as far as textiles and clothing is concerned are the complete elimination of tariffs, charges having equivalent effect and quotas over a 12-year period.[20] Thus the proposed EU agreement goes beyond the requirements of the UR, which does not eliminate tariffs. Immediate free access of all industrial goods, including textiles, would be provided upon entry into force of the agreement (Draft January 1996). In similar agreements, such as the one concluded with the East European countries, ATC products were excluded

Table 10.10 Degree of Egypt's utilization of yarns and fabrics quotas in EU markets, 1989–95

Percentage of actual Egyptian exports to quotas in EU markets						
	1989	1990	1991	1992	1993	1994	1995
Yarn	104.5	90.2	77.9	80.3	73.2	124.0	76.0
Fabrics	112.6	99.2	94.3	73.4	107.8	129.0	74.0

Source: Calculated from Cotton Textile Consolidation Fund Data.

from the immediate complete removal of quantitative restrictions. Instead it was agreed that restrictions on ATC will be removed within a period ending January 1998,[21] i.e. half the period agreed upon in the UR. The Tunisian agreement includes a joint declaration that textile products will be the subject of a special protocol to be concluded 'on the basis of the provisions of the arrangements in force in 1995'. This implies that the immediate abolition of quantitative restrictions (QRs) on industrial goods does not apply to textile products.[22]

Egypt is allowed to apply exceptional measures of limited duration – e.g. increasing or reintroducing tariffs – under specific constraints, to protect industries or sectors in serious difficulties. In addition, any party may take appropriate measures against dumping practices in accordance with Article VI of the GATT. Practical experience has shown that safeguards and anti-dumping provisions have been used as means of restricting trade and exports to the EU. East European countries have suffered from unfair application of these provisions to constrain increases in exports of iron and steel products. Some believe that quotas were a better alternative.[23] Similarly Turkish experience with textile and clothing exports to the EU supports the view that anti-dumping measures were overly applied to constrain exports to the EU.[24]

The rules of origin concerning the ATC products apply only to clothing; in other words, Egyptian yarns and fabrics will benefit from duty free access to the EU market whether cotton or yarn is originating in Egypt or elsewhere. Clothing exports from Egypt will benefit from duty free access to the EU market only if the fabrics used were either produced in Egypt or imported from the EU or a third country that has a free trade agreement with either Egypt or EU.[25]

10.3.2 *Potential direct effects of the agreement on Egyptian exports*

Removal of yarn quotas under the UR agreement will expose Egyptian exports to increased competition from countries such as India, Pakistan and Indonesia. Other potential competitors such as Argentina, Brazil, and Korea are not likely to challenge Egyptian yarn exports as they were far from filling their quotas during 1994–6.[26] Keen competition in fabrics can be expected from Thailand and Malaysia as these have exceeded their quotas to the EU. Other competitors from Asia, South America, Russia and Central and Eastern Europe have not filled their respective quotas and are not likely to threaten Egyptian export performance, *ceteris paribus*.[27]

The EU agreement will not provide Egypt with any additional preferential treatment beyond the extent to which exports from other countries will remain subject to EU tariffs. The scheduled reduction of these tariffs will lead to the erosion of preferences enjoyed by Egypt. This may explain Yeats (1994)[28] conclusion that Egypt will suffer a net loss from its textile and clothing liberalization under the UR agreement. The expected shift away from Egypt towards other suppliers will be much larger than any potential export increase Egypt could achieve in the EU market, unless Egypt's textile industry achieves greater efficiency in production.

Abolition of quantitative restrictions upon the entry into force of the EU partnership agreement will provide Egypt with an opportunity to increase its competitiveness in the EU markets – particularly for yarns and fabrics – compared to other countries except Turkey. However, this again requires exerting intensive efforts to increase efficiency by reducing costs and improving quality of production to benefit from enhanced export opportunities.

An important positive effect of the partnership agreement on exports is the potential increase in so-called outward processing activities. Since Egyptian clothing produced with EU fabrics will enjoy free access to the EU according to the rules of origin,[29] it is expected that European investors may increasingly engage in sub-contracting activities in Egypt by creating new productive units and providing the existing ones with fabrics, accessories, designs and the know-how to produce high value-added products to be exported to European markets. This kind of sub-contracting is already pursued by both the private and public sectors, but the scope for enlarging the scale of these operations is substantial.[30] Egypt's free zones and attractive incentives to investors to operate in new industrial areas provide opportunities for both foreign and local private investment.

Comparison with other countries reveals that after the conclusion of a partnership agreement with the East European countries, total outward processing activities significantly increased to account for about 18% of total Central and East European countries (CEEC) exports to the EU in 1993, up from 10% in 1989. For garments alone, such activities account for around 74.5% of CEEC exports to the EU, compared to 12.2% in Morocco, 16.5% in Tunisia and only 0.3% in Egypt in the same year.[31] Although these activities may improve the efficiency of domestic textile industries and promote exports, they are subject to various criticisms. The Moroccan experience suggests they may result in a dualism of the economy, as they install various production units alien to the rest of the economy and their externalities benefit the world rather than the domestic economy. On the other hand, new export opportunities may emerge for Egyptian fabrics to other countries which have concluded FTAs with the EU that allow for cumulation of the rules of origin.

10.3.3 *Potential impact on Egyptian imports*

The complete liberalization of trade in textile and clothing products will result in a surge of imports. If quantitative restrictions are removed according to WTO rules, no preferential treatment will be given to the EU products beyond that provided by the gradual elimination of tariffs on EU products. However, immediate removal of quantitative restrictions on EU imports will certainly give these products (fabrics and clothing) additional preferential access to the Egyptian market.

We do not expect that cotton yarn imports from the EU will significantly increase. The main current suppliers are Switzerland and Pakistan, and no quotas are imposed (the EU accounted for only 10% of Egypt's total yarn imports in 1994). Intermediate imports of fabrics may be diverted towards the EU as a result of the rules of origin. Imports of fabrics for final consumption and ready-made garments from the EU may also increase,[32] depending on the elasticity of these imports with respect to MFN tariff reductions within the World Trade Organization (WTO) framework. Trade diversion from other suppliers towards EU products will not occur in the first years of the agreement, as the reduction of these tariffs will be postponed to the later stages of implementation of this partnership at the request of the Egyptian government.

Egyptian imports of machinery and other intermediate inputs for the textile industry are not subject to quotas and face low tariff rates (5% for machinery, 10% for chemicals). Machinery and chemicals are essentially imported from Western Europe, Japan and the US. Trade diversion will occur to the extent that Egypt delays trade liberalization with other countries. However, this effect is likely to be very limited as prevailing tariff rates are very low. Overall, this effect will be beneficial to the extent it contributes to cost reduction in the textile industry.

The development of textile imports from the EU over time depends in large part on the pattern of tariff reduction that Egypt would follow. One possibility in this connection is that the same approach as Tunisia is followed, where tariffs on raw materials and capital goods are abolished first (over a period of five years), then tariffs on intermediate goods (yarn) over a period of twelve years starting from the date of entry into force of the agreement, while tariffs on final goods are eliminated over nine years starting in year 4 of the agreement. An alternative approach is to reduce all tariffs on all goods by a fixed – or varying – amount yearly over 12 years. A third approach is that implied by the UR: gradual reduction of tariffs on textile and clothing products till they reach 15% for yarn, 30% for fabrics and 40% for garments within ten years starting from the entry into force of UR agreements until 1 January 2005.

Egypt's negotiators seem to prefer the first back-loaded approach which would provide Egyptian industry with increased effective protection during the first years of the implementation of the partnership agreement. In fact, while this pattern of tariff reduction may assist Egyptian industry to restructure and to adapt to the new environment, the resulting increase of protection might create additional inefficiencies. Moreover, some argue that it might be more difficult for the government to start liberalization of the final products after providing them with increased protection: public and private producer may resist such measures.

Calculations have been made for the possible effect of the three alternative approaches on the ERP for textiles and clothing, as shown in Table 10.11. It appears that the first two approaches (options a and b) give similar results for cotton yarn, namely a gradual phasing out of all effective protection due to tariffs. However, the results differ for all other textile products. Gradual reduction of all tariffs implies a gradual phasing out of ERP to all activities, as shown in option b; while, according to the Tunisian model (option a), ERP will increase to reach a maximum by the end of year 3 for fabrics, ready-made garments and knitwear before starting to decline till complete erosion. The latter alternative (option a) might be less disrupting to the Egyptian textile industry as it allows 3–4 years to this industry to adapt to the new environment. On the other hand, this period is not long enough to have a damaging effect on the pattern of resource allocation. The results also

Table 10.11 ERP under various patterns of tariff reduction

	Year 0	Year 3			Year 6		
		a	b	c	a	b	c
Cotton yarn	90.9	66.3	62.9	70.5	47.1	41.9	55.2
Cotton fabrics	100.3	112.6	69.4	80.2	76.4	46.3	65.2
Knitwear	124.7	137.8	86.3	115.4	93.1	57.6	96.2
Ready-made garments	132.0	134.9	91.4	117.0	90.4	61.1	105.8

	Year 9			Year 12		
	a	b	c	a	b	c
Cotton yarn	21.4	20.9	39.9	0	0	39.9
Cotton fabrics	39.6	23.2	50.5	0	0	50.5
Knitwear	48.0	28.8	84.1	0	0	84.1
Ready-made garments	45.2	30.7	94.6	0	0	94.6

Year 0 = according to the tariff structure in 1995.
Year 3 and thereafter = the end of year (or the beginning of the following year)
a   tariff elimination according to the Tunisian model.
b   uniform tariff reduction till complete elimination by year 12 .
c   uniform tariff reduction over 10 years according to WTO.

imply that if the Tunisian approach is applied, imports of fabrics and clothing will not increase significantly during the first 3–4 years, while after that they will certainly increase at a higher rate in view of the declining protection.

The share of the EU total imports in Egypt from textile products – including woollen and silk products – and clothing reached around 31% in 1994, while tariffs revenues generated by the EU accounted for only 17% of the total tariffs revenues obtained from imports of spinning and weaving products.

Finally, the WTO approach to tariff reduction (option c) is more conservative than the first two approaches, as it does not lead to complete elimination of tariffs. Furthermore, it has the advantage of being non-preferential and hence does not discriminate between various groups of trade partners. Yet, the Tunisian model (option a) appears to provide cotton fabrics and clothing with higher protection than the WTO approach to tariff reduction until the end of year 3 of its implementation.[33]

10.4   Necessary changes to face the new environment

In relation to Egypt's exports the main beneficial direct impact of EU/FTA will stem from the elimination of existing tax exempt quotas, although these quotas have never been actually constraining Egyptian exports of cotton yarns and fabrics to EU. Egypt's export performance will thus depend crucially on improving its competitiveness *vis-a-vis* EU producers and other competitors in the Middle East and Eastern Europe. Improving the rate of capacity utilization and fostering productivity growth are necessary. Enlarging supply capacity and attracting new investments to textile and clothing activities are also necessary. However, this depends on what Egypt does to increase technical efficiency, improve the investment climate and reduce transactions costs.

On the import side, removal of tariffs on intermediate inputs and machinery from the EU are likely to reduce costs of production, but gradual removal of tariffs on textile and clothing imports from the EU will subject highly protected domestic production activities to increased competition. Two questions arise. First, will Egypt be able to compete with EU companies with respect to quality and price? Second, will Egypt be able to upgrade its infrastructure and reduce transaction costs during the transition period?

10.4.1 Spinning activity

In the area of cotton spinning, although value added at international prices is positive in all but one public sector company (see above), the activity is still economically disadvantageous due to high prices of cotton varieties with respect to yarn produced. Large public investments in upgrading, modernizing and enlarging spinning mills capacity were implemented in the 1980s, and there is currently evidence of overcapacity in spinning. Two alternatives can be envisaged:

1. Substitution of inexpensive short staple cottons for Egyptian varieties in spinning appropriate counts of yarn (of count 40 and less). Imports of short staple cotton were recently permitted and currently account for 15% to 20% of total consumption of spinning mills. However their use was restricted to spinning mills outside the delta region.[34] Furthermore, exports of yarns made of imported cotton is prohibited due to the belief that this might damage the yarn market. The argument is that foreign buyers are mainly attracted by the 'famous' Egyptian cotton entering the production of yarn rather than by the yarn itself. This is a myth, however, as the quality and specifications of the yarn produced are more important in attracting potential buyers than the raw material input for producing the yarn.
2. Specializing in spinning fine yarns out of Egyptian long staple varieties. While this is the niche that Egypt has traditionally chosen, it requires a level of perfection and accuracy that Egypt is not likely to attain within the medium term. Moreover, competition from European spinners would impede rapid expansion of market share of Egyptian yarns in EU markets.

The progress already achieved in producing blends of cotton and synthetic fibres, particularly in the private sector, illustrates the potential competitive edge which Egypt could enjoy given its domestic production of medium-long staple cotton (Giza 80) and of hydrocarbon feedstocks necessary to produce polyesters and other synthetics. The regional market – particularly in the Persian Gulf and Saudi Arabia – could also benefit substantially from Egyptian production of blends designed especially for use in hot climates.[35]

Technical assistance from the EU, within the context of the partnership agreement, e.g. from Italian spinners, could be sought to enhance the quality of yarn production, reduce waste rates in cotton use and more efficiently utilize prevailing capacity. The immediate liberalization of cotton imports to allow spinners to purchase lint cotton from least-cost sources is not only essential for efficient capacity utilization but also a precondition for liberalization of trade in yarns.

Removal of quantitative restrictions on yarn imports led to only a partial liberalization of these imports, which are still subject to a 30% tariff plus an additional surcharge. Immediate elimination – or at the minimum over a two-to-three year period – of these tariffs is feasible. This would put pressure on the domestic spinning industry, particularly in the public sector, to increase its efficiency. The negative impact of tariff elimination – or reduction – on producers would be easily matched by the benefits from lifting restrictions on cotton imports and use.

10.4.2 Weaving activity

Production of fabrics in Egypt was found to be profitable at international prices (see above), although Egyptian exports of fabrics to Europe are mostly raw fabrics (grey). Egypt appears to be well placed to serve the European market given low labour and transport costs, but the ability to export fabrics has been hampered by low quality of the weaving and finishing processes. The proposed partnership agreement may enhance the quality of these processes if EU firms are induced to provide up-to-date patterns, dyes and finishing requirements. A potential benefit from the agreement is the possibility of establishing regular marketing channels with European clothing manufacturers. Very much will depend in this connection on the efforts exerted by Egyptian producers to be able to deliver the quantities and quality demanded on time.

Domestically, Egyptian fabrics are too expensive. This is an essential reason for the inefficiency of clothing manufacturing in the public sector and helps to explain the reluctance of private sector manufacturers to use domestically produced fabrics in garment production. The rules of origin of the agreement will induce export-oriented garment producers to use fabrics that are domestically produced or originate in the EU. This again raises the question of efficiency improvement in weaving. This requires either using low-cost yarns to produce the prevailing quality of fabrics or using expensive yarns to weave special quality fabrics. A successful example of the first approach is that of fabric production for upholstery. Some private sector producers have succeeded in producing and exporting good quality textiles for upholstery. The second approach has not been tested and would require additional effort, particularly in the area of finishing.

These remarks suggest that the weaving process is not yet quite ready for complete liberalization. The weaving industry could take advantage of increased protection implied by the Tunisian pattern of phasing out tariffs on inputs first and then on final production to improve its finishing capabilities. Lack of adequate supervision and negligence from the part of workers could also be partly blamed for inadequate finishing. Phasing out of tariff protection of fabrics could be extended over a longer period than that of yarn, as domestic weaving capacity is not as readily available as in the case of spinning.

Rules of origin constraints and the great potential for increased garment production requires enlarging loom capacity in the weaving process.

This can only be achieved gradually. Prices of fabrics woven in the EU are relatively higher than in South and East Asia or the Middle East. Liberalizing trade with the EU faster than with other countries (as required by the UR agreement) will not necessarily divert trade to EU sources. A necessary condition is that the import price from the EU – including preferential or duty-free treatment – is lower than import price from other sources including the MFN tariff for the same products. Also, it will not necessarily create trade with Egypt: higher prices and quality of EU products may not fit the requirements of the Egyptian garment industry. However, EU fabrics will find their way to cater for the needs of more affluent Egyptians and may provide scope for manufacturing of brand name items under international labels.

10.4.3 Ready-made garments

Although garment making is in the public sector is at a great competitive disadvantage; it appears to be quite profitable in the private sector given the large increase in output and exports achieved in the 1990s. This diverging performance is in part a reflection of the fact that public sector companies rely primarily on expensive domestic cotton fabrics; the more flexible private sector has achieved cost reductions by using imported fabrics. In addition, private sector producers have increasingly succeeded in modernizing garment making through improving designs, production techniques and accessories used (such as buttons or zip-fasteners). Although the local market is nominally sheltered from foreign competition by bans on clothing imports, smuggling through free zones has partially exposed domestic production to foreign competition. Tariff on clothing items are as high as 70% and immediate removal of these tariffs would threaten this industry, particularly as it will have to use relatively expensive fabrics woven domestically according to EU/FTA requirements. Thus their liberalization should lag behind that of fabrics to allow this industry to adapt to the changing external conditions.

The prospects for growth in this area are quite promising in terms of production and exports. Opportunities for EU and local private investment are available in Egypt's free zones as well as in new industrial areas (such as the Tenth of Ramadan and Sixth of October), where availability of modern industrial infrastructure, tax holidays, preferential customs duties, and access to technical vocational training for workers provide attractive incentives to producers. European producers are already taking advantage of free zones in El-Ameriya to export clothing and fashion sportswear to France, Germany, the United Kingdom and even the United States.

The expanding private sector activity in this domain encompasses production of a diverse mix of products including suits, trousers, T-shirts, knitwear, underwear, mens', womens' and childrens' clothing, carpets and curtains. The partnership agreement would enhance such activities to the extent it would provide improved access to the best international fashion design, new production techniques, accessories, patterns, dyes and finishes as well as marketing and advertising services. This would have a significant effect on improving competitiveness of Egyptian-made products both internally and externally. It may further create niches among more affluent Egyptians and abroad for designer and brand-name items produced under licence in Egypt and marketed under international labels. To succeed within this agreement, distinct and differentiated Egyptian products must be created which have their own market niche.

Liberalization of trade in garments in the WTO context – as opposed to the EU agreement – is likely to threaten this domestic public sector monopoly by opening the market to cheaper products from Central and Eastern Europe, Turkey, and East and South Asia. Increased competition will compel public sector firms to enhance productivity by improving supervision, reducing waste, and improving quality control. Further reducing the cost of raw materials by upgrading the weaving process would improve their competitiveness *vis-a-vis* cheaper sources of garment supplies. EU garments, even if admitted duty-free, are not likely to be a serious threat to Egyptian garment-making given their high costs. However, in so far as prices for garments are lower than in Egypt, the threat of trade creation will be an additional spur to Egyptian producers to strive for greater efficiency and reduction in production costs or to pursue joint ventures with EU producers.

10.4.4 Other necessary changes

Changes of a more general nature must also be implemented to face the preferential opening towards EU markets. Some relate specifically to the structure of the textile industry and more particularly to that of the public textile sector, others involve reforms and restructuring of a more general nature. Over the 1986–92 period, in an effort to regain international competitiveness in textiles, the government launched a number of reforms. These included measures to increase cotton yields and production, freeing of cotton trade and textile export regulations, investment in new plants as well as measures to increase profitability of state-owned factories. The use of synthetic fibres, particularly polyesters, to make modern blends is also being encouraged.

Public investments directed to modernizing and upgrading the industry were heavily concentrated in spinning. This lead to overcapacity and to imbalances between various stages of production.[36] The global recession in textile markets, together with inflexibility in production and pricing decisions led to an accumulation of inventories (mostly of 30-count yarns) and a loss in competitiveness on the international market. Stocks are gradually being reduced through use in the weaving industry, but this is not sufficient to eliminate them. Moreover, the fabrics that are produced do not meet the needs of the local private garment industry as they are too expensive given their quality. As noted earlier, public sector garment manufacturing is compelled to use these fabrics, thus incurring losses in the process.

The excessive integration of the spinning and weaving processes and in many cases of the garment manufacturing in public sector companies reduces the flexibility in responding to rapidly changing market conditions and warrants decentralization of various production units and processes within each public sector company. It requires the dismantling of these huge entities into smaller independent production units to avoid cumulation of problems and their transfer to various units within the same company.[37] Disintegration of these large textile mills is also important for their effective privatization.

Another acute problem within this sector relates to the overstaffing of public textile companies which hinders their modernization without creating social and economic disruption. The EU/FTA may provide an opportunity to employ this excess labour productively in the highly labour intensive garment manufacturing stage, provided the necessary measures for improving patterns, designs and finishing are implemented.

Finally, there is a need to reduce costs and improve the quality of support services. A recent survey indicates that in knitwear, Egyptian manufacturers generally require a lead time of 2 to 5 months compared with only 15 to 25 days for firms in Brazil. These delays, which are in part the result of administrative 'red tape' barriers, impact negatively on export performance. Developing an up-to-date infrastructure for information on international markets and export channels is an essential prerequisite for improving world market access. Lack of appropriate and reliable information leads to weak marketing capabilities and inability to respond quickly to changes in demand in the international market. Removal of such obstacles would significantly improve the investment climate not only in textile activities but more generally in all production activities.

10.5   Concluding remarks

Egyptian textile and clothing manufacturing and exports are mostly constrained by domestic factors rather than by external conditions (market access). Egypt appears to have good export prospects in a wide array of products ranging from cotton yarns and fabrics to ready made garments and other made-up textiles. These prospects seem to be higher in EU markets than in other markets. However, this industry has traditionally been sheltered by escalating and high tariff and non-tariff barriers. This has allowed inefficient production to develop at all levels of the industry. The assessment of efficiency in this industry has been based on public sector data. Although there are indicators that the private sector performance has been better than that of the public sector, particularly in exports, high protection has perpetuated these inefficiencies all over the economy.

With increased trade liberalization resulting from implementation of the UR agreements and a free trade area with the EU, textile and clothing producers in Egypt will enjoy increased access to external markets. They will also face the challenge of domestic liberalization. This will require reform and restructuring within the industry as well as in the overall economic system. The main focus should be on increasing the value added of these activities by changing the product mix towards products with a higher unit value. This has always been the case in South and East Asian countries which shifted increasingly to manufacture higher unit value products to compensate the quota restrictions on their exports to the EU and US markets.[38] A complementary line of action is to seek to reduce unit costs by improving supervision, labour standards, control over waste and quality control.

In the area of spinning, both input and output mixes must be adjusted and firms be allowed the freedom to choose the least cost input mix, using imported cottons for spinning yarns of count 40 and less and Egyptian varieties for higher count yarns. To reduce cost further by reducing the cotton waste rate and the rate of defective output, technical assistance from EU spinners should be sought. Developing blends of cotton and synthetic fibres is another avenue to be pursued. In principle, tariff protection to this activity could be phased out within two years.

In weaving, increasing value added through developing dyeing, printing and finishing processes is essential. Improving quality and reducing cost is also crucial, as the agreement's rules of origin will not allow preferential access of exports of clothing and other made-up textiles to the EU unless made of domestically produced fabrics. The EU partnership agreement would also be helpful in facilitating access to patterns, improved dyes, and know-how through technical assistance, joint ventures or sub-contracting. Increasing capacity in weaving is necessary, but only feasible in the medium term. Thus, there may be a case for extending the period of tariff protection to this activity beyond that given to spinning. However, it should be clear to weavers that this protection is only temporary and will be phased out within three to four years.

Garment making appeared to be highly disadvantageous in the public sector, but it is quite profitable in the private sector, as witnessed by the large increase in output and exports. The more flexible private sector has reduced its costs by using low priced imported fabrics, it has further succeeded in modernizing garment making from knitted and non-knitted fabrics through improving designs, production techniques and accessories used. Prospects in this domain are very promising, However, they are constrained by the availability of low priced domestically produced fabrics. This further strengthens the argument for upgrading and enlarging the weaving process.

Restructuring the public sector companies is also a necessity. Dismantling these large public entities into smaller decision units is important for increasing their efficiency and reducing the problems associated with diseconomies of scale. This will further increase their flexibility and capacity to respond to changing internal and external environment.

These lines of action, together with more general reforms aimed at modernizing the economy, updating economic infrastructure, promoting private investment, reducing administrative barriers and enhancing competition will reduce transactions costs and boost industrial activities. Transparency of economic policies to be followed to liberalize the economy is essential. Producers in both the public and private sectors should be given clear signals as to the direction of economic policy.

The question should not be whether or not to liberalize or whether or not to integrate in the world economy or, transitionally, with the Mediterranean region, and at which pace. Rather, it should be what can be done to help update and restructure Egyptian industries to increase their competitiveness and allow them to face the challenge of increased globalization and regionalization of the world economy.

Appendix

1. Methodology for the calculation of DRC

DRC is calculated as follows:

$$DRC = \frac{\text{Economic cost of primary factor inputs}}{\text{(Value of output} - \text{value of traded inputs) at world prices}}$$

The denominator may be expressed either in foreign currency (\$), or in national currency (£E). In the first case, computed DRCs are to be compared to the exchange rate; if DRC is higher than the exchange rate, we conclude that the activity is not efficient as it would be cheaper to import the commodity than to produce it domestically; the domestic activity is paying more £E per $ worth of production than it would for imports. If the denominator is expressed in the national currency, then the DRC for any efficient activity should not exceed one. In brief, DRC value may fall into one of 3 ranges:

- DRC > 1, then the activity is not advantageous to the economy, as it is inefficient.
- 1 > DRC > 0, the activity is advantageous.
- 0 > DRC, then the activity is disadvantageous, as it involves foreign exchange loss since the value added at world prices would be negative. These case are referred to as NIVA.

The calculation of DRC requires the measurement of both value added at world prices, and economic opportunity costs of primary factor inputs.

1.1 Value added at world prices

This is defined as the difference between production and tradable inputs each at world prices:

1.1.1 Valuation of Production Production of any product is defined as the output designated for sale – whether in the local or export market – in addition to the amount produced and used internally by the companies to produce another product. For example, total of production yarn in a company is equal to the amount available for sale and the amount used in the weaving process. Most of the companies reports provide information on these two magnitudes. However, where they were not provided, we used an average input–output ratio computed from other companies to determine total production.

As for the valuation of products at world prices, all the reports of individual enterprises indicate the export prices (fob) of actually exported products. These prices were used to evaluate the company's total production of each product, although in some cases, these export prices were for different (better) qualities, which imply that the world value of the products is to some extent overestimated.

1.1.2 Valuation of Inputs As for inputs, a major problem is to allocate common inputs to individual products within each company, as all the companies are integrated units, and their accounts do not differentiate between various industrial processes. Direct inputs were easily allocated: cotton is allocated to cotton yarn, yarn to fabrics, fabrics to ready-made clothing and other made-up products. As for other inputs, such as electricity, fuel, packaging material, spare parts, chemicals, they were allocated to each product in proportion to the product share in the company's total production at domestic price.

This procedure was also applied to allocate the costs of factors of production (labour, capital and land).

The valuation of inputs at world prices was as follows:

For tradable inputs, most of the companies' reports included the cif prices of most imported inputs. In cases where such information was not available, a conversion factor (the ratio of average cif price to average domestic price) was applied to similar inputs falling within the same tariff category. On the other hand, export prices were applied on the exportable inputs, mainly cotton and fuel.

As for cotton, companies use different varieties of cotton each at a fixed price. Some of the companies' reports provide figures about the quantity used and domestic price of each variety. A weighted average export price has been derived – from CAPMAS foreign trade statistics – and applied to cotton inputs in different companies.

As for fuel, whereas some reports included detailed data on the fuel component, others provide an aggregate figure for fuel without specifying its components. Therefore, the detailed information was used to derive a weighted average price for fuel using CAPMAS statistics, to be applied to all companies.

As for electricity, the report of the Egypt Electricity Authority for 1995 indicates that about 50% of the costs of producing electricity was fuelled, while the other 50% could be approximately equally divided between labour and capital costs. Accordingly, half the domestic value of electricity used in the production activity was evaluated at its world price using again the CAPMAS fob price for fuel (mazout). The other half was treated as costs of primary factors and added to the numerator in its appropriate value.

1.2 Opportunity costs of primary factors of production

Labour costs In the companies' reports, labour is divided into five groups: production, workers industrial services, marketing, management and others. Only wages of production workers were used, assuming that they reflect their productivity and hence their opportunity costs. Wages include in-kind payments, bonuses and social security paid by the companies.

The opportunity cost of capital input consists of both the rate of return on capital – expressed by the shadow rate of interest – and the annual rate of depreciation of the capital assets. The financial liberalization implemented since the early nineties has resulted in interest rates that reflect to a large extent the economic rates. We assumed that shadow interest rate is about 15%, which is slightly higher than the average prevailing rate in 1995 for investment certificates or the long term treasury bills about 12%. As for depreciation, figures provided by the companies were used, and represent a very small fraction of total cost. Finally, shadow rent on land was arbitrarily calculated as 15% of the book value of land included in the companies' reports, which is highly underestimated as it ignores the sharp increase in land value in the areas where these companies are located.

2 Calculation of the ERP due to tariffs

$$\text{ERP} = \frac{DVA - WVA}{WVA} \times 100 - \left(\frac{DVA}{WVA} - 1\right) \times 100$$

where *WVA*, world value added, is the value added estimated using the fob and cif prices provided by the companies themselves, calculated as already described.

DVA, value added at domestic prices, is calculated as the difference between output and tradable inputs at domestic prices. Domestic prices are assumed to be equal to the world price + the amount of tariff per unit.

$$P_d = P_w + t$$

ERP has 3 ranges of value

ERP > 0, the activity is protected and attracts resources into it.

0 > ERP > –100, the activity is discouraged

–100 > ERP, the activity is highly protected because value added at world prices is negative.

References

Bruno, M.(1972), 'Domestic resource costs and effective protection, clarification and synthesis', *Journal of Political Economy*, January/February.

Chemonics International (1993), *Assessment of Potential Liberalization and Privatization of the Egyptian Cotton Textile Subsector*, Submitted to the Textile Industries Holding Company and the Ministry of Public Enterprises, Government of Egypt and to USAID/ Cairo, July.

Clément, Françoise (1990), 'Prospects for the Egyptian trade of textile products with the EU in the frame of the proposed partnership', Egyptian Center for Economic Studies (ECES), June.

Hoekman, B. and S. Djankov (1996), *'An Egypt–EU Trade Agreement: Issues and Policy Options'*, ECA/MENA Technical Department, World Bank, March.

Kaminski, B. (1994), 'The significance of the Europe Agreement for Central European industrial exports', World Bank Policy Research Working Paper 1314, June.

Kheir-El-Din, H. (1991), 'Economic efficiency of the cotton spinning industry in Egypt,' in *Productivity in the Egyptian Economy*, Proceedings of the Conference of the Economics Department, Faculty of Economics and Political Science, Cairo University, 1991.

Kirmani, N. (1996), 'The Uruguay Round and international trade in textiles and clothing', in Said El-Naggar, (ed.), *The Uruguay Round and the Arab Countries*, International Monetary Fund.

Krueger, A. (1972), 'Evaluating restrictionist trade regimes theory and measurement', *Journal of Political Economy*, January/February.

Meyanathan, S.D., (ed.), (1994), *'Managing Restructuring in the Textile and Garment Subsector, Examples from Asia'*, Economic Development Institute, World Bank, Washington, DC.

Ozdem, C. and O. Demirkol (1994), 'The Implication of the WTO Uruguay Round on Turkish Economy', Arab Experts Meeting on WTO Impacts, Analysis on Arab Economics, League of Arab States, Cairo, July.

UNIDO, Industrial Branch Profiles, various issues.

World Bank (1995), 'ARE: Egypt into the next century', Discussion Papers Report No. 14048 EGT, Washington, DC, May.

Yeats, A (1994), *Export Prospects of Middle Eastern Countries, A Post-Uruguay Round Analysis*, World Bank.

Further reading

Cline, William, (ed.) (1990), *The Future of World Trade in Textiles and Apparel*, Institute for International Economics, Washington, DC.

Erzan, R. and C. Holmes (1992), 'The restrictiveness of the Multi-fiber Arrangement on East European trade', Policy Research Working Paper 860, World Bank, Washington, DC, February.

Hamilton, Carl, (ed.) (1990), *Textiles Trade and the Developing Countries, Eliminating the ATC in the 1990s*, World Bank, Washington, DC.

Khedr, H. and H. Kheir-El-Din (1982), 'Economic efficiency of cotton production and ginning in Egypt', *Agricultural Development Systems Project*, ARE Ministry of Agriculture, University of California Economic Working Paper No. 104, 105, December 1982.

Trela, I. and J. Whalley (1990), 'Global effects of developed country trade restrictions on textiles and apparel', *Economic Journal,* 100, December.

Whalley, John (1994), *The UR and Textiles and Clothing*, Centre for the Study of International Economic Relations, Ontario, April.

Yang, Chang Po (1996), *Maximizing the Benefits From Free Trade with the European Union*, World Bank Resident Mission in Egypt, April.

Yang, Y. (1993), *The Impact of ATC Phasing out on World Clothing and Textiles Markets*, National Centre for Development Studies, Canberra.

Notes

The authors wish to thank Amel Rafit from ECES for her active research assistance in data collection and result calculation, and Françoise Clément for the background paper 'Prospects for Egyptian trade of textile products, with the EU in the frame of the proposed partnership,' June 1996. Thanks also to Sahar Nasr for helping in data collection on public sector companies, and to Lorenza Jachia from UNCTAD for providing trade data.

1. This industry is largely dominated by 31 public sector textile manufacturing companies of which 25 process cotton. These companies are mainly composed of large vertically integrated mills engaged in spinning, weaving, dyeing, finishing, garment making and even retailing. They operate under law 203 of 1991 and are distributed among three public holding companies (HCs) which have exclusive or majority ownership of the share capital of these affiliated companies (ACs). This law provides that HCs and ACs operate as other private sector companies incorporated under law 159 of 1981.

   In addition, 'mixed' companies – including El-Ameriya owned by Misr Bank, and Miratex owned by several public sector companies and the Iranian government – operate under Investment law 230 of 1989.

These public and 'mixed' enterprises dominate the textile industry. They account for all cotton spinning and for about 60% of weaving. On average they absorb about 80% of domestic cotton production, the remaining being exported. These companies are also involved in spinning and weaving of wool, jute and other fibres. However, since cotton is a predominant component of Egypt's textile industry, most analysis and disaggregated data reported in this paper refer to cotton textiles.

The private sector participation in weaving, and ready-made garments production has grown significantly to reach 55% of fabrics production and to exceed 85% of total production of garments during the 1990s according to Ministry of Industry figures. The private sector is composed of a large number of traditional small scale workshops and a smaller number of medium to large scale firms, many of which are joint ventures under law 230/1989. Data on the production of this sector by volume or value are sketchy and do not give an accurate picture of its relative importance in the textile industry.

2. According to the Egyptian Textile Consolidation Fund figures.
3. This share increased again to 21% in 1994 due to a cotton crop failure in both India and China, but fell in 1994 /5.
4. See background paper by Clément (1990).
5. Egypt is also subjected to quota restrictions on yarns and fabrics in the United States, which also imposes quotas for selected finished products (shirts, blouses, towels, and woollen trousers). As in the EU case, these quotas remain underutilized for most products.
6. Of course, this advantage is shared by other competitors in the Mediterranean region: Israel, Morocco, Tunisia, and Turkey, as well as by Central and Eastern European Countries (CEEC).
7. Revealed comparative advantage is calculated by the formula:

$$RCA = \ln \left(\frac{X_i}{X} \bigg/ \frac{M_i}{M} \right) \times 100$$

where X and M denote value of exports and imports respectively and the subscript i refers to a commodity group at the 2- digit HS classification level.
8. The RCA indices have been calculated on the basis of prevailing prices and domestic and external restrictions on imports and exports. Tariffs, quotas, bans, indirect taxes and subsidies could distort the results and affect the structure of international competitiveness. Any change in trade policy towards liberalization would have a direct impact on relative competitiveness of various product groups. Furthermore, efficiency improvements in domestic production would be reflected in costs and price reductions and hence on external competitiveness.
9. See, for example, the report prepared by the Secretariat of the 47th Plenary Meeting of the International Cotton Advisory Committee, Lima, Peru, October 1988.
10. Krueger (1972), pp. 51–3; Bruno, (1972), pp. 26–7.
11. The methodology is detailed in the Appendix to this chapter. Data was collected from the Follow-up and Performance Evaluation Reports on the individual companies for the year 1994/5.
12. See Kheir-El-Din (1991).
13. Note that these five companies incurred net financial losses in 1993/4 and in 1994/5.
14. It has been reported that the waste rate in some companies has exceeded (30%), while capacity utilization rates were sometimes as little as 40% and did not exceed 85% in 1993/4.
15. They were as high as 80% to 110%, but have been reduced in 1994 to a maximum of 70%.
16. According to data obtained from the international trade department of the Ministry of Supply and External Trade.
17. As mentioned in the report of the Egyptian delegation in UR negotiations.
18. Kirmani (1996).

19. As stated in the report of the Egyptian delegation in UR negotiations.
20. According to the proposed version as of January 1996. Egypt is proposing a 15 year transition period.
21. Kaminski (1994).
22. In Hoekman's study, Tunisia and EU will liberalize QR on ATC products according to the WTO agreements. See Hoekman and Djankov (1996), p.8.
23 Kaminski (1994) writes:

    'Some provisions of the FTA made it easier to erect extra barriers against CEE-5 exports. For instance trade in steel has been governed by QR and pricing arrangements. With the removal of these restrictions under the FTA, CEE-5 exporters have become more vulnerable to anti- dumping actions.'

24 See Ozdem and Demirkol (1994).
25 The provision that rules of origin apply to third parties having FTA with one of the members of the partnership is referred to as 'cumulation of the rules of origin'.
26 India has filled 107% of its yarn quota to EU in 1994/6, while Pakistan and Indonesia filled 150% and 130% of their respective quotas during the same period. However, Argentina only covered 33% of its quota in 1994/5, and the percentage quota utilization reached 6% in Brazil, 51% in Peru, 56% in Thailand, 22% in Turkey, 77% in South Korea (see Clément (1990)).
27 The rates of quota utilization for fabrics main exporters to EU for 1994/6 were as follows: Argentina 34%, Brazil 28%, Bulgaria 94%, Czech Republic 90%, Egypt 74%, Hong Kong 16%, Hungary 37%, India 93%, Indonesia 80%, Malaysia 101%, Pakistan 98%, Peru 24%, Poland 28%, Romania 34%, Thailand 108%, Turkey 71%, Singapore 5%, Slovakia 44%, South Korea 46% (see Clément (1990)).
28 Yeats (1994), pp. 40–2.
29 Note that clothing is not subject to any QR in the EU.
30 For example, in the private sector, products bearing the Italian knitwear brand Stefanel and the US brand Joval are produced, jeans under the Wrangler label as well as Van Heusen shirts are also manufactured. A substantial portion of these products is exported to the United States and the EU.
31 World Bank (1995), p. 115.
32 Egypt imports of ready-made garments from the EU accounted for about 12% in 1994, while fabrics were only 7%.
33 The elimination of tariffs on imports from the EU will certainly affect total tariffs revenues. Under the Tunisian approach imports with the higher tariffs – fabrics and clothing – will be gradually liberalized after year four, which means that during the first four years of the agreement, the decline in tariffs revenue will be very limited.
34 Restrictions on using imported cotton have recently been lifted.
35 UNIDO, Industrial Branch Profiles.
36 Study by Chemonics International (1993).
37 See for example some Far Eastern countries experience as in Meyanathan, S.D. and J. Ahmed, 'Managing restructuring in the textile and garment subsector: an overview', in Meyanathan (1994), pp. 14–15.
38 See for example Hill, H., 'The Indonesian textiles and garments industries structure, developments and strategies' in Meyanathan (1994), pp. 150–2.

11

The Egypt–EU Partnership Agreement and Liberalization of Services

Mahmoud Mohieldin
Egyptian Center for Economic Studies and Cairo University

11.1 Introduction

The term 'services' commonly refers to a variety of economic activities such as accounting, distribution, banking, insurance, tourism, health, education, transport, computer and information services, telecommunications and so forth. Services provide the essential linkages among economic agents and enable proper functioning of the market. Growth in the value of world trade in services has exceeded that of merchandise in recent years, reflecting advances in information, telecommunications and transport technology. These have transformed the services sector, from largely non-tradable activities with low productivity-growth potential, to a sector comprising a variety of fast-growing, knowledge-based products such as banking, value-added telecommunications, etc.

Two characteristics distinguish services from goods: First, *intangibility*: services change the 'condition' of a person or of a good belonging to an economic unit as a result of the activity of other economic unit(s).[1] Second, *non-storability*: services are consumed as they are produced.[2] Thus, service transactions usually require that the provider and consumer of the service interact, and often give rise to government intervention to reduce the quality uncertainty that may be associated with intangibility. A result is that, for effective liberalization, harmonization of national regulatory systems and agreements to recognize the standards of partner countries may be essential. Negotiations to liberalize trade in services and harmonization efforts may be more feasible in a regional arrangement such as the proposed Egypt-EU association agreement than in a multilateral context.[3]

This chapter addresses two questions that arise in the context of this agreement. First, will Egyptian service industries in general, and financial services in particular, be able to cope with liberalization? Second, what are the potential gains from such liberalization, or alternatively, to what extent do inefficient services impose a burden on Egyptian firms and put them at a disadvantage in global markets? Section 11.2 reviews recent developments in world trade in services, highlights the main impediments to trade imposed by governments and discusses their rationale. Section 11.3 discusses trade in services between Egypt and the EU and the services dimension of the proposed partnership agreement. In Section 11.4, the role of services in the Egyptian economy is explored. Section 11.5 analyses the Egyptian financial services industry. Section 11.6 concludes.

11.2 The state of services in international trade

Despite the inclusion of trade in services in every country's balance of payments, for a long time services were largely ignored by trade economists, reflecting the presumption that they were non-tradables. Since the late-1970s, however, the literature on trade in services has grown enormously. In part, this was in response to the absence of rules on international trade in services and the value of such trade. The need for physical proximity between the providers and recipients of a service implies that for trade to occur, often either the provider or the recipient of a service must move to the others' location (Sampson and Snape, 1985). The various options are shown in Table 11.1.

Five categories of policy instruments can be distinguished as impediments to services trade:

1. Quantity-based measures, which involve restriction of the volume or value of transactions.
2. Price-based measures.
3. Requirements of physical presence in the relevant market.
4. Measures concerned with standards, certification requirements and industry-specific regulations.
5. Government procurement and subsidization.

Table 11.1 Classification of services trade

	Consumer does not move	Consumer moves
Producer does not move	A (e.g. financial services)	B (e.g. tourism, education and health)
Producer moves	C (e.g. labour movements and foreign direct investment)	D (e.g. a tourist going to a foreign-owned hotel in a third country)

Source: Adapted from UNCTAD and World Bank (1994), Box 1.3., p. 9.

Quantitative restrictions and standards are the most important access restrictions in the services context. Although import tariffs rarely impede trade in services, price controls are common. These involve either price setting by government agencies and/or price monitoring and approval procedures. Barriers to trade in financial services include discrimination against services supplied to domestic customers by firms based abroad; prohibition on the establishment of branches by foreign providers; restrictions on the activities of foreign firms in the domestic markets (e.g. limits on the number and location of branches); and restrictions on the employment of foreign staff and their movement in the host country.

Such restrictions are imposed for different reasons.[4] First, the fact that industrial countries enjoy a comparative advantage in services has often motivated the protection of the financial service industry in developing countries. Even if a developing country manages to accumulate the physical and human capital required to become competitive in a service industry, *reputation* will be important in contesting markets. Thus, efficient new entrants in the market of international financial services may not be able to compete with well-established firms, especially when customers cannot easily differentiate between the products supplied by the new and old firms. The interaction between governments and firms may then determine the winners and losers of trade (Yoffie, 1993). Such infant industry arguments are bolstered by the experience of many developing countries, before and after independence, with foreign banks. These were accused of concentrating on short-term credit (usually directed towards financing of trade) and cream skimming.[5] Other reasons for establishing barriers to trade in financial services include a desire to control a key sector of the economy to safeguard national sovereignty and security, and the pursuit of policies favouring the employment of nationals (see Schultz, 1993). Whatever the rationale for discriminatory policies, the Uruguay Round of multilateral trade negotiations led to the creation of the General Agreement on Trade in Services (GATS) which has as its objective the progressive liberalization of trade in services. As discussed in the following section, this agreement is of particular importance in the context of the proposed partnership agreement between Egypt and the EU, as it is likely to govern the liberalization of trade in services between the two parties.

11.3 The partnership agreement with Europe and trade in services

To determine the magnitude of trade in services, a direct measure of the value of imports and exports of each internationally traded service is required. In the case of financial services, for example, this measure should include all fees and charges received by domestic banks from non-residents and must cover the value of all financial intermediation services. Currently no such data exist; indeed, in many cases the measurement of domestic financial service transactions leaves much to be desired.[6] Most of the data required for estimating trade flows are also unavailable for Egypt, as statistics on receipts and payments of foreign exchange do not distinguish between the different components of financial and banking services. As Egypt, along with its trading partners, starts to implement the recent changes to the IMF's Balance of Payments Manual, necessary statistics on trade in financial and other services may become available. Meanwhile, the shares of Egypt's receipts and payments of foreign exchange can be used to demonstrate the importance of trade in services between Egypt and the EU (Table 11.2).

11.3.1 Trade in services in the proposed partnership agreement

Tunisia and Morocco recently signed virtually identical association agreements with Europe. It is very unlikely that Egypt will reach a significantly different agreement in the area of trade in services. Neither the Tunisian nor Moroccan agreements make any specific commitments to liberalize trade in services. Both agreements only refer to the commitments and obligations of each party under the GATS.[7]

The GATS consists of three main elements. First, a framework agreement that lays down general principles and rules to be applied to all measures affecting services trade, including most-favoured-nation treatment (MFN). The second element, which is the heart of the agreement, consists of sector-specific commitments on national treatment and market access, listed in a schedule submitted by each country. The third is an understanding that periodic negotiations will be undertaken to liberalize trade in services. The GATS covers the four modes of supply distinguished in Table 11.1. This goes beyond transactions recorded in the

Table 11.2 Share of the EU in foreign exchange flows related to services, 1984/5–1993/4 (%)

Main traded services	Receipts	Payments
Insurance	11.83	4.57
Suez Canal tolls	25.83	–
Tourism	18.57	21.62
Interests, profits, etc.	15.25	31.99

Calculated from: CAPMAS, *Annual Bulletin of Foreign Exchange Receipts and Payments*, several issues.

Table 11.3 Commitments on market access for services (GATS)

Country group	Number of commitments in services	Services commitments as share of maximum possible (%)
High-income countries	2423	53.8
Developing countries	2159	17.2
North America	193	59.9
Latin America	738	15.3
Western Europe	2002	59.2
Central Europe	351	43.6
Africa	396	9.8
Middle East and North Africa	106	16.5
Asia	796	26.0

Source: Mohieldin and Wahba (1996), p. 5. The regional classification is that of the GATT Secretariat.

balance of payments, as local sales of foreign affiliates are included. However, unlike Part IV of the GATT, the GATS does not provide for favourable treatment of developing economies. It also does not impose a huge amount of obligations on them, unless they 'commit' themselves to do so in their offers.[8] The commitments of the Middle East and North African countries, including Egypt, do not imply much, if any, liberalization (Hoekman, 1995). The same conclusion then applies under the association agreements with Europe. MENA countries made limited commitments that covered only 16.5% of the maximum possible of their services sectors, while the EU scheduled 57% of its services (Table 11.3).

Mediterranean countries subjected only 6% of their services sectors to the national treatment and market access principles, as opposed to 26% for the EU. EU sensitivity towards services-related labour movement partly explains this limited commitment.

Egypt presented offers which are somewhat more comprehensive than those presented by most developing countries. Compared to the other five Arab GATS members, Egypt has the highest level of 'no restrictions' applied on market access and national treatment (Hoekman and Braga, 1995, p. 28). However, because of low sectoral coverage of commitments and due to the relatively more restrictive measures which apply to foreign commercial presence and natural persons in the scheduled sectors, a commitment to significant service liberalization is not evident.

11.4 Producer services in Egypt and competitiveness

The Egyptian economy is increasingly becoming services-based. The contribution of services to GDP, including social and producer services, increased from 51.5% in 1985 to 61.0% in 1994, with an average annual real growth rate of 1.3% during the 1990–4 period. This is higher than the growth rate of industry, which was only 0.3%. The sector's share in fixed capital formation averaged 46% during the 1982–92 period, and it employs more than 45% of the work force.[9] Exports of commercial services are estimated at $9.9 billion in 1994/5, i.e. almost double the value of merchandise exports. Thus, while Egypt was not listed among the 50 leading merchandise exporters in world trade in 1994, it ranks 26th in terms of commercial service exports. Table 11.4 illustrates the progress that Egypt has made in this respect since 1975 compared with selected countries. Egypt's revealed comparative advantage (RCA)[10] in commercial services has also been increasing, rising from 2.4 to 3.1 between 1985 and 1992 (Table 11.5).

In the absence of precise measures of relative competitiveness, Table 11.5 provides an indication of the variation in specialization in commercial services between the selected countries. The higher the RCA, the greater the observed competitiveness of the country; any value greater than one indicates relative specialization. In the Egyptian case this reflects Suez Canal dues, remittances of Egyptian workers abroad, and tourism.

Table 11.4 Leading exporters of world trade in commercial services

Exporter	Rank				Value (billion US$)	Share (%)
	1975	1980	1990	1994		
United States	1	2	1	1	178.2	17.0
France	2	1	2	2	91.8	8.7
Germany	4	4	3	3	63.1	6.0
United Kingdom	3	3	4	5	57.5	5.5
Japan	7	6	5	6	57.2	5.5
Italy	6	5	6	4	59.4	5.7
Singapore	17	15	12	12	25.7	2.4
Canada	12	14	13	15	17.6	1.7
Mexico	15	18	18	16	14.4	1.4
S. Korea	3	20	19	14	18.8	1.8
Taiwan	26	30	21	–	–	–
Turkey	36	57	23	24	10.0	1.0
Greece	20	22	24	25	8.8	0.8
China	–	28	26	–	–	–
Portugal	27	31	27	28	7.1	0.7
Egypt	32	29	28	26	8.0	0.8
Finland	24	27	29	32	5.4	0.5
Malaysia	47	41	31	31	6.3	0.6
India	28	26	32	27	7.5	0.7
Brazil	25	34	36	35	4.7	0.4
Ireland	34	39	37	30	3.6	0.3

Source: UNCTAD and World Bank (1994), p. 15 and World Trade Organization (1995a), pp. 15–16.

Table 11.5 Revealed comparative advantage in commercial services in selected countries

Country	1985	1990	1992
Egypt	2.42	2.96	3.1
Turkey	1.32	1.76	1.65
Tunisia	1.98	1.58	1.49
Morocco	1.72	1.58	1.36
Jordan	3.28	2.83	2.48
Mexico	0.84	0.81	0.76
S. Korea	0.96	0.74	0.66
Japan	0.65	0.66	0.61
United Kingdom	1.30	1.16	1.08
France	1.47	1.32	1.39
Italy	1.13	1.12	0.57
Germany	0.79	0.65	0.62
Greece	2.05	2.47	2.69
Spain	1.86	1.71	1.69

Calculated using data from International Monetary Fund (1995), International Financial Statistics Yearbook and Hoekman and Braga (1995), p. 32.

Despite Egypt's relative specialization in services, many producer services, such as insurance, telecommunications, ports and transportation are of low quality and/or high cost, in part because of state monopolies or state-dominated oligopolistic market structures. State monopolies in these sectors are protected by artificial barriers to trade, based on non-economic criteria such as national security and 'strategic' interests, which are exaggerated in some cases to justify state control. Lack of competition and contestability have resulted in poor quality and higher costs. Users of these services, especially exporters in the agricultural, manufacturing and services sectors, are put at a comparative disadvantage, given that they have to cope with higher transaction costs.[11]

11.4.1 The case of maritime transport

Despite Egypt's strategic location, its enormous spending on transport infrastructure, and the size of the sector,[12] both the quality and cost of the transport services remain unsatisfactory. Law 12 of 1964 created state monopolies across the board of all port services. Article 7 of this law determines that 'maritime transport activities, including freight forwarding, loading and unloading, catering of vessels, maintenance of maritime supplies, [..], shall be restricted to persons or entities registered by the Egyptian Public Organization for Maritime Transport, created by the Ministry of Transport to administer this law'.[13] Moreover, the share ownership between the state operating companies and port authorities and interlocking directorship have restrained competition and reduced incentives to maintain port facilities or to improve operating practices.[14]

The comparative cost of shipment and loading in Egypt in 1994 was higher than that of Jordan, Syria and Turkey by approximately 27%, 22% and 19% respectively.[15] Port service fees are some 30% higher than in other ports in the region. While freight costs to Europe, for example, are lower than other countries, the costs of loading and stevedoring are higher, which make the total cost in Egypt the highest compared to other countries in the region.[16] Transport costs account for 11% of the CIF cost of imports, and 10% of the cost of imported inputs, and hence reduce the ability of Egyptian exporting industries to compete internationally.[17]

Deregulation of potentially competitive transport activities and stimulating private sector participation are required to enhance competition. Private participation within an adequate regulatory framework has resulted in an improvement of the quality of provided services and lower costs in other developed and developing countries.[18] Although private provision of port and related infrastructure may not be economically efficient due to large sunk costs, operating and equipping facilities via leases and concessions would make services contestable.[19]

11.4.2 The case of telecommunications

Another example of high transaction costs and modest quality of service can be found in another state monopoly, ARENTO (Arab Republic of Egypt National Telecommunications Organization). Public Law 153 grants ARENTO exclusive responsibility for the establishment and operation of the national telecommunications network and for international interconnection.[20] As shown in Table 11.6, the revenue of the telecommunications sector as a percentage of GDP is quite high, ranking second after that of the UK. But while the high revenue in the case of the UK can be justified by performance and quality of service, this is not the case in Egypt.

Compared to the other countries, Egypt has the second lowest ratio of telephone lines per 100 inhabitants, and the longest waiting list and time required for installation of new lines. The state monopoly fulfils only 65% of the applications for new lines and is not addressing the large unexpressed demand. Previous studies[21] on the cost of service/rate emphasize that almost all services provided by ARENTO require significant price reform policy. The absence of such a policy and the continued transfer of revenues to other government ministries is jeopardizing the required expansion and maintenance of services. Due to the resulting budgetary constraints, ARENTO cannot deal with the persistence of underinvestment.

Table 11.6 Comparative data on telecommunications: Egypt and selected countries, 1994

Country	Revenue/ GDP (%)	Telephone lines per 100 inhabitants	Waiting list for telephone lines ('000s)	Satisfied demand (%)	Waiting time (years)
Egypt	2.2	4.26	1277.300	65	5.8
Morocco	2	3.75	107.700	90.2	0.7
Tunisia	1.5	5.38	126.000	79	2.8
Turkey	1.5	20.1	691.100	94.6	0.5
S. Korea	2.1	39.7	–	100	–
Mexico	2.1	9.25	196.900	97.7	0.2
France	1.8	54.74	–	100	–
United Kingdom	2.5	48.87	–	100	–
Germany	2.1	48.31	–	–	–
Italy	1.7	42.94	38.00	99.80	0.1

Source: International Telecommunication Union (1995), and the German–Arab Chamber of Commerce (1995).

As in the case of transport, competition and private participation are needed in the telecommunications sector in order to lower the cost of services and improve quality. These objectives can be achieved by a mix of the following measures:[22] commercialization of services and transforming ARENTO into a business-oriented organization; liberalization of the sector by allowing open entry and respecting market forces; and privatization through encouraging the private sector to invest in the infrastructure of the telecommunications sector. Of course, an appropriate regulatory regime must be put in place to ensure that new suppliers of services interconnect effectively with the incumbent. In a study of seven developing countries, Galal and Nauriyal (1995) have shown that in the absence of adequate regulation in the telecommunications sector, investment and productivity tend to be relatively low and returns of the private sector are relatively high. Chile illustrates that if problems of asymmetric information, pricing and commitment can be addressed through appropriate regulation, producers obtain reasonable rates of return, private investment increases, and consumer satisfaction increases.

11.5 The financial services industry in Egypt

As mentioned above, the proposed partnership agreement refers only to the GATS when it addresses the liberalization of trade in services.[23] The commitments of Egypt under the GATS regarding the liberalization of financial services are quite limited compared to its 'commitments' under the current Economic Reform and Structural Adjustment Programme, which was launched in 1991 with technical and financial support from the IMF and the World Bank.[24] This emphasizes our earlier argument that the degree of liberalization of trade in services under the partnership agreement is not sufficient to improve efficiency. Any meaningful reform must rely mainly on efforts undertaken domestically. In this section the main features of the financial system in Egypt are described. The formal financial system includes a shallow insurance market, an emerging securities market and a relatively active banking system.

11.5.1 Insurance

The insurance market comprises nine insurance companies, including one reinsurer, four insurance pools and the government insurance fund, in addition to 350 private insurance funds. Of the nine insurance companies four are state-owned. The market is dominated by three state-owned companies which manage 85% of general insurance and 94% of life insurance. Setting of entry barriers is left to the discretion of the Insurance Authority which decides if a company is eligible to enter the market or not. Foreign ownership is only allowed in free zones. However, under the GATS, foreign presence in domestic market in the form of joint ventures under the 49% rule will be allowed within five years.[25]

11.5.2 The Egyptian Securities Market (ESM)

The ESM, established in 1883,[26] was subjected to state intervention which had a devastating effect on its operations and its role in financial development. The size of the market, measured by the ratio of market capitalization to GNP, is 14%, low by emerging markets standards.[27] The ESM has been the source of less than 5% of new funding for both the public and private sectors during the period 1989–91. Further, only 3% of the £E 39 billion of savings were mobilized through the securities market during the 1989–91 period. These figures are in stark contrast to the performance of the market in the 1958–61 (pre-nationalization) period, when it provided 25% to 50% of new capital raised by the private sector alone.[28] Official attempts since the early 1970s to revive the ESM have not resulted in any meaningful improvement in performance. The market's negligible role in savings mobilization and its relative insignificance as a source of capital can be attributed to both demand and supply side problems.

Credibility is a major issue on the demand side. 'Egyptianization' in the 1950s, followed by nationalization, expropriation and sequestration in the 1960s, created a credibility problem that remains an important impediment after more than three decades. Furthermore, over the years, heavy losses in the remaining joint-stock companies in the 1970s and the 1980s, 'hit-and-run' activities which flourished in the early years of the open-door policy, and the sudden rise of Islamic investment companies which collapsed in the late 1980s have all had a negative impact. Moreover, the media has for a long time emphasized that heavy speculation, especially in the price of cotton in the early years of the ESM, was behind the bankruptcy of many wealthy families and the collapse of several businesses.

It is not the lack of investors or shortage of capital that explains the low profile of the ESM. The remarkable growth of the money market and the various inflation hedges that emerged in the last two decades reveal that there is a potential active demand for securities. The problem therefore is primarily on the supply side. These problems include:[29] the prevalence of state-owned enterprises (SOEs); relatively low costs of bank funding for enterprises; over-listing of closed companies with non-traded securities; limited variety of instruments; market illiquidity; unfavourable tax treatment of securities; inadequate information disclosure; absence of a uniform standard of accounting; and lack of anti-fraud measures. Many of these problems are currently under consideration by the government, and some of them, e.g. the capital gains tax, have already been resolved. The securities market is starting to sense the new government approach in reviving the activities of the market.

11.5.3 *The banking system*

The partial liberalization measures of the 1970s encouraged the establishment of foreign, private and joint-venture banks. The number of banks registered with the Central Bank of Egypt (CBE) increased from 7 in 1974 to 81 in 1995. The banking sector currently consists of 28 commercial banks, 4 of which are public; and 32 investment and business banks, of which 21 are branches of foreign banks. In addition, there are 21 specialized banks.[30] The increase in the number of banks resulted in a rise in the number of branches to 2,241 in 1995.[31] However the banking density, at 0.38, is still modest. Most bank branches tend to concentrate in Cairo, Alexandria, and the Suez Canal governorates. Branches of the public sector commercial banks dominate the banking system, especially considering public banks' participation in joint-venture banks, which is enforced by law.[32] Public sector commercial and specialized banks, excluding their part in joint-venture banks, accounted for 62% of total banking assets in 1991.[33]

This structure of the banking system and the geographic concentration of branches indicate a highly segmented market with a lack of competition. The relatively large branch networks of a few public sector banks allow them to dominate the process of savings mobilization from the public. Other banks target mainly big savers. Financial services are still basic with very limited innovation, though joint-venture banks are in a. better position. Public banks have been protected by an array of regulations and preferential treatment;[34] for example, branching by private banks was more restricted than branching of public sector banks, and pension funds of the public sector had to be deposited with public banks. Private banks were denied stakes in public sector companies.

The situation in government-owned financial intermediaries in Egypt before the 1991 reforms can be summarized as follows: low resource mobilization; low profitability; low capitalization ratios and insolvency; complicated bureaucratic procedures for loan processing, and operating inefficiency; allocation of resources on the basis of non-economic criteria; reduced autonomy; poor quality of personnel, overstaffing and weak management. To some extent this continues to be the case. Public banks in Egypt have been more prone to government interference in credit and planning decisions than private banks. Consequently they have had relatively high levels of non-performing loans, most of them theoretically government guaranteed. Incentives to maximize profits, or even to minimize losses, barely exist in public banks, with obvious implications for balance sheets as non-performing loans and bad debts were accumulated.

It is not just absence of competition, but the lack of contestability that is a source of the problem. Contestable markets (threat of entry) can promote efficiency, encourage innovation and give highly favourable welfare outcomes.[35] For a market to be contestable there should not be any significant entry barriers. In a contestable environment, the only way for incumbent firms to prevent additional entry is to offer no incentive for potential entrants. This can be achieved by efficient pricing and allocation of production among incumbent firms to eliminate significant excess profits. However, in practice there may be different barriers preventing potential firms from entering the market, even in the presence of high excess profits. Large economies of scale and high sunk costs, in addition to other entry costs, are examples. In the case of banking, government regulations through permits and licences are the most important barriers. The main reasons offered for such regulations are: concern about possible cream skimming by private and foreign banks; fear of establishment of dominant positions; concern about hit-and-run activities; a desire to protect the interests of the incumbent banks – especially the public ones; and attempts to prevent capital outflows. While some of these issues may justify restricting entry in the banking sector, such restrictions deny competent banks the opportunity to help improve the efficiency of intermediation.

An efficient market cannot be achieved in the absence of an adequate exit mechanism. Banks in Egypt are not allowed to fail. Unfortunately this has not been accomplished through prudential policy or measures that enhance the efficiency of banks. Instead, inefficient banks are allowed to continue to operate through support from the CBE and the rest of the banking system. Fear of public misunderstanding of the failure of one bank (implying that others might follow) made the banking system adopt a form of collective responsibility. Under this approach, insolvent banks were left to operate through support from the banking system; measures like restructuring, mergers or liquidation were not applied. The result was encouragement of inefficient banks to continue violating credit standards by high risk lending and bidding for deposits. Moreover, bank clients had no incentive to distinguish between efficient and inefficient, or sound and unsound banks.

However, the government is not formally obliged by law to protect deposits, and the extent of coverage is left to its discretion. Thus, it was felt that it may be better to transform the implicit deposit protection scheme in Egypt to an explicit one. A deposit insurance fund was established in 1993 but is not operating yet. Any deposit insurance scheme cannot operate effectively without satisfactory prudential measures to reduce moral hazard problems and improve the soundness of the banking system. In accordance with the financial reform programme, the banking units in Egypt were recapitalized and Basle guidelines were applied. However, bank supervision still suffers from various limitations.[36] First, the CBE does not enjoy reasonable autonomy from the government. Second, the huge increase in the number of operating banks was not matched by a corresponding increase in either the staff of the Bank Control department or its resources. Third, in many cases, the effective supervision of banks has been compromised by political pressure. Fourth, privileged private sector borrowers were also allowed to borrow despite their poor financial condition and insufficient collateral. In 1989, so-called sick balances reached 26% of total advances to private and investment sectors, of which 56.4% belonged to only 3% of defaulters.[37]

11.5.4 Intervention in the portfolio composition of banks

Banks in Egypt are required to hold a minimum of government securities as one of the components of the compulsory liquidity ratio. The liquidity ratio of 30%, imposed on domestic and foreign currency deposits, was introduced in 1958, and did not change until 1991 when it was reduced to 20% as part of the reform programme. Although the minimum liquidity ratio did not change over the 1960–90 period, the actual spread averaged

48.7%. Thus there was an average of 18.7% excess liquidity during the last three decades. In some years actual liquidity was more than double the minimum liquidity ratio. Excess liquidity reveals inefficiency in the intermediation process that forces banks to hold relatively high proportions of liquid assets.

The rise of excess liquidity in Egypt can be attributed to the inclusion of government securities and bonds in the components of the liquidity ratio, to the extent that they became major items in banks' portfolios. The rising usage of treasury bills by the government to finance its budget deficit, especially when the foreign credit market became more restrictive, increased their share in banks' portfolios. Banks were normally attracted to the risk-free treasury bills as they offer high, tax-free interest rates. Moreover, high liquidity ratios may reflect the monetary authority's concern regarding low capitalization and insolvency of some of the operating banks. They also indicate increasing perceived risk on the part of investors and banks.

11.5.5 High required reserves ratio

In Egypt, as in many other LDCs, the use of reserve requirements against bank liabilities goes beyond their traditional role as a monetary instrument and a prudential measure. They have been used to control the quantity of money and credit; affect the liquidity of the banking system; tax financial intermediaries; and most importantly, generate revenues to finance budget deficit.[38] High reserve requirements decrease loanable funds available for investment. Depending on the elasticities of demand for deposits and loans, the bank can pass part, or all, of the tax burden to depositors and borrowers in the form of a bigger spread between rates of deposit and lending.

Reserve requirements in Egypt were imposed on both local and foreign currency deposits in the form of reserve balances with the CBE. While required reserves on the former are not remunerated, on the latter they are at the LIBOR. The required reserve ratio was set by the CBE at a relatively low level in 1960 at 12.5%, until in 1962 it increased to 17.5% of deposits. During the period 1966–78 it rose to 20%, and then reached its high level of 25% during the period 1979–90. Under the financial reform programme it was reduced to 15%.

Given the levels of real deposit rates and required reserve ratio, the spread under zero-profit assumption[39] was 4 percentage points in 1990, i.e. before financial reform. However, the actual spread was as high as 8.4. The difference between the actual and zero-profit spread can be explained, in addition to bank profits, by high intermediation costs and banking inefficiency. The decline in the required reserve ratio to its current level of 15% was not reflected in a significant reduction in the spread. While the non-profit spread decreased to 1.43 in 1995, the actual spread was 6.12. This means that the difference between the actual and non-profit spread after financial reform has increased by 0.3 percentage points where it should decline. Such high spreads and significant differences between zero profit and actual spreads, before and after reform, are symptoms of lack of competition in the banking system and high intermediation costs.

The magnitude of reserve requirements indicates whether they are used for prudential purposes and as an instrument of monetary policy, or mainly for generating income for the budget. In developed economies the ratios of required reserves are much less than in LDCs. For Canadian chartered banks the reserve requirement is 10% on demand deposits, and the monetary authority has been considering a policy to phase out reserve requirements.[40] In the United Kingdom, the Bank of England imposes a reserve requirement ratio as low as 0.35% of deposits to finance its operations.[41]

It is widely accepted that the interest rate spread is a good proxy for competition and efficiency of intermediation. Despite the financial reform efforts, the Egyptian banking sector still suffers from inefficiencies and lack of competition which are negatively reflected in the mobilization of savings as well as funding of investment.

Thus, while reform measures in Egypt have focused on improving a few financial variables such as increasing nominal interest rates above inflation rates and reducing the required reserve and liquidity ratios, they have not been profoundly concerned with the uncompetitive conditions of the banking system. The remedy for these problems does not lie solely, or even necessarily, in changing the ownership of banks. It is rather the economic environment and mechanisms according to which public banks operate that emphasize the negative effects of inefficiency and hinder competition.[42] This is evident by the fact that the inefficiency of some private banks in Egypt may exceed, in particular cases, those of public banks.

11.6 Concluding remarks

The GATS, as a first multilateral attempt to establish disciplines for liberalization of trade in services, is only a start. A considerable amount of effort is required to achieve liberalization in the sensitive sectors of financial services, transport and telecommunications. In order to expand its sectoral coverage and reduce various restrictions on modes of supply, Egypt, as a developing country, needs to be convinced of the benefits of services liberalization. Relatively high transactions costs that result from inefficiencies in banking, telecommunications or transport, reduce the competitiveness of production sectors. The protection of intermediate services, in the interest of such objectives as political control, also has significant costs that hinder competitiveness. Efforts are required to modify the regulatory framework under which these sectors operate to allow for competition for the market and in the market. By removing barriers to trade in intermediate services, producers may have access to a variety of services that modern international markets can provide.

The sectoral coverage of Egypt's commitments under the GATS is relatively low. Restrictive protectionist measures continue to be applied in scheduled sectors, including financial services. As the Egypt–EU association agreement is not likely to go beyond the GATS, it will not result in significant liberalization of trade in services. In the case of financial services, liberalization of trade and allowing foreign firms to establish are not enough to weaken the monopolistic structure, or to improve efficiency in financial intermediation. The experience of Egypt, after approximately two decades of opening its financial market to foreign banks, illustrates that incumbent banks may squeeze out new entrants or collude with them. Further efforts are therefore required at the domestic level to improve competition in the financial market and reduce the role of the public sector.

In the context of the proposed agreement with Europe, Egypt has three options: First, to attempt to converge on the intra-EU situation, i.e. free trade; second, to negotiate specific arrangements for further liberalization of trade in services within the context of the agreement; and finally, to limit liberalization to whatever is negotiated over time in the GATS. The first is clearly too ambitious at this time, not just because of the implied commitments and obligations on Egypt, but also because the EU is unlikely to accept it. The second choice is the one Egypt should pursue. However, under the prevalent circumstances it is not unlikely that Egypt will follow the Tunisian–Moroccan path and 'choose the third-best'.

References

Arndt. H.W. (1984), 'Measuring trade in financial services', *Banca Nazionale Del Lavoro*, Vol. XXXVII.

Arab Republic of Egypt (1996), *The National Telecommunications Policy of the Arab Republic of Egypt*, Cairo.

Baumol, W., C. Panzar and R. Willig (1982), *Contestable Markets and the Theory for Industry Structure*, New York, Harcourt Brace Jovanovich.

Central Agency for Public Mobilisation And Statistics (CAPMAS), *Annual*

Bulletin of Foreign Exchange Receipts and Payments, several issues (from 1986 through 1995).

____ (1995), *Statistical Yearbook*, June.

Central Bank of Egypt, *Annual Reports*, several issues.

____ *Economic Review*, various issues.

Champ, B. and S. Freeman (1994), *Modelling Monetary Economics*, New York, John Wiley and Sons.

Egyptian Financial Group (1996), 'Egypt: a new age; guide to the Egyptian capital market'.

El-Refaie, F. (1996), 'The GATS and its implications on the banking sector in Arab countries', paper presented to the Conference of the Economic Department, Cairo University, January 1996.

Endres, A. and L. Altinger (1995), 'The scope and depth of GATS commitments', Mimeo.

Federation of Egyptian Industries (1995), 'Maritime transport services from the point of view of exporters: the problem and suggested solutions', November (in Arabic).

Fieleke, N. (1995), 'The soaring trade in "nontradables"', *New England Economic Review*, November.

Galal, A. and B. Nauriyal (1995), 'Regulation of telecom in developing countries: outcomes, incentives and commitment', *Revista de Analisis Economico*, Vol 10, No 2.

German–Arab Chamber of Commerce (1995), 'Egypt: business and production factor costs', October.

Germidis, D. and C.-A. Michalet (1984), *International Banks and Financial Markets in Developing Countries*, Paris, OECD.

Glaister, S., D. Starkie and D. Thompson (1990), 'An assessment: economic policy for transport', *Oxford Review of Economic Policy*, Vol. 6 no 2.

Hardy, C. (1993), 'Reserve requirements on monetary management: an introduction', International Monetary Fund working paper WP/93/35.

Hoekman, B. (1995), 'An assessment of the Uruguay Round Agreement on Services', in Will Martin and Alan Winters, (eds.), *The Uruguay Round and the Developing Economies*, Cambridge, Cambridge University Press, forthcoming.

Hoekman, Bernard and P. Sauve (1994), 'Liberalizing trade in services', *World Bank Discussion Papers*, Washington, DC, The World Bank.

Hoekman, B. and P. Braga (1995), 'Trade in services, the GATS and the Arab countries', Mimeo.

International Telecommunication Union (1995), *World Telecommunication Development Report*.

International Monetary Fund (1995), *Arab Republic of Egypt – recent economic developments*, Washington, DC, International Monetary Fund.

K & M Engineering and Consulting Corporation (1994), 'Policy reform and institutional development assessment', report for ARENTO.

Killick, T. (1993), *The Adaptive Economy: Adjustment Policies in Small, Low-Income Countries*, Washington, DC, The World Bank.

Mohieldin, M. (1995), 'Causes, measures and impact of state intervention in the financial sector: the Egyptian example', Working Paper 9507, Economic Research Forum For Arab Countries, Iran and Turkey.

Mohieldin, M. and J. Wahba (1996), 'The Uruguay Round and trade in financial services in the Arab countries', Discussion Paper in *Economics and Econometrics*, No. 9617.

Morris, F. et al, (1990), 'Latin America's banking system in the 1980s: a cross country comparison', World Bank discussion paper no. 81, Washington, DC, World Bank.

Moshirian, F. (1994), 'Trade in financial services', *The World Economy*, May, 17, 3, pp. 347–62.

Nathan Associates Inc. (1996), 'Egypt: options for increasing market competition in maritime port services', report prepared for the Government of Egypt.

National Bank of Egypt, *Economic Bulletin*, various issues.

Sampson, G. and R. Snape (1985), 'Identifying the issues in trade in services', *The World Economy* 8, June, pp. 171–82.

Schouten, B. (1995), 'Transaction costs to private exports', World Bank draft for discussion, February, Cairo, Egypt.

Schultz, S. (1993), 'Barriers in services trade: the state of negotiations and prospects', *Intereconomics*, September.

UNCTAD and World Bank (1994), 'Liberalizing international transactions in services', United Nations.

Whalley, J. (1995), 'Services in the Uruguay Round and beyond', UNCTAD Project on the Implications of the Uruguay Round on Developing Countries.

World Bank (1992), 'Egypt financial sector report-banking sector', draft-February.

＿＿ (1993), 'Egypt: financial policy for adjustment and growth', Report No. 10790-EGT, Washington, World Bank.

＿＿ (1994), *World Development Report*, Oxford, Oxford University Press.

＿＿ (1995), *Trends in Developing Countries*, Washington, DC, World Bank.

World Trade Organization (1995a), 'International trade trends and statistics', Economic Research and Analysis Division and Statistics and Information Systems Division.

＿＿ (1995b), 'Communication From the Arab Republic of Egypt'.

Yoffie, D. (1993), *Beyond Free Trade: Firms, Governments and Global Competition*, Boston, Harvard Business School.

The author is indebted to Amr Amin, Ahmed Galal and Bernard Hoekman for suggestions and discussions, and to Hala Fares for excellent research assistance.

Notes

1. *The Economist* magazine defines a service as 'something you can buy or sell but cannot drop on your foot'. *Law Journal Extra*, Vol. II, No. 1 (1996), p. 1.
2. Fieleke (1995), p. 25. These characteristics induced early economists like Adam Smith to state that services 'seldom leave any trace or value behind them'.
3. Hoekman and Sauve (1994), pp. 1–3.
4. For similar argument in the case of Arab countries see Mohieldin and Wahba (1996).
5. See for example Germidis and Michalet (1984).
6. On this issue see Appendix (A) in Whalley (1995) and Arndt (1984).
7. See Article 31 of the Association Agreement between Europe and Tunisia; which, in this respect, is identical to that of Morocco.
8. For further discussion of GATS commitments see Hoekman (1995) and Endres and Altinger (1995).
9. The World Bank (1995), p. 160 and the annual report of the Central Bank of Egypt (1995).

10. RCA is calculated as $[X_{ij}/Y_j]/[X_{iw}/Y_w]$, where X_{ij} are exports of product i by country j, Y_j are total exports of products by country j, and w stands for world trade, see Hoekman and Braga (1995), p. 7.
11. On this issue see Schouten (1995).
12. The relative importance of the transport, and means of communications, sector reached 6.7% of the GDP, if we include the Suez Canal the figure increases to 10.5%.
13. Cited in Nathan Associates Inc (1996), p. 38.
14. ibid., p. 5.
15. Federation of Egyptian Industries (1995), p. 15.
16. The shipment cost of a 40 ft container to Europe is US$ 1300, compared to US$ 1700 and US$ 1800 from Turkey and Cyprus, respectively (Schouten 1995, p. 37).
17. Nathan Associates, op. cit., p. 47..
18. See Glaister, Starkie and Thompson (1990), pp. 5–7.
19. World Bank (1994), pp. 120–1.
20. K & M Engineering and Consulting Corporation (1994), pp. 1–4.
21. See for example K & M Engineering and Consulting Corporation (1994), pp. 1–21.
22. See the position of ARENTO regarding these measure in Arab Republic of Egypt (1996), The National Telecommunications Policy of the Arab Republic of Egypt.
23. See for example article 31 of the EU agreement with Tunisia.
24. For a similar argument see El-Refaie (1996), pp. 27–30.
25. For further details see World Bank (1993), chapter VII and Egypt's schedules under the GATS. The author understands that the 49% rule is currently under revision.
26. The Egyptian Securities market was established in 1883 in Alexandria and then followed in 1890 by one in Cairo.
27. Egyptian Financial Group (1996), p. 51.
28. Central Bank of Egypt (1988), p. 254 and Central Bank of Egypt (1993), pp. 55–9.
29. See Mohieldin (1995) for further details of these issues.
30. Specialized banks include 1 industrial bank, 2 real estate, and 18 agricultural banks based in governorates, including the Principal Bank for Development and Agricultural Credit.
31. See Central Bank of Egypt, Annual Report 1994/5, p. 122.
32. While writing this paper the bank laws concerning this point were under revision.
33. See World Bank (1992), vol. 2, p. 27.
34. For further details see World Bank (1992), pp. 1–41.
35. For an analysis of contestable markets see Baumol, Panzar and Willig (1982).
36. For further discussion of this point see Mohieldin, op. cit., pp. 17–18.
37. National Bank of Egypt (1989), pp. 142–3.
38. See Morris, et al (1990), pp. 44–5.
39. In a perfectly competitive banking system in which profits are zero, the real interest rate spread can be calculated as follows: $i_1 - i_d = [k/(1-K)] \, i_d$; where K, i_1 and i_d are the required reserve ratio, lending rate and deposit rate respectively. Hence the spread increases if k increases. Also if deposit rate rises so does the spread. For further discussion of this issue see Mohieldin (1995), pp. 10–11.
40. Champ and Freeman (1995), p. 121.
41. See Hardy (1993), p. 10.
42. Killick (1993), p. 272.

PART IV
Policy Implications

12

Globalization, EU Partnership and Income Distribution in Egypt[1]

Ishac Diwan
The World Bank

12.1 Introduction

The Mediterranean Partnership initiative launched by the European Union (EU) at the Barcelona conference in 1994 is a multi-faceted attempt at deeper regional integration between the two shores of the Mediterranean. Its goal is to develop an area of free trade and cooperation among the countries of Europe, the Middle East, and North Africa. The initiative has moved fast – already Tunisia and Morocco have signed free trade agreements (FTAs) with the EU, Israel has deepened its existing FTA, and Turkey recently joined the European customs union. The Palestinians, Jordan, Egypt, Syria, and Lebanon are in the process of negotiating FTAs with the EU.

The question I try to address in this paper is the effect of the Association on income distribution in Egypt. Because the European economy represents such a large share of the world economy, opening up to Europe is in many aspects akin to opening up to the whole world. The FTA is therefore interpreted in this paper as a first step towards global integration. The paper also asks how the FTA can help to redress negative distributional effects related to globalization, and thus facilitate the social transition towards a more open economy.

Good research on income distribution, its variation through time, and the causes underlying such change must be grounded in solid empirical analysis. But work of this nature is very demanding in terms of data and effort. My approach here is less scientific, relying instead on an eclectic list of stylized facts, theoretical considerations, and research on other countries. As a result, conclusions are tentative, and the paper should be viewed as an attempt to structure the debate on some of the main issues that are likely to determine income distribution in Egypt over the next decade.

The chapter is organized as follows. Section 12.2 reviews the initial conditions and relates them to the policies of the past. The effects of the liberalization of trade and the ongoing globalization of capital markets, on income distribution in Egypt is analysed in Sections 12.3 and 12.4. Finally, Section 12.5 discusses the policy interventions that may, with the assistance of the EU, help reduce the negative impact of globalization.

12.2 Initial conditions: unemployment, poverty and the public sector

Egypt confronts a deep-seated employment problem that has the following symptoms: high unemployment, stagnant or falling wages, high public sector employment, and low returns to education. Poverty and inequality have also deteriorated in the last decade.

12.2.1 High unemployment

Since the early 1990s, unemployment has remained high at about 12–17%, with the exact figures depending very much on definitions. The unemployed are predominantly first-time job seekers, reflecting the rapid rise in labour supply as baby-boomers enter the labour market, and an implicit social contract that stresses seniority, with first-time entrants having to line up in order to get increasingly scarce modern sector jobs. This kind of unemployment tends to be of long duration. Unemployment is high among the type of workers that are over-represented in public service, especially those with medium levels of education (*see* Table 12.1).[2]

12.2.2 Falling wages

Formal sector wages appear to have declined in the mid to late 1980s and have stagnated since. In manufacturing, for which some data exists (from UNIDO), wages fell sharply, by some 40% on average between 1985 and 1995 (over the same period, GDP per worker remained flat; World Bank, 1995a). This reflects the tail end of the regional oil-based boom and bust cycle and the failure to find a new engine to pull labour demand.

12.2.3 High public sector employment

The state sector is a big employer in Egypt, employing about 35% of the labour force (about 25% in central government, and 10% in public enterprises). But while the public sector has been large in terms of numbers of

Table 12.1 Distribution of Egyptian workers by sector and education, 1988 (%)

Sector	Educational attainment (age 10 and above)					
	Below secondary		Above secondary		Total	
Government and public sector	38	*12*	62	*55*	100	*23*
Private non-agriculture	79	*29*	21	*21*	100	*27*
Agriculture	95	*55*	5	*8*	100	*43*
Unemployed	44	*4*	57	*25*	100	*7*
Total	74	*100*	26	*100*	100	*100*

Source: CAPMAS (1988)

employees, it has been increasingly poor in the wages offered. Government wages fell by some 50% between 1980 and 1992, but employment rose 80%, almost entirely by 1990 (Handoussa, 1992; Said 1996).

12.2.4 Low returns to education

Low returns to education is a feature of the Egyptian economy. Roughly, workers with secondary and post-secondary education have wages two and three times higher (respectively) than workers with no more than primary education. These ratios are among the lowest in the region (Figure 12.1).

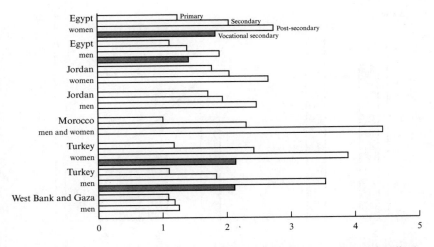

Figure 12.1 Returns to education (wage with schooling/wage without schooling)
Source: Angrist (1992); Assaad (forthcoming); Tansel (1992); World Bank (1994c, 1995b).

Education inequality tends to be much higher in the developing world (in Thailand for example, these ratios are respectively three and five).[3] Being a predominant employer of educated workers, the state of the public sector has had an important influence on this outcome. Cash wages are now lower in the public sector (Zaytoun, 1991; *see* Figure 12.2), but it seems that this is slightly reversed once the value of all benefits is taken into account (Assaad, forthcoming). There is evidence of wage compression over time, both within the public sector and between the public and private sectors (Zaytoun, 1991). In the public sector, the ratio of skilled/unskilled is smaller than in the private sector, while the difference for unskilled is smaller (Said, 1996). In comparison to the private sector, civil service pay tends to be more sensitive to seniority, less sensitive to performance, and less dispersed across skill levels. As a result, women, older workers, and workers with medium levels of education tend to earn higher wages compared to what they would command in the private sector (Asaad, 1996).

12.2.5 Relatively equal income distribution

Poverty levels, unlike unemployment, seem low by international standards. Using a conservative poverty line of $30 per person per month,[4] the World Bank had estimated average poverty at about 11% in 1990, compared with 28% in Latin America, despite lower average income there.[5] This reflects the relatively low degree of inequality in Egypt – much less than Latin America or the more unequal East Asian societies such as Malaysia, but

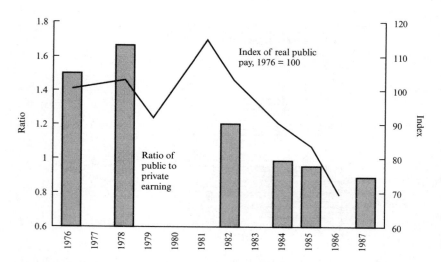

Figure 12.2 Public and private earnings in Egypt
Source: Zaytoun (1991)

still more unequal than formerly centrally planned countries, such as Hungary. This relative equality of income and spending probably reflects a combination of relatively equal asset distribution and substantial private transfers between households, that survey evidence elsewhere (for example from Jordan) finds to be well-targeted on the poor in most of the region.

12.2.6 But poverty and inequality are rising

Poverty has been rising fast in Egypt. Using a relatively high poverty line, Korayem (1994) finds that urban poverty rose from 30.4% in 1981 to between 36% and 49% in 1990. In the rural sector, the deterioration was even larger, with poverty rising from 29.7% to between 54.5% and 64.5%. This rise in poverty occurred despite a small rise in average incomes, reflecting some worsening in inequality.[6] These trends seem to have continued in the more recent past.

These stylized facts vividly illustrate that social conditions in Egypt have deteriorated in the last decade. In contrast, Egypt was among the fastest growing country in the world during the 1960s and 1970s. The state advocated modernity and 'the big push,' invested heavily in large infrastructure projects, built state industries and erected protective walls to nurture them during infancy, and sought shared growth and social mobility by encouraging education and initiating nationalization and land reforms. Fuelled by the regional oil boom, average growth per worker was about 5% a year during 1965–80 – not far below that of East Asia.

For the working population, this growth path brought large benefits. These flowed from two aspects of the development pattern, for both of which the public sector was key: policies that promoted the modern sector, especially through creation of millions of jobs in government services and protected public enterprises; and vigorous expansion in publicly-funded education, at all levels. Food and consumption subsidies were also broad, bringing benefits to the middle classes and the poor. Unskilled workers reaped gains from domestic and international construction booms. Education and public employment brought the promise of social mobility (Richards, 1995).

This set of policies was to a large extent financed by oil – a mixture of migrants flowing out to the oil centres, and oil money flowing in (grants and remittances). International migration was an integral part of Egypt's *de facto* growth and employment strategy during the past few decades. It was a potent source of labour demand, with important second round effects via the spending of foreign-earned income, that had a powerful effect on the bottom half of the income distribution.[7] When oil prices collapsed in the mid-1980s, the old sources of employment growth collapsed too. By the early 1990s, the public sector had stopped hiring;

migration as source of employment creation largely disappeared, and negative linkage effects became more important. Old forms of largesse – notably food subsidies – were cut drastically, falling from a high of 13% of GDP in 1983 to less than 2% in 1993. The private sector was hit by a rise in real interest rates and increased competition from imports.

Public employment and protected industrialization can be a source of economic and employment growth for a while (compare the rapid growth of many Latin American economies during the 1960s and 1970s). When there is a massive positive resource shock, it can be sustained much longer. But the combination of declining public sector revenues, rapidly expanding labour supply, increased urbanization, and large gains in education have made the old social contract unaffordable. When boom turned to bust, not only did past sources of employment growth – both national and international – disappear, but the unproductive nature of many of the jobs created became an unhappy and problematic heritage for the future.

As in Europe, large scale unemployment emerged because of the adverse shock – the dynamic of falling labour demand and continued rapid growth in supply. It has persisted because of the deep-seated expectations of the young – especially the educated young now in abundant rather than scarce supply, that a secondary certificate was the pathway to a 'good', modern sector job, and the capacity and willingness of families (especially non-poor ones) to support the unemployed. The old social contract is still present, if increasingly fragile, and within this contract it is the state that is expected to deliver jobs, especially to the educated (Richard, 1995).

Three groups – public sector workers, the unemployed and the rural poor – suffered most when boom turned to bust and the unsustainability of the old growth path and contract became exposed. With declining resources the spectre of distributional conflict is now rising. Meanwhile rising international integration is both creating opportunities and sharpening competition. In the international environment of the 1990s, failure to effectively integrate production structures via capital flows and trade will have high long-run costs. This means lost opportunities now, but more importantly, countries that fail to integrate risk falling further behind. In contrast, a more open international capital market can reward good policies with a large flow of capital and investment. And a more open international trading system offers important dynamic opportunities, freeing workers from the constraints imposed by domestic demand, and allowing for a growth strategy built on improved human resources and movement into higher productivity activities over time. But while increased integration can bring in large aggregate gains, it can also have important distributional effects, benefiting those whose products becomes more in demand, and hurting others who lose out to new competitors. Increased capital mobility also increases the risks of macroeconomic failure for the most vulnerable segment of society. The next two sections of this chapter focus on the effects of increased capital mobility and trade in order to clarify their distinct effects on incomes and distribution.

12.3 Opening up to international trade

Of the various channels of international integration, trade is probably the most important in the long run, but the least exploited in Egypt (*see* Figure 12.3). Meanwhile the world is in the midst of a profound opening. Economic reform is leading to the entry of huge pools of labour in South and East Asia, the former COMECON bloc and Latin America into world product markets. The Uruguay Round will lead to some further opening, including with respect to labour-intensive manufactures and agriculture (see Rodrik, 1994). The post-Uruguay Round international environment is likely to affect distribution negatively in Egypt. The liberalization of the Multi-fiber Arrangement will lead to lower prices of textiles, while partial liberalization of agriculture may lead to higher prices of food. Since Egypt exports textiles and imports food, it will suffer a negative terms of trade effect overall, although farmers would benefit if international price increases are passed on to them.[8]

These estimates of the effects of integration miss out, however, on the more important consequences of opening. In the East Asian experience, it was not terms of trade effects that brought extraordinary long run growth,

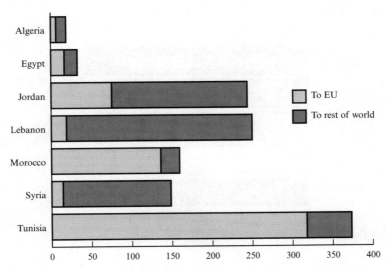

Figure 12.3 Per capita exports of manufactured goods in the Middle East and North Africa (US$)

but engagement in international markets – in association with sound domestic economic policies that allowed for large structural shifts in employment and large productivity growth. The key lies in the inter-relationship between openness, human capital, and the internal growth dynamic. While there will always be some place in the international division of labour, the real benefits from integration come from getting on to a path of rapid productivity growth and effective use of national skills.[9] In this respect, Egypt's labour force is well educated in relation to the country's income level (a reflection of past policies, *see* Table 12.2 and Figure 12.4), although there are serious concerns about the quality of such education. The real challenge is how to upgrade and use existing skills effectively.

Table 12.2 Mean years of schooling in the Middle East and North Africa

Country	1960	1990	1995
Algeria	1.74	5.06	6.37
Bahrain	n.a.	5.81	6.23
Egypt	2.75	4.94[1]	n.a.
Iraq	0.92	5.17	5.90
Jordan	1.56	6.56[1]	n.a.
Kuwait	n.a.	5.95	7.05
Morocco	0.38	2.48[1]	n.a.
Syria	2.17	5.86	6.66
Tunisia	1.32	3.58	4.22

1. 1987 figures
Source: Ahuja and Filmer (1995); Dubey and King (1994).

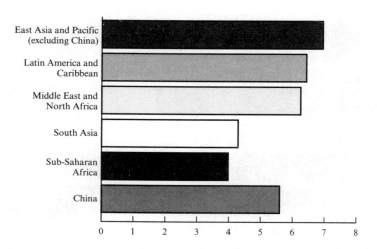

Figure 12.4 Mean years of schooling by region, 1985
Source: Barro and Lee (1993); Nehru, Swanson and Dubey (1993); ILO and updates.

At the same time, many countries within the region risk being left out of the global process of integration. The next decade represents perhaps the last opportunity for the region to open before the full force of competition from Asia comes to bear on them with the removal of the Multi-fiber Arrangement early in the next century. But while the old employment strategy that stresses education for an expanding public sector jobs is bankrupt and the need to open into a more integrated world becomes ever more urgent, some countries – notably Algeria and Syria – are in a fragile state of paralysis, needing new economic opportunities to tackle persistent poverty and unemployment but fearful of the adverse effects of opening on inefficient and unproductive current employment structures, especially in the government and public enterprise sectors. Others – Morocco, Tunisia, Turkey, and perhaps Jordan – are beginning to break out of this vicious cycle and have used opening as a means to do so. But they remain in the midst of the transition and fears over unemployment remain, as does large public sector employment. Egypt seems to stand somewhere in the middle.

While the gains for workers from East Asian-style use of international markets may provide compelling support for such an approach in the long run, most politicians are more concerned with getting from here to there. For this question, it is the transitional effects of opening that are likely to be of dominant concern. Opening involves changes in the pattern of demand for different products, with indirect effects on the pattern of demand for different categories of labour. It also involves an acceleration of the normal process of creation and destruction of jobs. It is useful to divide the effects into two: on public sector employment, for which the question of destruction of unviable jobs is key; and on the overall structure of labour demand for skilled and unskilled workers.

Effects on public employment are analytically easy but difficult in practice. Protected state enterprises in tradable activities, subject to the harsh winds of international competition, are likely to close or contract, in both cases shedding labour. Government employment and enterprise employment in services (utilities, for example) are shielded from the direct effects of competition, but there will be heightened pressure from the need for fiscal probity and higher quality services to raise productivity, layoff surplus labour and bring wage scales in line with the private sector. So the impact effects on public employment are likely to be negative.

In designing a strategy, the key question then concerns the implications of opening for the level and structure of private sector labour demand. The dominant popular view in rich countries is that opening leads to job losses, especially amongst unskilled workers, and is a cause of rising inequality in the United States and persistent unemployment in Europe. While few observers would deny that trade with low-wage countries is a source of some job loss, the weight of the evidence in fact suggests that such trade contributes only part, and probably a small part, of the employment problem in rich countries. Technological change, slow supply responses in the creation of skills, and the functioning of labour markets in Europe play larger roles.[10]

In low and middle income countries, fears of job losses are also common. But it is important to distinguish between two processes: the effect on opening the economy on the level and structure of labour demand once changes have worked their way through the system; and the likely acceleration of the process of job creation and destruction that a change in incentives will bring. For Egypt, the accelerated destruction of unproductive jobs is essentially the same as the public sector employment issue. The lasting effects on the structure of labour demand are, however, more complex.

The traditional view of economists is that opening in poorer countries would be unambiguously good for unskilled labour.[11] This was based on both theory and evidence. Poorer countries that opened up would be expected to trade and produce more in activities that intensively used their more abundant factors of production, unskilled labour, who would therefore stand to benefit most from liberalization, possibly at the expense of skilled labour. Evidence for the view that opening increases the relative demand for unskilled labour comes from data on the higher unskilled-labour content of exports compared with (protected) import substitutes in many countries, and from observed narrowing of wage differentials over time in export-oriented economies – especially the 'tigers' (Hong Kong, Korea, Singapore, Taiwan, and China).[12] Evidence of actual changes over time is probably more compelling for a government contemplating opening. Unfortunately, past work on these countries has generally failed to take account of shifts in relative supply of different categories of labour – and, as noted above, all of the economies were enjoying the fruits of previous educational expansion – nor of changes in labour market institutions. Moreover, more recent evidence, especially from studies of Latin American countries, commonly finds evidence of widening differentials – notably in Chile and Mexico, also in Costa Rica and Colombia – that were broadly coincident in timing with opening.[13] Attempts in some of these studies to control for effects of changes in relative supply of skills (in all cases there was an increase in the relative supply of skilled workers), confirm a shift in relative demand away from unskilled and toward skilled workers (Robbins, 1995).

How might opening lead to shifts in demand against the unskilled, when on the face of it, these are the abundant factor? The theory and evidence is still being disentangled, since most of the empirical work finding widening differentials is recent.[14] Three broad explanatory categories appear promising:

- First, widening differentials is a phenomenon that applies mainly to middle income countries that are intermediate in relative factor shares between rich and poor countries. Those countries are in fact experiencing the effects of the substantial increase in the international relative supply of unskilled-labour intensive goods due to the opening of Asian labour-intensive countries such as China, Indonesia, Bangladesh and India to trade.[15]
- Second, openness releases the market for skills from essentially domestic factors. Closed economies that invest heavily in education might run into significant relative price change against skills due to the expansion of the supply of educated workers. As the economy opens, the price of educated labour is going to be more strongly influenced by international trade, while unskilled wages may continue to be held down by large 'surplus' supplies of labour in low-productivity agriculture (Pissarides, 1995). This may explain what is happening in Eastern Europe during its transition to the market, and why inequality rose sharply in the past few years. It may also apply to Egypt with its low return to education and sharply reduced migration opportunities.
- Third, some categories of export – or features of exporting – may demand more skilled workers. It has often been argued that modern sector manufacturing requires at least basic education, in contrast to agriculture and informal sector services (Wood, 1994). This could be important for exports in which high quality is important. The same may apply to high-value agricultural production for rich country markets.[16]

Typically, however, the effects of growth on poverty have been much more important than on distribution. The regional experience in this respect is particularly telling. Changes in poverty in the region have generally been very sensitive to the overall economic cycle, but there have also been changes in inequality in recent times. Where average incomes rose between 1985 and 1990, as in Algeria, Morocco and Tunisia, poverty fell; where incomes fell, as in Iran and Jordan, poverty rose (Figure 12.4). There have also been changes in inequality in Morocco, Tunisia and Jordan. As measured by the Gini coefficient, inequality has fallen in Tunisia (from 43.5 in 1975–85 to 40.2 in 1990), risen slightly in Morocco (from 39.1 in 1985 to 39.6 in 1991) and risen strongly in Jordan (36.2 in 1986 to 43.3 in 1992). Thus, a lot of the reduction in poverty in Morocco and Tunisia was due to growth rather than redistribution effects (which were small and positive for Tunisia and small and negative for Morocco).[17]

The experiences of Morocco and Tunisia, the early trade reformers of the region, further illustrate both the opportunities and difficulties ahead. Following liberalization, labour demand rose fast in Morocco, with total employment increasing by about 5% a year in urban areas during 1984–94, manufacturing employment rising at 10%, and employment in the manufacturing export sector rising at a rate of 20% per year (World Bank, 1995a). But while employment expanded fast, measured average wages and productivity did not rise. The most plausible interpretation is that this was due to compositional effects with the relative expansion of lower-wage jobs. The manufacturing sector was small and protected in the past, it used capital intensively and employed skilled workers at high wages; these subsectors have been stagnant. The new jobs created in manufacturing exports were instead labour intensive and lower-wage. It is precisely this adjustment that allowed low-skill employment to grow so fast in these sectors and poverty to fall (Figure 12.5). In contrast, both wages and employment expanded slowly in firms producing for the internal market, although recently, the demand for skilled workers has started to rise.

In both countries, the net effects on inequality have been small. The demand for skills has fallen in the protected industries, but has started to rise in the export industries as a result of attempts to increase competitiveness with better technologies and management. In other words, what pushed inequality down may have been the effects of trade reform, but this was pushed up and neutralized by rising demand for skills and surplus labour. Indeed, it is striking that the two economies have higher returns to skills than Egypt, but still not unusually high by international standards (Figure 12.1).

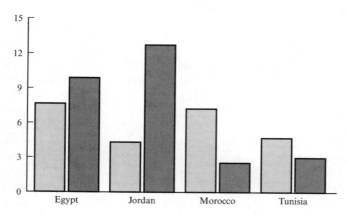

Figure 12.5 Population below poverty line (%)
Note: Poverty is defined as per capita monthly mean consumption below $30 in 1985 purchasing power parity dollars.
Source: Chen, Datt, and Ravillion (forthcoming).

The experience of Tunisia also illustrates the importance of structural change (Zouari-Bouattour, 1994). An analysis of employment change between 1984 and 1993, which decomposes job creation into within-sector productivity growth, structural shifts in employment and growth, finds that almost all sectors (except 'other services') enjoyed productivity increases, but there was net employment expansion as a consequence of growth in output and structural shifts. Rising within-sector productivity was particularly important in agriculture – the major low-productivity sector – and likely to be a major source of labour income growth for the poor. These changes accommodated, at rising average productivity, a large increase in female labour force participation between the ages of 20 and 44 (there is an offsetting effect for youths with increased time spent on education).

12.3.1 What does this mean for Egypt?

Opening may restore educational differentials. Beyond this, since Egypt falls around the bottom of the international income and wage levels, effects of opening are going to be positive on the relative demand for unskilled labour. Much will depend on agriculture which is of particular importance to the poor who mainly rely on income from unskilled labour on farms. Finally, we should re-emphasize that net effects during the transition will also depend on the dynamics of creation and destruction of jobs, especially the timing of destruction of old protected jobs.

- *The poor* The poor are likely to gain from opening, especially from the twin process of accelerated transfer of labour from agriculture to labour-intensive manufacturing and productivity increase within agriculture. Where there are terms of trade gains to farmers this will also be poverty-reducing. The process of growth expansion of labour demand for unskilled work was a key aspect in the dramatic fall in poverty experienced in both Morocco and Tunisia. It both accommodated the rise in female labour participation in both societies and allowed rural workers and workers in construction to get more productive higher-wage jobs. While average wages in manufacturing were stagnant or falling in Morocco, the new jobs were being created in activities that tended to tighten the labour market for poorer workers – those who got these jobs experienced significant rises in their wages.
- *Public sector workers* The effects on public sector employment are likely to be negative, so those that are laid-off will almost certainly suffer at least temporary losses. As the shifts in private sector demand emerge, there is potential for restoration of public sector wage differentials, benefiting the more productive public sector workers.

- *The unemployed* Net effects on the unemployed will reflect different phenomena. Some will gain from more dynamic job creation in new activities, but there will also be a temporary rise in new entrants to unemployment, to the extent that inefficient activities become less protected and governmental employment reform occurs. Both overall and educated youth unemployment is still high in Morocco and Tunisia, in part because of labour market rigidities in the modern sector, but also because of the persistence of expectations and support mechanisms referred to in the section above. However, they both have a much higher fraction of those laid off in the pool of unemployed. In 1991 Morocco had an unemployment rate of 12%, of which 55% had previously worked and 25% had secondary education. In contrast, Egypt had only slightly lower unemployment (11%), but only 23% of the unemployed had ever worked and 57% had secondary education.

The international and regional evidence suggests that opening can solve two long-run problems: it can *both* be good for unskilled labour demand *and* restore excessively compressed education differentials. However, the demand will be for productive, not unproductive, skills, and during the transition it is highly likely to be associated with: job losses for some of the educated presently in 'bad' jobs, problems of dealing with the relatively old who do not have productive or flexible skills, women who are over-represented in the public sector, and the educated young who have grown up with incorrect expectations of public sector job opportunities. Expectations can change, especially if government undertakes credible reforms both on opening up and on public hiring policies. In this respect, the role of capital flows is crucial.

12.4   Capital flows and investment

Capital flows will be an important complement to trade liberalization in affecting employment outcomes in the future. Workers need productive capital to raise their productivity, while movements of financial capital have a powerful immediate effect on macroeconomic activity, and so on wages and employment. However, the liberalization of capital markets also increases the share of GDP that accrues to capital, an asset that is unlikely to be distributed equally in Egypt. Even though the effect of capital flows on distribution are poorly understood internationally, I will try to make two points below: (i) rising capital mobility brings in opportunities, but also raises important distributional risks; and (ii) until recently it is likely to have had negative distributional consequences.

Egypt is one of the few countries that has liberalized the capital account before starting to reform the real side of its economy. One of the reasons for this unusual sequence is the importance of worker remittances in the economy, and the prevalence of capital flight under the financial repression of the past. Before the liberalization wave of the late 1980s, much of these flows occurred outside the banking sector, creating serious risks of financial collapse in the formal sector.

The open capital account brings in both opportunities and risks. Weak domestic conditions, in terms of politics, macroeconomics or microeconomics and business environment, will lead to paltry capital investment and vulnerability to destabilizing international capital flows. When capital flew out of the region in the 1980s, workers were left to pick up the bill. As with Latin America – only more so – capital controls proved feeble in preventing private outward capital flight when the going got rough. It is estimated that privately-owned foreign assets are equivalent to over twice GDP (Diwan and Squire, 1993). This represents a large tax on past growth, but also an opportunity for the future, since it represents a pool of resources that could be attracted back if the conditions were right internally.

Some of the potential has already been seen in the significant reflows of capital that occurred in the early 1990s, seduced by a combination of opening of the capital account, and the euphoria that flowed from the dual impulses of optimism over peace and the newfound international delight in 'emerging' markets (Diwan and Squire, 1995). This flow did benefit workers – overall economic activity was higher than it would have been in their absence and this helped the national labour market – but a large share of capital flows were sterilized and now sit safely in international reserves (and thus these flows did not end up creating many new jobs). As a result, aggregate investment has remained low, at below 20% of GDP (with less than half from private sources).

Conceptually, the effect of the liberalization of the capital account on poverty and income distribution is complex. There are two main forces working in opposite directions: on the one hand, the share of capital in GDP is likely to increase with the rise in real interest rates, exacerbating inequality. But on the other hand, capital inflows and investment can also rise, creating new jobs and reducing poverty. Until recently, the first effect may have been stronger, given the limited supply response.

Why has investment remained so low? The strategy of containment, whereby the public sector maintains its absolute size, leaving the task of growth to an emerging private sector, seems to have reached its limit. Instead of filling the void, much of the new jobs are low-wage low-productivity and often in informal markets. It is quite plausible that low investment is itself related to fears that reforms will remain stuck because of their potentially negative distributional effects; that is, until policy change in the real sectors passes the political test, the private sector will remain unconvinced that a new social contract more in line with current realities has emerged.

While the system now only benefits a (shrinking) minority of protected workers, it has created a web of interlocking interests that is hard to cut down. With 35% of workers in the public sector, the situation is not as bad in Russia or Eastern Europe, so the continuation of a status quo promises slow decay and rising poverty but no outward bankruptcy. But reform will not be as easy as in Latin America where the public sector was much smaller (about 15% of the labour force).

The weight of a large and increasingly poorer public sector is depressing new job creation and overall efficiency in many ways.

- Macroeconomic stability is at the constant mercy of wage increases for large numbers of underpaid public employees. In Lebanon in 1991, Turkey in 1993, and Mexico in 1995, wage pressures led to financial crises, and workers were left to pick up the tab. If public sector wages were to rise to their previous levels, the fiscal deficit would rise by about 5% of GDP. In addition, maintaining a large public sector taxes private sector growth.
- The feasibility of reform is also undermined because measures to increase labour efficiency, such as the liberalization of prices, investment, or trade will dramatically increase the losses of large state enterprises, unless part of the labour force is laid off.
- Public servants are underpaid, under-equipped, and work in overcrowded conditions, undermining the quality of core government services. The ratio of public investment to public salaries has nearly doubled in the past decade (Said, 1996). This shows in falling standards in schools and hospitals, as well as in customs operations or infrastructure maintenance. Many public employees hold multiple jobs, and petty corruption has risen. In order to increase efficiency, investment must rise, and wages must be decompressed. In turn, this is fiscally unfeasible until the public sector gets smaller.
- The high incidence of unemployment among skilled workers attests to the distortions introduced by the web of non-market based incentives – employment guarantees for graduates, subsidized higher education – that have corrupted the educational system. This is unlikely to change until the old social contract is clearly replaced by an acceptable new contract where the public sector does not play the role of employer of last resort.

The only way to permanently attract capital into long term investments, create jobs, and raise productivity is by putting in place a sound political and economic environment. In this respect, the policy stance towards international trade will be increasingly more important.

12.5 Assisting workers for change

Constructive change must rest on its social desirability. An acceptable new social contract is key, and its broad contours are starting to fall into place. But a road-map of how to get there in some acceptable way is the main challenge now. With their intricate kinship relations, households may be able to internalize some of the costs associated with rapid change, with young workers gaining from reforms compensating older parents that would have to retire earlier. But this is not enough in the face of systemic change. Mechanisms to facilitate the transfer of laid-off workers to new jobs, compensation for those hurt, and a policy framework supporting reductions in poverty will have to be important ingredients of a successful transition. Rather than spending more, the goal would be to shift resources from permanent public sector employment that undermines reform, to temporary programs that facilitate reform. It is precisely in helping and financing such transitional programs that the EU Initiative could help Egypt most.

Three types of policies can help during the transition: (i) policies that increase labour market flexibility to allow workers to find jobs where they are most productive, including reforming the labour code; (ii) passive policies that provide transfers to reduce income losses during layoffs (OECD countries spend 2–3% of GDP a year on such programs); and (iii) active policies to assist workers by equipping them for change. A key challenge in this connection is to capitalize on past successes in education and infrastructure, and salvage parts of the old industrial base, and to retrain workers whose skills have become outmoded. In Eastern Europe, governments now spend 1–5% of GDP a year on active labour market policies.

12.5.1 Re-regulating the labour market to increase flexibility

Labour policy in Egypt has been well-intentioned but misguided, seeking through labour regulations to support labour outcomes, but at best reaching a small minority of the work force. The current labour code in Egypt does not allow firms to fire workers for economic reasons. As a result, labour regulations are only applied in the public sector and in a small formal private sector. Labour policy has been irrelevant at best for small farmers who still account for the largest (and poorest) group; it has also been irrelevant for the large and growing number of workers in the urban informal sector and often ineffective for those who work in formal firms. This has created a two-tiered system where formal employees are over-protected and informal ones under-protected (Assaad, forthcoming). While this may have been a good second-best choice in the past, the challenge is to develop regulations that apply broadly to the economy as a whole, and not only in a small and protected modern sector. High and unenforced labour standards and decorative labour laws effectively preclude good regulations from being implemented and result in small and shrinking formal sectors. The informal sector is also implicitly taxed, but in different ways: it has no access to the credit system, and very little access to the legal system. Deregulation must therefore be part of the regulatory effort, the goal being to try to enlarge the modern formal sector.

12.5.2 Equipping workers for change

Even if there are no systemic barriers to mobility, labour markets are flexible, and wages adjust, workers must have resources to take advantage of new opportunities without losing their accumulated human capital in the process. The key issue is whether they have appropriate skills and access to opportunities and information. Various policy actions can help support labour mobility.

- *Skills imbalances* Jobs differ greatly in the skills they require, and workers whose jobs disappear often find that they lack the right skills for the jobs being created. This is exacerbated by the secular worldwide trend in labour demand toward workers with greater general skills and higher education. As a result, workers with firm specific skills and narrow specialization, but little general education have little chance of escaping unemployment. Most industrial and transition countries run public retraining programs. Evidence of their effectiveness is weak at best. If such programs are introduced, it is preferable to start with small experimental pilot projects first. While government subsidies make sense in the circumstances, strengthening the private sector as a provider of retraining can improve the effectiveness of retraining. As the Chilean experience demonstrates, systems based on distributing vouchers to targeted groups, allowing them to buy training services in a competitive market, can work particularly well. One area in which private provision and financing of retraining are unlikely to be adequate is the retraining of disadvantaged workers. Returns to such training are low, even though the externalities in terms of improved social cohesion can be high.
- *Public employment schemes* These can play a positive role as an anti-poverty measure. In periods of major change, although they do not improve the long-term prospects of participants, they can serve as a bridge between jobs. They are widely used in the Czech Republic for that purpose. There are examples of successful public support for apprenticeships in Germany and Japan, and of public employment for dropout minorities in Canada.

- *Supporting small businesses and startups* Countries have often tried to assist job losers by providing support to those wishing to start their own businesses. Many countries have experimented with special credit schemes and other programs to encourage the development of micro-enterprises. But such schemes have rarely been evaluated in a rigorous fashion. General experience with special credit programs in Sub-Saharan Africa and Latin America suggests that they have rarely brought benefits. In the industrial countries these schemes have been shown to be of interest only to a very small sub-group of the unemployed and have had significant displacement effects. In Egypt, it may be more useful to try to support existing small firms that operate in the informal sector with the provision of basic infrastructure and access to credit.
- *Wage subsidies* must be limited and very well controlled to play a positive role in periods of major change. In the industrial countries, they have proven ineffective in speeding up the adjustment process. There are substitution effects, whereby workers whose wages are subsidized replace those who are not covered by subsidies. Moreover, wage subsidies can easily undermine the reforms by keeping unprofitable firms afloat. Wage subsidies should be considered only in special cases where targeting is easy, such as in the case of depressed regions. When they are well controlled, they can be a less expensive alternative to transfers and yield a better outcome in terms of social cohesion.
- *Provision of information* Workers cannot take advantage of new opportunities unless they know about vacancies and wages. In many developing countries workers must rely on informal exchange of information to find new jobs. Job search assistance can help, but – although inexpensive – it is not a panacea. Even in the industrial market economies only a small percentage of job seekers (usually no more than 10% to 15%) get their jobs through public employment offices. Allowing private employment services to operate makes sense under all circumstances.
- *Compensating those hurt*[18] In the past decade, more than 50 countries used transfer schemes to assist in downsizing their public sectors. During major reorganizations, the desirable level of severance pay will usually be in excess of the compensation mandated under existing labour contracts. The early involvement of unions is crucial for success, and for fairness reasons, the offer should be open to all, or most, public sector employees. Ideally, programmes are voluntary, and a menu of options is offered, with workers allowed to choose freely among them. The possible options available on the menu include early retirement, cash offers, annuities, retraining programs, guaranteed wages backed by subsidies to new employers, and

remaining in the public sector (but possibly in another occupation). Offering a menu of exit options can help achieve better targeting at cheaper fiscal costs since each worker chooses the option he or she values most. But a potentially important disadvantage of voluntary exit programs is the adverse selection they are prone to. The fear is that the public sector would lose its best workers as a result of the voluntariness of the exit mechanism. However, this type of problem can be partially resolved by a proper use of vetoes.

In public enterprises restructuring, governments typically laid off redundant workers before privatization in order to allow new owners maximum flexibility in restructuring the enterprise. This is how it was done in Spain. But privatization can come first, leaving restructuring to the new owners. Often, there will remain constraints or firing or the level of wages. This gets reflected in lower sales price, so in effect, the government is implicitly paying the severance costs to the firm so it retains some redundant workers. This is the prevailing case in Central and Eastern Europe.

In sum, active labour market policies and compensations to those hurt by change are a necessary component of a reform program. They help maintain social cohesion in a period where the job destruction/job creation process intensifies, generating intense social dislocation. But given the depth of the problems, these policies are not a panacea and cannot be expected to smooth temporary losses perfectly. This means that policy must ensure that these losses remain indeed temporary. The credibility productivity growth that characterized open economies.

12.6   Concluding remarks

Egypt pursued an employment strategy that worked during the regional oil boom but collapsed afterwards. Some employment cycle was unavoidable, given that no one anticipated the scale of the oil cycle. But the pattern of growth chosen is now a disaster for employment, leaving the characteristic syndrome of high unemployment and high public employment. Past educational expansion contributed more to frustrated expectations of getting 'good' public sector jobs than to a dynamic of risks to both courses. The poor are the most robust potential beneficiaries, but least influential. Unemployment effects in transition are ambiguous. The political necessity and political risks of an opening reform are both clear. It is the only way to get onto a labour-demanding path and attract stable capital flows, but there will be some permanent and some temporary losers, especially among public sector workers. Employment-reducing reform of the public sector is unlikely and probably inadvisable before economic growth takes off, yet failure to reform could lead opening to end in a blaze of either fiscal crisis or growth-reducing fiscal repression of economic and social services. This implies that some gradualism may be important, provided the forces of conservatism do not undercut reform. It is in making this strategy possible, through both finance and technical assistance, that the European Initiative could make its most valuable contribution to facilitating Egypt's integration with the world economy.

References

Adams, Richard (1989), 'Workers remittances and income inequality in rural Egypt', *Economic Development and Cultural Change*, 38 (October), 45–71.

Ahuja, Vinrod and Deon Filmer (1995), 'Educational attainment in developing countries, new estimates and projections', Background paper for the World Development Report 1995, World Bank, Washington, DC.

Angrist, J. (1992), 'Wages and employment in the West Bank and Gaza, 1981–90', Maurice Falk Institute for Economic Research, discussion paper no. 92–02, Tel-Aviv.

Assaad, Ragui (1993), 'The employment crisis in Egypt: trends and issues', Humphrey Institute of Public Affairs, University of Minnesota.

____ (forthcoming), 'The effects of public sector hiring and compensation policies on the Egyptian labour market', *The World Bank Economic Review.*

Barro, R. and J. W. Lee (1993), 'International comparison of educational attainment', *Journal of Monetary Economics*, 32, 363–94.

CAPMAS (1988), *Statistical Yearbook.*

Chen, S., G. Datt and M. Ravallion (forthcoming), 'Is poverty increasing in the developing world? Review of income and wealth'.

Diwan, Ishac and Lyn Squire (1993), 'Public debts and private assets: external finance in a peaceful Middle East', *Middle East Journal*, 49(1), 69–88.

Diwan, Ishac (1994), 'Public sector retrenchment and severance pay: nine propositions', in S. Chaudhry, G. Reed, and W. Malik, (eds.), *Civil Service Reform in Latin America and the Caribbean*, World Bank.

Diwan, Ishac, Chang-Po Yang and Zhi Wang (1995), 'The Arab conomies, the Uruguayan Round predicament, and the European Union wildcard', The World Bank, Mimeo.

Dubey, A. and E. King (1994), 'A new cross country education stock series differentiated by age and sex', World Bank, Washington, DC.

Feenstra, Robert C. and Gordon Hanson (1994), 'Foreign investment, outsourcing and relative wages', University of California, Davis, Mimeo.

Handoussa, Heba (1992), *The Burden of Public Sector Employment and Remuneration: The Case of Egypt*, American University in Cairo, Cairo, Egypt.

ILO (1986), 'Economically active population, 1965–2025, Geneva, International Labor Office.

Korayem, Karima (1994), 'Poverty and income distribution in Egypt', Third World Forum, Cairo.

Krueger, A. O. (1983), 'Trade and employment in developing countries: 3 syntheses and conclusions', University of Chicago Press, Chicago.

Lawrence, Robert and Matthew Slaughter (1993), 'Trade and US wages: great sucking sound or small hiccup?' Faculty Research Series (R93–16), Kennedy School of Government, Harvard University.

Nehru, V., R. Swanson and A. Dubey (1993), 'A new database on human capital stock: sources, methodology and results', Policy Research Working Papers 1124, World Bank, International Economic Department, Washington DC.

Pissarides, Christopher (1995), 'Trade and the return to human capital in developing countries', *The World Bank Economic Review*, forthcoming.

Revenga, Ana and Claudio Montenegro (1995), 'North American integration and factor price equalization: is there evidence of wage convergence between Mexico and the US?', Brookings Institution, Washington, DC.

Richards, Alan (1995), 'Is unemployment a bourgeois luxury? The case of the Arab world'. UCSC Department of Economics Working Paper no. 313 (January), University of California, Santa Cruz.

Robbins, Donald (1995), 'Trade, trade liberalization, and inequality in Latin America and East Asia', synthesis of seven country studies', *The World Bank Economic Review*, forthcoming.

Rodrik, Dani (1994), 'Developing countries after the Uruguay Round', Columbia University, Department of Economics, New York.

Sachs, J. and H. Schatz (1994), 'Trade and jobs in US manufacturing', Brookings Papers on Economic Activity (Spring).

Said, Mona (1996), 'Public sector employment and labour markets in Arab countries: recent development and policy issues', Economic Research Forum Working Paper No. 9630, Cairo, Egypt.

Tan, Hong and Geeta Batra (1995), 'Explaining wage differentials: the role of employer investment in technology', *The World Bank Economic Review*, forthcoming.

Tansel, A. (1992), 'Wage employment, earnings and return to schooling for men and women in Turkey', Yale University Economic Growth Center, Discussion paper no. 661, New Haven, CT.

van Eeghen, Wilhem (1995), 'Poverty in the Middle East and North Africa', Mimeo, World Bank, Washington, DC.

Wood, Adrian (1994), *North-South Trade, Employment and Inequality: Changing Fortunes in a Skill-Driven World*, Oxford, Clarendon Press.

—— (1995), 'Does trade reduce wage inequality in developing countries?' Institute of Development Studies, University of Sussex, *The World Bank Economic Review*, forthcoming.

World Bank (1994), 'Kingdom of Morocco poverty, adjustment and growth: MENA region, country operations', Washington, DC.

—— (1995a), *World Development Report 1995*: 'Workers in an integrating world', No. 14086.

—— (1995b), 'Will Arab workers prosper or be left out in the Twenty-First Century?' Supplement to the *World Development Report 1995*: 'Workers in an integrating world'.

Zaytoun, Mohaya A. (1991), 'Earnings and the cost of living: an analysis of recent developments in the Egyptian economy', in Heba Handoussa and Gillian Potters, eds., *Employment and Structural Adjustment: Egypt in the 1990s*, Cairo, American University in Cairo Press.

Zouari-Bouattur, Salma (1994), 'Evolution de marche du travail Tunisien 1983–1993', Universite de Sfax.

Notes

1. This paper represents the views of the author, and not those of the World Bank or any of its affiliates. I would like to thank Michael Walton for useful discussions.
2. The share of young workers with secondary education among the unemployed is abnormally large at around 60%, while this group represents only 26% of the labour force (but they hold 60% of public sector jobs; in contrast, they constitute only about 20% of private non-agricultural sector employment). This pattern is also marked among educated women who are disproportionately employed in the public sector (71% of women with university degrees work for the state), and their chances of being unemployed are about five times larger than for men. (Asaad, 1993)
3. See World Bank (1995a), Box 5.1, page 39.
4. More precisely, this is a cut-off of $30 for average monthly per capita consumption in terms of 1985 purchasing power parity dollars. While a figure of $30 per month is a useful yardstick for international comparisons, most observers of the region would probably use a higher cut-off for absolute poverty.
5. See World Bank (1995b), Figure 4.
6. This is, for example, reflected in a rise of the Gini coefficient, especially in urban areas (from 32 to 38); Korayem (1994).
7. Although the poor tend to be under-represented amongst migrants, who generally have some education and resources to move, the indirect effects via tightening the labour market, private transfers and second-round spending impacts, undoubtedly contributed to poverty reduction (Adams, 1989)
8. The direct effects of the Uruguay Round on the Arab world are modest and negative, with a net loss of 0.2% of GDP per year. In the long run, once effects via migration are worked through, the consequences are negligible for agricultural and unskilled workers, and slightly negative for skilled workers (Diwan, Yang and Wang, 1995). My guess-estimate based on factor endowments is that the Egyptian case is likely to be similar in direction and perhaps a bit more marked in size.
9. Here, even Morocco and to a lesser extent Tunisia have lagged behind East Asian competitors, especially in productivity growth (World Bank, 1995a). It is noteworthy, however, that Turkey with the longest and deepest period of engagement in international markets, plus greater progress in policy aspects of integration with Europe, has a performance in productivity growth that rivals Indonesia and Malaysia.
10. Wood (1994); Lawrence and Slaughter (1993); Sachs and Schatz (1994).
11. In addition to the dynamic effects of getting on to a productivity and investment enhancing growth path emphasized above.
12. See especially Krueger (1983) for the first category of evidence, and Wood (1994), for a survey of the latter. See also World Bank (1995a), Figure 6.1, page 41 for a historical review of both types of cases.
13. See Revenga and Montenegro (1995).
14. See Wood (1995) for a survey and discussion.
15. China's exports to the EU have risen from 2.3% of the EU's total imports in 1985 to 4.9% in 1991. By one measure the relative price of labour intensive manufactures has fallen by 20% between the mid-1980s and early 1990s.
16. See Feenstra and Hanson (1994) for this argument.
17. At the same time, a measure of income dispersion (household income ratio of the top to bottom quintile) has risen in the three countries and especially in Jordan and Morocco (Jordan: 6.0 to 8.3 between 1986 and 1992; Morocco: 4.0 to 7.0 between 1985 and 1991; Tunisia: 7.0 to 7.85 between 1985 and 1990). See van Eeghen, 1995.
18. This section is based on Diwan (1994).

13

Egypt and the Partnership Agreement with the EU: The Road to Maximum Benefits

Ahmed Galal
Egyptian Center for Economic Studies

Bernard Hoekman
The World Bank and CEPR

13.1   Introduction

Paul Krugman has repeatedly made a very simple, important, yet often ignored point: magnitudes matter. Trade matters for employment and growth only if it accounts for a large percentage of GDP. The larger the percentage, the greater the dependency of the economy on its trading partners. Krugman used this argument forcefully to criticize such well-known authors as Thurow, who blamed Japan's restrictive trade policies, in his book *Head to Head* (1992), for the loss of American jobs. In 1993, the US only imported 11.4% of its GDP, and exported 10.4%; total imports from Japan equalled only 1.7% of GDP.

Applying Krugman's point to the Egypt–EU partnership agreement leads to the conclusion that it may make an important difference to growth and employment in Egypt. Exports plus imports were $17.5 billion in 1994 – or 35% of GDP. The 15 EU countries alone receive 50% of Egypt's exports, and some 40% of all imports originate in the EU. The agreement will entail dramatic changes in the degree to which the Egyptian economy is open to competition from EU countries, as Egypt will cut its tariffs on industrial imports from the EU to zero.[1] More fundamentally perhaps, Egypt is neither as developed nor free market-based as the US, which means that there is a premium on actions that foster integration into the world economy and signal the government's commitment to market-oriented reforms.

Given that the benefits of an agreement are largely endogenous, policy makers can make a big difference to the final outcome. We argue in this paper that the partnership will be most beneficial to Egypt if it is part of a coherent growth strategy. To develop this argument, we first set the stage by comparing Egypt's current economic growth strategy with the fast-growing economies. In Section 13.3 we explore how the partnership can enhance economic growth in Egypt. Section 13.4 discusses the implications of the agreement for different sectors. Finally, in Section 13.5 we highlight the domestic reforms necessary to enable Egypt to take full advantage of the agreement.

13.2   Is Egypt ready to take off?

Although Egypt's GDP growth rate has picked up in the last couple of years, per capita GDP has in fact declined by 3% a year over the period 1990–5. For Egypt to raise the standard of living of a population growing at about 2% a year and to begin catching up with higher income countries, it must grow by at least 7% per year for a sustained period of time.

13.2.1   What does it generally take to grow fast?

There is consensus that growth comes primarily from three sources:

1. The accumulation of human and physical capital.
2. The efficient allocation of resources.
3. Productivity improvement.

However, there is no consensus on how to realize these components of growth. The debate still rages, for example, over the extent to which resources should be allocated by markets as opposed to guided by government policy; how efficient governments are in picking winners; and the choice of policies to foster savings, investment and innovation. Searching for a growth strategy amounts in the final analysis to selecting appropriate economic institutions that support growth.

Broadly speaking, the evidence overwhelmingly discredits large-scale import substitution policies, large government, and central planning as effective strategies for economic growth. The collapse of the Soviet Union and the success of the export-oriented South-east Asian countries provides strong backing to this view. Evidence from cross-country growth regressions (e.g. Barro, 1991; and Levine and Renelt, 1992) suggests that two sets of variables are strongly associated with growth: factors reflecting initial conditions (e.g. per capita GDP, secondary school enrolment, income distribution, etc.), and policy variables (e.g. inflation, financial market development, etc.). This literature also supports the view that institutions matter, as measured by political stability, civil liberties and contract enforcement. Indeed, North has concluded that 'the inability of societies to develop effective, low-cost enforcement of contracts is the most important source of both historical stagnation and contemporary underdevelopment in the Third World' (1990, p. 54). Knack and Keefer (forthcoming), among others, find that property rights (measured by evaluations of contract enforceability, rule of law, and risk of expropriation) have a significant impact on investment and growth. Surveying the literature, Rodrik (1996) notes that equality also matters for growth through its impact on governance. Better governance follows from more egalitarian regimes because governments become less needy politically of redistributive policies for survival; they receive less lobbying pressure from different interest groups; and they have more time and greater incentives to ensure that the civil service is efficient in providing public goods (as opposed to imposing red tape and engaging in rent-seeking activities).

Finally, part of the literature dealing with growth-enhancing factors compares successful and unsuccessful country cases. One example of this literature is Sachs and Warner (1995), who found that the fastest-growing economies in the developing world were more open than those that did not grow as fast. Comparing Chile with the rest of Latin America, Büchi (1996) argues that Chile's success story can be attributed to three factors: stability (i.e. low inflation), structural changes (consistent with higher domestic savings and exports, more competition, and smaller government), and social programs to help the very poor.

The literature attempting to account for growth is extensive, and we do not intend a comprehensive review here. But the evidence is abundantly clear that beyond the initial conditions in a given country, policies matter.[2] Policies can foster the accumulation of capital, improve the allocation of resources, and contribute to productivity growth. Our reading of the literature and empirical evidence suggests that the key to the accumulation of physical and human capital is savings, domestic and foreign. The key to the efficient allocation of resources is openness of the economy to trade and financial flows. And the key to productivity improvement is competition (domestic and international), private ownership and the acquisition of technology. Savings, openness and competition are associated with other variables. Some of these relationships are highlighted below.

Savings and size of government

Large government expenditures correlate negatively with public savings (see Sachs, 1996). This is because large expenditures mean high marginal tax rates, which encourage tax evasion/avoidance, or monetary expansion with resulting macroeconomic instability. To mobilize savings and foster more rapid growth, the size of the government should not be too large. Lower government expenditures imply lower marginal tax rates on corporations and personal income. Low tax rates induce investment, especially if designed in a non-distortionary fashion to encourage reinvestment of retained earnings. As important, with respect to expenditures, the evidence suggests that net social returns are much higher when resources are used to finance basic infrastructure, health and primary education, as opposed to the maintenance of a large civil service, welfare spending, or subsidization of certain sectors (through the budget or through protection). Redistributive transfers are generally negatively correlated with growth. An important source of savings by individuals is for retirement. To motivate individuals to save, governments should give up generous pay-as-you-go state pension systems, if applicable. One example where this reform has been successfully implemented with positive implications on savings is in Chile (see Büchi, 1996, for details).

Smaller government, shifting expenditure away from redistributive transfers, and reforming pension systems are all policies that will increase savings. Provided there are incentives and channels to transform these savings into productive investment, this will stimulate growth. The accumulation of physical and human capital is the surest way to grow fast, as Krugman (1994) has argued in his widely-read article.

Openness of the economy and manufactured exports

Open economies tend to export more manufactured goods than less open economies, and are better at attracting and using technology (Sachs and Warner, 1995; Page and Underwood, 1996). Openness is generally interpreted to include currency convertibility, low import tariffs for intermediate inputs and machinery, and the absence of non-tariff barriers and taxation on exports (including duty free access to imports). Conversely, where the currency is overvalued, inflexible and/or non-convertible, where tariffs on intermediate inputs and machinery are high, and where exports are taxed heavily (because of import barriers and transaction-increasing costs), potential exporters find it more attractive to produce for domestic markets. The end result is a slow-growing economy, which is less efficient and dynamic than it might be otherwise.

How do openness and manufactured exports contribute to growth? The arguments, which are backed by empirical evidence, are straightforward. The key is competition, both from imports and export markets. This brings about more efficient allocation of resources and total factor productivity (TFP) growth through specialization, learning by doing, exploitation of economies of scale, and attracting new technology.

Competition and private sector-led growth

Openness is the shortest route to enhance competition, especially in the tradable sectors. Equally important, however, is the extent to which the economy is dominated by state-owned enterprises (SOEs). The greater the role of SOEs, the less competition will generally prevail in domestic markets. Governments typically carve out markets for SOEs by granting monopoly rights, imposing high trade barriers, providing access to capital that may not otherwise be available on commercial grounds, and assuring labour returns above the value of marginal product. Frequently, SOEs are large in size to the point of dominating their markets, even where they do not enjoy any formal monopoly rights.

For these reasons, privatization (combined with openness) is critical not only to improve productivity and increase investment, but also to increase competition. The gains in growth from privatization can be very substantial. Assuming SOEs account for 10% of GDP, privatizing just one half of the SOE sector can generate as much as a 1% increase in GDP (Galal et al, 1994).[3] A corollary of privatization is the associated change in the nature of the role of government. Instead of acting as an entrepreneur and owner of resources, its role shifts to a regulator to protect the consumers and the needy, enforce contracts and protect the functioning of markets. As noted below, improving the performance of the government in these areas is particularly important in the Egyptian context.

13.2.2 How does Egypt compare with fast-growing economies?

Egypt has undertaken substantial reforms in the 1990s. The budget deficit was reduced sharply, the growth of money supply curtailed, the exchange rate devalued and unified, and the capital account liberalized. Interest rates were freed and treasury bill auctions used to manage liquidity. Simultaneously, foreign trade was liberalized by virtually removing all quantitative restrictions on imports and reducing and rationalizing import tariffs. With a few exceptions, the maximum tariff was reduced from 160% in 1988 to 70% in 1994. In December 1993, the marginal tax rate was reduced from 65% to 48%, corporate dividends exempted to avoid double taxation, and the corporate tax rate lowered to 42% (with a further reduction to 34% for manufacturing). Inflation declined from 20% in 1990 to 8.3% in 1995. The current account deficit, excluding official transfers, declined from 6.8% of GDP in 1990 to 2.0% in 1995. International reserves increased to about $18 billion (18 months of merchandise imports) in 1995, thanks to a significant inflow of private capital. The success of the stabilization program was helped by debt forgiveness received in the wake of the Gulf War.

Notwithstanding this progress, per capita GNP growth averaged 2.8% per year between 1980 and 1993, compared to 5.3% for fast-growing Southeast Asian economies. This modest growth was essentially wiped out by population growth, leading to stagnation in the standard of living. Unemployment is relatively high (reaching 9.6% in 1995); investment is modest; and merchandise exports have in fact declined on average in the last few years, and remained less diversified than desirable (*see* Table 13.1).[4]

Egypt's lackluster growth performance relative to Southeast Asian economies reflects a much lower savings rate and significantly greater government expenditures, much of which does not go into infrastructure and similar public goods. Egypt's tariff rate is also much higher. Despite the liberalization program mentioned earlier, the average tariff fell only marginally (from 31% in 1988 to 28% in 1994).

The average collection rate (that is, trade taxes as a share of merchandise imports) is 50% to 100% higher in Egypt than in the comparator countries. SOEs account for a much larger portion of GDP in Egypt than in Southeast Asia, and the rate of growth of manufactured exports is much lower (Table 13.2).

A convenient way of summarizing the relative performance of the Egyptian economy is the efficiency index compiled by the Harvard Institute for International Development and the World Economic Forum for a sample of 49 countries. The index is the sum of three measures: openness of the economy to trade and financial flows; the size of government in the

Table 13.1 Selected economic indicators, 1989–95

	1989	1990	1991	1992	1993	1994	1995	Average 1989–95
Real GDP growth rate (%)	3.0	2.4	2.1	0.3	0.5	2.0	2.4	1.8
Real GDP per capita growth rate (%)	0.0	–0.6	–0.4	–1.4	–1.7	0.0	0.4	–0.5
Inflation (%)	16.7	17.5	22.4	19.4	10.4	8.2	8.3	14.7
Unemployment (% of labour force)	7.0	7.6	8.4	9.2	10.1	9.8	9.6	8.8
Investment (constant 1992 £E billions)	24.5	24.2	23.1	20.8	21.0	22.6	22.8	22.7
Investment (% growth rate)	0.0	–0.9	–4.6	–9.8	1.5	4.5	1.0	–1.2
Merchandise exports (US$ billions, 1992=100)	3.0	3.1	3.7	3.6	3.5	3.2	3.3	3.3
Exports growth rate (%, 1992 prices)	–17.8	5.1	19.7	–2.4	–2.9	–10.2	4.7	–0.6

Source: World Bank.

economy; and labour market flexibility. It gives a higher score for more openness, smaller government (measured by government expenditure to GDP, and various rates of taxation), and more flexible labour markets. According to this index, Egypt ranks 22nd on openness, 31st on size of government, and 40th on flexibility of labour markets (Sachs, 1996).

Perhaps more worrisome than the fact that Egypt is still a substantially closed economy compared with dynamic exporting countries is that the economy has become less integrated since the early 1980s. The change in openness (as measured by the ratio of population-adjusted trade to GDP) that occurred in the last decade was negative (Table 13.2), as compared to the increase that occurred in the majority of comparator countries.

The openness of an economy to international trade can also be measured by the level of trade barriers. On this basis, Egypt is also lagging behind comparators. Particularly noteworthy in this connection is that tariffs on raw materials and machinery are significant (some 10% on an import-weighted basis). The average nominal tariff on all imports in Egypt is currently about 30%. Although collected tariff revenue is substantially less (around 15%) because of exemptions, duty drawback and related policies, the use of such mechanisms gives rise to red tape costs and raises the dispersion of protection across firms and industries. Moreover, tariffs are complemented by a wide variety of other trade barriers.

Finally, the Egyptian economy is perceived to be overregulated, and contract enforcement is considered weak. According to a World Bank study

Table 13.2 Selected indicators of Egypt and fast-growing economies (percentage of GDP)

Country	Gross domestic savings 1993	Government spending 1995	Average tariff rate 1993[*]	Growth of manufactured exports 1985–92	Change in trade to GDP ratio 1980–83 to 1990–93	Average share of SOEs/GDP 1978–91
Chile	24.0	20.8	9.5	26.3	1.0	12.0
Hong Kong	31.0	16.6	0.0	21.4	19.1	n.a.
Indonesia	31.0	17.1	5.0	33.2	−1.4	13.0
S. Korea	35.0	20.3	4.0	14.1	1.4	10.2
Malaysia	28.0	30.6	6.0	29.2	5.7	n.a.
Singapore	47.0	20.4	0.4	20.2	11.1	n.a.
Thailand	36.0	22.1	9.0	33.7	3.3	5.4
Egypt	18.0[†]	36.5	15.0	1.0[‡]	−1.9	32.8

Sources: World Bank, *World Development Report* (1980, 1982 and 1995); *Government Finance Statistics Yearbook* IMF, (1994); UNCTAD Trade Analysis and Information System data, (1995); and World Bank, *Global Economic Prospects*, (1996).
[*]These are calculated as collected taxes on trade as a share of total merchandise imports.
[†]Gross national savings for 1993, as estimated by the World Bank. Gross domestic savings were only 6% of GDP.
[‡]Annual average growth over the period 1986–94.

(1995c), the perception of the administration of justice is that the system is simply too slow, expensive, and uncertain. In 1993/94, the clearance rate of commercial cases was only 36%, compared with 80% in Japan, and 88% in Belgium. A survey of private firms revealed that the most binding institutional constraints on private sector operation and investment were policy uncertainty, tax administration, access to finance, access to intermediate inputs, and labour regulation, in that order (Galal, 1996). Reducing policy uncertainty and the burden of tax administration and improving contract enforcement are therefore key elements to stimulate growth.

There is clearly much scope for improvement in policies. Against this background, it is useful to assess how an association agreement between Egypt and the EU will help relax some of these constraints, provide a step toward global integration, and signal government commitment to reform. In our view, the EU partnership should be viewed as a tool and component of a growth strategy that will help put Egypt on a sustained high growth path.

13.3   The partnership agreement and growth

Given the foregoing, in our assessment of the partnership agreement we focus on three growth-related 'integration' variables: trade openness, investment, and domestic competition. In each case, we identify the changes likely to be brought about by the agreement, and the implications of these changes for the Egyptian economy.

13.3.1 Trade

To what extent will the partnership agreement change the trade regime, giving industries access to lower-cost inputs and consumers access to lower-cost goods? With respect to tariffs, the agreement will enable enterprises to source inputs and machinery free of duty and to confront greater competition from EU sources. This will encourage investment and improvements in productivity. As far as non-tariff barriers are concerned, UNCTAD estimates that these apply to some 25% of imports of capital goods and raw materials (Lee, 1993). In practice, non-tariff barriers are mainly product standards (quality control) and various customs-related practices (valuation, classification, cumbersome procedures and 'red tape'). Some of these will be eliminated or reduced as a result of the implementation of the agreement. But the magnitude of the reductions depends importantly on the vigour with which this is pursued.

Quantifying the impact on the Egyptian economy of reducing trade barriers is difficult, as many effects are not readily measurable. The economic impact of preferential liberalization is conventionally broken down into two types – static and dynamic. The static impact is determined by the effect on allocation of existing resources; the dynamic effect takes into account the impact on the rate of factor accumulation (investment). The static welfare impact of trade liberalization is generally relatively small, because the efficiency gains that result from bringing domestic prices closer in line with world prices are offset by the loss in tariff revenue. Its magnitude depends on numerous variables, including the structure of domestic markets before opening the economy and the existence of economies of scale in production. The greater the market power of domestic firms and the less competition that prevails, the greater the increase in welfare resulting from liberalization. Much also depends on the type of trade barriers that are removed. Although all barriers raise the domestic price of goods above world levels, some trade barriers are sources of real resource costs that benefit no industry (e.g. inspection requirements and time-consuming customs procedures). Other barriers create rents for specific interest groups and therefore represent a transfer of income within society. For this reason, the net welfare gains from removing trade barriers involving real resource costs tend to be larger than from rent-creating barriers such as tariffs or quotas.[5]

The empirical evidence on Egypt's trade regime concludes that the prevalence of administrative barriers is significant (World Bank, 1995c). The study by Konan and Maskus (*see* Chapter 7) of the static effects of preferential liberalization *vis-à-vis* the EU strongly suggests that much of the welfare gain from a partnership agreement may be associated with a reduction in administrative barriers. Free trade with the EU – elimination of tariffs on EU imports combined with an assumed 1% increase in prices of Egyptian exports because of reduced incidence of testing and certification costs in the EU, as well as an 8% increase in export prices of agricultural produce and clothing – results in a welfare gain of only 0.2% of GDP. If it is assumed that the partnership agreement also reduces administrative costs incurred by traders – due to customs procedures, quality control, 'red tape' – the welfare gains rise to 1.8% of GDP.

A key issue, therefore, is lowering trade-related transaction costs. The partnership agreement will help achieve this to some extent, because it will involve some harmonization of regulatory regimes and administrative requirements relating to product standards, testing and certification procedures, and common documents for customs clearance (e.g. the EU's Single Administrative Document). The negotiation of mutual recognition agreements (e.g. for inspection and certification of goods), and coordination and cooperation on a wide variety of regulatory issues, are objectives of the agreement. To what extent these objectives will be achieved depends on the vigour with which they are pursued, and the extent to which the necessary institutions are created and/or restructured and upgraded.

The preferential nature of the trade liberalization that will be undertaken under the partnership agreement will lead to trade creation (replacement of domestic production with imports from the EU) and trade diversion (replacement of imports from outside the EU with European goods). Both of these effects imply that the EU share in Egypt's trade in manufacturing will expand. How much the EU's import market share will become depends on a number of factors, such as demand elasticities and domestic supply response. Konan and Maskus (1996) estimate that in the short run the volume of imports and exports will rise by some 20% and 30% respectively (no allowance being made for inter-sectoral reallocation of capital) and 30% and 40% in the long run (allowing for capital reallocation). These estimates do not allow for any dynamic effects. In so far as investment is encouraged, trade flows will expand more.

13.3.2 Investment

Fostering greater investment, including foreign direct investment (FDI), is a major objective of the Egyptian government. Inducing the repatriation of Egyptian capital abroad – estimated at $60-80 billion – is considered key for attracting investment from non-Egyptian sources (Bayoumi, 1996). Attracting FDI is important because it is a source of know-how and technology, creates employment, and fosters trade. The investment to GDP ratio is currently 17%, significantly below that of dynamic export-oriented countries, which often have double this figure or more. Moreover, FDI in Egypt is negligible compared to the flows going to emerging market economies. Measures of investor confidence (*Institutional Investor* country ratings) and the change in the ratio of FDI to GDP illustrate the problem. Investor ratings for Egypt were already relatively low in the early 1980s, and have declined since then (Table 13.3). Although in comparison to other countries the magnitude of inward FDI flows has been above average, the trend has been declining. Moreover, very little FDI has gone into export-oriented manufacturing activities.

Whether greater investment will be induced by the partnership agreement is an important – indeed, a crucial – question. Liberalization of trade under a partnership agreement may generate a number of beneficial dynamic effects. One is the indirect effect of the static allocative efficiency gain. For the given initial stocks of labour and capital, the increase in income following liberalization increases per capita savings, which in turn gives rise to greater investment (Baldwin, 1994). Investment may also be stimulated by the decline in trade costs and by general improvement of the incentives regime. Finally, an increase in the rate of accumulation of certain factors of production (knowledge, human capital) may occur.

Table 13.3 Measures of change in integration

	Change in *Institutional Investors* rating (1983–5 to 1993–5)	Change in ratio of FDI to GDP (1980–2 to 1990–2)
Egypt	–0.7 (35)	–0.04 (0.57)
High income countries	0.21 (81.8)	0.02 (0.32)
East Asia	–0.05 (56)	0.03 (0.12)
Latin America	0.21 (40.1)	0.01 (0.32)
MENA	–0.39 (39.2)	0.0 (0.26)
South Asia	–0.08 (25.9)	0.0 (0.0)
Sub-Saharan Africa	–0.03 (18.5)	0.0 (0.11)

Note: Figures in parentheses are the relevant levels in early 1980s that are the base from which changes are calculated.
Source: World Bank, *Global Economic Prospects*, 1996.

While little empirical evidence exists on the long-term growth effects of preferential liberalization, much is likely to depend on the extent to which an inflow of FDI is induced. The experiences of Portugal and Spain following accession to the European Community illustrate the possibility of significant medium-term investment effects if the macroeconomic environment is suitable. FDI in Portugal rose fourfold during the mid-1980s, while in Spain it more than doubled. In both countries, FDI centred on the finance, real estate and business service sectors, as well as on more traditional export-oriented sectors (such as textiles and clothing).[6]

To what extent will a partnership agreement improve the incentives to invest in Egypt? The partnership agreement can be useful in generating greater investment by influencing expectations and enhancing the credibility of reform by locking in the right of establishment. Granting a general right of establishment and guaranteeing national treatment would be an important signal in terms of improving the investment climate. But other impediments, such as the cost of financial intermediation, the tax burden and regulatory regimes, must also be addressed. It must also be recognized that a preferential trade agreement with the EU creates offsetting incentive effects for investment. On the one hand, the reduction in trade costs and the enhancement of competition will make the economy more efficient, and increase the trade of goods and services, providing investors with greater opportunities to exploit geographical and other advantages. On the other hand, the reduction in trade barriers reduces the incentive for inward FDI. As tariffs and other barriers to imports are eliminated, European firms no longer have a policy-induced reason to produce in Egypt. The greater the economies of scale in production, the greater the incentive may be to concentrate production in an EU location where a firm has access to many complementary service providers. The fact that a partnership agreement is simply a bilateral free-trade agreement worsens matters, as locating in an EU member (the 'hub') gives duty-free access to all countries with which the EU has concluded free trade agreements – virtually all its neighbours (sometimes called 'spokes'). As Egypt does not have comprehensive free trade agreements with all the countries in the region, and given the high transaction and transport costs that apply to intra-regional trade, firms that rely on imported inputs and export a significant part of their output confront a cost in locating in Egypt.

One implication of this is that it is very important that trade barriers are lowered with as many countries as possible, and with neighbouring countries in particular. Another implication is that opening up the service sector to foreign direct investors is important. Many services cannot be traded across frontiers, so the investment diversion incentives do not prevail. Foreign providers wishing to sell services in Egypt will generally have to establish a local presence. As efficient services are also an important dimension of raising the productivity of the economy, encouraging such investment should be a priority.

Improvements in TFP growth are another source of dynamic gains, which are likely to follow from the adjustment of domestic enterprises to the opening of the economy. Historically, Egypt has achieved relatively high rates of TFP growth, averaging around 2% over the 1960–90 period (Page and Underwood, 1996). More recently, however, TFP growth has been much lower, averaging 0.3% during 1982–92 (World Bank, 1994). The agreement with the EU may help boost TFP growth by facilitating the acquisition of technology. This may occur through a number of avenues: investments in new capital equipment as tariffs are eliminated; new inflows of FDI; technology licensing agreements (which may be stimulated in part through the adoption of stronger intellectual property protection); and more informal transfers of technology and know-how as linkages between European and Arab firms are facilitated. The last avenue may in part be attained through greater use of outsourcing arrangements, where goods are processed in Egypt and re-exported to the EU. This has been an important avenue of export growth for Central and Eastern European countries. Of the countries of the Middle East and North Africa, only Morocco and Tunisia have begun to exploit this export development channel. Egypt appears to make almost no use of such mechanisms. The reduction in administrative red tape and transaction costs that should emerge as the agreement is implemented should increase the ability of enterprises to pursue such contracting.

The strategy taken towards tariff liberalization will also affect investment incentives. In the Tunisian approach, tariffs on intermediates and capital goods are reduced first, and reductions in final goods are delayed until the second half of the transition period. An advantage of this approach is that it provides domestic industry with breathing space, and at the margin may provide greater incentives to invest in industries that continue to have guaranteed protection during the first phase of the transition. Thus, it may offset the possible downside related to the welfare cost of increasing effective rates of protection in the first part of the transition (Hoekman and Djankov, 1996).

13.3.3 Domestic competition

The partnership agreement contains a number of provisions that are intended to foster greater competition on the Egyptian domestic market and to ensure that foreign firms are not discriminated against. These include anti-trust disciplines for private parties (enterprises), competition policy rules for SOEs, restrictions on the reach and extent of industry-specific subsidies, and intellectual property right (IPR) protection.

The Tunisian partnership agreement requires the adoption of the basic competition rules of the EU, in particular with respect to collusive behaviour, abuse of dominant position, and competition-distorting state aid in so far as these affect trade between the EU and Egypt. Implementing rules are to be adopted by the Association Council within five years (as opposed to three under the Europe Agreements). Until then, GATT rules with respect to countervailing of subsidies will apply. If the same approach is followed as in the agreement between the EU and Tunisia, for the first five years after entry into force of the partnership agreement, Egypt will not be subject to the rules on state aids (subsidies). Anti-dumping rules remain applicable to trade flows between Egypt and the EU, despite the agreement by Egypt to apply EU competition disciplines. In addition to the various provisions imposing concrete competition disciplines, the partnership agreement contains language pertaining to harmonization/coordination of regulatory regimes.

Compared to the impact of eliminating tariffs on EU industrial products, these provisions are likely to have a much smaller impact on domestic competition. More important than the disciplines that are incurred is what has been left off the agenda (at least in the cases of Tunisia and Morocco). The issue of granting and guaranteeing the right of establishment was already mentioned; at the time of writing it appeared that the agreement between the EU and Egypt did not include commitments in this area. Service-related bottlenecks can prohibit manufacturing or food-processing industries from exploiting their comparative advantage. Stimulating competition and providing industries and traders with access to lower-cost, higher-quality services are therefore of great importance. Numerous studies have illustrated the drag on efficient production and export expansion imposed by high service and transactions costs in Egypt. These include excessive insurance fees, high port service costs, losses caused by unnecessary waste and breakage of goods due to low quality transport and storage, and unavailability or excessive costs of value-added telecommunications services (World Bank, 1994; 1995a,b). Allowing entry into service activities should help offset these various costs. Although the government may not be willing to open all services to foreign competition, it may wish to consider liberalizing access to a number of major sectors where foreign investment is likely to materialize. Examples include trade and distribution, business and professional services, and telecommunications. In some of these sectors the large investment required to improve output (both quantity and quality) will probably require private participation.[7]

13.4 How will the agreement affect agriculture, industry and services, and thus growth?

What does the partnership agreement imply for individual sectors? What will it do in terms of inducing enterprises to improve productivity and adopt best practices? Clearly, more competition will allow some industries to expand and cause others to contract. This process of reallocating resources to their most efficient uses is fundamental to enhancing economic growth. It is of course difficult to predict how specific sectors will be affected, as much depends not only on industry-specific initial conditions but also on the flexibility of the labour market and on the investment response by the private sector. However, data on current patterns of protection, import penetration and export sales on a sectoral basis provide some information on the possible impact of the agreement.

Overall, the absence of significant liberalization of agriculture by the EU, and the lack of immediate action on services by Egypt implies that most of the policy changes will impact primarily on manufacturing. Moreover, it can be argued that the lack of free trade in agricultural produce significantly reduces the benefits of a partnership agreement for Egypt. Agriculture is an important sector of the Egyptian economy, accounting for almost 20% of GDP and over 35% of employment. Vegetables and fruits dominate Egypt's exports of agricultural produce, standing at $200 million in 1994, of which 40% went to the EU. However, agriculture accounts for less than 5% of total exports (Egyptian agricultural exports account for less than 0.08% of total EU imports of such products). Also, many of Egypt's major agricultural import items do not originate in the EU. Only 13% of Egypt's $870 million of cereal imports came from the EU, and only 7% of the $277 million of vegetable fat imports. Egypt will not lower tariffs on these items, which reduces the potential for trade diversion. It also provides Egypt with some negotiating leverage, which the Egyptian negotiating team has made efforts to employ. What will be achieved in this connection remains to be seen.

Beyond the immediate impact of the agreement, both agriculture and the service sector will be affected indirectly, as relative prices of factors and goods and services change. The absence of agricultural liberalization by Egypt implies that the effective rate of protection (ERP) for agriculture rises over time. This is because farmers benefit from cheaper manufactured inputs into their production process (fertilizers, equipment, etc.). Indeed, currently agriculture is effectively taxed (Table 13.4). As tariffs on industrial goods are gradually reduced, the ERP for agriculture rises above zero, and greater value added is generated. A similar effect occurs for services. Even if allowance is made for the fact that services are protected because of entry restrictions, service activities are currently effectively taxed because the average level of import protection applying to manufactures is substantial. As tariffs are lowered, the ERP for service sectors rises. Agriculture and services therefore benefit in terms of protection from the reduction in trade barriers on manufactured goods. Indeed, for many service sectors ERPs may rise significantly. This implies that there is a need for reducing barriers to competition in services that goes beyond the need for efficient services noted earlier. Without policies to reduce ERPs in services, investment incentives may become skewed (Table 13.4).

With respect to manufacturing, data on trade openness and levels of protection are helpful in identifying the adjustment pressures that are likely to emerge for different sectors. Industries benefiting from high levels of protection, with low imports as a share of domestic consumption and/or limited exports as a share of output, are the most likely to confront significant adjustment pressure. Examples of such sectors include clothing, leather, footwear and furniture (Table 13.4). Much depends on the export capacity of the industry involved. The greater the export share of an industry, the more efficient it is likely to be, as this is a necessary condition for contesting world markets.

Although imports of clothing will increase substantially following the decline of quantitative restrictions, segments of the domestic industry are already exporting substantially, and the industry should be able to maintain its current output (Konan and Maskus, 1996). Moreover, the ERP for this industry remains high even after full implementation of the agreement. The leather, paper and printing, chemicals and machinery industries also have significant export sales, and should therefore find it easier to adjust to a more competitive domestic environment. Most of these industries also confront substantial import competition. Other industries already subject to import competition include food processing, wood products, rubber and plastics, ceramics and glass, and transport equipment. However, in some instances this comprises components or inputs that are processed/assembled in Egypt. As tariffs on the final goods involved are lowered, the incentive to engage in such processing will decline; this is particularly likely to be seen in the motor vehicle sector, which consists of assembly operations.

A useful measure of the impact of the agreement on individual industries is the magnitude of the change in effective protection. The greatest absolute declines will occur for footwear, ceramics, furniture, glass and glass products, paper and printing, transportation equipment, clothing and food processing (in that order). However, of these sectors, footwear, ceramics, and clothing will continue to benefit from relatively high ERPs at the end of the 12-year transition to free trade with the EU. In contrast, furniture, paper and printing and transportation equipment – which all have high ERPs at the present – will end up with negative effective protection. It can also be observed that the dispersion in protection across sectors continues to be high, both within manufacturing, and as noted earlier, between manufacturing and the services sectors.

In other words, the partnership agreement will contribute to opening the Egyptian economy, reducing transaction costs, subjecting domestic firms to greater competition, and possibly attracting more FDI. The negotiator can strive for a better agreement for Egypt, and the government can help viable industries in the adjustment process. More important perhaps, the government can adopt other complementary policies at home to maximize the gains from the agreement.

13.5 Policy reforms to take full advantage of the agreement

Egypt has the potential to join the club of fast-growing economies. It has the human capital, an advantageous geographical location, and a diversified industrial base. As noted previously, significant progress has been made on macroeconomic variables. Being a poor economy also helps. Poorer economies can expect to grow faster than richer countries because of lower capital-labour ratios and higher rates of return on new investments, both of which attract investment, and because poorer countries can take advantage of technological advances already made by the richer countries.

Convergence tendencies, however, are not automatic. Much depends on whether policy makers adopt appropriate economic policies and institutions. Before looking at what the Egyptian policy makers could do to capitalize on and complement the partnership agreement in the medium term, it is useful to consider the savings-investment possibilities in Egypt in the short run.

Table 13.4 Protection and trade shares, 1994

Sector	Nominal tariff	ERP*	ERP† Year 2010	Imports/ Apparent consumption	Exports/ Domestic output
Agriculture				%	%
1. Vegetable foodstuffs	2.5	−5	4	18.3	2.3
2. Other vegetable products	6.7	−5	8	0.4	0.7
3. Animal products	4.4	18	64	2.0	0.4
Mining and quarrying					
4. Oil	8.2	−21	−29	31.1	79.0
5. Other	7.0	−5	−10	31.0	2.1
Manufacturing					
6. Food processing	6.8	59	−11	29.1	1.9
7. Cotton ginning	17.3	9	−23	12.2	40.9
8. Cotton spinning/weaving	23.3	38	−24	10.9	22.7
9. Clothing	53.7	147	77	0.3	9.6
10. Leather	34.8	13	−22	1.5	5.7
11. Shoes	51.8	267	33	1.1	0.1
12. Wood products	8.1	54	−20	48.8	0.7
13. Furniture	46.9	107	−10	0.2	4.2
14. Paper and printing	13.3	52	−29	32.5	6.9
15. Chemicals	8.9	−12	−64	43.2	6.7
16. Petroleum refining	7.1	45	−25	9.4	13.8
17. Rubber/plastic	15.6	16	−10	38.7	4.9
18. Ceramics	43.5	98	36	23.9	3.9
19. Glass	29.6	91	4	25.7	4.7
20. Mineral products	18.1	21	−10	4.7	0.1
21. Iron, steel	17.2	9	2	16.8	3.3
22. Machinery	17.9	20	−28	61.3	15.0
23. Transport equipment	41.2	65	−20	55.3	4.6
24. Other	19.3	23	−8	45.4	9.6
Manufacturing average		51	−9		
Services					
25. Construction		−64	58		
26. Electricity, gas		−116	-45		
27. Transport, storage		−25	43		
28. Hotels, restaurants		−42	20		
29. Communications		−15	25		
30. Finance		−10	11		
31. Distribution		−9	8		
32. Insurance		−4	5		
Services average		−36	16		

*Effective rate of protection in 1994, including an assumed 15% tariff equivalent for services.

†Assumes full implementation of the partnership agreement but no reduction in service tariff equivalents.

Source: Konan and Maskus (1996) and Hoekman and Djankov (1996).

13.5.1 Savings and investment in the short run

We start with the assumption that Egypt should grow by at least 7% annually. This requires three things:

1. Boosting the investment rate from about 17% of GDP to 27%, and securing corresponding increases in savings – domestic and foreign – to finance it.
2. Allocating resources to their most efficient uses.
3. Invigorating the efficiency of the capital stock, current and new.

All this must be achieved without compromising financial stability.

All told, there is some room for mobilizing additional savings in the short run, mainly from privatization of SOEs and attracting more FDI. However, mobilizing savings and investment to levels comparable to those of the fast-growing Southeast Asian economies is out of reach in the short run. For Egypt to make the quantum shift necessary to achieve a sustainable rate of growth of 7%, a significant shift in orientation is necessary. Higher domestic savings can come from the government sector, the SOE sector, or the private sector. Experience has shown that the response of private sector savings is both uncertain in magnitude and duration, and generally follows growth. Greater government savings will require higher taxes or lower expenditure. Higher taxes would be inconsistent with efforts to induce investment, while the room for reducing government expenditure is narrow, given that real wages of the civil service have already been eroded and unemployment in the country is high. In addition, the budget will, in any event, lose revenue from tariff cuts. Accordingly, the scope for higher government savings in the short run is limited. This leaves the SOE sector as the main potential source of higher domestic savings. Additional savings from privatization, liquidation of loss-making companies, and reforming the remaining SOEs would amount to some two percentage points of GDP.[8] But the privatization process is universally slow, and such savings will take time to materialize.

Investment minus domestic savings equals the current account. A current account deficit can by financed by: (i) running down reserves, (ii) borrowing more from abroad, or (iii) attracting more foreign direct investment. Egypt's reserves are currently at US$ 18 billion, equal to 18 months' import cover. A target of 12 months' cover would allow for room to run down reserves to about US$ 15 billion (which could be the average import level as growth picks up). But this can only provide a one-off source of savings (of, say, 4–5% of GDP). Borrowing from abroad, though feasible to some degree, would add to the debt service burden in the future (the current level of foreign debt is about US$ 32 billion, or 60% of GDP). This leaves FDI as the most likely candidate for providing additional savings in the short run. Of the ten percentage point increase in aggregate investment needed to boost growth, about half would have to be financed by FDI. This would amount to about £E10 billion or US$2.9 billion in annual inflows of FDI, which is several times the current inflow. The policy effort required to attract such flows is considerable and unlikely to be feasible in the short run.

13.5.2 Complementary policies to achieve high sustainable growth in the medium run

How then can Egypt make the desirable quantum shift in policies to achieve the rapid and sustainable growth achieved by the fast-growing countries? To reiterate, Egypt is in a good position to adopt such reforms. It has a stable policy environment and financial stability (inflation is less than 10%; reserves are significant). The key problems are that the size of the government is too large to induce savings; markets are too closed to promote exports of manufactured goods; and domestic competition is impeded further by the dominance of SOEs. The partnership agreement with the EU will help somewhat in relaxing some of these constraints, but significant changes that go beyond the agreement are needed to move ahead.

Savings, investment and size of government

Perhaps the most important disincentive to greater savings and investment is the size of the public sector. The role of the state in Egypt is pervasive. As noted already, government expenditure is 36%, compared to 21% in the fast-growing economies. The size of the SOE sector relative to GDP is 33%, compared with the world average for developing economies of 11% (World Bank, 1995d). Not surprisingly, domestic savings are about half the average for the fast-growing economies. To increase domestic savings, there is no way but to reduce the size of government expenditure and taxes, as well as the size of the SOE sector.

Lower taxes would not only increase savings, it would also help to increase investment. A necessary condition is that the environment is conducive. To improve the environment, there is a need for simplifying and unifying the investment law. This simplification, however, should not be pursued by giving multiple and distorting incentives for all variety of reasons that are hard to implement fairly, as envisaged in the current draft company law (or investment law). Rather, it should be pursued by further reduction and unification of corporate tax rates, and providing infrastructure in new industrial geographical locations deserving promotion, to address the problem of congestion in large cities. Inducing investment could also be pursued effectively by tax administration reform, with a view to reducing discretion in implementation. To partially offset the reductions in corporate tax rates, effort should be made to modernize the tax system and move quickly on VAT to widen the tax base. In the process of restructuring taxes and expenditure, effort should be made to spend less on re-distributive transfers and more on primary education, health and infrastructure projects not undertaken by the private sector.

The gradual reduction of tariffs that will be implemented under the partnership agreement will result in a reduction in the effective level of taxation and a fall in government revenues (assuming away any offsetting revenue effects resulting from greater economic activity). Here, the government has two choices: (i) seek to replace the lost tariff revenue through the imposition of alternative indirect taxes (such as GST or a future VAT), or (ii) reduce expenditures in line with the gradual fall in tariff revenue. In our view, the latter option is in the best interests of the economy from a growth perspective. Tariff revenue from the EU in 1994 was $800 million. Taking into account that EU import market share will expand, the revenue loss at the end of the transition is likely to be in the order of $1.0 billion, or 2% of GDP. This is not negligible, but alternative sources of savings (income) are readily available, privatization being the most important.

Openness and manufactured exports

As mentioned before, Egypt's tariffs are high; the collected average being more than double that of many fast-growing economies. Efficiency gains as well as the shift of resources into export sectors require a gradual pre-announced lowering of tariffs on goods that originate in non-EU countries in order to expose domestic firms to international competition. Free zones, tax holidays, and other selective types of liberalization will not help. The objective must be – taking into account the constraints – to convert the whole country into a free zone or something close to one. More uniform tariffs and tariff reductions must be introduced, given the evolving regional environment and the imminent conclusion of the partnership negotiations with the EU.

A significant reduction in MFN tariffs will reduce potential trade diversion induced by the partnership agreement, subject industries to greater competition and thus induce efficiency-enhancing measures. Simulation models show that there are opportunity costs associated with preferential liberalization. For example, Konan and Maskus (1996) conclude that if Egypt were to extend free trade to the world, welfare would increase by 2.6% of GDP. Alternatively, if a uniform, non-discriminatory tariff of 10% were imposed, welfare would rise by 2.3%. This illustrates the gains that can be obtained by extending the partnership agreement gradually over time to the rest of the world.

Reducing hub and spoke investment diversion incentives is also important, otherwise a free trade agreement may create incentives for firms *not* to invest in Egypt but to locate in the centre (hub) of the network of EU trade agreements (i.e. Europe). Trade barriers against regional trading partners should be eliminated as rapidly as possible to encourage investment by domestic and foreign firms that are interested in servicing regional markets and want to benefit from Egypt's geographical location and relatively diversified industrial base. The government is cognisant of this issue and has initiated talks with neighbouring Arab countries to agree on common rules of origin. It is necessary to go beyond this and pursue regional free trade.

With respect to the exchange rate, it may have been wise to use the rate as a nominal anchor of reform to curb inflation in the early stages of the economic reform programme. However, the current policy is not sustainable in the medium run. Accumulated appreciation will eventually reduce the competitiveness of exports, and encourage consumption by increasing imports, thus lowering domestic savings, investment and growth. Moreover, as the economy approaches fuller employment, fixing the exchange rate means that domestic prices will rise, which will give rise to further real exchange rate appreciation. The cost of deferring devaluation and adoption of a more flexible exchange rate policy can be very high. Cardoso (1996) illustrates the dire consequences of flawed exchange rate policy by citing the Chilean crisis in the late seventies and early eighties (where GDP dropped by 14%) and the 1994 Mexican crisis (where GDP dropped by 8%). Egypt should not travel that path. The exchange rate issue should be addressed sooner rather than later, especially since delay would make it harder to adjust. The government could gradually move from a fixed exchange rate regime to a crawling peg regime, whereby the Egyptian pound is linked to a set of hard currencies. This type of reform has recently been adopted by countries such as the Czech Republic.

Competition and private sector-led growth

The partnership agreement with the EU will progressively increase the competitive pressure on industrial producers through trade liberalization. However, with the size of the SOE sector in Egypt being three times the average of developing countries, competition will almost always be compromised. To enhance competition, privatization of at least two thirds of the current SOE sector enterprises should be pursued. Privatization will increase the efficiency of utilizing existing capital stock and arrest the flow of resources to unviable enterprises (both of which would increase savings). It would also signal the withdrawal of government from certain sectors of economic activity. Equally important, privatization would increase private investment and attract FDI.

While the sale of the companies already trading on the stock market may serve as a start, attracting FDI requires a 'landmark' privatization. In other words, privatization would have to be widened to encompass infrastructure, particularly telecommunications and port services (which would help improve the efficiency of exports). The sale itself can be conditioned upon commitment to expand on the part of the buyers, as happened in Chile and Mexico.

For privatization to be successful in enhancing domestic savings and attracting foreign investment, two main conditions have to be met. First, privatization in infrastructure should be preceded by introducing competition in potentially competitive markets, unbundling existing companies, adopting appropriate regulatory rules (for example, with respect to prices and interconnection) and creating genuinely independent regulatory bodies. Second, the revenue from privatization should be used to retire public debt. This will relieve the government budget from the burden of servicing the debt, and thus enhance public savings.[9]

13.6 Conclusions

The partnership agreement has the potential of playing a catalytic role in increasing the openness of the Egyptian economy, attracting FDI, and signalling the government's commitment to reform. The agreement is a tool, not an end in itself. It must be used to help achieve what Egypt needs most: a high rate of economic growth. This will not be achieved through the partnership agreement alone; rather, the partnership agreement should be just one (albeit important) component of a broader growth strategy. To reduce uncertainty it is crucial that the long-term policy path is spelled out clearly and debated publicly.

Increasing savings and investment in productive activities is key in the medium term. For this, Egypt should increase public sector savings (by reducing the size of the public sector) and reducing the tax burdens (by lowering tax rates and improving tax administration). In addition, a comprehensive privatization effort is crucial for fostering national savings (public and private), encouraging private sector investment and the repatriation of flight capital. Greater openness and exchange rate reforms are also essential for fostering savings and domestic competition and promoting manufactured exports.

The partnership agreement will help in encouraging investment and improving the allocation of resources. The impact and usefulness of the partnership agreement will be greatest if its reach extends to investment (guaranteeing the right of establishment) and the liberalization of service markets. The right of establishment is critical for capital inflows.

Liberalization of services is required to enhance domestic competition, expand investment opportunities, and provide domestic manufacturers with the low-cost, high-quality producer services they need in order to be able to compete on world markets.

Preferential liberalization is in principle a suboptimal approach to reducing trade barriers, as it gives rise to trade diversion. The greater the elimination of transaction costs in the context of the partnership agreement, and the more liberalization is generalized to all trading partners over time, the more such diversion will be offset. This implies a leveraging of the partnership agreement. Simulation studies – of both Egypt and other countries in the region – show that the adjustment costs of a nondiscriminatory approach to liberalization are not significantly higher than what will be incurred under the partnership agreement. However, the additional gains are substantial.

Last but not least, the set of recommended policy reforms should be designed and pursued in a credible, comprehensive and consistent fashion to be successful. The policy initiatives have to be *credible* to evoke a sustained investor response (especially from foreign investors) and overcome cynicism bred by years of patchy implementation and wavering commitment. They have to be *comprehensive* to have their full impact and signal that the effort is not selective and piecemeal. Finally, they have to be *consistent* to ensure that they can be implemented without being derailed by internal contradictions.

References

Bajo-Rubio, Oscar and Simon Sosvilla-Rivero (1994), 'An econometric analysis of foreign direct investment in Spain', *Southern Economic Journal*, 61, 104–20.

Baldwin, Richard (1994), *Towards an Integrated Europe*, London, CEPR.

Barro, Robert J. (1991), 'Economic growth in a cross section of countries', *Quarterly Journal of Economics*, 106, 407–44.

Bayoumi, Gamal (1996), 'Secrets of the negotiation rounds on the Association Agreement between Egypt and the European Communities, and its impact on Egyptian industry and agriculture', Interview in *Al Ahram*, 28 April.

Büchi, Hernan (1996), 'Chile's success story: a recipe for Egypt', Distinguished Lecture Series, the Egyptian Centre for Economic Studies.

Cardoso, Eliana, (1996), 'Lessons from the Mexican crisis for reforming economies', Distinguished Lecture Series, the Egyptian Centre for Economic Studies.

Diwan, Ishac (1996), 'Distributional consequences of the EU Agreement', in this volume.

Galal, Ahmed, Leroy Jones, Pankaj Tandon, and Ingo Vogelsang (1994), *Welfare Consequences of Selling Public Enterprises*, New York, Oxford University Press.

Galal, Ahmed (1996), 'Which institutions constrain economic growth in Egypt the most?', Working Paper 001, the Egyptian Centre for Economic Studies.

Hoekman, Bernard and Simon Djankov (1996), 'Towards a free trade agreement with the European Union: issues and policy options for Egypt', in this volume.

Knack, Stephen and Philip Keefer (forthcoming), 'Institutions and economic performance: cross-country tests using alternative institutional measures', *Economics and Politics*.

Konan, Denise and Keith Maskus, (1996), 'A computable general equilibrium analysis of trade liberalization using the Egypt CGE-TL model', in this volume.

Krugman, Paul (1994), 'The myth of Asia's miracle', *Foreign Affairs*, November/December.

Lee, Jong-Wha (1993), 'International trade, distortions and long-run economic growth', IMF Staff Papers, 40, 299–328.

Levine, Ross and David Renelt (1992), 'A sensitivity analysis of cross country growth regressions', *American Economic Review*, September.

North, Douglas (1990), *Institutions, Institutional Change, and Economic Performance*, New York, Cambridge University Press.

Page, John and John Underwood (1996), 'Growth, the Maghreb and the European Union: assessing the impact of the free trade agreements on Tunisia and Morocco', in this volume.

Rodrik, Dani (1996), 'Understanding economic reform', *Journal of Economic Literature*, 34, 9–41.

Sachs, Jeffrey and Andrew Warner (1995), 'Economic reform and the process of global integration', in W. Brainard and G. Perry (eds.), Brookings Papers on Economic Activity, Vol. 1.

Sachs, Jeffrey (1996), 'Achieving rapid growth: the road ahead for Egypt', Distinguished Lecture Series 3, the Egyptian Centre for Economic Studies.

Subramanian, Arvind (1995), 'The effects of the Uruguay Round on Egypt', International Monetary Fund, Mimeo.

Thurow, Lester (1992), *Head to Head: The Coming Battle among Japan, Europe, and America*, New York, Morrow.

World Bank (1994), 'Private sector development in Egypt: the status and the challenge,' World Bank Resident Mission, Cairo.

____ (1995a), *Economic Policies for Private Sector Development*. No. 14067 EGT, Washington, DC, World Bank.

____ (1995b), *Claiming the Future: Choosing Prosperity in the Middle East and North Africa*, Washington, DC, World Bank.

____ (1995c), Country Economic Memorandum, Washington, DC, World Bank.

____ (1995d), *Bureaucrats in Business: The Economics and Politics of Government Ownership*, Oxford University Press.

____ (1996), Country Economic Memorandum: India, Washington, DC, World Bank.

Yeats, Alexander (1996), 'Export prospects of Middle Eastern countries', World Bank Policy Research Working Paper 1571.

The views expressed here are those of the authors, and are not meant to represent the views of the World Bank or ECES.

Notes

1. In contrast, under its commitments made in the WTO context, Egypt will not be obliged to change its current tariff regime at all. The average rate at which tariffs have been bound in the GATT is some five percentage points above the 1994 applied tariffs (Subramanian, 1995).
2. Of course, some initial conditions are reflections of past policies, e.g. human capital, income distribution, etc.
3. In a country like Egypt, where the size of the SOE sector relative to GDP is about 33%, the magnitude of the gains from privatization is likely to be even more significant. For a recent analysis of the impact of SOEs on the economy, see World Bank (1995d).
4. Although a significant change has occurred in Egypt's composition of exports since the 1960s (cotton used to account for almost 50% of total exports, compared to some 4% currently), diversification and growth in non-traditional exports has lagged behind. According to UN statistics, Egypt's total merchandise exports in 1994 were $5.5 billion, of which some 50% went to European countries. Some 50% of Egypt's exports are comprised of oil and oil products. Agriculture/food accounts for another 5%. Manufactures represent only one-third of total merchandise exports. Exports of manufactures have been expanding – high growth items in recent years include aluminum, clothing, iron/steel, chemicals and furniture (Yeats, 1996). For most industries, however, the value of goods shipped abroad accounts for less than 0.5% of total exports. This is the case for 75% of the 2-digit categories of the Standard International Trade Classification. Given the diversified industrial base that exists in Egypt, this weak export performance illustrates both the need for efficiency-enhancing reforms and the potential that exists for expanding exports significantly once Egyptian enterprises begin to confront greater international competition.
5. Note that some administrative barriers may not differentiate between sources of imports. If these barriers are reduced or removed in the context of the partnership agreement, they will also reduce the costs of trade with non-EU countries. This will further increase the gains from the agreement.
6. Bajo-Rubio and Sosvilla Rivero (1994), in an econometric analysis of the Spanish case, find a positive relationship between EU accession and FDI inflows.
7. Despite the importance of the role of the state in economic activity and competition, no real disciplines are imposed under the partnership agreement with respect to the role of the state.
8. This is a conservative estimate, and is based on a simulation carried out for India (see World Bank, 1996).
9. The proceeds should not be used to restructure public enterprises, save the necessary cost of facilitating privatization (e.g. labour compensation).

Index